"*The Globalization of NATO* by Mahdi Darius Nazemroaya is magnificent, erudite and devoid of the ethnocentrism to which one has become so accustomed from Western authors. The book deals with what doubtless are the most important and relevant issues of the day for all those committed to saving life and protecting Mother Earth from rampant human irresponsibility and crime. There is no other book that, at this particular time, I would most heartily endorse. I think Africans, Near Eastern peoples, Iranians, Russians, Chinese, Asians and Europeans generally and all the progressive Latin American countries of today will find a much needed reinforcement and support for their peaceful ideals in this excellent must-read book."

—MIGUEL D'ESCOTO BROCKMANN,
Former Foreign Minister of Nicaragua and
President of the 63rd Session of the United Nations General Assembly

"We are far away from the principles and objectives for which the United Nations was created and the decisions of the Nuremberg Tribunal stipulating that some state actions can be considered crimes against peace. Nazemroaya's book, in addition to reminding us that the role of the United Nations has been confiscated by NATO, elaborates the danger that the North Atlantic Treaty represents to world peace."

—JOSÉ L. GÓMEZ DEL PRADO,
Former Chairman of the United Nations Working Group
on the Use of Mercenaries

"Through carefully documented research, Mahdi Darius Nazemroaya analyzes the historical and geopolitical evolution of NATO from the Cold War to the post 9/11 US-led 'Global War on Terrorism.' This book is a must read for those committed to reversing the tide of war and imperial conquest by the world's foremost military machine."

—MICHEL CHOSSUDOVSKY,
Professor Emeritus of Economics, University of Ottawa and
Director of the Centre for Research on Globalization (CRG), Montréal, Canada.

"Mahdi Darius Nazemroaya's prolific writings give us a comprehensive understanding of the character of the military thrust and it's all out, no holds barred STRATEGIC plans and moves to invade, occupy and plunder the resources of nations, inflicting unprecedented barbaric acts on civilian populations. He is one of the prescient thinkers and writers of contemporary times who deserves to be read and acted upon by people with a conscience and concern for humanity's future."

—VISHNU BHAGWAT,
Admiral and former Chief of the Naval Staff of India

"A very timely book. Yes, US-led NATO is globalizing, like the US-led finance economy. No doubt also for it to protect the latter, the "free market." It is a classical case of overstretch to help save the crumbling US Empire and Western influence in general, by countries most of whom are bankrupt by their own economic mismanagement. All their interventions share two characteristics. The conflicts could have been solved with a little patience and creativity, but

NATO does not want solutions. It uses conflicts as raw material it can process into interventions to tell the world that it is the strongest in military terms. And, with the help of the mainstream media, it sees Hitler everywhere, in a Milosevic, a bin Laden, a Hussein, a Qaddafi, in Assad, insensitive to the enormous differences between all these cases. I hope this book will be read by very, very many who can turn this morbid fascination with violence into constructive conflict resolution."

—JOHAN GALTUNG,
Professor Emeritus of Peace Studies and Sociology, University of Oslo and Founder of the International Peace Research Institute in Oslo (PRIO), the Galtung-Institut, and the Transcend Network, Oslo, Norway.

"This is a book really necessary to understanding the role of NATO within the frame of long-term US strategy. *The Globalization of NATO* by Mahdi Darius Nazemroaya not only provides an articulate analysis on the Atlantic Alliance: it is the best modern text devoted to the hegemonic alliance. With this book Nazemroaya reconfirms his ability as a brilliant geopolitical analyst."

—TIBERIO GRAZIANI,
President of the Institute of Advanced Studies in Geopolitics and Auxiliary Sciences/ L'Istituto di Alti Studi in Geopolitica e Scienze Ausiliarie (IsAG), Rome, Italy.

"Nazemroaya is an unbelievably prolific writer. What has often amazed many is his almost nonstop writing on extremely important issues for the contemporary world and his analysis about the globalization of NATO. What amazes many of us in other parts of the world are his seemingly limitless depth, breadth and the thoroughness of his knowledge that has been repeatedly appearing in his work. We are deeply indebted to Nazemroaya's humble, tireless and invaluable contributions through his fearless, insightful and powerful writings."

—KIYUL CHUNG,
Editor-in-Chief of *The 4th Media* and Visiting Professor at the School of Journalism and Communication, Tsinghua University, Beijing, People's Republic of China.

"The Journalists' Press Club in Mexico is grateful and privileged to know a man who respects the written word and used it in an ethical way without another interest other than showing the reality about the other side of power in the world. Mahdi Darius Nazemroaya gives voice to the "voiceless." He can see the other side of the moon, the side without lights."

—CELESE SÁENZ DE MIERA,
Mexican Broadcaster and Secretary-General of the Mexican Press Club

"With his very well documented analysis, Mahdi Darius Nazemroaya has conducted a remarkable decryption of the strategies implemented by NATO—in the interests of the United States, the European Union and Israel—to expand its military grip on the world, ensure its control over energy resources and transit routes, and encircling the countries likely to be a barrier or a threat to its goals, whether it be Iran, Russia or China. Nazemroaya's work is essential reading for those that want to understand what is being played out right now on the map in all the world's trouble spots; Libya and Africa; Syria and the Middle East; the Persian Gulf and Eurasia."

—SILVIA CATTORI,
Political Analyst and Journalist, Geneva, Switzerland.

THE GLOBALIZATION OF NATO

BY

MAHDI DARIUS NAZEMROAYA

FOREWORD BY

DENIS J. HALLIDAY

CLARITY PRESS, INC.

ISBN: 0-9852710-2-7
        978-0-9852710-2-2
E-book: 978-0-98353353-3-5

In-house editor: Diana G. Collier
Cover: R. Jordan P. Santos

Library of Congress Cataloging-in-Publication Data

Nazemroaya, Mahdi Darius.
  The globalization of NATO / by Mahdi Darius Nazemroaya.
      p. cm.
  Includes bibliographical references and index.
  ISBN-13: 978-0-9852710-2-2 (alk. paper)
  ISBN-10: 0-9852710-2-7 (alk. paper)
  1. North Atlantic Treaty Organization. 2. North Atlantic Treaty
Organization--Membership. 3. Unipolarity (International relations)
4. United States--Strategic aspects. 5. Eurasia--Strategic aspects. 6.
Geopolitics. 7. Security, International. I. Title.

  UA646.3.N44 2012
  355'.031091821--dc23

                        2012027472

                    Clarity Press, Inc.
            Ste. 469, 3277 Roswell Rd. NE
                Atlanta, GA. 30305 , USA
            http://www.claritypress.com

Sometimes we take time for granted, believing that many things in our individual or collective lives are constant and will always be there and that time will never erode or whisk them away from us. I dedicate this to the memory of Khodadad Nazemroaya of Sadeh. He was my grandfather, a brilliant chemist, a dedicated family man, and a loyal husband. The world is a better place for having him.

DIS•MAN
KH•NAZEMROAYA•SADEH•II•IVERIANUS
V•C•ET•P•F
ET•BENE•MERENTI
NAT•PROV•ASPADANA
DORMIAS•SINE•QVRA

TABLE OF CONTENTS

ACKNOWLEDGEMENTS / 10

FOREWORD   A UN Assistant Secretary-General's Warnings / 12
                by Denis J. Halliday

CHAPTER 1   An Overview of NATO Growth: Prometheanism? / 16
CHAPTER 2   EU, NATO Expansion and the Partnership for Peace / 28
CHAPTER 3   Yugoslavia and the Reinvention of NATO / 67
CHAPTER 4   NATO in Afghanistan / 114
CHAPTER 5   NATO's Mediterranean Dialogue / 134
CHAPTER 6   NATO in the Persian Gulf: The Gulf Security
                Initiative / 153
CHAPTER 7   Claiming the Post-Soviet Space / 165
CHAPTER 8   NATO and the High Seas: Control of Strategic
                Waterways / 175
CHAPTER 9   The Global Missile Shield Project / 192
CHAPTER 10   NATO and Africa / 208
CHAPTER 11   The Militarization of Japan and the Asia-Pacific / 252
CHAPTER 12   The Drive into Eurasia: Encircling Russia,
                China, and Iran / 266
CHAPTER 13   The Eurasian Counter-Alliances / 279
CHAPTER 14   NATO and the Levant: Lebanon and Syria / 304
CHAPTER 15   America and NATO as Rome and the Peninsular
                Allies / 331
CHAPTER 16   Global Militarization: At the Doors of World War
                III? / 340

ENDNOTES / 367
FIGURE CREDITS / 394
INDEX / 395

FIGURES: CHARTS, DIAGRAMS, AND TABLES

Table 1.1	NATO During the Cold War
Table 1.2	New Members of NATO, After the Cold War
Table 2.1	Eastern Partnership Countries and Russia
Table 2.2	European Neighborhood Policy Program
Table2.3	Participants in Partnership for Peace that Entered NATO
Table 2.4	Current Participants in Partnership for Peace
Table 2.5	Progressive Steps Towards NATO Membership?
Chart 2.1	NATO Outreach and Partnership
Diagram 2.1	Euler Diagram of NATO within Europe's Security Architecture
Table 3.1	Albania and the Former Yugoslavia
Chart 3.1	The Formation of Yugoslavia
Table 3.2	Euro-Atlantic Integration of Albania and the Former Yugoslavia
Chart 3.2	The Disintegration of Yugoslavia
Table 5.1	Mediterranean Dialogue Members
Table 6.1	ICI Members and their NATO Participation
Table 12.1	NATO and its Global Alliance Network
Table 13.1	Collective Treaty Security Organization Member States
Table 13.2	Shanghai Cooperation Organization Member States
Table 13.3	Diversity of the Eurasian Alliances
Table 16.1	The Eurasian Entente and its Global Alliance Network
Table 16.2	Global Peacekeeping Operations in 2010
Chart 16.1	The Share of World Military Expenditures Among NATO Countries
Chart 16.2	Military Expenditures: NATO versus the World
Chart 16.3	The Military Expenditures of the Eurasian Powers and their Allies

MAPS

Map I	History of NATO Enlargement
Map II	EU and the Eastern Partnership Countries
Map III	NATO and Partnerships in 2004
Map IV	Former Yugoslavia
Map V	NATO in Bosnia Under SFOR

Map VI   NATO in Kosovo Under KFOR
Map VII   NATO in Afghanistan Under ISAF
Map VIII   NATO in 2004
Map IX   The Mediterranean Sea
Map X   The Situation Around the Strait of Hormuz
Map XI   The Caucasus and Central Asia
Map XII   The Commonwealth of Independent States
Map XIII   The String of Pearls: Chinese Naval Bases
                in the Indian Ocean
Map XIV   The Missile Shield Project
Map XV   Russia's View of the European Missile Shield
Map XVI   NATO and the CSTO
Map XVII   Shanghai Cooperation Organization
Map XVIII   NATO Operations in 2006
Map XIX   NATO Operations and Missions in 2009
Map XX   The Bolivarian Bloc

ACKNOWLEDGMENTS

I am indebted to a great many people. Firstly, I would like to thank Diana G. Collier and Clarity Press, my publisher in the US. They have given me the space and freedom that I needed to work on this manuscript in tandem with my teaching duties at Carleton University, ongoing research, social science seminars, and various institutional commitments. It was a real tightrope act. Secondly, it is a real honor to have my foreword written by the man who spoke out against the corruption of the United Nations and its Security Council when he was assistant secretary-general. I thank Denis J. Halliday for taking the time in between his travels to write my foreword. Thirdly, I thank Jordan Santos for the fantastic cover, which catches the thematic essence of this book.

I cannot avoid mentioning the Department of Sociology and Anthropology at Carleton University either. I am grateful for the accommodations they made for me. In 2011, I had arrived to Carleton almost directly from the war theater in Libya. The process of decompressing was at times a hard and troubled one. It is an understatement to say that being on the receiving end of bombs, bullets, and mortal threats is an unpleasant one. My mind also goes to the physicist Jeff Schmidt and the two opening lines in the introduction of his critique on the socialization of professionals: "This book is stolen. Written in part on stolen time."* My critique of NATO has also been written in part on stolen time—time taken from other places or points in my life. I labored on the creation of this book by allocating time from other aspects of my life, including nullified office hours at Carleton University's Department of History.

I owe a debt of gratitude to my dear friend and colleague Michel J. Chossudovsky, professor emeritus of economics at the University of Ottawa and the director of the Centre for Research on Globalization, for his support throughout the years. I am grateful to him for always giving me the leeway I have needed. Reverend Miguel d'Escoto Brockmann, the former foreign minister of Nicaragua and the former president of the UN General Assembly, and his niece and former deputy chief of staff at the United Nations, Ambassador Sofía Clark, have my heartfelt appreciation and gratitude for their support. I am also indebted to Omar Kraya, Joseph Mroué, Robert Rassi, and Naser Al-Sharif for their support. Despite different and clashing perspectives at times, they always listened and challenged me for explanations. My debt to them is inexpressible. Likewise I am grateful to Stefanos Samonas, Maria Gandolfo, Paul Pavlovic, Ilija Mikasinovic, Thomas-Matthew Halton, Marie-Hélène Cholette, Ivaylo Grouev, Walid Mourad, John Baker, Maximilian Potemkin, Roger Taguchi, Henri Sader, André Hanna, Christopher Lajoie, Roy Murgich, Briton J. Amos, and Grandmother Nazemroaya. My work also owes a degree of debt to the work of others before me who also made critical assessments of the Cold War and the shift in NATO. The metaphor "standing on the shoulders of giants" comes into mind as the best way to describe this.

Finally, I would like to thank Misho Bogdanic, Navid Babaei, and Michael Kaminski for their disagreements and hostilities towards the simplistic discourses on the western side of the Atlantic "pond" that have for years painted the Soviets simply as aggressors. To Michael I am very grateful for giving me access, well over a decade ago, to the library and archives of his late father, a Polish historian, from which I acquired documents and books about the Soviet Union that helped me understand the Soviet system and the USSR's world-view. It seems like things have gone full circle; it is of extraordinary coincidence that many years onward I have found myself actually writing as an expert for one of the very publications that I so intently read from Kaminski's library as a young man.**

*   Jeff Schmidt, *Disciplined Minds: A Critical Look at Salaried Professionals and the Soul-Battering System that Shapes their Lives* (Lanham, MD: Rowman and Littlefield, 2000), p.1.

**   The books that I am talking about are the *Opposing Viewpoints* series of educational textbooks, which now belong to Cenage Learning. The first textbook in the series that I read was about the Soviet Union, while the one that I wrote for is about Libya.

A UN ASSISTANT SECRETARY-GENERAL'S WARNINGS

BY DENIS J. HALLIDAY

Martin Luther King, Jr. said that "those who love peace must learn to organize as effectively as those who love war." Tragically the leaders of the NATO countries do love war and the arms profits from warfare. Clearly, they are very well organized. To thinking people, the current expansion of NATO is eroding the minds of politicians while infusing fear into the minds of real people. The new arms race and massive expenditures on weapons in a time of growing global hunger, poverty and unemployment is poisoning international relations, further reinforcing corruption of decision making in the UN Security Council and undermining the wellbeing of billions of world citizens. For change, we must turn to youth throughout the world who have the courage to organize and protest injustice, inequality. Their in-the-street demands for the right to expect peace, social justice and a sustainable future is negated everyday NATO is enabled to expand into an unauthorized world police force with illicit and dangerous military credentials. Ineffective as a peacekeeper although the UN has become, NATO has no proven interest whatsoever in peace and non-violent coexistence. Warfare is the most profitable business of all. The military arms industry keeps entire economics afloat. Peace would put NATO out of the large scale and rewarding killing business.

In one of his great movies, James Dean played the part of a rebel without a cause. He was a young thug, violent of manner with questionable purpose, who appeared not to fully understand his own aggression. Today NATO is a much more dangerous thug, very violent in manner with questionable purpose but financed and backstopped by an empire in demise. NATO understands its own aggression as a device to encircle the world with military capacity, gift the arms manufacturing corporations amongst its member states with permanent demand

and openly threaten states it deems to have potential for competitive leadership. A redundant military alliance today long after the Cold War passed, NATO constantly seeks new resources, new weapons and new members to pursue violence against non-existent enemies, creating opportunities for warfare that require nothing more than dialogue, cooperation in a mature and civilized manner. There is nothing mature or civilized about NATO, or its leadership.

Of course NATO can be viewed from various different angles. Looking from China and Russia, it must appear to be a dangerous fiction of collaboration by countries that have no reason to be frightened or feel threatened. These two large sovereign states must see NATO as an opportunistic alliance looking for enhanced hegemony and power. Astonishingly, NATO is tolerated by the same European countries that know the unacceptable horrors of total warfare and have no inclination to return to a living hell. Others like Canada, Australia and the USA that have no in-country experience of modern war are cavalier with the young human resources at their disposal. They seduce young people into their military forces with handsome financial rewards, and call them heroes when they lose their lives for nought. Extraordinarily, some are awarded citizenship posthumously.

As an Irishman, the NATO presence is an unwanted danger to the EU project of active togetherness. To the EU states committed to genuine peacekeeping NATO is an affront. It represents the economic and hegemonic need of American regimes in Washington to continue the occupation of Europe with troops and weapons, including nuclear. Instead, the US should be disarming, and investing in the poverty of its own people, dealing with its economic collapse and adjusting to the pain of a declining empire facing its demise. To most EU members, committed to socialism-light and the use of revenue for the social wellbeing of citizens, NATO has become a redundant, extravagant and unwelcome military toy that gobbles up human and financial resources to no positive end. Worse, under the constant pressure of corporate arms dealers, funding for presidential elections and pathetically beribboned generals NATO has strayed beyond the scope of the original post-World War II alliance into threatening sovereign states such as Iran where dialogue, together with homegrown solutions would likely suffice. And not just suffice, but resolve issues without loss of innocent life, hugely damaged civilian infrastructure and the horror of nuclear weapons.

Further, the United Nations Charter and terms of reference of the Security Council contained in Chapter VII, Article 41 calling for nonviolent action is undermined by a standing NATO military force that anxiously seeks warfare. Perhaps "undermined" is not the right word, when the same villains driving NATO from Washington, London and Paris make up the majority of the five permanent and veto wielding member states of the UN Security Council. Already corrupted by the self-serving vested interests of the Permanent Five, the employment of NATO as a onetime, but no longer regional peacekeeping force is nepotistic at its very worst. The vested interests within the Security Council are now entrusted to NATO forces which are led and supplemented by the USA military budget to destroy sovereignty, infrastructure and most importantly innocent lives on a catastrophic scale as we have seen recently in Libya. NATO has demonstrated it can no longer be trusted as a peacekeeping entity by the UN. Genuine humanitarian intervention, or R2P as it is known, can never again be entrusted to NATO forces. Clearly NATO has no objectivity in a situation such as the much needed protection of the Palestinian civilian people from Israeli occupation, violation of their human rights and its endless multi-diverse forms of violence.

The danger to global equilibrium is a growing NATO being expanded further by American and British ambitions into a monster military force of world proportions, way beyond any Atlantic or European alliance. NATO expansion, intrusive military hardware, such as cyber technology/ interference and the murderous capacity of drones is threatening North/ South peace. The creeping slime of NATO expansion into Asia, the attempt to surround Russia, China and others can only end badly for the billions of human beings involved. The recent mini-US occupation of Australia, the interference in the ASEAN countries by US arms dealers and naval forces, the menacing presence of US aircraft carriers in the Indian Ocean, the South China Sea and the Strait of Malacca should remind historians of just why the Japanese considered it necessary to attack Pearl Harbor to end the US naval strangle hold imposed upon them.

Surely we do not want another global conflagration, started in the Middle East over US protection of energy sources, the poison of Israeli occupation in violation of international law, or internal change within Arab states. The change that is needed is an end to the comfortable US/EU relationships with absolute monarchs, dictatorships and military regimes blindly financed by Washington. The human rights and wellbeing of the people of this extraordinary and ancient region of the world appear to have no value in the military-conditioned minds of Western democracies, the very states that provide the backbone of much of NATO's interference and deadly use of force.

The issues for us all, and in particular our young people willing to organize is how to stop NATO's growth into a global power, thereby endangering real human security that does not come from the barrels of many guns, or the use of depleted uranium, or the employment of killer drones and nuclear weapons. Instead, we need a massive reduction in financial resources wasted on military capacity so such monies can be focused on the elimination of the crushing poverty and hunger whereby over two billion persons live with an unacceptable low quality of life. Ending the violence against the environment, the good health of which we humans all depend needs focus and resources. We must all learn to accept that real people do not want war, they want love, justice, education and opportunity for better lives now and for their children in the future.

Somehow, the younger amongst us need to demand of their leaders the abolition of nuclear weapons, an end to the use of depleted uranium, and the employment of deadly drones. Legislators must be convinced to re-allocate tax monies from the military craw into social needs and opportunities for education, investment in human wellbeing with sustainable growth. We must demand an end to the vast divide between rich and poor, the 1% and the 99%, and insist upon the introduction of greater equality amongst all persons, including women and men. A greater focus and understanding of what human-rights-for-all means would move us forward.

NATO as it expands today is absolutely not what the world of struggling economies and deprived populations require. It is nothing, but a negative force. It is undermining an already fragile United Nations. NATO has not been appointed policeman for the globe. It is self-serving, lacks integrity, has demonstrated its leadership cannot be trusted and creates nothing positive. It only yields destruction and human poverty, insecurity and misery. NATO must be abolished!

Nazemroaya's book is a must-read for any European or other NATO state citizen who wants to understand the danger the American-driven Alliance presents to world harmony and peace. I would hope that having done so, the reader would accept appropriate responsibility for actively pursuing ways to terminate this war machine that seeks out opportunities for warfare for all the wrong reasons. To those readers who realize they are targeted for NATO treatment now or in the future, worry and turn that worry into pragmatic means to confront the Alliance, not with military violence, but with dialogue that shows strength and commitment to global coexistence. If together we cannot demonstrate the advantages to humanity of a world without redundant militarism, we are lost. Reading this book, may be the first step to finding ourselves before it is too late.

DENIS J. HALLIDAY,
UNITED NATIONS ASSISTANT SECRETARY-GENERAL
(1994-98)

CHAPTER 1

AN OVERVIEW OF NATO GROWTH: PROMETHEANISM?

...NATO has been transforming from its Cold War and then regional incarnation of the 1990s into a transatlantic institution with global missions, global reach, and global partners. This transformation is most evident in Afghanistan where NATO is at work, but the line we've crossed is that that [sic.] "in area/out of area" debate that cost so much time to debate in the 1990s is effectively over. There is no "in area/out of area." Everything is NATO's area, potentially. That doesn't mean it's a global organization. It's a transatlantic organization, but Article 5 now has global implications. NATO is in the process of developing the capabilities and the political horizons to deal with problems and contingencies around the world. That is a huge change.

**–US Assistant Secretary of State
for European and Eurasian Affairs Daniel Fried (2007)**

Opposing Viewpoints on NATO

The North Atlantic Treaty Organization (NATO) is perhaps the world's foremost military alliance. Definitely, it is the best known military alliance on the face of the planet. It is a household name and one that frequently is heard in news reports and policy debates. NATO has grown out of a small collective of Western European countries huddling with Canada under the protective umbrella of the United States of America at a time when the US, along with the Union of Soviet Socialist Republics (USSR) was one of two global superpowers. Both the US and USSR, the main victors to step out of the rubble in the aftermath of the Second World War, were engaged in a global faceoff for hegemony and influence that had divided the European continent into two main blocs, the American-led Western Bloc and the Soviet-led Eastern Bloc, also called the Soviet Bloc. Within the context of this faceoff, NATO and the Warsaw Pact would later be born. While the Warsaw Pact was dissolved in 1991, NATO has since become a mounting force in the international arena in the process of cementing itself as a truly global institution and military force ready to operate anywhere on the map, inside and outside of the Euro-Atlantic Zone.

The Alliance has been viewed in many ways, and continues to be, by its proponents and opponents alike. Its name can arouse intense and varying emotions, from anger and hatred to pride and Cold War nostalgia. It has united and divided people in support and opposition in diverse ways. NATO forces have waged war on three continents, have standing forces ready on four continents, and have in one way or another been actively involved in all the inhabited continents of the world. NATO's supporters see it as an indispensable foundation for the multi-layered security architecture of the Euro-Atlantic Zone, which encompasses the US, Canada, and Europe with the North Atlantic as its geo-political core. Conversely, the critics of the Atlantic Alliance point out that it has long since overstepped its mandate and Euro-Atlantic boundaries by operating "out-of-area." These critics, whether they are activists, members of the global intelligentsia, or politicians, see the North Atlantic Treaty Organization as a menace and a genuine threat to global peace and security. They see the Atlantic Alliance as a destabilizing factor in international relations and as a tool to impose US and EU objectives on those nations outside of the Atlanticist orbit.

New Post-Cold War Mandates and Zones

For years after the disbanding of the Soviet-dominated Warsaw Pact and the collapse of the USSR, NATO was viewed as a relic of the Cold War. With the threat of a Soviet invasion from Eastern Europe against Western Europe gone, NATO had lost its raison d'être. Analysts like James Chace, a former editor of the Council on Foreign Relation's journal, *Foreign Affairs*, labelled NATO a dinosaur and a dead organization. Chace proposed that NATO be turned into an international police force with responsibilities that included peacekeeping and monitoring elections. Other influential US figures like Ronald Asmus, Zbigniew Brzezinski, Richard Kugler, and Steven Larrabee, through White House and establishment publications, all postulated that NATO had to expand and go beyond its boundaries or become obsolete and wither away like a dried up plant. Still others like Ira Straus talked about the entry of a reformed and subdued Russia into NATO. As Straus put it:

> When I wrote in 1985 about the hypothetical possibility
> of Eastern Europe and Russia joining NATO, people
> thought I had lost my mind. Even today when one talks

about Russia joining NATO, it sounds in the West like the wolf joining a flock of sheep. Currently, in Russia, the phrase is put the other way around—it is a sheep (Russia) joining a pack of wolves (the West) that are gobbling up Russia.[1]

Straus was boldly refuted by many who did not want to surrender Russia's image as an enemy and saw NATO as not just an anti-Soviet, but an anti-Russian alliance. In wider terms the Alliance also began to be referred to as the embodiment of the anachronistic mentalities of that ideological era, which saw the world divided parachronistically in terms of "us and them" and black and white.

Ideas about NATO's anachronism began to change after a series of secessionist wars in the disintegrating and devolving Socialist Federal Republic of Yugoslavia that saw NATO conduct several military campaigns in the Eastern European region of the Balkans. NATO intervened militarily in Bosnia-Herzegovina in 1995. Next it waged an aerial war over the fate of the predominantly Albanian-inhabited Serbian province of Kosovo against the Federal Republic of Yugoslavia in 1999. In 2001, NATO boots were deployed on the soil of the former Yugoslav Republic (FYR) of Macedonia, which the Atlantic Alliance's Kosovo Liberation Army (KLA) allies had been destabilizing. Yet, the dying Yugoslavia was neither the start nor the end of NATO military intervention. In 1991, NATO had been silently involved in major military operations in the Gulf War that brightened the eyes of Pentagon strategists as they considered the future possibilities of using the Atlantic Alliance in other regions of the world. The military interoperability of the NATO members that fought in Iraq also rekindled their zeal.

The events in the Balkans during the 1990s would be followed by the US-led invasion of Taliban-controlled Afghanistan in the same year as the NATO deployment into Macedonia. NATO agreed to support the US in the "Global War on Terror" after Article 5, the collective defense article of the treaty, was invoked by the US government in the aftermath of the attacks of September 11, 2001. In the same year, NATO launched a policing mission to control the Mediterranean Sea called Operation Active Endeavor and agreed to manage the military mission in Afghanistan by taking control of the International Security Assistance Force (ISAF) in 2003. This allowed the US and UK to focus on Iraq. Despite the opposition of Washington's Franco-German partners, the Atlantic Alliance was also informally involved in Iraq in 2003. NATO conducted air operations around Iraq that it claimed were intended to defend Turkey, should Iraq attack it. NATO would also assist the deploying of the military forces of Poland, which aided the US and UK in the invasion and occupation of Iraq by supplying about two hundred soldiers. Subsequently, in 2004, NATO accepted what was a US request for further involvement in Anglo-

American occupied Iraq. This lasted until 2011 and was conducted under what was termed "NATO Training Mission–Iraq."

In the 1990s there were continuous references by US policymakers and Pentagon officials to Islam and a coming conflict with Muslims. Insofar as the "Red Menace" of Marxism had been defeated during the Cold War, the conceptualization of a new enemy began taking shape. This would take form as the "Green Menace" of Islam within a Straussian *weltanschauung*. Secretary-General Willem Claes of Belgium would actually go so far as to say that Islam had become NATO's new threat. The military planners of the Pentagon and NATO also began contemplating missions to places in Africa like Somalia, Rwanda, and Congo. In 1994, one senior US officer made the following statement to a forum at the Miller Center for Public Affairs:

> What if [the NATO allies] are called on to promote stability outside of the European area? What if the [United States] decides that if NATO cannot get involved in places like Somalia or Rwanda, then it is no longer furthering [American] interests, thus leading the United States to present the alliance with an ultimatum—either move out or we'll pull out? That scenario is no longer totally implausible as it was during the Cold War.[2]

From 2001 to 2011 the Alliance's commanders expanded its out-of-area operations even further by taking on naval missions in the Indian Ocean. In conjunction, NATO naval vessels and jets also began operations off the coastlines of Africa and the Arabian Peninsula under such missions as Operation Allied Provider in 2008 and Operation Allied Protector in 2009 in the name of regional anti-piracy and maritime surveillance. The Alliance also became busy over African skies as it began to taxi African Union troops into places like Sudan and Somalia. NATO's leaders were expressing more and more interest in the African continent. In 2011, North Africa entered the out-of-area fray as NATO launched a military campaign against the Libyan Arab Jamahiriya and openly engaged in regime change operations under the banner of a humanitarian operation mandated by the United Nations Security Council.

By 2001 onward, if it had not been already apparent in the late-1990s, it was clear that NATO was no longer just a defensive pact intended for mutual defense. It was operating in more than five different regions of the world from the valleys of Afghanistan to the skies of East Africa and the waters off the coasts of Cuba and Greenland. The new NATO was an organization actively pursuing combat missions and international policing duties of airspace and international waters. NATO was publicly taking it on itself to impose what its political leaders have claimed to be the maintenance of international law and stability.

Atlanticist Growth: Expanding the Bloc

NATO was founded on April 4, 1949 by the signing of the Washington Treaty in what was then the Departmental Auditorium, and now the Andrew W. Mellon Auditorium. The agreement was signed by the foreign ministers of twelve countries from both sides of the Atlantic Ocean: Paul-Henri Spaak (the Kingdom of Belgium), Lester B. Pearson (the Dominion of Canada), Gustav Rasmussen (the Kingdom of Denmark), Robert Schuman (France under the Fourth Republic), Bjarni Benediktsson (the Republic of Iceland), Carlo Sforza (Italy), Joseph Bech (the Grand Duchy of Luxembourg), Dirk Uipko Stikker (the Kingdom of the Netherlands), Halvard Manthey Lange (the Kingdom of Norway), José Caeiro da Matta (Portugal), Ernest Bevin (the United Kingdom of Great Britain and Northern Ireland), and Dean Acheson (the United States of America). Under Article 5 of the Washington Treaty, also commonly referred to as the North Atlantic Treaty, each signatory and ally agreed that an armed attack against one or more of them would be considered an attack against them all collectively. In reality the North Atlantic Treaty was a US security guarantee, which included the nuclear arsenal of the US as the single global nuclear power, to protect the rest of the Atlantic Alliance.

The Washington Treaty was primarily the work of the US, Britain, Canada, and France. The French would never be totally satisfied with the final draft, because it excluded their colonies as a zone of defense for the Atlantic Alliance. The Belgians too wanted the Belgian Congo included as a zone of defense. In the end the colonial possessions of the Western European states were excluded from the zone of defense outlined by the draft. Algeria, however, was included. This was because Algeria at the time was a direct department (province or state) of Metropolitan France. Concerning the zone of defense, the Washington Treaty stated:

Article 5

The Parties agree that an armed attack against one or more of them in Europe or North America shall be considered an attack against them all and consequently they agree that, if such an armed attack occurs, each of them, in exercise of the right of individual or collective self-defense recognized by Article 51 of the Charter of the United Nations, will assist the Party or Parties so attacked by taking forthwith, individually and in concert with the other Parties, such action as it deems necessary, including the use of armed force, to restore and maintain the security of the North Atlantic area.

Any such armed attack and all measures taken as a result thereof shall immediately be reported to the Security Council. Such measures shall be terminated when the Security Council has taken the measures necessary to restore and maintain international peace and security.

Article 6

For the purpose of Article 5, an armed attack on one or more of the Parties is deemed to include an armed attack:

- on the territory of any of the Parties in Europe or North America, on the Algerian Departments of France, on the territory of or on the Islands under the jurisdiction of any of the Parties in the North Atlantic area north of the Tropic of Cancer;

- on the forces, vessels, or aircraft of any of the Parties, when in or over these territories or any other area in Europe in which occupation forces of any of the Parties were stationed on the date when the Treaty entered into force or the Mediterranean Sea or the North Atlantic area north of the Tropic of Cancer.

Since its 1949 inception, NATO has drawn the bulk of European states, not to mention Turkey, under its umbrella in one way or another. The Atlanticist growth and the spreading out of the Atlantic Alliance have taken place through six rounds of eastward and southward expansion in continental Europe and its geographic periphery, which includes Anatolia. We would have to consider it seven rounds of membership expansion, if the entry of the German Democratic Republic (East Germany) in 1990 into NATO by means of German reunification is counted. Four rounds of the Atlantic Alliance's expansion took place during the Cold War during which, in comparison, it had accepted fewer states.

The first round of Atlanticist expansion occurred in 1952 when the two rival Aegean and Mediterranean states of Greece and Turkey were admitted into the ranks of the Alliance about one month before the North Atlantic Council selected Britain's Hastings Ismay as its first secretary-general on March 24. Two years later, in 1954, the Federal Republic of Germany, commonly referred to as West Germany, would join the Alliance. The inclusion of West Germany into the ranks of the

MAP I

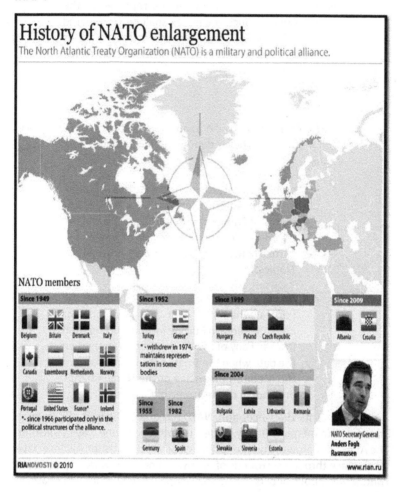

History of NATO enlargement
The North Atlantic Treaty Organization (NATO) is a military and political alliance.

NATO members

Since 1949
Belgium, Britain, Denmark, Italy
Canada, Luxembourg, Netherlands, Norway
Portugal, United States, France*, Iceland
*- since 1966 participated only in the political structures of the alliance.

Since 1952
Turkey, Greece*
* - withdrew in 1974, maintains representation in some bodies

Since 1955   Since 1982
Germany   Spain

Since 1999
Hungary, Poland, Czech Republic

Since 2004
Bulgaria, Latvia, Lithuania, Romania
Slovakia, Slovenia, Estonia

Since 2009
Albania, Croatia

NATO Secretary General **Anders Fogh Rasmussen**

RIANOVOSTI © 2010   www.rian.ru

Atlantic Alliance would lead to the formation of the Warsaw Pact by the Soviet Union and its allies in the Eastern Bloc. A year later, in 1955, NATO formed the North Atlantic Assembly, which was renamed as the NATO Parliamentary Assembly (NATO PA) in 1999, as a consultative body to the North Atlantic Council made up of parliamentarians from NATO countries. The next country to join the Alliance, and the last during the Cold War period, would be the Kingdom of Spain in 1982, which was already a NATO ally before its membership. The North Atlantic Treaty Organization would not accept any more new members for almost another two decades after the end of the Cold War in 1991.

TABLE 1.1

NATO During the Cold War

Country	Allied Power	Axis Power	Entry Date
Original Members			
Belgium	Yes	No	4 April 1949
Canada	Yes	No	4 April 1949
Denmark	Yes	No	4 April 1949
France*	Yes	No	4 April 1949
Iceland	Yes	No	4 April 1949
Italy	No	Yes	4 April 1949
Portugal	Yes	No	4 April 1949
Netherlands	Yes	No	4 April 1949
Norway	Yes	No	4 April 1949
United Kingdom	Yes	No	4 April 1949
United States of America	Yes	No	4 April 1949
Post-1949 Members			
Germany, Federal Republic of (West Germany)	No	Yes	23 October 1954
German Democratic Republic (East Germany)	No	Yes	3 October 1990†
Greece	Yes	No	18 February 1952
Spain	Neutral	Neutral; Pro-Axis	30 May 1982
Turkey	Yes‡	No	18 February 1952

*Algeria was a part of Metropolitan France at the time; the North Atlantic Treaty also included Algeria as a zone of defense.

† When East Germany united with West Germany on October 3, 1990, it became a part of NATO.

‡ Turkey was mostly neutral throughout the Second World War and only joined the Allies at the very end of the war in Europe on February 23, 1945.

In the post-Cold War period, the next round of expansion for NATO would be a watershed moment. It would also be part of a contiguous trend. Under the fourth round of expansion, the first countries to be accepted into NATO would be former Eastern Bloc adversaries: the Czech Republic, Hungary, and Poland. These former Soviet satellites were the three most developed and industrialized Eastern Bloc countries after the USSR and East Germany. Their accession as members in the military bloc was accepted by the North Atlantic Council on March 16, 1999. This was merely a few days before the Atlantic Alliance went to war with the Federal Republic of Yugoslavia on March 24. Eager to prove their allegiance, all three new NATO members quickly provided their ample support against Belgrade.

In 2004, about a year after the US and UK invaded and occupied Iraq, seven more new members from Eastern Europe would be accepted into the ranks of the Atlantic Alliance. This round of expansion would be significant too for several reasons. In the first place, these new members of NATO all supported the Anglo-American invasion of Iraq in 2003 and proved themselves to be ardent supporters of militaristic US foreign policy. This put them at odds with France and Germany. US Defense Secretary Donald Rumsfeld even commented on the rift by pointing out that these new NATO members were on the side of Washington and not Paris and Berlin during the trans-Atlantic rift over Iraq. In much publicized statements which angered French President Jacques Chirac and German Federal Chancellor Gerhard Schröder, Secretary Rumsfeld casually stated that the orbit of NATO in the European continent was shifting eastward towards these future members. As far as Rumsfeld and the Pentagon were concerned, France and Germany were part of the "old Europe."[3] On March 29, 2004, just over a year after Rumsfeld's statements, the states of "new Europe"—Bulgaria, Romania, Slovakia, Slovenia, and the three Baltic States of Estonia, Latvia, and Lithuania—became fully fledged members of NATO. Donald Rumsfeld was right about the importance of these members for the Pentagon and American military operations. By this time both Romania and Bulgaria were becoming important hubs for US military operations and movements extending from the Balkans to the Middle East and Central Asia. *The New York Times* would verify this by publishing a text by Lawrence J. Korb, a former US assistant secretary of defense, saying:

> The Pentagon is smitten with Romania. And Poland. And Bulgaria too. The Defense Department is considering closing many, if not all, of its bases in Western Europe—which are primarily in Germany— and to shift its troops to Spartan new sites in the former Soviet bloc. Already we are told that the First

Armored Division, now on the ground in Iraq, will not
return to the bases in Germany it left in April [2003].
And Gen. James Jones, the head of the European
Command [of the United States], said this month that
all 26 Army and Air Force installations in Germany,
except for the Air Force base at Ramstein, might be
closed. In effect this could mean transferring five army
brigades, some 25,000 troops, to the East [meaning to
NATO's relatively new Eastern European members].[4]

Because of their geo-strategic importance to the US, by 2006 General
David McKiernan, one of the military commanders of the US Army in
Europe, would state "Bulgaria and Romania are war-proven allies of the
United States." [5]

After 2004, the next round of expansion for the Atlantic Alliance
would not happen until 2009 when Albania and Croatia would be admitted
to NATO. By the start of 2012, the North Atlantic Alliance's ranks included
twenty-eight countries—twelve of which had joined after the collapse of the
Soviet Union and the end of the Cold War. Bosnia-Herzegovina, Montenegro,
and the former Yugoslav Republic (FYR) of Macedonia currently all have
what are called Membership Action Plans (MAPs), which is the final step
before accession into the ranks of the military bloc.

TABLE 1.2

New Members of NATO, After the Cold War*

Country	Ex-Communist	Ex-Warsaw Pact	Entry Date
Albania	Yes	Yes	1 April 2009
Bulgaria	Yes	Yes	29 March 2004
Croatia†	Yes	No	1 April 2009
Czech Republic‡	Yes	Yes	16 March 1999
Estonia§	Yes	Yes	29 March 2004
Hungary	Yes	Yes	16 March 1999
Latvia§	Yes	Yes	29 March 2004
Lithuania§	Yes	Yes	29 March 2004
Poland	Yes	Yes	16 March 1999
Romania	Yes	Yes	29 March 2004
Slovakia‡	Yes	Yes	29 March 2004
Slovenia†	Yes	No	29 March 2004

*The end of the Cold War is operationalized as 1991.
†Formerly part of the Socialist Federal Republic of Yugoslavia
‡ Formerly part of Czechoslovakia until 1992.
§ Formerly part of the Union of Soviet Socialist Republics (USSR) until
1991.

NATO Expansion and the Push into the Eurasian Heartland

Since the end of the Cold War the North Atlantic Treaty Organization has continued its indefinite expansion breaching the boundaries of the former Soviet Union by incorporating the Baltic States of Estonia, Latvia, and Lithuania. This caused alarm and great agitation in the Russian Federation. The Kremlin began to ask if the Cold War was over, why was the Atlantic Alliance still in place and even expanding? Nor have the North Atlantic Treaty Organization's expansionist aims stopped at Russia's Baltic doorstep. NATO has been involved in a long courtship with other states in the post-Soviet space. The Atlantic Alliance has been particularly involved in engaging both the former Soviet republics of Georgia and Ukraine in membership bids as a result of the color revolutions that changed the political orientation of both republics. The 2003 color revolution in Georgia known as the Rose Revolution would lead to the election of Mikheil Saakashvili on January 4, 2004 as the new president of Georgia. In Ukraine, Viktor Yushchenko would become the president in 2005 as a result of his country's 2004 color revolution known as the Orange Revolution. While the Georgian government under Saakashvili remains dedicated to entering NATO, Ukraine no longer does with the election of Viktor Yanukovych as president. NATO has also made gestures to the Republic of Azerbaijan and Kazakhstan for membership and greater cooperation. The Atlantic Alliance has expressed its desire to enter the Caucasus and Central Asia and after the Istanbul Summit in 2004 has even assigned a special envoy for these strategic regions. The Republic of Azerbaijan has remained silent on the subject, wishing to avoid friction with its larger neighbors, Russia and Iran. Like Armenia and Belarus, Kazakhstan on the other hand has made it clear that it will not join NATO. Nonetheless, this expansion process has become a major issue of concern for the Russian Federation, Russia's allies in the Commonwealth of Independent States (CIS), and other states, including the People's Republic of China and the Islamic Republic of Iran.

For Russia and other international actors the issue of NATO expansion alone has not been the subject of their growing concerns. NATO's transforming—even dynamic—mandates that have taken on peacekeeping, international policing, and counter-terrorism have all caused concern. NATO military intervention has especially rattled the nations of the world outside of the Euro-Atlantic Zone. Russia and a growing number of other states view these activities with more and more suspicion as they see NATO being used in self-serving ways by its members, particularly Washington. Coupled with its continuing expansion and its operations outside of its mandated zone, the Alliance's post-Cold War reinvention has become a cause of worry for these countries. Their questions essentially gravitate not only around NATO's function and its zone of operations. They also bring issues of international law and strategic balance into the foreground. To many of its worldwide critics and opponents, ranging from activists like Chicago's Rick Rozoff and Sweden's Agneta Norberg to Leonid Ivashov, the former chief of the Russian Armed Forces, the Alliance now ranks among the biggest dangers to world peace. NATO's missile shield project led by the US has also aggravated the situation. Its military presence in the Balkans has now lasted over two decades, while in Afghanistan it has lasted over a decade. The Alliance's handling of the war in Libya has caused a stir in international relations. In Libya, the Alliance deliberately overstepped the UN mandated no-fly zone and illegally sent soldiers onto the ground. After the toppling of the Jamahiriya in Tripoli and the capture and murder of Muammar Qaddafi in the Libyan city of Sirte, it was revealed that NATO operatives and forces had been on the ground from the start of the conflict in Libya. The Alliance is increasingly being viewed as a geo-political extension of America, an arm of the Pentagon, and a synonym for an evolving American Empire.

By the start of 2012, it is clear that NATO is determined to expand its membership circle and to expand its mandate. Its operations are global and its partnership agreements include countries like Japan, Australia, Israel, and the United Arab Emirates. Ultimately NATO is slated to become an institutionalized global military force. Foreshadowing this in 2010, NATO Secretary-General Anders Fogh Rasmussen told reporters that the Atlantic Alliance was going to have "undivided global responsibility" and that NATO in the future "will have no place for geographic zones of responsibility."[6] Russia has even accused the Alliance of trying to supplant the United Nations. Moreover, part of the objectives of NATO as a global military alliance is to ensure the "energy security" of its member states and what its critics call desires for "invulnerability." What this signifies is the militarization of the world's arteries, strategic energy routes, maritime traffic corridors used by oil tankers, and international waters. Nevertheless for every action there is a reaction and NATO's actions have given rise to opposing trends. The Atlantic Alliance is increasingly coming into contact with a zone of Eurasia that is in the process of emerging with its own ideas and alliance. What this will lead to next is the question of the century.

CHAPTER 2

EU, NATO EXPANSION AND THE PARTNERSHIP FOR PEACE

The first and most important area where change must come is in further developing our ability to project stability to the East.
—NATO Secretary-General Manfred Wörner (1993)

The Taxonomy of European States and Non-European States

Article 10 of the Washington Treaty specifically conditions entrance into NATO on the basis that any acceding state be a European country. This brings into question the concept of what European identity is and what forms European characteristics in a country. This is not a straightforward matter at all. There is much more to being European than geography, but it is also not purely a political, cultural, or sociological issue either. It is a mixed package of subjectivity and interlinked objectivity, which is dynamic and changing.

Physiographically, it has to first categorically be stated that Europe is not a real continent, but really part—and a large peninsula, as some geographically categorize—of the Eurasian landmass in unison with Asia, which by the same token is not a real continent either. Rather than delving into the question of what defines Europe, which is a treatise in itself, we should emphasize the fact that Europe has been a shifting entity and polity. One can also trace this metamorphosis with ease in a cross-examination of older atlases. Looking through atlases from the 1900s up until the present, we notice that the outer boundaries and the geo-political concept of Europe have been in shift and expanding.

Countries like Cyprus and Armenia that are geographically located in Asia have been redefined as European states. Some scholars and policy makers justify this on the basis of historic and cultural ties, which are not matters of argument for the purposes of this text, but the same case is also being made for including several other countries with no territorial ties to Europe, such as the settler-state of Israel. We can even develop this argument much further. Culturally, the Greek Cypriots and Armenians are not very different from either Turks or Iranians. The same is true of the cultures in mainland Greece and Italy. Greeks and Turks have far more cultural similarities than do the Greeks and the Scandinavians, such as the Swedes and the Norwegians of Northern Europe. In fact, aside from religious and political differences, the cultures of places like Armenia, Georgia, Iran, Turkey, Greece, Albania, and Italy are invariably very much the same. Yet, Europe has been redefined to include Cyprus, Armenia, and the Republic of Azerbaijan through a mixed package of historical, cultural, and political justifications. This is also increasingly true in respect to countries like Kazakhstan even though only a portion of Kazakhstan's territory lies in Eastern Europe. The basis for the argument of including Kazakhstan in Europe is that it has strong cultural ties to Russia and Ukraine due to their common Soviet history, Kazakhstan's large population of Eastern Slavs, the use of the Russian language, and the effects of the process of Russification on the Kazakhstani state.

The point here is that Europe is not a purely cultural or geographic phenomenon. This shifting of Europe is a process tied to Foucauldian governmentality. Institutions and the ideas they project on society have a large effect on geo-political discourse. In this regard, there is a multi-layered drive to expand so-called European institutions such as NATO, the European Union, and all the organizations complementing them. Aside from the reference to NATO with its North American members and Turkey, why would the European Union be called a "so-called European institution" in this chapter, one may ask? The answer is simple. The EU makes the pretentious claim that it is the sole body of and basis for Europe, overlooking all else in Europe that is outside of its scope. In reality the EU has worked to either absorb or erase any other European alternatives to itself, especially in the Balkans and the European portions of the former USSR. Moreover, it should also be committed to memory that the EU is not the sole representative of the European continent or of European civilization. Europe is not the EU and the EU is not Europe. Nor is Europe an interchangeable name or entity with the EU. Countries like Russia, Belarus, and Ukraine all stand outside of the EU's boundaries, though less so for countries like Moldova, Switzerland, and Serbia. Europe is a far more diverse place, though increasingly less so, than a land collectively symbolized by the EU.

Now nearing full circle to the subject of NATO's growth, Europe has been expanding its borders because of institutional expansion, which represents the politico-economic spreading out of the Western Bloc's frontiers after the collapse of the USSR and the Eastern Bloc. This also helps explain the current project to redefine Europe and to expand it conceptually, intellectually, socially, culturally, politically, economically, militarily, and institutionally. This is a multi-layered process involving various organizations and initiatives that are helping to cultivate this expansion.

Within this venture, NATO and the EU complement one another. NATO and EU expansion go hand-in-hand, which means there is a partnership between the military push and the economic push, which are both tied together under political collaboration. In this chapter the pattern of the process will be revealed. Now going full circle, Article 10 of the Washington Treaty applies to European countries, but is not intent on stopping expansion on the basis of what was defined as Europe in 1949. The concept of Europe is not static in the long-term, as has been discussed, and will allow for new interpretations of Europe. Nor is the concept of Europe a fixed definition within the Washington Treaty. We are already witnessing a restructuring of the boundaries of Europe as countries like Kazakhstan, Uzbekistan, Kyrgyzstan, and Tajikistan were admitted into the Organization for Security and Cooperation in Europe (OSCE) and other European bodies. Nor is the Washington Treaty itself beyond amendment or inflexible as the North Atlantic Council has shown. Moreover, NATO has wasted no time in cultivating the grounds for growth into an expanded Europe. This has translated into the Partnership for Peace Program (PfP) and the Mediterranean Dialogue (MD), which complement EU expansion, including the two main categories of the EU's European Neighborhood Policy (ENP).

The Twin Pillars of NATO

Before the advent of Nicolas Stéphane Sarkozy in the Élysée Palace as president of France, the Atlantic Alliance could concretely be conceptualized as an alliance divided into two main pillars formed by two intra-NATO camps. Sarkozy's policies have helped muddle the boundaries of the two intra-NATO alliances, but they still exist. These internal axes of the Atlantic Alliance are the Anglo-American Alliance formed by the US and the UK and the Franco-German Entente formed by the French Republic and Germany. Together both intra-NATO alliances accounted for approximately 55% of the world's total military expenditures in 2011, while the rest of NATO accounted for about 9.8% of the world's military spending in the same year.[1] Both these axes evolved around economic, political, and military contours that were forged by both historical and socio-cultural realities. Moreover, the wavering Franco-German Entente is a continental European entity, whereas the Anglo-American Alliance is the very incarnation of Atlanticism, maritime trade, and the overseas legacy of Britain and its empire. The Anglo-American side also forms the heart and vanguard of Atlanticist ideology, while the Franco-German side has always had a strong pan-Europeanist tradition and leanings towards Eurasianist tendencies, including such concepts as a strategic axis between Paris, Berlin, and Moscow. Together these two intra-NATO alliances form the centers of gravity for the world of NATO within the existing Euro-Atlantic Zone.

Originally the Franco-German Entente evolved through the partnership of France and West Germany after the Second World War on the basis of France's adamant determination to be independent from the United States of America. It started when French President Charles de Gaulle's unremitting demands that a tripartite directorate be created between France, Britain, and the United States to manage the Western Bloc were rejected by Washington and London in 1958. After the unification of West and East Germany in 1990, the Franco-German partnership strengthened further and spawned the European Economic Community (EEC), becoming one of the driving forces for political pan-Europeanism. France and a unified Germany were the engines of the evolving structure of the European Common Market, which would later become the modern European Union. By extension Western European countries like the Kingdom of Belgium, the Republic of Austria, and the Grand Duchy of Luxembourg are members of the Franco-German camp.

The strategic axis formed by Washington and London is formulated on the vestiges of Britain's overseas colonies and territories, which essentially fell under US control. In this regard, countries like Australia and Canada fall within the orbit of the Anglo-American camp. As a reflection of the Anglo-American camp's colonial history, many of the nations in its axis are also part of the Anglosphere or English-speaking world where the English language is either the de facto (practical) or de jure (official) language of state. Countries like the Philippines, Japan, South Korea, and Guam that have all in the past fallen under the military control and occupation of the US are also closely aligned to this Anglo-American axis. Moreover, Anglo-American ties are very intimate with Israel, which is their creation and strategic pin in an important geo-strategic junction of the world. Unlike the Franco-German Entente, the base of the Anglo-American Alliance is outside of Eurasia and is more fixated on an Atlantic zoning. This also becomes apparent after one considers the island nature of Britain in addition to the geographic situation of the US in the continent of North America. This reality is additionally reflected in the naval strength of the UK and the US. In classical geo-political terms, this in itself is a reflection of Atlanticist sea-power versus Eurasian land-power.

Because of these geographic realities, Atlanticism is the geo-political ideology that has shaped US and UK security architecture and conceptions about international relations. This has led to a view that differentiates Britain from the rest of Europe, which in turn had led to objections to the Anglo-American "belief that England [is] an Atlantic rather than a European [state] and must be allied, or even federated, with the United States and must remain isolated from Europe" by some among the Anglo-American elites like Carroll Quigley who have seen this as shortsighted and counter-productive.[2] When members of the British intelligentsia like George Orwell and Halford J. Mackinder referred respectively to the perpetual war of "Oceania" against Eurasia and the spreading of "oceanic freedom" from the sea-powers into the heart of Eurasia, they are referring to the Atlantic nature of the Anglo-American Alliance.

The Trans-Atlantic Fault Lines:
Atlanticism, pan-Europeanism, and Eurasianism

Despite the memberships of Paris and Berlin in the Atlantic Alliance, Atlanticism is not an instinctive or inherent geo-political paradigm for either France or Germany. Both the French Republic and the Federal Republic of Germany are continental European states and at one point each was a major force in its day in the European mesocosm of Eurasia. Before the ascendancy of the US and Russia in European affairs, the rivalry between the forerunners of modern Atlanticism on one side and pan-Europeanism and Eurasianism on another side historically played themselves out between Britain and these two states. Entities like Napoleonic France, as the First French Empire was called, and the Imperial German Realm, as the German Empire that evolved out of Prussia was called, were bitter rivals of Britain. London's objectives always leaned towards a policy of preventing the "Continentals," the precursor term for pan-Europeanists and Eurasians, from uniting. With this strategic perspective in mind London always tried to play the French, Germans, Austrians, Ottomans, and Russians against one another. Whenever one would get too strong, Britain would side against it and work with the others to keep a strategic balance on the so-called "Continent."

A discussion of NATO expansion must also start with an understanding of the Atlanticist, Eurasianist, and pan-Europeanist paradigms and the rivalry between the Anglo-American and Franco-German pillars of NATO where these geo-political currents come into play. To do this we must refer back to the European Union once more. The EU is the materialization of a long-term regionalized pan-Europeanist goal in Western Europe. Even the Brussels Treaty, which was replaced by the ideas of American, British, and Canadian Atlanticist figures through the Washington Treaty, is a reflection of the goal of uniting Europe in social, political, economic, and defensive terms under pan-Europeanism. European unification in itself can develop primarily in three different directions under three distinct geo-political trends. European unification can (1) fit within an Atlanticist paradigm and amalgamate the entity of Europe with North America; it can (2) fit as a building block within a larger Eurasianist project of uniting all the regions of Eurasia; or it can (3) pursue a purely European course keeping a distance from both paradigms and the geo-political poles that embody them. In theoretical terms, a united Europe could be an equal partner with either Atlanticists or Eurasianists from centers of power outside of the polity of Europe. In practice, the European nations within the North Atlantic Treaty Organization have selected pan-Europeanism under the umbrella of Atlanticism. The current geo-political composure of the EU is a dichotomy; the EU is a pan-Europeanist project under Atlanticist contours within the Euro-Atlantic Zone. NATO is also a representation of this pan-Europeanism within the contours of an overarching Atlanticist architecture.

Aside from economics, the rivalry between the Anglo-American and Franco-German sides has been based on efforts by Paris and Berlin to maintain the pan-Europeanist integrity of the integration project in Europe from total subordination to Atlanticism under the helm of their Anglo-American allies. This intra-NATO rivalry has also been played out in the field of ideological paradigms, but is a rivalry that is built on the basis of power politics where France and Germany have worked to maintain their autonomy in order to create a realm in Europe and its periphery for themselves. Nothing brings this to mind better than Gaullist doctrine and its political offshoots in France and Franco-German efforts to insulate Europe from US strategic designs against the Kremlin and Eurasia. Anglo-American efforts to push France out of Africa and to prevent the French from creating their own nuclear weapons worked to fasten Paris on its geo-strategic course away from full-fledged Atlanticism. In this sense France has had one foot in and one foot out of NATO most the time until the ascendency of Sarkozy into the Élysée Palace.

Gaullism has been described as a deluded view of French grandeur by its critics and as a doctrine of independence, flexibility, and self-dependency by its advocates. According to the historian Theodore Draper there are four versions of Gaullism that would emerge in France.[3] The first and original version is the Gaullism of Charles de Gaulle and the other three versions of Gaullism can be called neo-Gaullism; these are the Gaullisms, or arguably pseudo-Gaullisms, of Georges Pompidou, Valéry Giscard d'Estaing, and François Mitterrand.[4] Despite everything that Mitterrand had said before the French presidential elections in 1980, his Gaullism proved to be a fraud. The concept of Gaullism started when Charles de Gaulle and French officials became increasingly disenchanted with the US and the Anglo-American Alliance. Africa, the Anglo-American nuclear monopoly, the concept of a strategic deterrence, and economics all served to change the course of France. Whereas French Prime Minister Henri Queuille was an enthusiastic supporter of US involvement in Europe and trans-Atlantic ties, Charles de Gaulle began to manipulate them to serve French interests. In regard to Africa, its importance for France has to be emphasized. France has always seen the Maghreb and West Africa as part of its sphere of influence, even after the loss of its colonies. The French African colonies were of such importance to Paris and French business interests that Jacques Godfrain, the former French cabinet minister responsible for Franco-African relations, declared years later: "[France is] a little country, with a small amount of strength [but] we can move a planet because we have relations of friendship and intimacy with 15 or 20 African countries."[5]

Before the Second World War had even ended the US had started plans for increasing its post-war influence at the expense of France and other Western European colonial powers. This included the securing of uranium resources in Africa, particularly the Belgian Congo, to maintain the US nuclear monopoly. This put Washington and Paris at odds over Africa and would lead to resentment among certain French elites. Both France and the US were aware of the gas and oil reserves in Africa and the French even created the Petroleum Research Office for the purpose of extracting oil and gas in 1945. In 1953, a few years later, Paris would issue oil exploration licenses to four French companies in Africa. Due to its fears of both US encroachment and African demands for independence Paris would even form the Common Organization of the Saharan Regions or the *Organisation Commune des Régions Sahariennes* (OCRS) to maintain its control over the resource-rich portions of its African territories that had oil, gas, and uranium. The uranium in the OCRS would be important for guaranteeing French independence through the creation of a nuclear strategic deterrent and as a riposte to the Anglo-American monopoly over NATO's nuclear weapons that the US refused to share with France. Tensions would worsen as US efforts to carve a sphere of influence in Africa at the expense of France included arms transfers to Tunisia and Morocco that ended up being used in Algeria against the French military. President de Gaulle's Anglo-American NATO allies would also refuse repeated requests to expand NATO's area of defense to include France's colonies in Africa in an effort to help the French prevent the loss of their African empire. On the basis of these differences Gaullism emerged in the French Republic.

The intra-NATO rivalries that exist within the Atlantic Alliance have led to several schisms within NATO that at times appeared to threaten the continuation of the Atlanticist project. In 1959, Charles de Gaulle delivered his famous speech in Strasbourg about a unified Europe from the coastline of the Atlantic Ocean to the Ural Mountains in the

Soviet Union as part of France's push for the creation of a third pole (or a sub-pole) rising from within the contours of the Altanticist architecture dominating Western Europe. It was in this time frame that President de Gaulle would look to West Germany for help in counter-balancing Anglo-American influence in the Western Bloc and Europe. He would also go on to make the decisions to remove France from the Atlantic Alliance's Anglo-American dominated integrated military structure in 1966 and remove French forces from the command of NATO. Moreover, France would ask foreign troops and military units from other NATO members to depart from its soil. Paris would also push forward the scientific work for creating its own nuclear weapons program and establish the European Atomic Energy Community (Euratom) to break the Anglo-American nuclear monopoly. As a result of the Gaullist actions, the Atlantic Alliance's headquarters was relocated from Paris to Brussels, Belgium.

The last major crisis on the basis of these intra-NATO rivalries would be on January 22, 2003 as a result of the Anglo-American plans to invade Iraq. Belgium, France, and Germany would obstruct the Anglo-American desires at the North Atlantic Council for initiating supportive NATO operations in Turkey to supplement their plans for the invasion of Iraq. The divisions would lead to angry demands from the US Congress that France be ostracized and removed from all of NATO's decision making mechanisms. US Senator Carl Levin would even propose that a model like that of the EU, on the basis of population weight instead of the consensus system in the North Atlantic Council, be instituted to marginalize the Franco-German side from ever obstructing US plans again. Publicly Paris and Berlin argued that military operations would work against diplomacy with Baghdad, but in reality their opposition to NATO deployment in Turkey was formulated on the basis of Franco-German and Anglo-American economic rivalries. In the end, however, the Anglo-American side would get its way by taking the question of the operations in Turkey to NATO's Defense Planning Committee, which excluded France, on February 16, 2003. NATO Secretary-General George Robertson of the UK could also have made a decision to deploy NATO forces into Turkey unilaterally, following the precedent of Secretary-General Joseph Luns of the Netherlands, claiming his own decisions to be final unless there was unanimous opposition to it from NATO's members. Moreover, the war in Iraq ultimately worked against Franco-German interest in dominating Europe.

Eurasianism has not been defeated or banished in France and Germany just because both republics are situated in the Atlanticists' camp. Since the election of Nicolas Sarkozy, however, France has adopted a stronger Atlanticist attitude and moved closer to its Anglo-American allies. In 2009, Sarkozy even reintegrated France into the NATO command structure that Charles de Gaulle had removed it from in 1966. Although the rise of Sarkozy and Angela Merkel has undermined Franco-German autonomy, Paris and Berlin have never abandoned alternatives to Atlanticisim for themselves and the EU or, if need be, ruled out a day when the EU would be synchronized within the contours of a Eurasianist project led by Russia. Russia, as the primary Eurasianist actor on the European chessboard, is very well aware of this and continues to engage with France, Germany, and the EU in the hope that they will develop the EU within the contours of Eurasianism and not an Atlanticist axis. The Common European Economic Space (CEES) that is intended to create a common market between the EU and the Russian Federation is tied to this objective of uniting Eurasia from Lisbon to Vladivostok and Beijing, as are discussions about the possibility of a future merger between the EU and the Common Economic Space or Single Economic Space of the Eurasian Union that Belarus, Kazakhstan, and Russia have formed.

Before 2003, Moscow was also working with Paris and Berlin to help strengthen the euro as a rival to the US dollar. In part, the Anglo-American invasion of Iraq in 2003 was a blow to greater pan-Europeanist autonomy and the Eurasianist project of integrating Europe into Eurasia. Saddam Hussein had begun selling Iraqi oil in euros which challenged the US dollar and the petro-dollar system, but the Anglo-American invasion put a stop to this. This is one of the main reasons that the UK and US invasion infuriated the Franco-German Entente which, with the help of Russia, created a worldwide political firestorm for London and Washington. Both France and Germany, however, had to make a settlement with their Anglo-American allies. Soon after the invasion of Iraq the Franco-German side held talks with the UK and US in 2003 and 2004 that resulted in a cancellation of pre-war Iraqi debts to France and Germany. France alone cancelled 80% of Iraq's $6.4 billion (US) debt on December 21, 2005.[6] To the dismay of Russia and other international actors, both the Anglo-American and Franco-German sides would eventually realize that they had need of one another.

In the Shadow of NATO Expansion: US support for EU Expansion

Traditionally, the three major powers in the EU are France, Germany, and the UK: the so-called "EU-3." Yet, these three EU states are not alone in their dominance over the European Union. Aside from the influence of Italy, the US in practicality is the EU's fourth power. Moreover, the Anglo-American Alliance has worked throughout the years to entrench the EU within an Atlanticist framework to maintain US influence over the EU. Thus, while the EU may be viewed as the creation of France and Germany, it has become a shared body between them and their Anglo-American partners. Without giving recognition to the fact that the EU is a creature of France, Germany, Britain, and the US, it is hard to conceptualize the Anglo-American foreign policy objectives that are being implemented through EU expansion. Like a bridgehead, this expansion by the EU acts as an expansion of the Atlanticist polity into Eurasia.

The so-called "special relationship" between the US and the UK also fits into this schematic. While the Gaullists in France and Western Europe have always seen Britain as a Trojan horse working for the US, British political elites have always prided themselves on this "special relationship" and seen the United Kingdom as a strictly Atlantic country tied to the US. Albeit the US needs no one to voice its opinions in the EU, the British government has traditionally acted as if it were performing that task. Washington has indeed acted by means of—or more properly with—London to influence the direction of the EU like a Trojan horse. This essentially makes the US a de facto power in the EU—to say nothing about the funneling of money to the European Central Bank (ECB) and the $2 trillion (US) direct investments of the United States in Europe.[7] Other mechanisms including the US domination of NATO and several international financial institutions along with control over the policies of newer EU members—the "new Europe" which mattered more than "old Europe" to George W. Bush, Jr. and Donald Rumsfeld if one recalls the first chapter of this book—also allow Washington to exert itself as a power not just over but within the EU.

Up until 2003, within the pan-Europeanist and Atlanticist framework of Europe the Franco-German Entente mainly had the political upper hand. To keep this influence France had always tried to prevent the UK from too often being a part of certain aspects of European integration. Charles de Gaulle and the Gaullists in France using their veto had even prevented Britain from entering the European Economic Community, the precursor to the EU, until Georges Pompidou let Britain enter in 1973. On the other hand, the Anglo-American Alliance has always held military sway due to the primacy of the Pentagon. In 2011 alone, the Anglo-American Alliance accounted for about 48% of the world's total military expenditures, while the Franco-German sided accounted for about 7%.[8]

It is this political-military imbalance that has created an oscillating relationship for both sides, maintaining their alliance and the integrity of NATO. France and Germany with their allies are still the principal forces within the EU. It should be understood at this point that when international analysts talk about rifts or arguments between the EU and the US they are mostly talking about disagreements or rivalries between the Franco-German Entente and the US, as well as the UK by extension of the Anglo-American Alliance. NATO on the other hand is the inverse of this relationship. The Atlantic Alliance is dominated by the

Anglo-Americans, specifically the US. Just as one conceptualizes that the EU serves the interests of the United States, one must also recognize that Franco-German interests in NATO can be served if they fall within the contours of Atlanticism and US interests. A case in point is NATO intervention in the Balkans, which benefited Germany greatly. In the former Yugoslavia, Germany and the US worked hand-in-hand to reduce the former Yugoslav states to military garrisons and economic territories. Thus, France and Germany are unhappily dependent in military terms on the US through NATO. On several occasions the creation of an EU defense strategy has been part of past Franco-German attempts to gain control over the EU and undermine Anglo-American military influence in the Euro-Atlantic Zone. The last attempt was during the invasion of Iraq when France, Germany, Belgium, and the Grand Duchy of Luxembourg held a meeting on the issue. The subject was so corrosive that Tony Blair, the prime minister of Britain, said that it was a return to the divisions of the Cold War in Europe.

Despite the intra-NATO rivalries, Anglo-American geostrategic planning recognizes that France and Germany are crucial for Atlanticist influence over Europe and for post-Cold War expansion into Eurasia. Theodore Draper would go so far as to assert: "Without France, Western Europe is a political and geographic amputee."[9] Atlanticists also recognize the predominance of the Franco-Germans in the EU. This is also another reason why the intra-NATO rivalry has had its limits and both sides have been willing to negotiate with one another. In 1997, one of the top geostrategists of the US, Zbigniew Kazimierz Brzezinski, stressed the pivotal role that the Franco-German dominated EU would play in expanding the Euro-Atlantic Zone and Atlanticism into the heart of Eurasia. Like many of his colleagues at the Council on Foreign Relations (CFR), Brzezinski has also contended that EU expansion is equivalent to the clandestine expansion of US influence. In this regard he has written:

> Unlike America's links with Japan, NATO entrenches American political influence and military power on the Eurasian mainland. While the allied European nations [are] still highly dependent on [American] protection, any expansion of Europe's political scope is automatically an expansion of U.S. influence.[10]

According to James Arthur Salter, a former British cabinet minister, these aims have also been part of a much older Anglo-American strategy of using Europe as a means of spreading their sphere of influence globally through "regional leagues" or blocs; the seeds of this process may have been set into motion in 1930 when France proposed through the Briand

Memorandum that a "European Federal Union" be created.[11] This is why Brzezinski, a former cabinet secretary as the US national security advisor in the Carter Administration, has insisted that Paris and Berlin should never be alienated from the US. Without the strategic cooperation of France and Germany the task of expanding US influence into Eurasia would be drastically crippled. It is on this basis that people like Richard Kuger, Brzezinski's colleague at the RAND Corporation, have advocated more of an equal footing between the US, Britain, France, and Germany; they have even advocated putting the UK aside in favor of France.

Over the years EU expansion has also served a secondary purpose for the Anglo-American Alliance. It has diluted and undermined the strength of the Franco-German Entente and cemented the EU in an Atlanticist course. In context of US interests, Brzezinski has explained EU expansion thus:

> A wider [EU] and an enlarged NATO will serve the short-term and long-term interest of [American] policy. A larger [EU] will expand the range of American influence without simultaneously creating a [EU] so politically integrated that it could challenge the United States on matters of [strategic] importance, particularly in the Middle East.[12]

Arguably, the outcome of this is dependent on the rate or velocity of the EU's expansion. A fast rate of EU expansion, but not exceedingly fast, serves Anglo-American interests by not allowing their Franco-German allies to consolidate power within the European Union and to commandeer it, which could result in a breakout of the EU from its current Atlanticist trajectory or in the partnering of the EU with the Euransianists and their geo-political project. Steadier rates of EU expansion are in the best interests of the Franco-German Entente and give time for Paris and Berlin to build their influence among acceding nations and newer EU members. This is one of the reasons why there were major tensions between Britain and France over EU expansion in Eastern Europe. This is also the reason why the US openly meddled in EU affairs and demanded the entry of several Eastern European countries, such as Poland, into the European Union. The entry of Turkey into the EU, which both the governments of the United States and the United Kingdom support, would also greatly dilute the influence of France or Germany.

TEXT BOX

European Union Milestones

1950: France proposes integrating the coal and steel industries of Western Europe.

1951: Six countries set up the European Coal and Steel Community (ECSC): Belgium, France, Italy, Luxembourg, the Netherlands and West Germany.

1957: The Treaties of Rome are signed, creating the European Atomic Energy Community (Euratom) and the European Economic Community (EEC).

1967: The institutions of the three European Communities (the ECSC, the EEC and Euratom) are merged. Three new institutions are formed: the European Commission, the Council of Ministers and the European Parliament.

1970: Following a decision taken in 1969 by the European Council, the Werner Report lays down the first blueprint for an economic and monetary union comprising the then six Member States of the EEC.

1979: The governments and central banks of the now nine Member States create the European Monetary System (EMS). Its main feature is the exchange rate mechanism (ERM), which establishes fixed but adjustable exchange rates between the currencies.

1986: The idea of an economic and monetary union is revived in the Single European Act (SEA).

1988: The European Council confirms the objective of achieving Economic and Monetary Union (EMU).

1989: The negotiations of the Treaty on the European Union begin. It amends the European Community. In particular, it includes provisions on the introduction of EMU and the establishment of the European Central Bank.

1992: The Maastricht Treaty is signed and creates the European Union.

2002: Introduction of the euro.

Based on information from the European Central Bank

EU Expansion: The European Neighborhood Policy

Borders are not necessarily physical. When removing fine lines of separation, meaning borders, what is left, other than some form of harmonization or assimilation? The European Neighborhood Policy (ENP) is a means for expanding the European Union, and by extension the Euro-Atlantic Zone, by creating additional layers for Altanticist expansion, like the Union for the Mediterranean (UfM). The ENP was first outlined by the European Commission when it was deliberating on the concept of a "wider Europe" during the same timeframe as the Anglo-American invasion of Iraq in March 2003. The chronology of these two events falls into line with Euro-Atlantic expansionism. The European Commission subtly elucidated these expansionist intentions in its official texts when describing the ENP:

> The European Neighborhood Policy (ENP) was developed in 2004, with the objective of avoiding the emergence of new dividing lines between the enlarged [European Union] and our neighbors [in Eastern Europe, Caucasia, and the Mediterranean] and instead strengthening the prosperity, stability and security of all concerned.[13]

Special attention should be given to the European Commission's stated "objective of avoiding the emergence of new dividing lines between the enlarged [European Union]" and its neighbors in the Balkans, the former USSR, and the non-European areas of the Mediterranean Basin.[14] The ENP program covers EU relations with Algeria, Armenia, the Republic of Azerbaijan, Belarus, Egypt, Georgia, Israel, Jordan, Lebanon, Libya, Moldova, Morocco, the Palestinian Authority, Syria, Tunisia, and Ukraine. Furthermore, the ENP is divided into two streams, one covering the south or Mediterranean—called the EU's neighbors to the south—and the other governing the east or the former republics of the USSR in Eastern Europe and the Caucasus—called the EU's neighbors to the east. The latter is called the Eastern Partnership (EaP) while the former is called the Euro-Mediterranean Partnership (EURMED), formerly the Barcelona Process. EUROMED has resulted in the formation of a Mediterranean Union or, more properly called by its official name, the Union for the Mediterranean (UfM), which was co-launched in July 2008 by Nicolas Sarkozy and Egypt's former dictator Mohammed Husni (Hosni) Mubarak. Heretofore the Eastern Partnership had not launched any direct program for any formal regional organization, but it has strengthened and complemented the Black Sea Synergy (BSS) that was launched in the Ukrainian capital of

Kiev in February 2009. The BSS is built on various regional concepts in the Black Sea including the Black Sea Forum for Partnership and Dialogue, which was launched by pre-EU Romania in 2006. The Eastern Partnership has also sought cooperation with the Russian Federation through the Northern Dimension program, which was established in 1999. The non-EU countries involved in this program are Russia and the Scandinavian countries of Iceland and Norway.

The ENP also provides funding to EU neighbors through what it calls "financial instruments." The European Neighborhood and Partnership Instrument (ENPI) for macro-economic reforms and economic restructuring is one of these financial instruments. This includes the privatization of the national economies of the countries participating in the ENP program. For example, after the harrowing 2006 Israeli war on Lebanon, the corrupt Lebanese government of Fouad Siniora agreed through the European Union-Lebanon ENP Action Plan and the ENPI to accelerate the privatization of the Lebanese economy. The ENPI also serves to streamline and standardize the EU's neighbors' policies with those of the EU. The ENPI began operating among the EU's eastern neighbors in 2007 and replaced the Technical Assistance for the Commonwealth of Independent States (TACIS) program, which was designed to help transform the economies of the republics of the former USSR into countries espousing capitalist economic principles. This program was launched as a means to prevent these post-Soviet economies from developing autonomously or integrating with Russia or in a Eurasian direction. Among the EU's southern neighbors, the ENPI has replaced the 1995 MEDA I and 2000 MEDA II, which themselves had replaced the bilateral financial instruments that the EU had in place with the non-European Mediterranean countries under the Barcelona Process. From the years 2007 to 2010, the EU was projected to give the Kingdom of Morocco 654 million euros, Algeria 220 million euros, Tunisia 300 million euros, Egypt 558 million euros, the Palestinian Authority 632 euros, Syria 130 million euros, and Israel 8 million euros in league with their reforms and development projects intended to help open their doors to EU customers and business interests. These funds were intended to restructure the local economies, open up their markets, privatize, and integrate with the EU while encouraging these countries to sell their assets to companies from the EU.

The ENPI are additionally far more policy-oriented than both the TACIS and the MEDs. They are designed to manipulate national political and economic policies in recipient countries. Along the same lines as the EU's southern and eastern initiatives, the ENPI are categorized into those ENPI covering the "east," meaning Eastern Europe and the former USSR, and those ENPI covering the "south," meaning the non-European countries of the Mediterranean Basin. The process has resounding resemblances to World Bank and International Monetary Fund (IMF) programs. ENP funding has been administered to all the EU's geographic frontiers through so-called democratization programs, stabilization initiatives, and humanitarian programs that include food aid. Recipients of ENP funding include Ukraine, Moldova, Georgia, and Arab countries like Morocco and Jordan. In 2007 the executive arm of the EU also formed the Neighborhood Investment Fund. The purpose of the Neighborhood Investment Fund, which will be active until 2013, is to support international financial institution (IFI) lending from such organizations as the World Bank and the European Bank for Reconstruction and Development (EBRD) in ENP partner countries. Since 2002, the EU's European Investment Bank has been heavily involved in the Arab countries of the Mediterranean under the mandate of the ENP and the Facility for Euro-Mediterranean Investment and Partnership (FEMIP). This also further cultivates the chains of privatization and opens the Mediterranean to Euro-Atlantic control and expansion.

Key to the ENP program and its financial instruments are the bilateral agreements called Action Plans made between the EU and ENP partners. The Action Plans essentially restructure the neighboring states and open their doors to the political and economic influence of the EU. Russia is included in the ENP on a special basis through a strategic partnership agreement that covers four common spaces between the Russian Federation and the EU. In 2011, there were four holdouts that did not activate the Action Plans that the EU had unilaterally designed for them. These countries were Algeria, Belarus, Libya, and Syria. These states have not fully opened their doors to Euro-Atlantic expansion. Although relations appear cordial with Algeria, this is one of the reasons that these four states have faced US, EU, and NATO hostility in one way or another. Libya for example refused ENPI funding and remained an observer in the EUROMED, though this may change due to the recent regime change. These initiatives are actually conquest by means of financial and economic control. Neighboring states are coerced into accepting them and if coercion fails then military might is used.

One feature of the ENP is the Stabilization and Association Process (SAP) which includes the so-called stabilization of national economies through Action Plans drawn by the EU involving country reports. SAP agreements have been made with Albania, Bosnia-Herzegovina, Croatia, Montenegro, Serbia, and the former Yugoslav Republic (FYR) of Macedonia. EU assistance and aid to these nations in the Balkans is tied to conditionalities that are drawn up by the European Commission in Brussels, which includes the privatization of state infrastructure and its purchase by British, French, German, Dutch, Italian, Canadian, and American companies amongst others. The SAP has been accused of being part of the modus operandi of the EU and US for moving into the conflict zones they themselves have created. Along with similar agreements and devices, the SAP can also be called a form of neo-colonialism and imperial expansion like the entire ENP. Countries are either smashed or eroded and then swallowed up and incorporated into larger organizations or entities in the process of expanding the Euro-Atlantic Zone. The SAP in this regard is part of the expansion formula of the Atlanticist sphere of influence. It has proceeded by encouraging the SAP candidates in the Balkans to quickly open up their economies, integrate, and eventually become full-fledged EU members. The process establishes a contractual relationship between the EU and the SAP candidate countries. This imposes legal obligations on the SAP candidate states that force them to open up their national economies and to privatize their state infrastructure. State loans and economic arrangements are also made by the EU for the candidate states, which further put them under the economic control of the primary EU powers. The words conflict, post-conflict, and stabilization are linked together in this discourse. Where war brings instability, the economic and political tutelage of the EU and US are presented as bringing stability and prosperity. Both are systematic steps of the same formula.

The Eastern Partnership and Russia

The Eastern Partnership (EaP) was launched on May 7, 2009 and was an initiative that the governments of Poland and Sweden are credited for drafting. It is a specific program designed as an additional layer of the ENP. Although the EaP does not promise or preclude EU membership, it is directed at making sure that the former Soviet countries of Belarus, Moldova, and Ukraine in Eastern Europe and Armenia, the Republic of Azerbaijan, and Georgia in the Caucasus open their borders and are integrated with the EU. An additional dimension of the EU's EaP is the aim of restructuring the public institutions of the republics of the former USSR under the Comprehensive Institution Building Program to match those of the EU. This can be viewed as an audacious form of institutional colonization tied to economic and political absorption into the Euro-Atlantic Zone. This is why the EaP has been met with hostility by several of these republics which view this as a slow breach of their sovereignty and as a soft invasion. Russia, which refuses to join the EaP, has openly accused the EU of acting in a neo-colonial manner and trying to impose its expansion in Eastern Europe.

There is also a simultaneous competitive process tied to the tensions between Russia and the EU over the EaP. Russia wants these nations that are the focus of the EaP to join the Eurasian Union, which is modeled on the EU. Belarus is already a member of the Eurasian Union.

TEXT BOX

EUROPEAN NEIGHBORHOOD POLICY (ENP)

In the Balkans – Albania and the former Yugoslavian States

- Stabilization and Association Process (SAP)

In the former USSR – Ex-Soviet Eastern European and Caucasian States

- Eastern Partnership Program (EaP)

In the Mediterranean Basin – Israel and the Arab States of the Mediterranean Sea

- Euro-Mediterranean Partnership (EUROMED)

Strategic Partnership with Russia

- Common European Economic Space (CEES)

TABLE 2.1

The Eastern Partnership Countries and Russia

Country	Russian Ally	Position on EU Membership	Eurasian Union Membership
Armenia	Yes	Not Interested	Interested in Joining
Azerbaijan, Republic of	No	Interested in Joining	Interested in Cooperation
Belarus	Yes	Not Interested	Member
Georgia, Republic of	No	Interested in Joining	Not Interested
Moldova	Neutral	Interested in Cooperation	Interested in Cooperation
Russia -		Not Interested	Member
Ukraine	Yes	Interested in Cooperation	Interested in Joining

MAP II: EU and the Eastern Partnership Countries

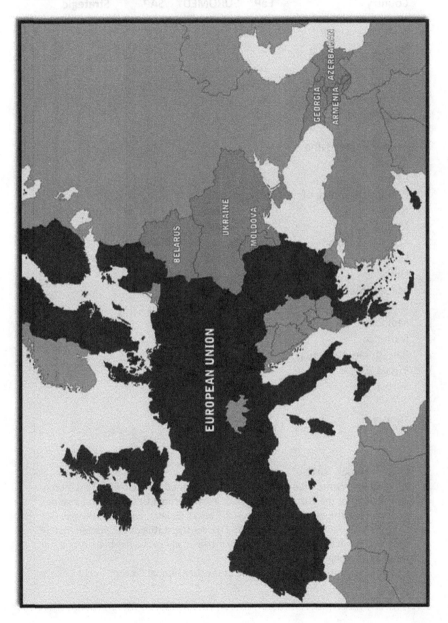

TABLE 2.2

| Country | European Neighborhood Policy Program* | | | |
	EaP	EUROMED†	SAP	Strategic Partnership
Albania	-	-	Yes	-
Algeria	Yes	-		-
Armenia	Yes	-	-	-
Azerbaijan, Republic of	Yes	-	-	-
Belarus	Yes	-	-	-
Bosnia-Herzegovina	-	-	Yes	-
Croatia	-	-	Yes	-
Egypt	-	Yes	-	-
Georgia, Republic of	Yes	-	-	-
Israel	-	Yes	-	-
Jordan	-	Yes	-	-
Kosovo - Serbia	-	-	Candidate‡	-
Lebanon	-	Yes	-	-
Libya	-	Observer§	-	-
Macedonia, FYR of	-	-	Yes	-
Montenegro	-	-	Yes	-
Moldova	Yes	-	-	-
Morocco	-	Yes	-	-
Palestinian Authority	-	Yes	-	-
Russia	-	-	-	Yes
Serbia	-	-	Yes	-
Syria	-	Yes	-	-
Tunisia	-	Yes	-	-
Ukraine	Yes	-	-	-

* As of February 2012
† The Union for the Mediterranean (UfM) is formed on the basis of the Barcelona Process or the Euro-Mediterranean Partnership (EUROMED) and includes the non-EU European states of Albania, Bosnia, Croatia, and Montenegro.
‡The dispute between Serbia and the EU over the status of the predominately Albanian-inhabited Serbian breakaway province of Kosovo has been a factor in formally delaying certain EU programs.
§ Libya is likely to join under the rule of the Transitional Council.

Georgia has ruled out joining the Eurasian Union. Ukraine is central in this process, because both US and NATO strategists have believed since 1992 that if Ukraine should become lodged fully within the orbit of the Kremlin that hostilities with Russia would lead Moscow to make an attempt to regain its lost influence in Europe. This has led to intense competition between Russia and NATO over Ukraine.

Looking beyond the EU's diplomatic jargon and all the noise, it is clear that expanding the borders of the European Union is the mission of the ENP. The ENP follows the directives of the European Security Strategy, a strategic EU document that was put together by the Franco-German Entente. This document only emerged in Brussels on December 12, 2003 after a series of meetings between the Anglo-American and Franco-German pillars of the North Atlantic Treaty Alliance. As mentioned earlier, it was around this time on December 16, 2003 that both Jacques Chirac and Gerhard Schröder would also officially cancel Iraq's debts to France and Germany. It is also no mere coincidence that the puppet Interim Iraqi President Ghazi Al-Yawar visited NATO Headquarters just prior to this on September 16, 2003. These events can be perceived as the start of the rapprochement between the Franco-German and Anglo-American sides that resulted in an agreement to co-manage the Middle East and North Africa. In other words, the European Security Strategy is a product of a tactical Franco-German and Anglo-American agreement to create spheres of influence around Europe.

NATO's important 2006 summit in Riga, Latvia also furthered this agreement by building on it and lifting it from the EU level to the NATO level. It was not accidental either that the securing of energy resources was a main theme of the Atlantic Alliance's conference in Riga; this fell in line with the objective of co-managing the resources of the EU's periphery from North Africa to the Caucasus between the two intra-NATO alliances. In the European Security Strategy emphasis is placed on the central importance of NATO as the embodiment of military cooperation between America and the EU and on the objective of establishing a "rule-based international order" (debatably "rule *by* law" and not the "rule *of* law") globally through international regional bodies such as the UN Security Council, the Association of Southeast Asian Nations (ASEAN), MERCOSUR, and the African Union.[15]

The European Security Strategy provides the roadmap for redefining the European Union's security borders in concert with both Franco-German and Anglo-American interests. In 2006 this was widely advertized by EU officials who emphasized that the EU's security borders started in the Middle East and the Mediterranean. The European Security Strategy in fact states:

> The United States has played a critical role in European integration and European security, in particular through NATO. The end of the Cold War has left the United States in a dominant position as a military actor. However, no single country is able to tackle today's complex problems on its own.[16]

It essentially states that the EU must be a full partner in the Atlanticist project with the US. To add to this, the Anglo-American and Franco-German sides have been in the process of merging as a means to end their intra-NATO rivalries. This also includes the ultimate aim of merging the economies of the EU and North America into a single trans-Atlantic market; this would be formally agreed upon by German Federal Chancellor Angela Merkel, US President George W. Bush, Jr., and European Commission President José Manuel Durão Barroso through an EU-US pact on trans-Atlantic trade and market standardization signed on April 30, 2007.[17] This had been something that had long been advocated by officials on both sides of the Atlantic Ocean, according to Brzezinski: "[A] Free Trade Agreement, already advocated by a number of prominent Atlantic leaders, could also mitigate the risk of growing economic rivalry between a more united [European Union] and the United States."[18] Another example of this merging process is the outcomes of the 2010 Anglo-French Defense and Security Cooperation Treaty. Under the treaty both Paris and London will share their aircraft carriers, pool their military resources, and have joint military forces, closer arms industry cooperation, joint defense equipment projects, joint military facilities, integrated nuclear weapons programs, and will jointly develop nuclear submarines, assess cooperation on developing military satellites, and develop unmanned aerial drones.[19]

The EU security document additionally declares the global ambitions of the European Union:

> As a union of 25 states with over 450 million producing over a quarter of the world's [gross national product] (GNP), and with a wide range of instruments at its disposal, the European Union is inevitably a global player. In the last decade European forces have been deployed abroad to places as distant as Afghanistan, East Timor, and the [Democratic Republic of the Congo].[20]

This means the Euro-Atlantic Zone will expand. More importantly, the security document replicates Anglo-American dogma, but in a somewhat vague way, even preemptively tackling threats abroad, in what has come to be known by political scientists as the Bush Doctrine.[21] "Good governance" is also declared as a goal to be imposed on the EU's eastern neighbors and southern neighbors, respectively in the former USSR and Mediterranean Basin.[22] Moreover, the document ultimately calls for higher defense spending, upgrading the military sector, pooling the armed forces, militarizing the EU's civilian sector, harnessing EU civilian programs to help military intervention, and aligning the EU with NATO in what will one day amount to integration.[23]

The Partnership for Peace:
NATO Expansion within the Framework of EU Expansion

The ties between NATO and the EU should be very hard to overlook at this stage. It should be clear that EU and NATO expansion go hand-in-hand, jointly expanding the Euro-Atlantic area together in harmony. The US position has always been that NATO members should be a part of the EU, the Council of Europe, or other similar institutions centered around Europe. This process should also be viewed as an expansion of both Anglo-American and Franco-German influence. The expansion of NATO precedes EU expansion and paves the way for EU membership, even though, for purposes of explanation, we looked at the EU first. NATO is even the older of the two organizations.

NATO also opens the door to gradual expansion through various programs and instruments. As the Eastern Bloc began to unravel in 1990, NATO began steps to absorb the Warsaw Pact countries. Among the first steps for NATO expansion was the creation of the North Atlantic Cooperation Council (NACC) on December 20, 1991 as a round table between NATO and the former Warsaw Pact countries. Soviet membership in the NACC was transferred to Russia almost at the very start. From 1992 onward most of the former republics of the USSR joined the NACC. At one point the Russians began proposing that the NACC be separated from NATO and used as a forum in the Organization for Security and Cooperation in Europe (OSCE). Members of the NACC and all non-NATO states belonging to the OSCE were later invited by NATO to join the Partnership for Peace Program (PfP), as a means of establishing bilateral political and military relations with the North Atlantic Treaty Organization. Jacques Lévesque of the Center for the Study of Foreign Policy and Security at the University of Québec in Montréal (UQAM) has argued that "Russia decided to join, hoping to slow the process from within."[24] NATO describes PfP thus: "It is a program of practical bilateral cooperation between individual Partner countries and NATO, designed to allow Partner countries to build up an individual relationship with NATO, while choosing their own priorities for cooperation."[25] The creation of the PfP was also a practical means of absorbing the OSCE within an overlapping NATO mechanism.

The PfP program was formally embarked upon by the Atlantic Alliance on January 10, 1994 following a US proposal made several months earlier. The program was opened to any European or former Soviet country without major preconditions. To join all PfP members had to make their military budgets transparent and open to review. This allowed NATO to monitor their defense programs and to approximate their strengths. Moreover, any PfP member had to subordinate their defense ministries to civilians and politicians. In many cases the military officers and defense ministries of the former Warsaw Pact nations were opposed to the direction that the new breed of Eastern European politicians, supported by the US and Western Europe, wanted to take their countries. These military officers could have challenged their selling off of state assets and the subordination of Eastern European economies by launching coup d'états. By subordinating Eastern European defense ministries to politicians supported by the US and Western Europe, the threat posed by these military officers was effectively sidelined and neutralized. At the same time NATO began education programs aimed at changing the mindsets and institutional cultures of the national armed forces of the countries of the former Eastern Bloc.

PfP would work to bring the new republics of the former Soviet Union and the other former members of the disbanded Warsaw Pact into the orbit of NATO. It effectively did not give them full NATO membership, but let them have one foot in the door of the Atlantic Alliance in what some saw as a bureaucratic compromise in the North Atlantic Council among those that wanted to expand NATO's membership and those that wanted no new members. It postponed expansion, but did not put potential members in limbo either. Besides, rapid expansion of NATO would have been unnecessarily provocative to Russia and could have helped hoist hostile figures into the Kremlin. Moreover, behind closed doors, those that were opposed to the entry of the former Warsaw Pact nations into NATO argued that these Eastern European countries did not share the same political culture or values as NATO members. In a manner of speaking, they argued that the former Warsaw Pact countries were premature for NATO membership.

In effect the PfP worked to prepare and transform the former Warsaw Pact nations to make them a better fit. It was predominately not a question of "if" a country would join NATO, but a question of "when." In this context, when the PfP was initiated, it was also complemented by parallel political and economic reforms in Eastern Europe. According to Joseph Kruzel, a former Pentagon official responsible for NATO, all PfP members who desired NATO membership were told that they would only be allowed to enter NATO when they had fully adopted capitalist economies, popularly and misleadingly referred to as "market democracies," and had readily changeable governments.[26] Critics may argue that this was a means to make the PfP nations susceptible to color revolutions, to make them more penetrable rather than more democratic. In addition the PfP gave time to the US and its Western European allies to weed out any politicians and political parties in the Eastern European countries that they found to be unfavorable. If NATO were to admit some of these countries into its ranks as they stood, it would have been faced with potentially allowing the entry of communist-led nations into the organization which may have refused to accept "market democracy."

The NACC would eventually be succeeded by the Euro-Atlantic Partnership Council (EAPC) on May 29, 1997. EAPC would work to advance the PfP and further Euro-Atlantic integration and cooperation. The PfP would later be expanded to include the republics of the former Socialist Federal Republic of Yugoslavia. Bosnia-Herzegovina, Montenegro, and Serbia all joined PfP in 2006. Twelve participants in NATO's PfP would eventually become members of NATO. These former PfP participants are Albania, Bulgaria, Croatia, the Czech Republic, Estonia, Hungary, Latvia, Lithuania, Poland, Romania, Slovakia, and Slovenia. All of them are formerly communist states and almost all are former members of the Warsaw Pact. Aside from Albania and Croatia,

TABLE 2.3

Participants in Partnership for Peace that Entered NATO*

Country	PfP Entry Date	EU Entry Date	NATO Entry Date
Albania	23 February 1994	-	1 April 2009
Bulgaria	14 February 1994	1 January 2007	29 March 2004
Croatia	25 May 2000	2013 set for accession	1 April 2009
Czech Republic	10 March 1994	1 May 2004	16 March 1999
Estonia	3 February 1994	1 May 2004	29 March 2004
Hungary	8 February 1994	1 May 2004	16 March 1999
Latvia	14 February 1994	1 May 2004	29 March 2004
Lithuania	27 January 1994	1 May 2004	29 March 2004
Poland	2 February 1994	1 May 2004	16 March 1999
Romania	26 January 1994	1 January 2007	29 March 2004
Slovakia	9 February 1994	1 May 2004	29 March 2004
Slovenia	30 March 1994	1 May 2004	29 March 2004

* As of February 2012

all these nations have additionally become members of the European Union. In summary, NATO's Partnership for Peace works as a means to open the doors of membership into the Atlantic Alliance for participating countries through a phase-based variety of programs or tools that involve reforms in the participant countries. The PfP has served as a NATO apprenticeship program promoted by the Pentagon. It has also served as a means of preventing any alternative security architecture to NATO from emerging in Eastern Europe.

NATO's Other "Outreach Programs"

Following a similar course to the PfP, NATO also developed the Mediterranean Dialogue (MD) in 1994, the Istanbul Cooperation Initiative (ICI) in 2004, and several special relationships. While the PfP can be viewed as NATO's equivalent to the EU's EaP and EU programs for the Balkans, the Mediterranean Dialogue and the ICI can be viewed as NATO's equivalents to the EU's Euro-Mediterranean Partnership. Overall, these NATO programs can be compared to the EU's ENP. The patterns are the same. A similar pattern is even repeated with the Russian Federation. Just as Russia has a strategic partnership with the European Union, it also has a similar strategic partnership with NATO. This strategic partnership between both parties is based on an agreement signed between the Russian Federation and the North Atlantic Treaty Organization on May 27, 1997 in Paris, France. When the Global War on Terror started, NATO and Russia increased some of their cooperation on the basis of a common enemy. It is within the framework of this 1997 agreement that the NATO-Russia Council was created on May 28, 2002. Over the years, however, NATO-Russia cooperation has diminished to symbolic levels in many aspects as tensions have mounted between Washington and Moscow. Ukraine and several other countries also maintain strategic ties to NATO; the Atlantic Alliance has the NATO-Ukraine Commission and NATO also has special relationships under the framework of bilateral relations with what NATO officials formerly called the "Partners Across the Globe" and now refer to as the Contact Countries (CC) or Global Partners.

The Contact Countries: NATO's "Global Partners"

Aside from Mongolia, Contact Countries are either countries that have been occupied or are close US allies in the Asia-Pacific region. Both Afghanistan and Iraq are Contact Countries; after both were invaded militarily by the US and its allies, their new governments signed bilateral agreements with NATO. Several of the US and NATO's strategic allies in the Asia-Pacific region are included in the list of Contact Countries because of the bilateral agreements of cooperation and coordination they have signed with the Alliance. These countries are the Commonwealth of Australia, Japan, the Republic of Korea (South Korea), and New Zealand.

NATO has been active in Pakistan since 2001 as an extension of its war in Afghanistan, giving rise to the term "AfPak," designating both as a single NATO theater. A NATO earthquake relief mission took place in Pakistan from October 2005 to February 2006 and Islamabad is also a member of the Afghanistan-Pakistan-ISAF Tripartite Commission. Alliance forces frequently militarily strike Pakistan, specifically the Pakistani Federally Administered Tribal Areas (FATA). Despite this Pakistan is one of the Contact Countries.

The Republic of Colombia may also become a Contact Country. Colombia is a closet US ally in South America and has been working closely with several NATO members, including Britain. Much of this collaboration has been aimed at combating the agrarian Marxist peasant militia movement known as the Fuerzas Armadas Revolucionarias de Colombia (FARCO), or Revolutionary Armed Forces of Colombia in English, and countering the influence of the Bolivarian Republic of Venezuela in Latin America. In 2007 Colombian Defense Minister Juan Manuel Santos travelled to the US and EU for discussions about military cooperation.[27] It is in this context that the government of President Alvaro Uribe signed a bilateral military agreement with the Pentagon in 2009 that has allowed the US military to use seven of Bogota's military bases. Three other NATO members—Britain, France, and the Netherlands—also have military infrastructure in the Caribbean and Latin America. The meetings between Colombian and NATO member officials has also resulted in the deployment of Colombian troops to Afghanistan under the command of NATO.

TEXT BOX

THE NATO OUTREACH PROGRAMS

In the Balkans – Albania and the former Yugoslavian States
- Partnership for Peace (PfP)

In the former USSR –
Ex-Soviet Eastern European and Caucasian States
- Partnership for Peace (PfP)

In the Mediterranean Basin –
Israel and the Arab States of the Mediterranean Sea
- Mediterranean Dialogue (MD)

In the Persian Gulf –
Gulf Cooperation Council (GCC) Countries
- Istanbul Cooperation Initiative (ICI)

Strategic Partnership with Russia
- NATO-Russia Council under the Partnership for Peace (PfP)

Strategic Partnership with Ukraine
- NATO-Ukraine Commission under the Partnership for Peace (PfP)

In Other Parts of the World
- Contact Countries (CC)/Global Partners

1. Asia-Pacific Region: Australia, Japan, New Zealand, South Korea

2. Central Asia: Afghanistan, Mongolia

3. Middle East: Iraq

4. The Indian Sub-Continent/South Asia: Pakistan

MAP III: NATO and Partnerships in 2004

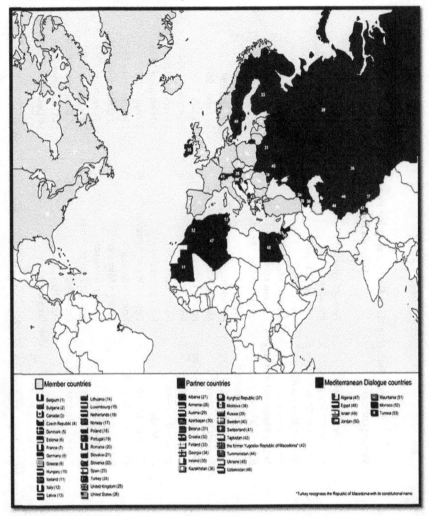

☐ Member countries

Ⴊ Belgium (1)
Ⴊ Bulgaria (2)
Ⴊ Canada (3)
Ⴊ Czech Republic (4)
Ⴊ Denmark (5)
Ⴊ Estonia (6)
Ⴊ France (7)
Ⴊ Germany (8)
Ⴊ Greece (9)
Ⴊ Hungary (10)
Ⴊ Iceland (11)
Ⴊ Italy (12)
Ⴊ Latvia (13)

Ⴊ Lithuania (14)
Ⴊ Luxembourg (15)
Ⴊ Netherlands (16)
Ⴊ Norway (17)
Ⴊ Poland (18)
Ⴊ Portugal (19)
Ⴊ Romania (20)
Ⴊ Slovakia (21)
Ⴊ Slovenia (22)
Ⴊ Spain (23)
Ⴊ Turkey (24)
Ⴊ United Kingdom (25)
Ⴊ United States (26)

■ Partner countries

Ⴊ Albania (27)
Ⴊ Armenia (28)
Ⴊ Austria (29)
Ⴊ Azerbaijan (30)
Ⴊ Belarus (31)
Ⴊ Croatia (32)
Ⴊ Finland (33)
Ⴊ Georgia (34)
Ⴊ Ireland (35)
Ⴊ Kazakhstan (36)

Ⴊ Kyrghyz Republic (37)
Ⴊ Moldova (38)
Ⴊ Russia (39)
Ⴊ Sweden (40)
Ⴊ Switzerland (41)
Ⴊ Tajikistan (42)
Ⴊ the former Yugoslav Republic of Macedonia* (43)
Ⴊ Turkmenistan (44)
Ⴊ Ukraine (45)
Ⴊ Uzbekistan (46)

■ Mediterranean Dialogue countries

Ⴊ Algeria (47)
Ⴊ Egypt (48)
Ⴊ Israel (49)
Ⴊ Jordan (50)

Ⴊ Mauritania (51)
Ⴊ Morocco (52)
Ⴊ Tunisia (53)

*Turkey recognises the Republic of Macedonia with its constitutional name

TABLE 2.4

Current Participants in Partnership for Peace*

Country	Signing Official	Official's Post	Entry Date
Ukraine	Anatoly M. Zlenko	Foreign Minister	8 February 1994
Moldova	Mircea Ion Snegur	President	16 March 1994
Georgia, Republic of	Alexander Chikvaidze	Foreign Minister	23 March 1994
Azerbaijan, Republic of	Heydar Ali-Reza Aliyev	President	4 May 1994
Finland	Heikki Haavisto	Foreign Minister	9 May 1994
Sweden	Märta Margaretha af Ugglas	Foreign Minister	9 May 1994
Turkmenistan	Boris Shikhmuradov	Deputy Prime Minister	10 May 1994
Kazakhstan	Kanat B. Saudabayev	Foreign Minister	27 May 1994
Kyrgyzstan	Askar Akayev	President	1 June 1994
Russia	Andrey V. Kozyrev	Foreign Minister	22 June 1994
Uzbekistan	Saidmukhtar Saidkasimov	Foreign Minister	13 July 1994
Armenia	Vahan Papazian	Foreign Minister	5 October 1994
Belarus	Uladzmir Syanko	Foreign Minister	11 January 1995
Austria	Alois Mock	Foreign Minister	10 February 1995
Malta	Guido de Marco	Deputy Prime Minister	26 April 1995†
Macedonia, FYR of	Branko Crvenkovski	Prime Minister	15 November 1995
Switzerland	Favio Cotti	Foreign Minister	11 December 1996
Ireland (Éire)	David Andrews	Foreign Minister	1 December 1999
Tajikistan	Sharif Rahimov	Ambassador to the EC	20 February 2002
Bosnia-Herzegovina	Nebojša Radmanović	President	14 December 2006
Montenegro	Filip Vujanović	President	14 December 2006
Serbia	Boris Tadić	President	14 December 2006

* As of February 2012

† Malta withdrew from the PfP (October 27, 1996); it then reactivated the agreement on March 20, 2008.

Chart 2.1: NATO Outreach and Partnership

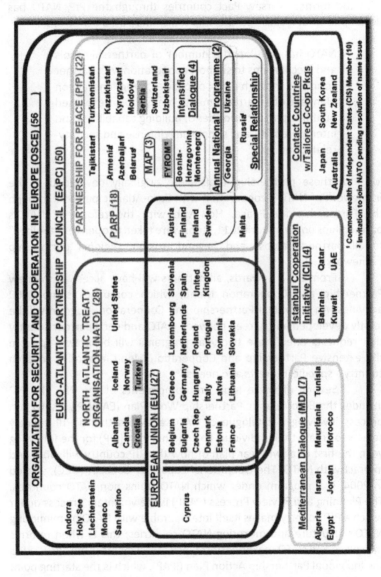

ORGANIZATION FOR SECURITY AND COOPERATION IN EUROPE (OSCE) (56)

Andorra
Holy See
Liechtenstein
Monaco
San Marino

EURO-ATLANTIC PARTNERSHIP COUNCIL (EAPC) (50)

NORTH ATLANTIC TREATY ORGANISATION (NATO) (28)

Albania
Canada
Croatia

Iceland
Norway
Turkey

United States

EUROPEAN UNION (EU) (27)

Cyprus

Belgium
Bulgaria
Czech Rep
Denmark
Estonia
France

Greece
Germany
Hungary
Italy
Latvia
Lithuania

Luxembourg
Netherlands
Poland
Portugal
Romania
Slovakia

Slovenia
Spain
United Kingdom

PARTNERSHIP FOR PEACE (PfP) (22)

PARP (18)

Tajikistan¹
Armenia¹
Azerbaijan¹
Belarus¹

Turkmenistan
Kazakhstan¹
Kyrgyzstan¹
Moldova¹
Serbia

Switzerland
Uzbekistan¹

MAP (3)
FYROM²
Bosnia-Herzegovina
Montenegro

Intensified Dialogue (4)

Annual National Programme (2)
Georgia
Ukraine

Russia¹
Special Relationship

Austria
Finland
Ireland
Sweden

Malta

Contact Countries w/Tailored Coop Pkgs

Japan
Australia

South Korea
New Zealand

¹ Commonwealth of Independent States (CIS) Member (10)
² Invitation to join NATO pending resolution of name issue

Istanbul Cooperation Initiative (ICI) (4)

Bahrain
Kuwait

Qatar
UAE

Mediterranean Dialogue (MD) (7)

Algeria
Egypt

Israel
Jordan

Mauritania
Morocco

Tunisia

NATO's "Partnership Tools"

On the basis of the forums and cooperation NATO established with the former Warsaw Pact countries through the PfP, NATO has developed what it calls "partnership tools." In NATO's own words:

> NATO has developed a number of partnership tools and mechanisms to support cooperation with partner countries through a mix of policies, programs, action plans and other arrangements. Many tools are focused on the important priorities of building capabilities and interoperability, and supporting defense and security-related reform.[28]

Most of these partnership tools were originally developed in the framework of NATO's cooperation with Euro-Atlantic partners through the Partnership for Peace. However, with the reform of NATO's partnerships policy in April 2011, steps were taken to open the "toolbox" to all partners, across and beyond existing regional partnership frameworks.

From 2012 onwards, all partners will have access to the new Partnership and Cooperation Menu, which comprises some 1600 activities. An Individual Partnership and Cooperation Program will be jointly developed and agreed between NATO and each partner country that requests one. These two-year programs will be drawn up from the extensive Partnership and Cooperation Menu, according to each country's specific interests and needs.[28]

Several of these tools are components of the PfP. The PfP includes the Euro-Atlantic Partnership Work Plan (EAPWP), a selection process involving a catalogue of NATO activities that a PfP country selects to create their Individual Partnership Plan (IPP) for the following year, the first of a two-year plan of how the PfP country will work and interact with NATO. The Operational Capability Concept (OCC), started in 2004, is a program under which NATO trains non-NATO countries. The Planning and Review Process (PARP) is the voluntary process under which a PfP country makes itself interoperable with NATO by mimicking NATO's structure and mirroring NATO countries; this is when reforms take place and NATO makes performance assessments. After the PARP is the Individual Partnership Action Plan (IPAP), which is the starting point to entry into the Atlantic Alliance.

During the 2002 summit in the Czech capital of Prague, NATO launched the IPAPs. According to NATO:

> Individual Partnership Action Plans (IPAPs) offer
> partners the opportunity to deepen their cooperation
> with NATO and sharpen the focus on domestic reform
> efforts. Developed on a two-year basis, these plans
> include [...] objectives and targets for reforms on
> political issues as well as security and defense issues.
> They are designed to bring together all the various
> cooperation mechanisms through which a partner
> country interacts with the Alliance. Since the launch
> of the IPAP in 2002, six countries have chosen to
> develop IPAPs with NATO. The development of IPAPs
> is open to all partners, on a case-by-case basis, upon
> approval of the North Atlantic Council.[29]

An IPAP is essentially an individualized cooperation program between NATO and a non-NATO country. Armenia, the Republic of Azerbaijan, Bosnia-Herzegovina, the Republic of Georgia, Kazakhstan, Moldova, Montenegro, and Ukraine have all attained IPAPs with NATO. Armenia, Kazakhstan, Moldova, and Ukraine have categorically stated that they will not use the IPAPs as a means of becoming NATO members and are satisfied with their PfP membership. So has the Republic of Azerbaijan, but Baku could eventually embark on a road towards membership and already has a special relationship with both the US and NATO. Ukraine's position has changed due to the electoral victory of Viktor Yanukovych and the Party of Regions against the Orangist camps of Victor Yushenko and Yulia Tymoshenko. Along with the government of the former Yugoslav Republic (FYR) of Macedonia, the governments of Bosnia-Herzegovina, the Republic of Georgia, and Montenegro all openly want entry into NATO.

Intensified Dialogue with NATO is the next highest level of cooperation and interaction after an IPAP between a non-NATO country and the Atlantic Alliance. Intensified Dialogue builds on the IPAPs and opens the doors for a Membership Action Plan (MAP). MAPs are the last step a country must take before joining NATO. Bosnia-Herzegovina, the Republic of Georgia, Montenegro, and Ukraine are presently engaged in the Intensified Dialogue process with NATO. Intensified Dialogue was also offered to Serbia in 2008 without solicitation from the Serb government, because of the popular dislike of NATO within the general Serbian population as a result of the war between Serbia and NATO.

TABLE 2.5

Progressive Steps Towards NATO Membership?*

Country	Partnership for Peace	Individual Partnership Action Plan (IPAP)	Intensified Dialogue (MAP)	Membership Action Plan (PfP)
Armenia	5 Oct.1994	16 Dec. 2008	-	-
Azerbaijan, Republic of	4 May 1994	27 May 2005	-	-
Belarus	11 Jan. 1995	14 May 1955	-	-
Bosnia-Herzegovina	14 Dec. 2006	10 Jan. 2008	3 April 2008	22 April 2010
Georgia, Republic of	23 March 1994	29 Oct. 2004	21 Sep. 2006	-
Kazakhstan	27 May 1994	31 Jan. 2006	-	-
Macedonia, FYR of	15 Nov. 1995	-	-	24 April 1999
Moldova	16 March 1994	19 May 2006	-	-
Montenegro	14 Dec. 2006	24 June 2008	3 Aril 2008	4 Dec. 2009
Serbia	14 Dec. 2006	-	Offered†	-
Ukraine	8 Feb. 1994	22 Nov. 2002	21 April 2005	-

* As of February 2012.

† At the NATO summit in 2008 in Bucharest, Romania the Atlantic Alliance offered Serbia, without any solicitation by the Serbian government, for the chance to start the intensified dialogue with NATO.

Becoming a NATO Member and the Membership Action Plan (MAP)

Accession into the North Atlantic Treaty Organization has changed since the Cold War period. On the basis of Article 10, a country merely needs to be invited by the North Atlantic Council and deposit their instruments of accession, meaning legal treaty document, with the US federal government to become a NATO member. As outlined during NATO's 2002 Prague Summit in the Czech Republic, membership accession now takes places by means of a step-by-step process that has been outlined by the North Atlantic Council and falls into the framework of the PfP.

Since the foundation of the PfP the North Atlantic Council has admitted twelve PfP countries into the ranks of NATO. Insofar as the PfP countries actually outnumber NATO members, this has changed as the PfP has opened up the process of phased entry into the Atlantic Alliance. We will now examine the path to membership through the MAP.

As the first step of accession, interested candidate countries must give formal confirmation to NATO Headquarters in Brussels about their intention to join NATO. The criteria set by the Atlantic Alliance is that interested countries must also be able to contribute to NATO's budget and meet all the military, legal, political, and technical obligations that NATO puts forward for them through the North Atlantic Council. This includes any reforms that are needed to meet NATO's requirements and military standards, which can continue into NATO accession. These requirements are put together on the basis of a consensus reached by all NATO members. The process is not apolitical; a country's constitutional name or foreign policy can be subject to demands by NATO members. For example, Greece has prevented the former Yugoslav Republic (FYR) of Macedonia from joining NATO on the basis of a naming dispute between the two republics.[30] On the basis of these requirements for entry, the North Atlantic Council then sets a timetable for the candidate country and transmits an invitation to it. Technocrats also come into the picture to monitor reforms and give direction to the candidates.

The second step is the delivery of an official letter of intent by the government of the country that wishes entrance into the ranks of NATO. Attached to the letter will be a formal document outlining the interested country's objective of becoming a NATO member and a timetable with benchmarks and schedules of any reforms that are needed for Atlantic Alliance membership. The third step is the signing of accession protocols between NATO and the interested country. These documents are amendments to the Washington Treaty. Upon signing and ratification, the candidate country becomes a formal member of the military bloc. The fourth step is the domestic ratification of the accession protocols by all the different members of NATO, then lastly accession of the candidate country on the basis of its domestic procedures. After this is done, the invited country will deposit its instruments of accession with the US State Department, which is the legal depository of the Washington Treaty, and enter NATO.

Within this process of accession, step five is whatever the national procedure is for joining treaties/organizations. It may be by an executive order or through the country's legislature. In this process, the Membership Action Plan (MAP) comes into play and is central. MAP was established on April 24, 1999. It is a voluntary process through which a non-NATO country accedes into the Atlantic Alliance by taking the advice and assistance of NATO in restructuring itself. It is divided into five sections or chapters as NATO calls it. These chapters are (1) political and economic issues, (2) military issues, (3) resource issues, (4) security issues, and (5) legal issues. The first chapter is of particular importance:

> 1. Aspirants are offered the opportunity to discuss and substantiate their willingness and ability to assume the obligations and commitments under the Washington Treaty and the relevant provisions of the Study on NATO Enlargement. Future members must conform to basic principles embodied in the Washington Treaty such as democracy, individual liberty and other relevant provisions set out in its Preamble.
> 2. Aspirants would also be expected:
>> a. to settle their international disputes by peaceful means;
>> b. to demonstrate commitment to the rule of law and human rights;
>> c. to settle ethnic disputes or external territorial disputes including irredentist claims or internal jurisdictional disputes by peaceful means in accordance with OSCE principles and to pursue good neighborly relations;
>> d. to establish appropriate democratic and civilian control of their armed forces;
>> e. to refrain from the threat or use of force in any manner inconsistent with the purposes of the UN;
>> f. to contribute to the development of peaceful and friendly international relations by strengthening their free institutions and by promoting stability and well-being;
>> g. to continue fully to support and be engaged in the Euro-Atlantic Partnership Council and the Partnership for Peace;
>> h. to show a commitment to promoting stability and well-

being by economic liberty, social justice and environmental responsibility.[31]

It is because of this first chapter that the Republic of Georgia has been obstructed in attaining a MAP as President Saakashvili pursues entry into the North Atlantic Treaty Organization. The ethnic disputes and the territorial problems in Georgia that ultimately resulted in the recognition of the breakaway republics of Abkhazia and South Ossetia by the Russian Federation in 2008 have prevented Tbilisi from becoming a NATO member. Aside from Moscow's fervent objections and opposition to it, Georgian membership in NATO will be further obstructed until NATO makes amendments or becomes flexible on the topic. Presently the Balkan states of Bosnia-Herzegovina, the former Yugoslav Republic (FYR) of Macedonia, and Montenegro all have MAPs. MAPs have also been applied to every country that has entered or wanted to enter NATO after the 1999 round of NATO enlargement that saw the accession of the Czech Republic, Hungary, and Poland before NATO's war with Yugoslavia over the breakaway province of Kosovo. Albania, Bulgaria, Croatia, Estonia, Latvia, Lithuania, Romania, Slovakia, and Slovenia all had different MAPs on their individual roads to NATO membership.

TEXT BOX

THE STEP-BY-STEP PROCDURE TO NATO MEMBERSHIP

Step 1: Accession talks

Step 2: Invitees send letters of intent to NATO

Step 3: Accession protocols are signed

Step 4: Accession protocols are ratified by NATO countries

Step 5: NATO invites the candidate to join

Step 6: Invitees join NATO in accordance with their national procedures

Step 7: Invitees become NATO members

*Based on the accession process as outlined during NATO's 2002 Prague Summit

---

Diagram 2.1: Euler Diagram of NATO within Europe's Security Architecture

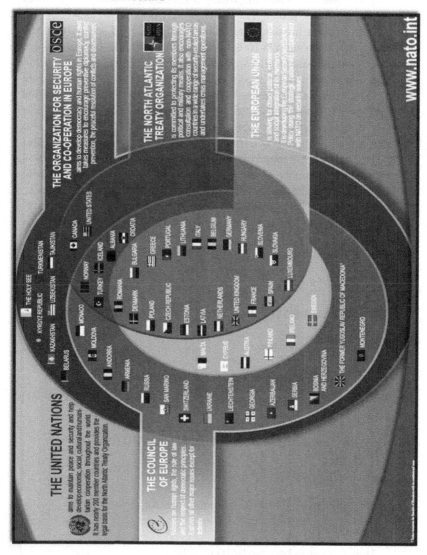

CHAPTER 3

YUGOSLAVIA AND THE REINVENTION OF NATO

The Yugoslav crisis demonstrates not NATO's irrelevance but its vitality and its potential. For the first time in history we are both acting out of area and, through our commitment to conduct air strikes, poised for actual combat operations.
—NATO Secretary-General Manfred Wörner (1993)

The "Stay-Behinds" and NATO

In this chapter we turn to the Balkans region of Eastern Europe and what was once the major regional power of Yugoslavia (Jugoslavia). For our purposes we will not delve deeply into the history of this regional power, but examine its decline and its role in the globalization of NATO. Before we do this, however, a factor referred to as the "stay-behinds" must be examined.

By the end of 1991, the communist states had collapsed and NATO no longer had an official enemy. The famous *bon mot* used to describe NATO's function, "to keep the Russians [*sic.*; that is, the Soviets] out, the Americans in, and the Germans down," by Hastings Lionel Ismay—NATO's first secretary-general, one of the partitioners of India, and Winston Churchill's chief military aid during the Second World War—was no longer applicable. Russia and the former Soviet republics were all down for the count. No massive external military threat to the Western Bloc existed and there no longer was an ideological communist bogeyman. In fact, NATO documents no longer used the word "threat" in their language; the word "challenge" had come to replace it in all of the Atlantic Alliance's documents.[1]

The Atlantic Alliance and the Western Bloc had actually become confident enough to reveal some of their darkest secrets during the wrapping up of the Cold War. News began to come out about the stay-behind organizations and cells of NATO inside Western Bloc countries. Closely aligned to the concept of a "deep state," these organizations, which are popularly referred to as "Gladio," were intelligence, military, and paramilitary formations that were created at the end of the Second World War. The US and NATO also recruited former Nazis and other fascists from Scandinavia and Iberia to Italy and Turkey. Their purpose was to act as sleeper cells that would stay behind in enemy territory where they would become operational and conduct acts of sabotage, assassination, and terrorism should a Western Bloc country become allied to the USSR and/or become communist either through external force, internal revolution, or democratic elections. Midway through the Cold War all Western Europe, including all neutral states, had stay-behind forces in place.[2] What was created to act as a resistance movement in the face of Soviet occupation ended up becoming something else altogether. Although the existence of the stay-behinds was denied during the Cold War, there no longer was as much importance placed on keeping them secret. *The Guardian* revealed the following in 1990:

> "I can say that the head of the secret services has repeatedly and unequivocally excluded the existence of a hidden organisation of any type or size," the Italian Minister of Defence, Giulio Andreotti, told a judicial inquiry in 1974 into the alleged existence of a secret state army.
>
> Four years later, the scene repeated itself in front of judges investigating a fascist bombing in Milan.
>
> Last month, however, Andreotti—now Prime Minister—confirmed the now infamous Gladio organisation had indeed existed since 1958, with the sanction of the political authorities, as a paramilitary "clandestine network" prepared to fight a Warsaw Pact invading army.[3]

The stay-behind units in Italy, however, were revealed to be actively operating against Italian citizens and interfering in internal politics through coercion and violence:

> A briefing minute of June 1, 1959, reveals Gladio was built around "internal subversion". It was to play "a determining role ... not only on the general policy level of warfare, but also in the politics of emergency".

In the 1970s, with communist electoral support growing and other leftists looking menacing, the establishment turned to the "Strategy of Tension"—with Gladio eager to be involved.

General Gerardo Serravalle, a former head of "Office R", told the terrorism commission that at a crucial Gladio meeting in 1972, at least half of the upper echelons "had the idea of attacking the communists before an invasion. They were preparing for civil war."

Later he put it more bluntly: "They were saying this: 'Why wait for the invaders when we can make a pre-emptive attack now on the communists who would support the invader?'"

The idea is now emerging of a Gladio web made up of semi-autonomous cadres which—although answerable to their secret service masters and ultimately to the Nato-CIA command—could initiate what they regarded as anti-communist operations by themselves, needing only sanction and funds from the existing "official" Gladio column.

General Pietro Corona, head of the "R" office from 1969-70, told the Venice inquiry about "an alternative clandestine network, parallel to Gladio, which knew about the arms and explosives dumps and who had access to them". General Nino Lugarese, head of SISMI from 1981-84 testified on the existence of a "Super Gladio" of 800 men responsible for "internal intervention" against domestic political targets.[4]

The murder of Aldo Moro in 1978, the leader of the Christian Democrats of Italy, by the so-called Second Red Brigades (RB) just before he was about to create an Italian coalition government that would include the Italian Communist Party (PCI) was a milestone moment for the stay-behinds.[5] Though it should have been viewed as an act that was counter-productive and therefore unlikely to have been perpetrated by them, militant communists were said to have killed the man who was going to empower Marxists in Italy. According to Daniele Ganser, a Swiss researcher and former professor of history at the University of Basel, the violent acts and covert operations of the stay-behind cells would falsely be attributed to socialists and communists with the systematic purpose of discrediting them in the eyes of the broader public.[6] Ganser's account of the Gladio in Italy is worth quoting:

In Italy, on 3 August 1990, then-prime minister Giulio Andreotti confirmed the existence of a secret army code-named "Gladio"—the Latin word for "sword"—within the state. His testimony before the Senate subcommittee investigating terrorism in Italy sent shockwaves through the Italian parliament and the public, as speculation arose that the secret army had possibly manipulated Italian politics through acts of terrorism.

Andreotti revealed that the secret Gladio army had been hidden within the Defense Ministry as a subsection of the military secret service, SISMI. General Vito Miceli, a former director of the Italian military secret service, could hardly believe that Andreotti had lifted the secret, and protested:

> "I have gone to prison because I did not want to reveal the existence of this super secret organization. And now Andreotti comes along and tells it to parliament!" According to a document compiled by the Italian military secret service in 1959, the secret armies had a two-fold strategic purpose: firstly, to operate as a so-called "stay-behind" group in the case of a Soviet invasion and to carry out a guerrilla war in occupied territories; secondly, to carry out domestic operations in case of "emergency situations".

The military secret services' perceptions of what constituted an "emergency" was well defined in Cold War Italy and focused on the increasing strength of the Italian Communist and the Socialist parties, both of which were tasked with weakening NATO "from within". Felice Casson, an Italian judge who during his investigations into right-wing terrorism had first discovered the secret Gladio army and had forced Andreotti to take a stand, found that the secret army had linked up with right-wing terrorists in order to confront "emergency situations". The terrorists, supplied by the secret army, carried out bomb attacks in public places, blamed them on the Italian left, and were thereafter protected from prosecution by the military secret service. "You had to attack civilians, the people, women, children, innocent people, unknown people far removed from any political game," right-wing terrorist Vincezo Vinciguerra explained the so-called "strategy of tension" to Casson.

> "The reason was quite simple. They were supposed to force these people, the Italian public, to turn to the state to ask for greater security. This is the political logic that lies behind all the massacres and the bombings which remain unpunished, because the state cannot convict itself or declare itself responsible for what happened."[7]

Maybe out of fear and cowardice or maybe as a political tactic, Prime Minister Andreotti revealed that Italy was not alone in having secret armies:

> In a public speech in front of the Italian Senate on November 9, 1990, Andreotti stressed once again that NATO, the United States and numerous countries in Western Europe including Germany, Greece, Denmark and Belgium had been involved in the stay-behind conspiracy. To prove this point, classified data was leaked to the press and the Italian political magazine Panorama published the entire document, 'The parallel SID—Operation Gladio' which Andreotti had handed to the parliamentary Commission. When France tried to deny its involvement in the international Gladio network Andreotti mercilessly declared that France as well had secretly participated in the most recent Gladio ACC meeting which had taken place in Brussels but a few weeks ago on October 23 and 24, 1990. Thereupon, somewhat embarrassed, also France confirmed that it had been involved in Gladio. The international dimension of the secret war could no longer be denied and the military scandal swept across Western Europe. Following the geographical zones of NATO membership it thereafter crossed the Atlantic and also reached the United States. An Italian parliamentary commission investigating Gladio and the Italian massacres in 2000 concluded: 'Those massacres, those bombs, those military actions had been organised or promoted or supported by men inside Italian state institutions and, as has been discovered more recently, by men linked to the structures of United States intelligence.'[8]

Thus, the events in Italy are what led to investigations throughout Western Europe that would reveal local stay-behinds existed in every Western Bloc country and lead back to NATO:

> The clandestine network, which after the revelations of the Italian Prime Minister was researched by judges, parliamentarians, academics and investigative journalists across Europe, is now understood to have been code-named 'Gladio' (the sword) in Italy, while in other countries the network operated under different names including 'Absalon' in Denmark, 'ROC' in Norway and 'SDRA8' in Belgium. In each country the military secret service operated the anti-Communist army within the state in close collaboration with the CIA or the MI6 unknown to parliaments and populations. In each country, leading members of the executive, including Prime Ministers, Presidents, Interior Ministers and Defence Ministers, were involved in the conspiracy, while the 'Allied Clandestine Committee' (ACC), sometimes also euphemistically called the 'Allied Co-ordination Committee' and the 'Clandestine Planning Committee' (CPC), less conspicuously at times also called 'Coordination and Planning Committee' of NATO's Supreme Headquarters Allied Powers Europe (SHAPE), coordinated the networks on the international level. The last confirmed secret meeting of ACC with representatives of European secret services took place on October 24, 1990 in Brussels.[9]

It did turn out, however, through the work of the Belgian Parliament that the origin of the stay-behinds preceded NATO:

> Given the strength of the Communist parties in several countries of Western Europe, NATO had engaged in secret non-orthodox warfare ever since its creation in the years following the Second World War. According to the findings of the Belgian parliamentary investigation into Gladio, secret non-orthodox warfare even preceded the foundation of the alliance. As of 1948, non-orthodox warfare was coordinated by the so-called 'Clandestine Committee of the Western Union' (CCWU). According to the press all Gladio 'nations were members of the "Clandestine Committee of the

Western Union" (CCWU) and participated regularly in its reunions through a representative of their respective secret service. The secret services are generally in direct contact with the S/B structures.'

When in 1949 the North Atlantic Treaty was signed, CCWU was secretly integrated into the new international military apparatus and as of 1951 operated under the new label CPC. At that time European NATO headquarters were in France and also the CPC was located in Paris. Like the CCWU before it the CPC was concerned with the planning, preparation and direction of non-orthodox warfare carried out by the stay-behind armies and Special Forces. Only officers with the highest NATO security clearances were allowed to enter CPC headquarters were [*sic*.] under the guidance of CIA and MI6 experts the chiefs of the Western European Secret Services met at regular intervals during the year in order to coordinate measures of non-orthodox warfare in Western Europe.[10]

Nonetheless, it was clear that the Anglo-Americans, particularly the US, were dominating the stay-behinds. The picture painted by all the evidence shows that Aldo Moro was murdered because he had disagreements with Washington. Eleonora Chiavarelli, Moro's widowed wife, later confirmed that her husband had meet with Henry Kissinger and an unidentified US intelligence official, who threatened him about pursuing the idea of bringing the Italian Communists into his cabinet in a national unity government.[11] In 2008, the news came out that the US government with the collaboration of the Italian Interior Ministry did want Moro killed. *The Daily Telegraph* put it this way:

> An American envoy has claimed that he played a critical role in the fate of Aldo Moro, the former Italian prime minister who was murdered by terrorists in 1978.
>
> Steve Pieczenik, an international crisis manager and hostage negotiator in the State Department, said that Moro had been "sacrificed" for the "stability" of Italy.
>
> In a new book called We Killed Aldo Moro, Mr Pieczenik said he was sent to Italy by President Jimmy Carter on the day that Moro was kidnapped by the Red Brigades, a far-Left terrorist group.

Moro, who had been prime minister for a total of more than five years between 1963 and 1976, was snatched at gunpoint from his car in Rome.[12]

The US fear was that should the Italian Communists gain power in Rome then Italy would eventually withdraw from the Atlantic Alliance. This could lead to the demise of NATO. This is why the US and NATO used the stay-behinds in Italy to eliminate Aldo Moro. More evidence has also revealed that the US was clandestinely using the stay-behinds to conduct domestic terrorist operations in Western Europe as a means of manipulating the public and shaping the direction of Western Bloc politics. This evidence includes testimonies by high-ranking intelligence officials:

> US intelligence services instigated and abetted rightwing terrorism in Italy during the 1970s, a former Italian secret service general has claimed.
>
> The allegation was made by General Gianadelio Maletti, a former head of military counter-intelligence, at the trial last week of rightwing extremists accused of killing 16 people in the bombing of a Milan bank in 1969—the first time such a charge has been made in a court of law by a senior Italian intelligence figure.
>
> Gen Maletti, comannder [*sic.*] of the counter-intelligence section of the military intelligence service from 1971 to 1975, said his men had discovered that a rightwing terrorist cell in the Venice region had been supplied with military explosives from Germany.
>
> Those explosives may have been obtained with the help of members of the US intelligence community, an indication that the Americans had gone beyond the infiltration and monitoring of extremist groups to instigating acts of violence, he said.
>
> "The CIA [Central Intelligence Agency], following the directives of its government, wanted to create an Italian nationalism capable of halting what it saw as a slide to the left and, for this purpose, it may have made use of rightwing terrorism," Gen Maletti told the Milan court. "I believe this is what happened in other countries as well."
>
> The general has been living in South Africa for the last 21 years as a fugitive from Italian justice. He has been sentenced to 14 years imprisonment for

leaking a secret service document to the press and last year received a 15-year sentence for obstructing justice. He was granted a special 15-day immunity from arrest to enable him to give evidence at the trial for the bombing of a bank in Milan's Piazza Fontana, the atrocity that inaugurated the "strategy of tension", a series of bombings intended to shift the country's political centre of gravity to the right.

"The impression was that the Americans would do anything to stop Italy from sliding to the left," Gen Maletti said during an interview at his Milan hotel.[13]

Yugoslavia, the "Land of the South Slavs"

Yugoslavia was a country formed by the aspirations of the ethnic Slavs of the Western Balkans to unite into one country and realm. After the end of the First World War, Yugoslavia was formed in 1918 when three states united. Initially the Kingdom of Montenegro and the Kingdom of Serbia united with one another, to be joined shortly afterwards in their unification by the newly independent State of Slovenes, Croats, and Serbs that emerged out of the remnants of Austro-Hungary. The third state's very name, the State of Slovenes, Croats, and Serbs, betrayed the fact that its political and cultural center of gravity was Vienna, Austria. The Kingdoms of Serbia and Montenegro on the other hand had been under Ottoman domination for centuries and had different centers of gravity. The pan-Slavic union of these three states resulted in the creation of the Kingdom of Serbs, Croats, and Slovenes. The name of the new kingdom would only be used up until 1929 but the rearrangement of the order in which Serbs, Croats, and Slovenians were mentioned in, betrays a new political orbit. From 1929 onward the Kingdom of Serbs, Croats, and Slovenes would be called the Kingdom of Yugoslavia. In practice, Yugoslavia had been the name that the country had been called by its inhabitants from the beginning for ethnographic reasons.

The Yugoslav Kingdom would find itself in a hard spot when the unfinished business of the First World War and its unfair settlements resulted in the rise of Adolph Hitler, Benito Mussolini, and a whole series of fascist leaders in Europe. Following the examples of Hungary, Romania, German-controlled Slovakia, and Bulgaria during the Second World War, the government of Yugoslavia would align itself with Germany and the Axis. On 25 March 1941, Prince Paul Karadordević, the regent of Yugoslavia, joined the Axis, but under the terms that it would not fight in the war. The move would be highly controversial in Yugoslavia and galvanize Serbs and Croats. A palace coup removed Prince Paul from power soon after Yugoslavia became a member of the Axis. This prompted a German and Axis invasion of the Yugoslav Kingdom, which resulted in the creation of a German-controlled Croatia that was technically an Italian protectorate run by the Croatian revolutionary movement, the Ustaša. Guerilla fighting would erupt in Yugoslavia against the Germans and their allies. This was led mostly by the royalist Chetniks, composed mainly of Serbian nationalists, and the Marxist-dominated Partisans. Both groups would also fight one another as well as the Ustaše, the Germans, and other Axis forces.

The Partisans to their credit were the only pan-Yugoslav resistance force in the country that had a vision of a plural federal republic for all the ethnic groups of Yugoslavia. They and their leader and field commander Marshal Josip Broz Tito would eventually come to control Yugoslavia in 1943. Yugoslavia was quickly reconstituted as a federal state comprised of the six South Slav federal states of Slovenia, Croatia, Bosnia and Herzegovina, Montenegro, Serbia, and Macedonia. The makeshift name of Democratic Federal Yugoslavia was used until the question of whether the country was a republic or a kingdom was settled. The answer came on November 29, 1945, when Yugoslavia was declared a republic. The country was officially renamed the Federal People's Republic of Yugoslavia and would continue to use this name until it would be renamed the Socialist Federal Republic of Yugoslavia in 1963.

Enter NATO: Interventionism in the Balkans and the End of Yugoslavia

Economic disparity began to arise towards the end of the Cold War in Yugoslavia and the Eastern Bloc. Talking about the economic transformation that would take place, professor of economics and international development Michel Chossudovsky writes:

> The end of the Cold War has had a profound impact on the global distribution of income. Until the early 1990s, Eastern Europe and the Soviet Union were considered as part of the developed "North"—i.e. with levels of material consumption, education, health, scientific development, etc. broadly comparable [or superior] to those in the OECD countries. Whereas average incomes were on the whole lower, Western scholars, nonetheless, acknowledged the achievements of the Eastern Bloc countries, particularly in the areas of health and education.
>
> Impoverished as a result of the IMF-sponsored reforms, the countries of the former socialist Bloc are

CHART 3.1

The Formation of Yugoslavia

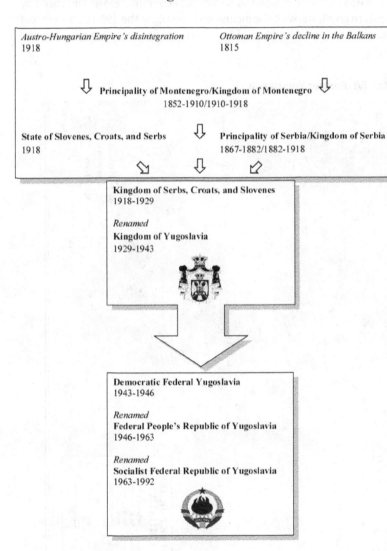

Austro-Hungarian Empire's disintegration 1918	*Ottoman Empire's decline in the Balkans* 1815

⇩ Principality of Montenegro/Kingdom of Montenegro ⇩
1852-1910/1910-1918

State of Slovenes, Croats, and Serbs ⇩ Principality of Serbia/Kingdom of Serbia
1918 1867-1882/1882-1918

⇨ ⇩ ⇗

Kingdom of Serbs, Croats, and Slovenes
1918-1929

Renamed
Kingdom of Yugoslavia
1929-1943

Democratic Federal Yugoslavia
1943-1946

Renamed
Federal People's Republic of Yugoslavia
1946-1963

Renamed
Socialist Federal Republic of Yugoslavia
1963-1992

77

now categorized by the World Bank as "developing countries", alongside the "low" and "middle-incomes countries" of the [developing world].[14]

Yugoslavia faced a major economic crisis and a sharp drop in living standards that was induced by disastrous economic reforms imposed by Western creditors, with the inclusion of the US, in the 1980s. Lost in most the accounts of the breakup of Yugoslavia are how economic decline and

Map IV: Former Yugoslavia

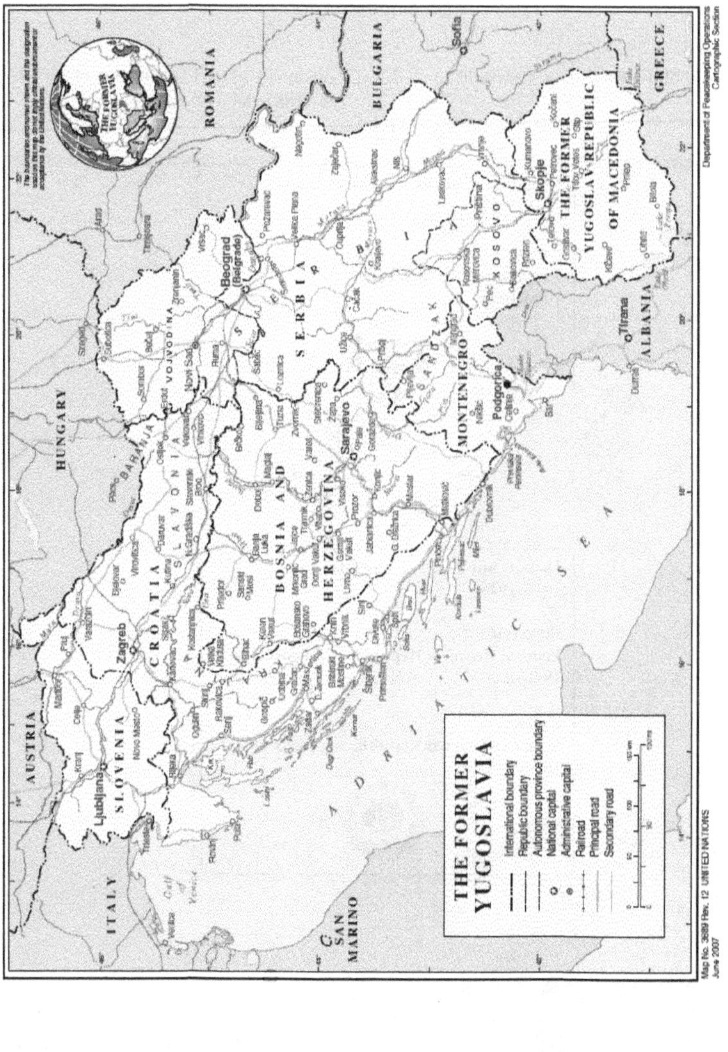

foreign debt were used to manipulate and exacerbate ethnic and social cleavages, feeding secessionism. Instead a narrative of deeply rooted historical differences and hatred has been fostered as the primary force that brought about the demise of Yugoslavia. The economic degradation of Yugoslavia was systematic and calculated:

> Yugoslavia's implosion was partially due to US machinations. Despite Belgrade's non-alignment [during the Cold War] and its extensive trading relations with the European Community and the US, the Reagan administration had targeted the Yugoslav economy in a "Secret Sensitive" 1984 National Security Decision Directive (NSDD 133) entitled "US Policy towards Yugoslavia." A censored version, declassified in 1990, elaborated on NSDD 64 on Eastern Europe issued in 1982. The latter advocated "expanded efforts to promote a 'quiet revolution' to overthrow Communist governments and parties," while reintegrating the countries of Eastern Europe into a market-oriented economy.[15]

Thus the Yugoslav economy was dealt a crippling blow that would result in an externally induced implosion:

> These reforms, accompanied by the signing of debt restructuring agreements with the official and commercial creditors [from the Western Bloc], also served to weaken the institutions of the federal state, creating political divisions between Belgrade and the governments of the Republics and the Autonomous Provinces. "The [Federal] Prime Minister Milka Planinc, who was supposed to carry out the program, had to promise the IMF an immediate increase of the discount rates and much more for the Reaganomics arsenal of measures..." And throughout the 1980s, the IMF and World Bank periodically prescribed further doses of their bitter economic medicine as the Yugoslav economy slowly lapsed into a coma.[16]

The disintegration of the once strong Yugoslav industrial and worker-managed public sectors and the erosion of all social programs followed in piecemeal steps, while Yugoslavia's debt restructuring agreements not only increased foreign debt, but also mandated a currency devaluation, wage freezes, and sharp cuts in government spending on social programs like education, which in turn made Yugoslav living standards and quality of life plummet and costs of living go up.[17] To service the national debt, the Yugoslavian federal government began to redirect and suspend its transfer payments to the constituent republics and the autonomous provinces of Kosovo and Vojvodina.

This resulted in the empowerment of nationalists and the secession of Slovenia and Croatia in June 1991 followed by the Slavic Macedonians (Skopjians) later that same year.[18] From 1991 onward a bloody process of balkanization would start. The ethnic communities that in many ways were virtually indistinguishable became galvanized and manipulated through identity allegiances into fighting one another, particularly in the Socialist Republic of Bosnia and Herzegovina, where Bosniaks, Serbs, and Croats—if one believes they are separate ethnic groups—had all co-existed in unity for hundreds of years. In 1990, three nationalist and virtually exclusivist parties would be elected in Bosnia laying the ground work for division. These parties were Alija Izetbegović's Party of Democratic Action for the Bosniaks, the Bosnian branch of the Serbian Democratic Party, and the Bosnian branch of the Croatian Democratic Union.

Although not homogenous, Serbs, Croats, Bosniaks, and Montenegrins are essentially the same ethnic group with variations that can be compared to those of the ethnic Germans in Austria and Germany (refer to Table 3.1 for consultation). All four groups speak Serbo-Croatian, albeit with variations in dialect which reflect regionalism and the historical dividing lines of the different empires they fell under. Faith and religious differences are the primary forms of differentiation between these groups. While the Bosniaks are Muslim, the Croats are Roman Catholic Christians and the Serbs and Montenegrins are Eastern Orthodox Christians. Without this difference in faith, the relationship between the Bosniaks and the Serbs and Croats would be more like the relationship of the Montenegrins and the Serbs, a relationship forged by differences based on belonging to a different political entity. This is a topic of particular importance in the balkanization process. Because of the centrality of Bosnia-Herzegovina within Yugoslavia and its location as an ethnographic merging point, its fate would affect the other Yugoslavs. At first federal forces—the Yugoslav People's Army— would try to maintain order, but they too began to disintegrate as the country disintegrated and Belgrade was forced into accepting the divorce and independence of the secessionist republics. In 1992, Bosnia-Herzegovina would finally declare its independence, which would incite major fighting that would draw in the Federal Republic of Yugoslavia in support of the Bosnian Serbs and Croatia in support of the Bosnian

Croats. This would ultimately lead to the military engagement of NATO in its first "official" combat mission.

TABLE 3.1

Albania and the Former Yugoslavia

Country	Main Language	Muslims	Orthodox Christians	Catholic Christians
Albania	Albanian	70%	20%	10%
Bosnia-Herzegovina	Serbo-Croatian	52%	31%	15%
Croatia	Serbo-Croatian	1.3%	4.4%	88%
Kosovo - Serbia	Albanian	90%	6%	3%
Macedonia, FYR	Macedonian Slavic*	35%	64%	1%
Montenegro	Serbo-Croatian	19.1%	72%	3.4%
Serbia	Serbo-Croatian	3.2%	85%	5.5%
Slovenia	Slovene	2.4%	2.3%	58%

*Macedonian Slavic or Slavo-Macedonian is considered a dialect of Bulgarian by some linguists.

The Politics of Identity

The Slavic or Slavonic people are divided into three major groups: the Eastern Slavs, the Western Slavs, and the Southern Slavs. The Eastern Slavs are comprised of the Russians, Ukrainians, and Belarusians. The Western Slavs are mainly comprised of the Poles, Czechs, and Slovaks. The Southern Slavs are the Yugoslavs. Yugoslav literally means "South Slav." In ethnic terms all Slovenians, Croats, Bosniaks, Serbs, Montenegrins, and Slavic Macedonians are Yugoslavs regardless of their political views about the former country of Yugoslavia. Bulgarians are ethnically also Yugoslavs in the sense that they are Southern Slavs. The discussion about the nomenclature of the South Slavs becomes complicated, because Yugoslav is additionally a national label. Thus, ethnic Romanians and Albanians in the country of Yugoslavia were also Yugoslavs by citizenship while they were not ethnically Yugoslavs. In 1971, to help sort this out, quotation marks were added to distinguish ethnic "Yugoslavs" from those with Yugoslav citizenship—which was written without quotation marks.

For hundreds of years the Slavic peoples of the Western Balkans were under the control of non-Slavs; this was predominately under the High Porte of the Ottoman Empire and later the Habsburgs and what would become the monarchic union of Austro-Hungary. Since the schism between the Latin-dominated Roman Catholic Church based in Rome and the Greek-dominated Eastern Orthodox Church based in Constantinople (present-day Istanbul), the inhabitants of the region predominately became Christians divided amongst the confessions of Eastern Orthodoxy and Roman Catholicism. The difference between Croatians and Serbs is an example of this ecclesiastical split. While Croats were influenced by Rome, their ethnic kin the Serbs were in the cultural orbit of the East Romans or Byzantines. These differences were also enunciated through the scripts used by the Roman Catholic "Yugoslavs" and the Eastern Orthodox "Yugoslavs." Croats, like Slovenes, would use Latin, while the Serbs would use Cyrillic, like the Slavic Macedonians and Bulgarians.

As the Ottomans expanded into the Balkans, Islam was added to the picture as many of the inhabitants of the region became Muslims. Large communities of local Muslims, which have survived until this day, would come to dominate and flourish in Albania, Bosnia-Herzegovina, Bulgaria, and Macedonia in the Ottoman period. Amongst the "Yugoslavs," specifically in Bosnia-Herzegovina, this would be the basis for the evolution of the Bosniak identity. For this reason, until this day Bosniaks are colloquially called "Bosnian Muslims." In parallel the inhabitants of the westernmost areas of the region fell into the orbit of Habsburg Austria and through the influence of the Austrians continued to practice Roman Catholicism, while gravitating towards German culture. While those Slavs in the Austrian and later the shared Austrian and Magyar (Hungarian) orbit continued to use the Latin script, the Slavs in the Ottoman orbit either continued their commitment to the Orthodox Church or practiced Islam, while using the Cyrillic and now Arabic scripts.

The double standards that have been used to divide the Socialist Federal Republic of Yugoslavia are apparent when examined on the basis of the interest of NATO powers. The US and EU stance on identity was inverse to that of the former Yugoslavia when the so-called "Twitter Revolution" erupted in 2009 in the former Soviet republic of Moldova. This exposes how the Atlanticist powers manipulate identity allegiances in their political favor.

During the riots of the Twitter Revolution the Moldovan government angrily pointed out the use of Romanian and EU flags by the protesters as they stormed government buildings as a threat to

Moldova's independence and as part of a push for the political takeover of Moldova by Romania. Most Moldovans are ethnically and linguistically Romanians, but the use of the Romanian flag has a political tag to it and a subliminal meaning. The media in the US and the EU were quick to report that the Moldovan government disliked the use of Romanian flags and has tried to continuously suppress Moldova's Romanian identity. The reporting on Moldova during the protests and riots made sure to emphasize that Moldavian, which is the official name of the language of Moldova, is really Romanian. Yet, in the case of Bosnia-Herzegovina the same media and governments did the opposite, and distinctively tried to alienate or separate the Bosnian dialect of Serbo-Croatian from that of Serbia as a totally separate language. Nor have any of the members of the Atlantic Alliance ever really contested the claims of a Montenegrin language and ethnicity. Instead both the US and the EU have supported this differentiation process between Montenegrins and Serbs. This helped end the last remaining political bonds of Yugoslavia as the Federal Republic of Yugoslavia devolved into the Union of Serbia and Montenegro in 2003 and finally ended when Montenegro declared independence on June 3, 2006. No real discussions have ever taken place about the shared identities and heritage of the Yugoslav people.

The above assessments being made about the Montenegrin identity are not intended to imply that Montenegrins or the Bosnians do not possess a distinct identity and history. The Montenegrins had formed their own separate country for hundreds of years while the other Serbs were under Ottoman control. Montenegrins are a distinct grouping, but they do not form a separate ethnic group or language. In addition, the branch of Eastern Orthodoxy in Montenegro is represented by the Serbian Orthodox Church. Yet, through a manipulated political process a Montenegrin Orthodox Church has been created. Similar to the position of the Vatican on the Roman Catholic Church of China, because of the manipulated discourse behind the creation of the Montenegrin Orthodox Church, it is not recognized as a legitimate church by all Eastern Orthodoxy. Scratching under the surface one will find that the support for this Montenegrin Orthodox Church was used by local Montenegrin elites working with the Atlanticists to justify their nationalist rhetoric and alienate their own people from the Serbs, thereby empowering themselves.

Sociologically, the core of the matter is that the major NATO powers have objectified the people of the former Yugoslavia through dividing practices, leading to differential classifications, and finally the subjectification or internalization of prescribed and manufactured identities or new ethnic tags. The same is true of African countries like Rwanda where both the Bantu groups of the Hutu (Abahutu) and Tutsi

(Watutsi) were artificially divided on the basis of height by the former Belgian and German colonial administrations as a means of externally creating and manufacturing identities and tribalism which could be used as a means to divide them. This demonstrated how individual personality or self-conceptualization could be changed dynamically under very traumatic situations, such as war, making individuals very open to suggestions and to forming new self-concepts based on these suggestions very rapidly. Individual societies can be shaped or socially engineered through shock therapy in the form of war, sanctions, and economic restructuring. This is why national heritage and cultural sites in Iraq and the former Yugoslavia, such as the museums and national symbols, were deliberately destroyed by the NATO powers—to make way for new identities.

A similar modus operandi to that in Yugoslavia was employed through the confessionalization of the Iraqi identity amongst Shiite Muslims and Sunni Muslims, while the ethnic differences between the Arabs and Kurds have been aggravated for years by the Anglo-American Alliance. In addition to the predominately Sunni Muslim Kurds, Iraq has wrongly been portrayed as having two sectarian groupings among the Arabs, Shiite and Sunni, portrayed as if they were outright separate ethnic groups. This is a re-run of what happened in the former Yugoslavia, specifically Bosnia-Herzegovina, on the basis of a difference in religion. People who once saw themselves as ethnic Yugoslavs have been redefined as Bosnian Bosniaks (though the media still calls them Muslims, using their religion), Bosnian Serbs, and Bosnian Croats.[19]

The majority of Austrians are Roman Catholic, while Germany is mixed between Protestants in its northern areas and Roman Catholics in its southern areas, but this has not resulted in the manufactured creation of two separate ethnic identities. No one disputes that Austrians are ethnic Germans. Nor does being a Catholic or Protestant automatically exclude you from one group. On the contrary, the confessional differences between Germany and Austria have resulted in different states. Yet, new ethnic identities have been manufactured on these grounds in the former Yugoslavia. While the EU has grown and advocated an acceptance of pluralism in a united Europe, it has promoted a conflictual differentiation in the nations outside of its sphere in the European continent. These countries outside of the Euro-Atlantic Zone have systematically been divided and fallen apart. Czechoslovakia and the former Soviet Union are additional examples. On the other hand, German unity was supported because it brought East Germany into the Euro-Atlantic orbit. The Romanian identity of Moldova is also supported because it will bring Moldova into the Euro-Atlantic orbit. A

Yugoslav identity, however, was not supported, because it was keeping Yugoslavia outside of the Euro-Atlantic orbit.

Recalling the historic discourse of Europe, one realizes that the Austrians as ethnic Germans have been denied unification with Germany. This first happened after the First World War when Austro-Hungary was dismantled: whilst the Wilsonian concept of the nation-state was being applied to dividing Eastern Europe and the Middle East, it deliberately excluded the Germans. The Treaty of Versailles and the Treaty of Saint-Germain-en-Laye were both forthright in prohibiting unification between Austria and Germany, which was a popular idea until after the Second World War. After the surrender of Germany in the Second World War, the US, UK, France, and USSR partitioned Austria from Germany on the basis of the claim of undoing Adolph Hitler's 1938 Anschluss. This falls into line with what Lord Ismay meant when he famously said "keep the Germans down." From this point on pan-German views were curbed through discouragement and repression, equated with Nazism and silenced.

These considerations about identity politics should be a facet in any of the foci on the historic discourse of modern nation-building in Eastern Europe and the former Soviet Union. Why have the national aspirations of the Flemish in Belgium or the Basques in the Pyrenees never been recognized, while Czechoslovakian secession from the Austro-Hungarian Empire was recognized by Washington even before the Czechs and Slovaks declared it themselves? The same can be said about the support of the Obama Administration for the secession of South Sudan from the Republic of Sudan. Two standards are clearly being applied. While the Moldovans are portrayed as Romanians, the Yugoslavs are not portrayed as a single people. Moreover, the self-serving idea of engrained hatred between peoples outside of the US alliance is naturalized, while it is not for those within it. Serbs and Croats are said to have had a timeless animosity, as are Shiite Muslims and Sunni Muslims, while nothing comparable using the language of hate is said about those cleavages within the Euro-Atlantic Zone. These differences in themselves are also used to de-politicize the political and class based natures of any of these tensions. Moreover, the conduct of the Atlantic Alliance in its differentiation and labelling exercises cannot be excused as merely ethnocentric mistakes or unconscious exceptionalism. The politics of identity are fully knowingly used as dividing techniques and as a means of controlling states.

The Destabilization of Bosnia and Herzegovina

The Carrington-Cutileiro Plan, more properly known as the

Lisbon Agreement, began the ground work to divide Bosnia-Herzegovina along ethnic lines in 1991. On October 15, 1991 the Bosnian Parliament approved a Memorandum on Sovereignty, which alienated the Bosnian Serbs. The Bosnian Serbs reacted by forming a separate parliament in Banja Luka on October 24 called the Assembly of the Serb People in Bosnia and Herzegovina. On November 9, 1991 a communitarian referendum was held on the issue of secession from Yugoslavia among the Bosnian Serb community. Almost unanimously, the November referendum opted for preserving Yugoslavia. On January 9, 1992 this same assembly proclaimed the Republic of the Serb People of Bosnia and Herzegovina and declared it a constituent of Yugoslavia. They would also be supported in their objectives of preserving Yugoslavia by Bosniaks such as Fikret Abdić, who would later flee the country and be charged with war crimes in Croatia.

On February 29, 1992 a referendum, on the basis of the Memorandum on Sovereignty, for the independence of the Socialist Republic of Bosnia-Herzegovina from the Socialist Federal Republic of Yugoslavia was started. The referendum lasted until March 1 and was controversial; it was boycotted by the Bosnian Serbs who were politically and legally in opposition to Bosnian secession from Yugoslavia. They also claimed that on the basis of the communal power sharing agreement the referendum was illegal, because it did not consider the equal weight of one of the three communities in Bosnia-Herzegovina. Shorty after the referendum the leaders of the three main Bosnian communities would endorse the ethnocratic Carrington-Cutileiro Plan to try and resolve internal tensions; on March 18, 1992, Alija Izetbegović, representing the Bosnian Bosniaks, Mate Boban, representing the Bosnian Croats, and Radovan Karadžić, representing the Bosnian Serbs, signed the agreement. Alija Izetbegović, however, would withdraw his signature ten days later after consultations with US Ambassador Warren Zimmermann, a key backroom figure in the breakup of Yugoslavia. Izetbegović was determined to establish a Muslim state for the Bosniak majority, but his zeal was the subject of US and NATO manipulation that saw him involved in *realpolitik* with them that actually ended up hurting his own community the most. The Bosnian Serbs then declared their own independence with the military support of what would become the newly formed Federal Republic of Yugoslavia, which paired Montenegro with Serbia as the remaining republics of the federation

The Bosnian Serbs would form what would become the Republika Srpska. They would also form their own army with the support of Belgrade and fight against the newly formed Bosniak-dominated Bosnian military, the armed force of the Republic of Bosnia and Herzegovina. The Croats on the other hand would align with Croatia and form their own military force, the Croatian Defense Council. Agreements between the Croats and Serbs to divide up Bosnia-Herzegovina would result in armed combat between the Republic of Bosnia and Herzegovina and the Croat entity of Herzeg-Bosnia. Thus, a three-way war would take place. In 1994, the Bosniaks and Croats in Bosnia would align themselves against the stronger Republika Srpska with the creation of the Federation of Bosnia and Herzegovina following the Washington Agreement, a ceasefire deal between Herzeg-Bosnia and the Republic of Bosnia and Herzegovina, signed on March 18, 1994. The agreement created a confederate alliance between Croatia and the Federation of Bosnia and Herzegovina against the Bosnian Serbs and Yugoslavia.

NATO Enters Bosnia: From Sky Monitor to Operation Deny Flight

Almost from the very onset, the war in Bosnia was characterized by news reports of ethnic cleansing. Before Bosnia-Herzegovina even declared its independence and the main fighting started the UN Security Council passed UNSC Resolution 743 on February 21, 1992. This mandated the creation of the United Nations Protection Force (UNPROFOR) and its deployment to Croatia and Bosnia-Herzegovina. By the end of the year, on October 9, the UN Security Council passed UNSC Resolution 781, creating a no-fly zone over Bosnia-Herzegovina.

This led to NATO's Operation Sky Monitor, where NATO would patrol Bosnian airspace and passively monitored violations of the no-fly zone. The NATO operations started on October 16, 1992. NATO documented these violations and gave them to the UN. The UN Security Council passed UNSC Resolution 816 on March 31, 1993 as a result of hundreds of violations of the no-fly zone documented by NATO. The UNSC Resolution opened the door to military force by allowing NATO to police Bosnian skies. Operation Sky Monitor ended on April 12, 1993 transforming into NATO's Operation Deny Flight, which would also come to include air support duties for UN ground troops and air offensives against Bosnian Serb ground targets. This coincided with UNSC Resolution 836, which was passed on June 4, 1993 allowing UNPROFOR to engage the Bosnian Serbs and any other local forces in combat. Shortly after, NATO and the Western European Union set up a naval blockade of the Adriatic named Operation Sharp Guard on June 15, 1993 as a means of controlling the maritime traffic coming and going to the former Yugoslavian republics.

Operation Deny Flight is important, because it would result in NATO officially fighting for the first time and engaging in combat operations. NATO authorized its jets to attack coordinates given by

UNPROFOR under Operation Deny Flight on February 9, 1994. The Atlantic Alliance would also deliver an ultimatum to the Bosnian Serb forces surrounding Sarajevo to which they were to submit or face a major bombing campaign. The Bosnian Serbs were obliged to retreat, but this would not prevent a major air campaign materializing in 1995. The process was actually one of gradual escalation as NATO increased its presence through phased operations. Before, in the lead up to the major bombing campaign, NATO jets fought an air battle over the airspace southeast of Banja Luka on February 28, 1994. Six of the Republika Srpska's J-21 Jastrebs in violation of the no-fly zone would be attacked and four shot down by US Air Force F-16s. From this point on the Atlantic Alliance would begin to flex its muscles more and more in Bosnia-Herzegovina. The following month, UNPROFOR requested NATO air support. Once the mechanisms were worked out NATO would actively make air strikes against the Republika Srpska's armed forces. The first such attacks on April 10 and 11 against Bosnian Serb posts near Gorazde by the US Air Force were the Atlantic Alliance's first official offensive airstrikes. Furious at the role of NATO and outside interference in what they saw as a domestic dispute over the right of self-determination, the Bosnian Serbs began attacking UNPROFOR and taking UN troops as hostages to prevent airstrikes. The Bosnian Serbs demanded that NATO and the UN stop interfering in the civil war to tilt the balance of power against them.

The Bosnian Arms Embargo

NATO gradual escalation was part of a careful scheme to weaken all three sides inside Bosnia so that none of the three sides could resist NATO's advances in the Balkans. The Bosniaks were not NATO's dupes either as many critics of NATO think; Bosniaks were just as much targets as were Serbs. The Bosniaks even worked with Iranians against the US at times:

> James Woolsey, director of the CIA until May 1995, had increasingly found himself out of step with the Clinton White House over his reluctance to develop close relations with the Islamists [that is, the Bosniak side or their allies]. The sentiments were reciprocated. In the spring of 1995, when the CIA sent its first head of station to Sarajevo to liaise with Bosnia's security authorities, the Bosnians tipped off Iranian intelligence. The CIA learned that the Iranians had targeted him for liquidation and quickly withdrew him. [20]

No side was also allowed to gain a true strategic advantage or be militarily independent. The arms embargo in Bosnia—that was breached secretly by the US, Israel, Turkey, Germany, and others—was actually used to regulate and manipulate the flow of arms into the Slavic country.[21] The Dutch professor Cees Wiebes, through unrestricted access to the files of the Netherland's intelligence service on the Bosnian War, has disclosed these findings:

> Rather than the CIA, the Pentagon's own secret service was the hidden force behind these operations. The UN protection force, UNPROFOR, was dependent on its troop-contributing nations for intelligence, and above all on the sophisticated monitoring capabilities of the US to police the arms embargo. This gave the Pentagon the ability to manipulate the embargo at will: ensuring that American Awacs aircraft covered crucial areas and were able to turn a blind eye to the frequent nightime [sic.] comings and goings at Tuzla [of arms smugglers].
>
> Weapons flown in during the spring of 1995 were to turn up only a fortnight later in the besieged and demilitarised enclave at Srebrenica. When these shipments were noticed, Americans pressured UNPROFOR to rewrite reports, and when Norwegian officials protested about the flights, they were reportedly threatened into silence.[22]

The arms embargo was used as a tool to keep the three sides weak and dependent. When one side became too strong their flow of arms would be cut or re-routed to another side.

The Colonization of Bosnia: From Srebrenica to the Dayton Accords

During Operation Deny Flight a British Sea Harrier over Gorazde and a US F-16 over Mrkonjić Grad were shot down by the Bosnian Serbs on 16 April and June 2, 1995. Soon after the downing of the US F-16, the Bosnian Serbs would move into the so-called UN Srebrenica Safe Area on July 11, 1995. The official NATO narrative is that UN troops agreed to withdraw from Srebrenica and let the Bosnian Serb forces take care of the local Bosniaks, but that once the Bosnian Serbs entered the area they slaughtered about 8,000 Bosniaks in the worst massacre in Europe after the Second World War.

The Srebrenica Massacre, however, has been described as follows by critics of NATO intervention in Yugoslavia:

Both the scale of the casualties at Srebrenica and the context surrounding the July 1995 killings there have been misrepresented in official reports from governmental and non-governmental organizations as well as in the mainstream media. Senior UN military and civilian officials, NATO intelligence officers, and independent intelligence analysts dispute the official characterization by the ICTY of the fall of Srebrenica and the evacuation of this "safe area" population as a unique atrocity in the Bosnian conflict and as a case of genocide. The contention that as many as 8,000 Bosnian Muslim men and boys were executed in the span of one week, that the Srebrenica massacre was the "single worst atrocity" of the wars in the former Yugoslavia, and the "worst massacre that occurred in Europe since the months after World War II," has no basis in available evidence and is essentially a political construct.[23]

The most senior UN official inside Bosnia-Herzegovina, Philip Corwin, would also lend his voice to these critics saying that the events in Srebrenica were distorted for political gain. He would disturbingly write:

At the time, I was the highest ranking United Nations civilian official in Bosnia-Herzegovina. In my book, Dubious Mandate, I made some comments on that tragedy. Beyond that, I decried the distortions of the international press in their reporting, not only on that event, but on the wars in Yugoslavia (1992-95) in general. I expressed the wish that there could have been, and must be, some balance in telling the story of what actually happened in Srebrenica and in all of former Yugoslavia, if we are to learn from our experience.[24]

After the Bosnian Serb takeover, the events of Srebrenica would be used and warped to justify a massive NATO response on the basis of public outrage. Bosniak leaders would also refuse to give the Red Cross the names of people who had fled Srebrenica, thus resulting in an inflated number of missing people, and the number of dead would also later turn out to be significantly lower than originally reported.[25] Bill Clinton had actually instructed Alija Izetbegović that 5,000 Bosniaks would need to be sacrificed to bring NATO into the war as a combatant:

According to the UN Secretary-General's 1999 assessment: "Some surviving members of the Srebrenica delegation have stated that President Izetbegovic also told that he had learned that a NATO intervention in Bosnia and Herzegovina was possible, but could occur only if the Serbs were to break into Srebrenica, killing at least 5,000 of its people. President Izetbegovic has flatly denied making such a statement." (See The Fall of Srebrenica (A/54/549), Report of the Secretary-General pursuant to General Assembly resolution 53/35, November 15, 1999, para. 115 [...]) This UN report does not mention that there were nine others present at that meeting, and that one of them, Hakija Meholijic, a former chief of police in Srebrenica, has stated that eight of them (all those living) "can confirm" the Clinton suggestion.[26]

Moreover, Washington presented the UN Security Council with questionable documentation about the events in Srebrenica:

[T]he United States presented to the United Nations in August 1995, giving supposed photo documentation of massacres in July [1995]. None of the reported photos showed killings, bodies, graves being dug, or bodies being removed and reburied—all but one of our six articles mention only the photo showing a group of assembled prisoners and a subsequent photo showing a nearby field with ground recently dug or disturbed. One article mentions a photo of a backhoe digging, where the Serbs "might have been trying to hide evidence," but "the effort was either botched or frost and rain exposed bones that were sitting just below the surface." None of the six quote Madeleine Albright's statement in August 1995 that "We will be watching," which suggests that special attention would be given to providing satellite evidence. None of the six ask obvious questions, such as: with an acknowledged interest in providing evidence of Serb executions why are there no photos of corpses, burials in process, and trucks carrying away several thousand bodies to new grave sites as later alleged? This lack of media interest in satellite-based evidence is especially notable as the media were claiming a "huge Serb effort to hide bodies by moving and reburying them." They never ask why the photos have been kept out of public view or challenge this secrecy. The failure to even raise such questions reflects the gullibility of journalists who know the truth in advance of gathering relevant facts, and who therefore serve as de facto propagandists.[27]

The Srebrenica Massacre would result in NATO officially launching its first combat mission in August 30, 1995 under the name of Operation Deliberate Force, which would result in the major offensive that the Republika Srpska wanted to avoid. The NATO attack, in reality a sustained war involving hundreds of warplanes and thousands of military servicepersons, would last until September 20, 1995.

NATO systematically weakened the Bosnian Serbs and Croatian Serbs, because they wanted to keep Yugoslavia intact. Granted, there were atrocities committed by all sides, but it was the Serbs who were vilified. This was because of their objective of keeping as much Yugoslavian territory united within one political entity as they could. If it were not for NATO intervention, they would have succeeded. By waging war on Serb forces, NATO opened the door for Operation Mistral, a military offensive by the Croatian military, Bosnian Croats, and Bosnian Bosniaks against the dramatically weakened Bosnian Serbs that would see their military defeat. The war was over by December 14, 1995. The Dayton Accords would be stamped out less than a week later on December 21, 1995.

NATO deployed 60,000 troops into Bosnia-Herzegovina while the Dayton Accords were being drafted in a military base in Ohio. Bosnia-Herzegovina would be transformed into a NATO garrison. The Dayton Accord and the acceptance of the foreign-drafted Bosnian Constitution effectively transformed Bosnia-Herzegovina into a modern protectorate. Under its new constitution, a neo-colonial administration was imposed on Bosnia-Herzegovina under the watchful eye of the Atlantic Alliance. The country could only be legally run by non-Bosnians and the actual head of the Bosnian government would be the individual holding the Office of High Representative of Bosnia-Herzegovina, effectively a colonial governor that would be assigned by the European Union to manage the country from Sarajevo.[28] Moreover, the Office of the High Representative and the Special Representative of the European Union in Bosnia-Herzegovina have been held by the same person since 2002.[29] At the same time the Office of the Principal Deputy High Representative has always been held by a US official answering to Washington.[30] The Bosnian Central Bank became headed by a foreigner who was always selected by the US, EU, and IMF in tandem.[31] The Bosnian Central Bank could not even issue credit or issue its own currency under the guidelines of the Bosnian Constitution.[32] Most Central Banks in Euro-Atlantic countries are in private hands, and there is no constitutional law saying that their central banks must only be run by foreign citizens, but Bosnians were constitutionally barred from holding office in their own central bank.

NATO turns to Kosovo and Metohija

After Bosnia-Herzegovina, the Atlantic Alliance would turn its attention to the predominantly Albanian-inhabited Serbian province of Kosovo and Metohija, which since the Ottoman invasion of Serbia had become the symbolic heart of the Serbian nation. This would result in NATO imposing a no-fly zone over the Federal Republic of Yugoslavia and essentially demanding Serbia renounce its sovereignty over the province. The Kosovo War would become NATO's second military confrontation. The war would be waged by the Alliance under the name of Operation Allied Force. NATO attacks would officially start on March 24, 1999 and end on June 10, 1999.

Map V: NATO in Bosnia under SFOR

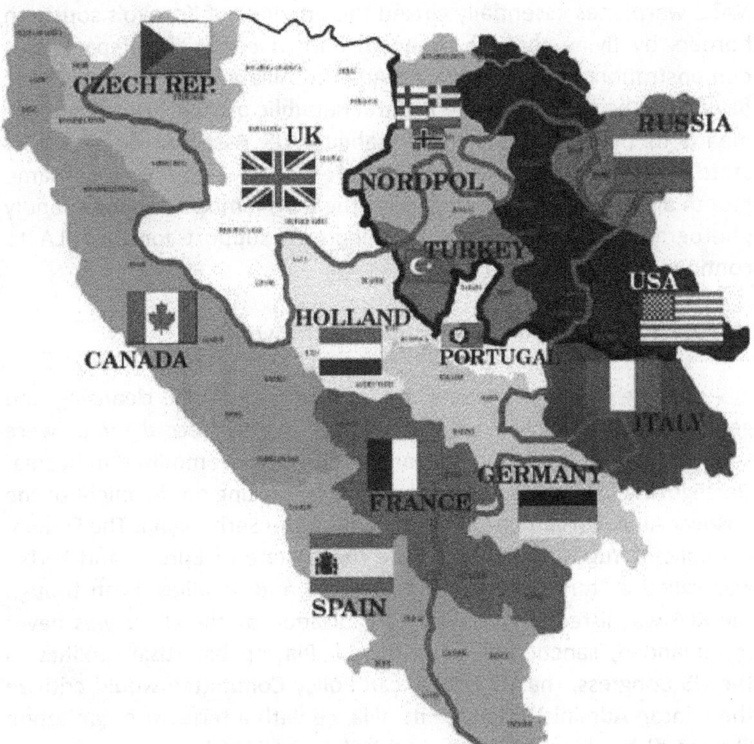

The roots of the war are based in the tensions that began to rise in Kosovo with the breakup of Yugoslavia, the economic demise of the country, and the fuelling of sectarianism. As a result, criminality began to rise due to poverty in Kosovo, as it did in the neighboring states of Albania and the former Yugoslav Republic (FYR) of Macedonia. Eventually the Kosovo Liberation Army (KLA) would be formed mainly by a group of Kosovar Albanians. The KLA would be tied to criminal enterprise and start enforcing tributes from local inhabitants in different parts of Kosovo. Soon a mixed crime war and insurgency would break out between the Serbian police and the KLA. Despite the fact that the US State Department had listed the KLA as a terrorist organization, the US and NATO would tacitly throw their support behind the KLA and its destabilization campaign against the Serbian police.

The fighting between the KLA and Serbian police worsened to a point where the Yugoslav military was called in. The US and its Atlanticist allies appointed themselves as overseers for resolving the conflict. NATO supported the KLA by trying to intimidate Belgrade through military exercises. In a show of major air power the Atlantic Alliance executed Operation Determined Falcon on June 15, 1998. NATO warplanes essentially circled the province of Kosovo's southern borders by flying through Albanian and Macedonian airspace in a demonstration of airpower. The Atlantic Alliance called the muscle flexing on the borders of the Federal Republic of Yugoslavia a gesture meant to promote peace and stability. US Assistant Secretary of State Richard Holbrooke threatened Yugoslav leaders that same month and then held meetings with the KLA, famously taking friendly photographs. This indicated Washington's support for the KLA to continue its fighting.

NATO's "Humanitarian Intervention" in Kosovo

The Serbs, who had been accused of ethnic cleansing and genocide and publicly appeared to have a track record for it, were soon accused of repeating the same crimes they committed in Bosnia-Herzegovina in Kosovo. The media began reporting on the plight of the Kosovar Albanians and began to demonize the Serbs again. The Federal Republic of Yugoslavia became the rogue state of Europe and Serbia was called a "terrorist nation" by the US and its allies. Even though the KLA was listed as a terrorist organization by the US, it was never reprimanded, sanctioned, or criticized. Playing bipartisan politics in the US Congress, the US Republican Policy Committee would criticize the Clinton Administration for its alliance with a terrorist organization like the KLA, which was also cited as being trained and sponsored by the Iranians in an attempt by Tehran to get a strategic foothold in the Balkans from Sarajevo to Pristina.[33]

The Yugoslav military was forced to withdraw from Kosovo by the US and NATO, but the KLA continued to launch attacks with the encouragement of Washington. The KLA was encouraged to attack as a means of instigating Serbian retaliation to open the door for a NATO attack. In the words of BBC reporter Allan Little:

> When news of a massacre in the Kosovan village of Racak reached Washington, Madeleine Albright's reaction was immediate.
>
> "Spring has come early," the US Secretary of State told Sandy Berger, the National Security Adviser, after hearing that the corpses of 45 ethnic Albanians had been found following an attack by Serb forces. Ms Albright, the West's most influential anti-Serb hawk, was quick to grasp that the atrocity could be used with great effect to stiffen international resolve against President Slobodan Milosevic of Yugoslavia.
>
> But only now has a detailed new investigation revealed how Ms Albright and the leaders of the rebel Kosovo Liberation Army took such dramatic advantage of the "Racak effect".
>
> "It was the kind of event we wanted to avoid," she told me recently. "But the fact that it had happened meant that it had to be a galvanising event and we had to move the Allies as rapidly as we could."
>
> Ms Albright was not alone in turning the Serb atrocity into a tactical advantage. Hashim Thaci, the young guerrilla who emerged as the KLA leader, had also begun to think of international opinion as potentially the strongest weapon in his otherwise ineffective armoury. The rebels had already provoked Serbian retaliation, targeting police and military patrols in hit-and-run ambushes, then melting back into the civilian population. At Racak, the week before the massacre, the rebels killed four Serb policemen. The response was predictable. "We knew full well that any armed action we undertook would trigger a ruthless retaliation by Serbs against our people," Mr Thaci has now admitted. "We knew we were endangering civilian lives, too, a great number of lives."
>
> Ms Albright and Mr Thaci made their candid

admissions to me as I compiled a BBC documentary to mark the first anniversary of a war which the West presented as a moral crusade against ethnic cleansing but which, in reality, was much more complex.

KLA commanders and their political backers in Washington understood how effectively civilian casualties would stoke international outrage—particularly among Western allies whose thinking was driven by the guilt of having hesitated over neighbouring Bosnia.

In late 1998, Milosevic signed up to a ceasefire that curtailed the number of Serb police in Kosovo and required the withdrawal of Yugoslavian troops to barracks. Milosevic faced Nato bombing if he failed to comply. He did comply.

But the KLA had not been asked to undertake anything. Because it threatened force against Milosevic only, the agreement enabled the rebels to perpetuate the cycle of violence while recruiting, re-arming and regrouping. They even filled the trenches vacated by the Serbs. The ceasefire monitors had no stick to wield against the KLA. "This became a problem with the Serbs," recalls one British monitor. "They said to us, 'Hang on, the deal was that we withdrew from these places, so can you please get these KLA out of the trenches we were in a month ago?'"

Even on the North Atlantic Council, Nato's governing body, there was profound scepticism about rebel intentions. Confidential minutes taken by one member nation on November 13, 1998, speak of the KLA as "the main initiator of the violence which is threatening the ceasefire arrangements". [34]

In March 1999, NATO began demanding that the Yugoslav military and Serb police leave the province of Kosovo. It also accepted the Czech Republic, Hungary, and Poland as new members. The accession of Hungary created a direct border with the Federal Republic of Yugoslavia. All this would lead the federal government in Belgrade to decree an emergency on March 23. The next day the Atlantic Alliance would start its first "humanitarian war." The war marked a turning point, because NATO acted unilaterally without any UN approval. Russia, China, India, and many other states would condemn the war. Greece, following the precedent it set in Bosnia-Herzegovina, would not join its

NATO allies in the Kosovo War. There would also be a big backlash over the war, which was unpopular among the populations of many NATO countries like Italy, Greece, and Spain.

The bombing did not limit itself to military targets. Civilian infrastructure was heavily bombed throughout the Federal Republic of Yugoslavia. Although Montenegro declared neutrality and refused to recognize the Yugoslav federal government's March 23 emergency decree that would allow it to instate a military draft, it too was bombed by NATO forces.[35] The Chinese Embassy in Belgrade was also deliberately bombed in violation of international laws; the Atlantic Alliance attacked the Chinese because they were communicating with the Yugoslav military and they were "suspected of monitoring the cruise missile attacks on Belgrade, with a view to developing effective counter-measures against US missiles."[36] The economy of the Federal Republic of Yugoslavia would be destroyed as NATO bombed factories and economic sites. Other civilian infrastructure bombed included hospitals and schools. Civilian casualties were high. The war resulted in a few thousand Yugoslav deaths in its less than one-month span. NATO bombs would even kill the Kosovar Albanians that the Atlantic Alliance had been professing to protect.

Operation Allied Force barely hurt the Yugoslav military. It punished the civilian population. NATO did not win the war by defeating the Yugoslavian military; it won by forcing Belgrade's surrender by attacking civilians. NATO also left behind a deadly legacy. During the war untargeted cluster bombs and depleted uranium were used that will affect civilians henceforth. The bombing of industrial sites with chemicals also resulted in major ecological damage.

The NATO Protectorate of Kosovo: From KFOR to Independence

A NATO protectorate was established in Kosovo. The war ended in the withdrawal of Yugoslav forces from Kosovo and the establishment of a United Nations Interim Administration Mission in Kosovo (UNMIK), which has run Kosovo's affairs from 1999 until the present. From that point on Kosovo's fiscal and economic policy has been governed by the US and EU. UNMIK economically de-linked Kosovo from Yugoslavia by replacing the Yugoslav Dinar with the German Mark on September 9, 1999.[37] UNMIK also encouraged the people of Kosovo to do business using multiple foreign currencies, thereby helping to undermine Yugoslavia.[38] Despite the fact that it was still officially a part of Yugoslavia and Serbia, Kosovo would also switch to the euro in 2002; UNMIK never even entertained the idea of a local currency in Kosovo.[39] In reality UNIMIK would be dominated by the EU and most of its administration would be assumed by the European Union Rule of Law Mission in Kosovo (EULEX) in December 2008. Following the model of the Dayton Accords and the restructuring of the Bosnian state under the watchful eye of NATO soldiers, NATO forces would enter under the Kosovo Force (KFOR).

The US and NATO wasted no time in establishing a military footing in Kosovo, which would be pivotal for the invasions of Afghanistan and Iraq in 2001 and 2003. Camp Bondsteel would become one of the Pentagon's most important military bases and transit points for its operations into the Middle East and Central Asia. Furthermore, via KLA attacks, the Atlantic Alliance would also push out the Russian peacekeepers which Moscow wanted to use to safeguard Serbian and Russian interests. Once the Serbian authorities were evicted by NATO the KLA started targeting non-Albanians and anyone that opposed it:

> In Kosovo, this one-sided propaganda and NATO control unleashed serious and unremitting anti-Serb (along with anti-Roma, anti-Turk, anti-dissident-Albanian) violence, helped along by the willingness of the NATO authorities to look the other way as their allies—the purported victims—took their revenge and pursued their long-standing aim of ethnic purification.[40]

The Kosovo War would also bring about the last chapter of Yugoslavia. The bonds between Montenegro and Serbia were also weakened by the war. The Federal Republic of Yugoslavia would be reconstructed as the Union of Serbia and Montenegro in 2003 until its dissolution in 2006, which would spell the final death of Yugoslavia.

On February 17, 2008, Kosovo would go on to declare its unilateral independence from the Republic of Serbia. President Fatmir Sejdiu, Prime Minister Hashim Thaçi, and Speaker of Parliament Jakup Krasniqi all marked the occasion with speeches inside and outside of the Kosovar Parliament. Many in Kosovo's ethnic Albanian majority celebrated what they believed was a shift towards self-determination. Yet, the truth of the matter is that the Kosovar declaration of independence was a declaration of dependency. Without any remorse Kosovar leaders transformed their land into a colonial outpost of Franco-German and Anglo-American interests. The declaration of independence also formally made NATO troops and EU police agents the formal administrators of law and order in Kosovo.

The actions of the Alliance and its KLA allies in Kosovo opened a Pandora's Box setting a dangerous precedent for recognizing states outside of the framework of international law. China quickly voiced disapproval out of fear that Taiwan (Chinese Taipei) would declare independence under the precedent set by Kosovo. The Republic of Azerbaijan, Indonesia, Sri Lanka, Sudan, Spain, Georgia, and Russia also all voiced opposition because of their own secessionist movements. Although the conditions leading to it are different, Moscow's recognition of Abkhazian and South Ossetian independence is a symmetrical move to US and EU recognition of Kosovar independence.

The Criminalization of Kosovo: The Drug Trade and Organ Harvesting

The criminalization of neighboring Albania and the ex-Yugoslav republics would take place with the economic takeover and dissolution of Yugoslavia and the installment of complicit political leaders in the Balkans. This has been a parcel of Euro-Atlantic integration and the US government played a direct role in this process. While the name Albania had become synonymous with crime throughout Europe at the expense of ordinary Albanians, the Council for Europe would go so far as to call Kosovo a "mafia state." The KLA, which by all means was not the only organization involved in criminal activities inside the former Yugoslavia, would be exposed for its involvement in the trafficking of weapons, narcotics, and people.

On the drug front, heroin was the main drug that the KLA exported in connection with Turkish and Italian criminal syndicates. After the KLA takeover of Kosovo under NATO's protection the news of their involvement with drugs began surfacing internationally:

> The KLA has taken control of all city administrations, and the UN has integrated the bulk of the 10,000 rebels into the Kosovo Provisional Corps, a militia with official policing powers and a mandate to ensure inter-ethnic stability. But far from promoting ethnic harmony, the KLA itself stands accused of instigating much of the anti-minority violence. Its popularity among Kosovars has dropped sharply.
>
> There is another question that continues to dog the KLA, and raises still more doubts about the legacy of the war—the question of drugs.
>
> A mass of evidence over the years has suggested the KLA got much of its funding from sales of heroin, and enjoyed intimate links with the Italian Mafia and Albanian heroin barons.
>
> The involvement was so great that the KLA played

a part in feeding the heroin craze that has raged across Western Europe and North America during the 1990s.[41]

The links of organized crime also showed that a network involving Albania and the CIA existed:

"The close relationship between (KLA leader Hashim) Thaçi and the Tirana government, which has a reputation for corruption and has been linked by Western diplomats to drug trafficking, is one of the factors that disillusioned many former (KLA) fighters who were interviewed in Germany, Switzerland and Austria," said the report.

The KLA's relations with the Albanian regime were overseen by a shadowy figure named Xhavit Haliti. One of the group's founders, he was the rebels' head fundraiser. Now he is a top lieutenant to Thaçi and a member of the advisory council that assists the UN administration in Kosovo.

He is also the provisional Kosovo government's ambassador to Albania, where he was said by ethnic Albanian and Western observers to have ties to the underworld, the London Guardian reported Sept. 3.

He has also collaborated with Albanian secret police agents to silence dissenters in Kosovo, according to current and former KLA commanders and Western diplomats cited in the New York Times report of June 25. The London Guardian also mentioned ties to Albania's secret police: it said the KLA's own spy service had been "aided" by Albanian and U.S. intelligence services.

Michael Levine, a 25-year veteran of the DEA who left in 1990, said he believes there is no question that U.S. intelligence knew about the KLA's drug ties.

"They (the CIA) protected them (the KLA) in every way they could. As long as the CIA is protecting the KLA, you've got major drug pipelines protected from any police investigation," said Levine, who teaches undercover tactics and informer handling to U.S. and Canadian police forces, including the RCMP. [42]

KLA people trafficking would involve kidnapping and murder

and be tied particularly to the illicit sex industry and human organ sales. Even Carla Del Ponte, the Swiss attorney-general who was appointed chief prosecutor of the International Criminal Tribunal for the former Yugoslavia (ICTY) by the UN, would acknowledge that at least 300 people had been kidnapped by the KLA and taken to neighboring Albania in 1999 where their organs were extracted. Hashim Thaçi, the former head of the KLA who would become the premier of Kosovo, would be directly incriminated by Carla Del Ponte and others in the murderous black market organ harvesting operations. Individuals personally involved in the organ harvesting would also testify privately about the illicit organ trade: "one of whom 'personally made an organ delivery' to an Albanian airport for transport abroad, and 'confirmed information directly gathered by the tribunal.'"[43]

The Council of Europe would also add its voice to the accusations against Prime Minister Thaçi and the KLA and additionally point out that the officials from NATO nations that would be responsible for the breakaway Serbian province after the Kosovo War would look the other way. On December 12, 2010, their provisional report would state some of the following points:

1. The Parliamentary Assembly was extremely concerned to learn of the revelations of the former Prosecutor at the International Criminal Tribunal for the Former Yugoslavia (ICTY), who alleged that serious crimes had been committed during the conflict in Kosovo, including trafficking in human organs, crimes which had gone unpunished hitherto and had not been the subject of any serious investigation.

2. In addition, according to the former Prosecutor, these acts had been committed by members of the "Kosovo Liberation Army" (KLA) militia against Serbian nationals who had remained in Kosovo at the end of the armed conflict and been taken prisoner.

3. According to the information gathered by the Assembly and to the criminal investigations now under way, numerous concrete and convergent indications confirm that some Serbians and some Albanian Kosovars were held prisoner in secret places of detention under KLA control in northern Albania and were subjected to inhuman and degrading treatment, before ultimately disappearing.

4. Numerous indications seem to confirm that, during the

period immediately after the end of the armed conflict, before international forces had really been able to take control of the region and re-establish a semblance of law and order, organs were removed from some prisoners at a clinic in Albanian territory, near Fushë-Krujë, to be taken abroad for transplantation.

5. This criminal activity, which developed with the benefit of the chaos prevailing in the region, at the initiative of certain KLA militia leaders linked to organised crime, has continued, albeit in other forms, until today, as demonstrated by an investigation being carried out by the European Union Rule of Law Mission in Kosovo (EULEX) relating to the Medicus clinic in Pristina.

6. Although some concrete evidence of such trafficking already existed at the beginning of the decade, the international authorities in charge of the region did not consider it necessary to conduct a detailed examination of these circumstances, or did so incompletely and superficially.[44]

The news about the organ harvesting operations of NATO's allies would go mostly unnoticed by NATO leaders, who for the most part stayed silent, choosing to look the other way. Investigation requests were ignored, and the charges were discredited because the names of witnesses were kept a secret. Despite Bernard Kouchner's denials and attacks on the reports about human organ trafficking, a classified UN document obtained by the channel France 24 revealed that UNIMIK and the UN knew about organ trafficking in NATO-garrisoned Kosovo as early as 2003.[45] A leaked confidential UN report involving testimonies from KLA fighters from Kosovo and Montenegro stated:

The captives taken to central Albania were again moved, in small groups, south of Burrel that was set up as a makeshift clinic. There, medical equipment and personnel were used to extract body organs from the captives, who then died. Their remains were buried nearby. The organs were transported to Rinas airport near Tirana (approximately 75 kilometers southwest of Burrel) and flown abroad. Other captives taken to the house/clinic near Burrel included a small number of females from Kosovo, Albania, and eastern Europe. [...] the transports and surgical procedure were carried out with the knowledge and/or active involvement of mid-level and senior KLA officers as well as doctors from Kosovo and abroad. The operation was supported by men with links to Albanian secret police operatives of the former government of Salih Berisha.[46]

Kouchner, who was the former head of UNIMIK and later the French foreign minister under Sarkozy, would also be accused of participating in the organ trafficking by the families of people who were kidnapped and murdered for their organs.[47] It is also suspected that the KLA is linked to Israel's organ harvesting industry either directly or by means of Turkish and Italian channels.

Greater Albania: Myth, Moral Panic, or Real Possibility?

Discussions of a Greater Albania began to lead to alarmism and sociological moral panics in the Balkans during the 1990s. It should not be overlooked that racist and Islamophobic prejudices and biases in many cases have been tied to the alarmism about a Greater Albania. The sounding of these alarms has led to a series of moral panics (feelings that a threat is emerging against a society and its values) in relation to ethnic Albanian minorities, despite the fact that these Albanian populations are usually destitute and marginalized, and in many cases the victims of the so-called "nationalist" Albanian militias and organized crime within Albanian populations. To add to this, political forces and nationalists in Greece and the former Yugoslavia have tried to use fear of Albanian minorities as a ticket for political gain and support. In other words, the fears of Albanian expansionism can be explained as a politically and socially manufactured fear that has been drawn on as a means of self empowerment by certain groups and people.

Turning to the reverse side of the coin, there are also legitimate fears in the Balkans tied to Albanian irredentism. In the 1990s, the discussions of a Greater Albania began to gain popularity at the same time that ethnic Albanian militias began to form in the Yugoslav republics of Macedonia, Montenegro, and Serbia. In Albanian communities, nationalism was also being used as means of distracting the Albanian people from their miseries and their exploitation by their own leaders and the organized criminal groups thriving in their communities. The US and NATO sought to use the resurgence of Albanian nationalism as a means of tightening their grip in the region through a tactic of divide and conquer. In this context, Albanian leaders—which are some of the closest allies of the US—have been tacitly supported by the US in their dreams of forming a Greater Albania or a Balkan economic zone

TABLE 3.2

Euro-Atlantic Integration of Albania and the Former Yugoslavia

Country	NATO Status, Respective Date	EU Status, Respective Date
Albania	Member, 1 April 2009	Partner, 1, 8 February 2008
Bosnia-Herzegovina	Candidate, 22 April 2010	Membership Applicant, 28 April 2009
Croatia	Member, 1 April 2009	Partner, 18 February 2008
		Acceding State, 9 December 2011
		EU Entry slated for 1 July 2013
Kosovo – Serbia	–	–
Macedonia, FYR of	Candidate, 24 April 1999	Candidate, 18 February 2008
Montenegro	Candidate, 4 December 2009	Candidate, 17 December 2010
Serbia	Offered Candidate Status, 2008 *	Candidate, 1 March 2012
Slovenia	Member, 29 March 2004	Member, 1 May 2004

* NATO offered Serbia, without any solicitation by Serbia, for the chance to start the intensified dialogue with NATO.

controlled by Albanian business interests that even NATO allies like Bulgaria fear.[48]

NATO in the Former Yugoslav Republic of Macedonia

The former Yugoslav Republic of Macedonia would not be spared from the criminalization process and became part of an illicit trade corridor in the Balkans:

> A triangular trade in oil, arms and narcotics had developed largely as a result of the embargo imposed by the international community on Serbia and Montenegro and the blockade enforced by Greece against Macedonia. In turn, the collapse of industry and agriculture had created a vacuum in the economic system which boosted the further expansion of illicit trade. The latter had become a "leading sector," an important source of foreign exchange and a fertile ground for the criminal mafias.
>
> [...]
>
> The trade in narcotics and weapons was allowed to [deliberately] prosper despite the presence, since 1993, of more than 800 American troops at the Albanian-Macedonian border with a mandate to enforce the embargo. [...] The revenues from oil and narcotics were used to finance the purchase of arms (often in terms of direct barter): "Deliveries of oil to Macedonia (skirting the Greek embargo [in 1993-1994]) can be used to cover heroin, as do deliveries of Kalashnikov rifles [...] in Kosovo."[49]

The biggest beneficiaries of the criminalization of Albania and the former Yugoslavia would be Wall Street and the financial conglomerates.[50] In this regard organized criminal enterprise has always been subordinate to organized capital.

The strengthening of the KLA would soon have a direct impact on the former Yugoslav Republic of Macedonia. The Macedonian arm of the KLA, called the National Liberation Army (NLA), would soon begin conducting attacks inside Slavic Macedonia like the KLA did in Kosovo. KLA men and weapons would be transferred to the NLA. NATO would pressure Skopje into accepting the Ohrid Framework Agreement overseen by the US and the EU on August 13, 2001. Under the terms of the understanding the government in Skopje would open its borders for

Map VI: NATO in Kosovo under KFOR

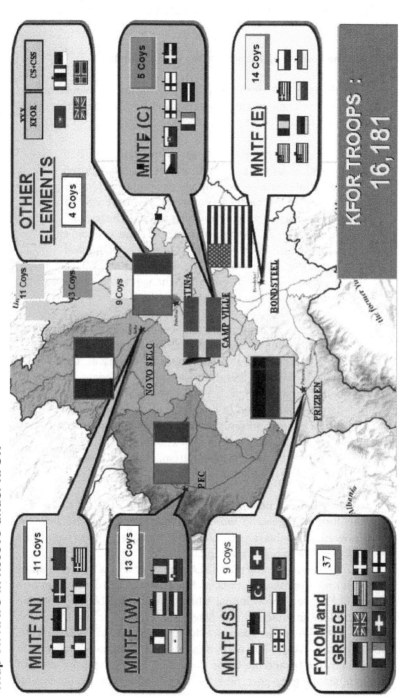

official NATO intervention under the name Essential Harvest. According to NATO:

> Operation "Essential Harvest" was officially launched on 22 August [2001] and effectively started on 27 August [2001]. This 30-day mission involved the sending of approximately 3500 NATO troops, with logistical support, to disarm ethnic Albanian groups and destroy their weapons.[51]

The Atlantic Alliance had supported the NLA, and later the Albanian National Army (ANA), as a means of getting a foothold in Macedonia. In fact when the Skopjian military began a major offensive against the NLA, there were threats by NATO to stop the attacks. One observer described the events unfolding in Macedonia after the empowerment of the KLA in 1999 as thus:

> To make everything even more tragic, all of this is taking place in front of the eyes of NATO and KFOR, respectively. Where will Macedonia end up in the security sphere, and what will happen to its territorial integrity and NATO verbal obligation to guarantee its security, is perhaps best demonstrated by the information from the commander of a border post in the Kicevo region. He is informing his superiors that, after a recent exchange of soldiers for a criminal, members of [NATO and UNIMIK] have several times brazenly entered Macedonian territory and arrogantly ridiculed their Macedonian colleagues by stating that "if they want and whenever they want, they can get kidnapped". [52]

In fact, the NATO forces from Kosovo operating in KFOR rescued the NLA fighters. An unidentified informed source on the ground at the time explained:

> When the terrorists were defeated and showed a white flag, the OSCE and NATO were in panic and ordered us [the Macedonian authorities] to stop immediately the [military] action. Swedish Foreign Minister Ana Lindth and the European leaders were hysterical, threatening us with economic sanctions, etc. Furthermore, the OSCE and KFOR entered

> Aracinovo and 'saved' 500 terrorists together with
> their weaponry and took them to another village
> from where they are now attacking again, killing
> civilians and undertaking ethnic cleansing in several
> Macedonian villages... NATO forbids us to defend
> ourselves when we are attacked; our territory is
> brutally abused by the terrorists. We have tried to
> defend ourselves, and they have saved the terrorists
> in air-conditioned buses. That has provoked harsh
> reaction of the Macedonian people.[53]

US officials would claim in a fantastic excuse that NLA fighters using tanks forced US soldiers to hand over the captured NLA fighters.[54] This is not possible, because the NLA did not have heavy weapons such as armored vehicles, tanks, and jets. Furthermore, the US and NATO could have easily tracked any tanks.

Operation Essential Harvest would see the transformation of Slavic Macedonia into another NATO garrison in the Balkans. It would later give way to Operation Amber Fox, which would start on September 23, 2001. Three hundred NATO troops from Operation Essential Harvest would be joined by seven hundred more NATO soldiers under the new German-led mission that was originally supposed to last three months, but would last until December 15, 2002.[55] This operation would lead to the establishment of a NATO office in Slavic Macedonia and to Operation Allied Harmony, which would begin on December 16, 2002 and last until March 31, 2003. The latter operation worked to restructure the Skopjian military and insure Skopjian ties to the Atlantic Alliance:

> NATO's presence after 15 December [2002] was two-
> fold; [1] its operational elements provided support
> for the international monitors; [2] its [civilian and
> military] advisory elements assisted the government
> in taking ownership of security throughout [the
> former Yugoslav Republic of Macedonia].[56]

Since NATO involvement in its country, Skopje has become a client of the Atlantic Alliance, pursuing Euro-Atlantic integration like the rest of the former Yugoslavia. All the ex-Yugoslav republics are actively seeking both EU and NATO membership, if they have not already got them (see Table 3.2). Serbia is the only exception, which has declined NATO membership. Slovenia is both a NATO and EU member while Croatia joined NATO in 2009 and is slated to join the EU in 2013.

CHART 3.2

The Disintegration of Yugoslavia

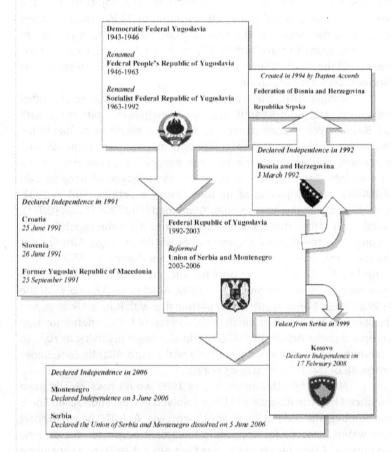

Democratic Federal Yugoslavia
1943-1946

Renamed
Federal People's Republic of Yugoslavia
1946-1963

Renamed
Socialist Federal Republic of Yugoslavia
1963-1992

Created in 1994 by Dayton Accords

Federation of Bosnia and Herzegovina

Republika Srpska

Declared Independence in 1992

Bosnia and Herzegovina
3 March 1992

Declared Independence in 1991

Croatia
25 June 1991

Slovenia
26 June 1991

Former Yugoslav Republic of Macedonia
25 September 1991

Federal Republic of Yugoslavia
1992-2003

Reformed
Union of Serbia and Montenegro
2003-2006

Taken from Serbia in 1999

Kosovo
*Declares Independence on
17 February 2008*

Declared Independence in 2006

Montenegro
Declared Independence on 3 June 2006

Serbia
Declared the Union of Serbia and Montenegro dissolved on 5 June 2006

NATO 2.0: The Reinvention of the Atlantic Alliance in the 1990s

As the Cold War started wrapping up in the late 1980s and early 1990s, with events like the fall of the Berlin Wall in 1989 and the deposing of Romania's Nicolae Ceaușescu from power in 1989 taking place, more people began to question the purpose, function, and existence of NATO. Many started demanding that NATO be disbanded. NATO was also obsolete in the eyes of a vast array of the public. All types of literature started being produced arguing for disbanding NATO and projecting an identity crisis within the organization over its purpose without the USSR and its Warsaw Pact allies. It is quite fitting to note that the Atlantic Alliance produced two new strategic concepts in this period: one in 1991 and the next in 1999. The former was used to take strategic advantage of the demise of the USSR and the dissolution of the Warsaw Pact and the latter to chart NATO's trajectory into the next century as a global force. At a summit in 1990, NATO's leaders announced the release of the new and unclassified Strategic Concept document, plans to transform NATO, to expand the Alliance, and the creation of the North Atlantic Cooperation Council (NACC) to absorb the former Warsaw Pact countries.

Initially NATO tried to reinvent itself with a mandate of conflict prevention and Euro-Atlantic security management, but then, with the Bosnian War, began marketing itself as a player in humanitarian operations, including peacekeeping, and intervention. Arms control, expansion, and an insistence that the geographic peripheries of the Euro-Atlantic Zone needed to be tamed and engaged all became part of NATO's new projection of its role. During meetings held in 1991, NATO began planning to assemble "Combined Joint Task Forces (CJTFs), multilateral forces that include air, land, and maritime capabilities."[57] According to the discussions, the forces would be Anglo-American at the cores; this was directly tied to an important change in NATO strategy caused by the Gulf War. The bureaucratic jargon for expansion began to be molded more intensively.[58] In 1999, Articles 36, 37, and 38 of the 1999 Strategic Concept pushed for partnership with Russia, Ukraine, and the states of the Mediterranean littoral on top of NATO's determination to expand under Article 39. NATO would also begin justifying its right to intervene and deploy militarily outside of the Euro-Atlantic Zone under Article 48 of the 1999 Strategic Concept.

NATO's fiftieth anniversary in 1999 would have chiefly gone unnoticed had the Alliance not been involved in Operation Allied Force and bombing the Federal Republic of Yugoslavia. As NATO began to chart new waters, reasons for opposition towards it began to take on new dimensions. Many people were dead set against military intervention being married to humanitarianism. NATO's offensives in Yugoslavia had publicly disturbed them, as well as the Alliance's growing involvement in international politics as an active player. The question of international law also became a major focal point for opposing the Atlantic Alliance; after all NATO had intervened in a civil war in Bosnia-Herzegovina to change the balance of power against the Bosnians Serbs, who would have won the civil war and made sure that Bosnia remained a member of Yugoslavia if NATO had not interfered.

NATO also began to look for new threats. Despite the fact that NATO's mandate of defending Western Europe from a Soviet invasion was fundamentally moot after the dissolution of the Warsaw Pact and the collapse of the Soviet Union, the Atlantic Alliance persevered. While the Soviets and state communism melted away, NATO would first find new adversaries in the Balkans. Almost as if events were unfolding from a script, John Woodworth, the former US deputy assistant secretary of defense, would admit in 1996 that the future focus of NATO would be on the Balkans—as this chapter has examined in a chronological overview—and then on the parts of the world inhabited by Muslims and nuclear proliferation, which will be examined anon.

NATO in the Gulf War and the Preparations for the "Long War"

NATO's out-of-area military engagement did not start with Yugoslavia; it only became publicly apparent in Yugoslavia. It actually started in the Middle East. Few are fully aware that NATO had been silently involved in the Persian Gulf in 1991 and that in reality the wars in Iraq and Yugoslavia were all NATO wars. On the other side of the Atlantic Ocean, President George H. W. Bush, Sr. remained sinisterly silent about the US-directed NATO stay-behind forces while the news broke out in Italy and Europe about these clandestine organizations in the 1990s. Bush Sr. refused to make any statements or to involve the US in the matter. That was because the US was mustering all its forces and preparing its allies for a war with Iraq. The North Atlantic Council's Defense Planning Committee in Brussels called for the withdrawal of the Iraqi Army from Kuwait and even released a statement asking all the Atlantic Alliance's members to "further support this continuing effort, in line with evolving requirement."[59] What is being addressed herein is much more than Operation Ace Guard, which was executed by NATO to protect Turkey. It is worth quoting Colonel Samuel Nelson Drew of the US Air Force, a military officer attached to the US contingent in NATO:

> [F]rom 1989 to 1991, NATO members also became involved in the largest military operation in the history of NATO's existence: the Gulf War. Had it not been for NATO's contributions to moving military personnel and equipment from Europe to the Gulf and supplying equipment such as Patriot missiles to Turkey and Israel, the United States would have been unable to prosecute that war in the manner it did. As a matter of fact, the entire "end-run" strategy would have been impossible had it not been for NATO allies and the breakup of the Warsaw Pact. There weren't enough heavy lifters in the [Pentagon's] inventory to transport tanks at high speeds overland in the desert to carry out the end-run around the flanks of the Iraqi army. The German government responded favorably

to our request for such vehicles, but it was a matter of serendipity that they had just acquired the military inventory of the former East Germany, including an abundance of tank-transport vehicles.

All of those things coming together at one time and the tremendous support from NATO did not receive due attention in the American press. During the remaining two years that I worked in the alliance, I was surprised by the opinions expressed by a number of members of Congress that visited NATO. We would brief them on what NATO was doing and how it was advancing, or attempting to advance, [American] policy goals. But when we mentioned NATO's role in the Gulf War, they would say, "Wait a second, NATO wasn't a player in the Gulf War." We would then itemize the examples of cooperation we had received through the alliance; the number of times we made a request and got 15 positive answers from our allies; the massive transfer of [Germany's] transportation network that enabled us to move a corps out of Europe and into Saudi Arabia; and the deployment of air elements from the ACE (Allied Command-Europe) mobile force from Central Europe—where everyone had assumed it would be used—to Turkey, in order to deter a potential Iraqi attack in Turkish air space.[60]

The events in Iraq would be used to upset and reframe "the beliefs of most NATO experts about how the alliance might be used in the future."[61] The former chairman of the US House Delegation to the NATO Parliamentary Assembly, Douglas Bereuter, also acknowledged this:

Although NATO was not officially involved in Desert Storm, without the NATO underpinnings that stood behind the British, French, and American cooperation, coalition objectives would have been much more difficult to achieve. It would have also been much more difficult for any country to aid the Kurds [militarily] in northern Iraq.[62]

The former military head of NATO, General John Galvin, while addressing a question about Yugoslavia, would also acknowledge this:

NATO can act, as was evident in the Gulf War that followed the end of the Cold War. Gulf War forces were comprised primarily of NATO member forces that had experience working together, with similar training, doctrine, organization, and the ability and political-military sense to carry out missions. For this reason we were successful in the Gulf War.[63]

Even the Atlantic Alliance's strategies were applied in the Gulf War. The forward-defense strategy of deep strikes—which was adopted in 1984 against the Warsaw Pact and refocused NATO's attack tactics from the frontlines to rear-echelon forces before those forces could be moved to the frontline—were used against Iraq in the Gulf War.[64]

The fact that Somalia in the Horn of Africa erupted into civil war, Iraq was attacked, the USSR collapsed, and Yugoslavia began to disintegrate all in 1991 says something important about the changes that were sweeping the geo-political environment. The 1990s were actually a time spent in preparation for bringing about the globalization of NATO and the conflicts of the next two decades. The US was preparing to raise the tempo of its "long war" into Eurasia and the World-Island—the Eurasian and African landmasses combined—by taking advantage of the geo-political void that the death of the USSR would leave. It is on the basis of the Gulf War against Iraq that NATO's military intervention in Yugoslavia took place. Military planners saw NATO action and realized that the Atlantic Alliance was a powerful weapon and tool for reshaping countries and regions. Moreover, the intervention of NATO into the Socialist Federal Republic of Yugoslavia was systematically executed in gradual phases in a piecemeal overarching operation, because NATO officials knew that an all-out invasion during the disintegration of the country would result in a massive guerrilla war against US and NATO troops.[65] It was from the starting point of Yugoslavia that the concept of humanitarian intervention and new techniques for perception management would enter the public discourse and gain some currency: "Official deceptions about events in Bosnia and Kosovo surely paved the way for false reports about mass weapons in Iraq, which were faithfully echoed by news organizations in the early years of the Iraq war."[66] The stages were set for a new chapter for the North Atlantic Treaty Organization.

CHAPTER 4

NATO IN AFGHANISTAN

The Americans want us to continue fighting but not to win, just to bleed the Russians [sic., the Soviets].

— Mohammed Ismail Khan,
Afghan Mujahedeen commander in Heart (1986)[1]

September 11, 2011: A Pretext for the Occupation of Afghanistan?

It was foretold in the previous decade that NATO would focus on the lands inhabited mostly by Muslims after its engagement in the Balkans. The attacks of September 11, 2011 in the US would make this a reality. While the 9/11 attacks were recognized as an act of terrorism rather than an act of war against the United States by another country, Article 5 of the NATO Charter on mutual defense would nonetheless be invoked by the Atlantic Alliance on the following day, September 12. NATO members decided that, if it was determined that the attack against the US was directed from outside of the United States, the Alliance would see it as an attack on all members. Thus each member publicly stood in solidarity with the US as the mainstream media in the NATO states began to prepare their publics for military retribution and war. At the same time the other NATO members, particularly those attached to the Franco-German Entente, gave themselves some latitude in responding, permitting them the freedom to decide how to assist the US in its upcoming war by stating that each US ally is responsible for determining what response it deemed necessary and that collective action would be taken after further consultations by the North Atlantic Council.

Osama bin Laden and his Al-Qaeda network were immediately blamed by the US, which used the opportunity to turn on its own purported allies, the Taliban regime, in Afghanistan, initially a creation of the CIA and the Pakistani Inter-Services Intelligence (ISI). The Bush Jr. White House had even been funding the Taliban that year; Washington had given the Taliban a "gift" of $43 million (US) just in the month of May.[2] While Osama bin Laden was supportive of the 9/11 actions he conveyed the message several times that he was not involved. Associated Press had this to say:

> On Wednesday, bin Laden congratulated the people who carried out the deadly terrorist strikes in the United States, but denied that he was involved, Palestinian journalist Jamal Ismail said. He spoke with a bin Laden aide early Wednesday by satellite telephone.[3]

According to *Reuters*, Osama bin Laden denied any ties to the attacks in a message conveyed by the Taliban envoy to Pakistan:

> Afghanistan's ruling Taliban movement said on Thursday that Saudi-born dissident Osama bin Laden had told them he had no role in Tuesday's terror attacks in the United States.
> "We asked from [*sic*.] [Osama bin Ladin], (and) he told (us) we don't have any hand in this action," Taliban ambassador to Pakistan Mullah Abdul Salam Zaeef, told Reuters in an interview.
> He said also that the hardline Islamic Taliban movement was prepared to cooperate with the United States in investigating those believed responsible for the devastating attacks.[4]

The Saudi national would even send a message on the Arabic satellite news network Al Jazeera denying responsibility for the attacks.

Despite the fact that the Taliban offered to hand Osama bin Laden over if provided with solid admissible evidence, Washington attacked Taliban-controlled Afghanistan on the grounds that Mullah Omar, the mysterious leader of the Taliban, was sheltering him and refusing that demand.[5] The Taliban's offer was renewed again several times and they started to include offers of a trial in Afghanistan.[6] While being attacked, the Taliban even offered during a secret meeting in Pakistan in mid-October, to hand over Osama bin Laden without any evidence from Washington.[7]

The Guardian, in a September 22, 2001 article, actually brought to light that the Taliban had received threats of a US attack two months before 9/11:

> Osama bin Laden and the Taliban received threats of possible American military strikes against them two months before the terrorist assaults on New York and Washington, which were allegedly masterminded by the Saudi-born fundamentalist, a Guardian investigation has established.
>
> [...]
>
> The warning to the Taliban originated at a four-day meeting of senior Americans, Russians, Iranians and Pakistanis at a hotel in Berlin in mid-July [2001]. The conference, the third in a series dubbed "brainstorming on Afghanistan", was part of a classic diplomatic device known as "track two".[8]

The US had conducted a Pentagon-led inter-agency simulation of an invasion of Taliban-controlled Afghanistan called Unified Vision 2001 in May 2001.[9] According to the Pentagon's own *American Forces Press Service*: "[The participants] took their experiences in Unified Vision back to their commands and put them to use as the [different] commands created plans for operations Enduring Freedom and Noble Eagle."[10] Despite the fact that there is very little chance involved in military planning, the Pentagon casually presents all this as a forecast of the first war of the 21st Century.[11] In the words of the assistant director of the Pentagon's Joint Experimentation Directorate: "Nostradamus couldn't have nailed the first battle of the next war any closer than we did."[12] It is worth noting that the war in Afghanistan was described as the "first battle of the next war" in the above statement made in 2002.

The primary interest of the US and UK in 9/11 was a pretext to swiftly move into Afghanistan. Their war would officially start on October 7, 2001 under the name Operation Enduring Freedom. On September 9, 2001, immediately prior to the Anglo-American invasion of Taliban-controlled Afghanistan the head of the Northern Alliance, Ahmed Shah Massoud, was assassinated. Despite the rhetoric from US politicians about Massoud being an ally, Massoud's assassination was too good to be true for Washington. After the end of the Cold War, the US had supported the Taliban against him and Massoud saw the US as being treacherous. With Massoud out of the way, the Northern Alliance was free to form an alliance with the US. Until this day it is alleged in Afghanistan that the US was involved in his murder.

From the Balkans to Central Asia: Atlanticism on the March

The Anglo-American invasion of Afghanistan in 2001 quickly turned into a NATO war on the basis of Article 5. It is worth noting, as

Canadian political scientist Carl Hodge does, that NATO actually did not do all the heavy lifting in Afghanistan:

> The fighting campaign in Afghanistan, however, was in reality conducted almost entirely by the United States with the Afghan North Alliance as junior partners and the cooperation of the government of [General Pervez Musharraf in] Pakistan was more critical to the completion of the campaign than any of the NATO capitals.[13]

Likewise, there is a good argument to be made that without the Afghan ground forces loosely called the Northern Alliance, the conflict might have taken a different course. It was these Afghan forces—allied or tied to Iran, Russia, Tajikistan, and India—that did most of the fighting against the Taliban's forces.

As a result of the US war in Afghanistan and its stationing of troops in Central Asia, the US military presence in the Balkans was trimmed down. Here lies the crux of the matter and the challenge that NATO faces in practice: "while the Alliance was constituted to defend Western Europe and North America, its leaders had *global* interests and commitments."[14] Now not only were the other US allies forced to mobilize their forces to replace US soldiers in the Balkans, but they had to also mobilize their military resources and power to help the US in its expanding campaign(s). This would become very clear as the US expanded its war from Afghanistan into Iraq in 2003 and its NATO allies faced even more pressure to increase their presences in Afghanistan.

NATO's role in Afghanistan was less pronounced at the start of its deployment in 2001 and 2002. It would unofficially run the International Security Assistance Force (ISAF) under US oversight. ISAF was originally established by the UN Security Council on December 20, 2001 as an international force to help Afghanistan, but the domination of NATO states made it a de facto NATO force. Its mandate first covered the Afghan capital of Kabul and its surrounding environs, but this would change as the US would have to focus outside Afghanistan, leaving its allies to assume combat missions in Afghanistan on its behalf. ISAF and NATO's role would become more visible in Afghanistan once this happened and the US decided to channel its military resources from Afghanistan into Iraq in 2003. In a direct correlation to the Anglo-American invasion of Iraq, NATO assumed command of ISAF on August 11, 2003.

The Geographic Placement of Afghanistan on the Eurasian Chessboard

Afghanistan's location has always been significant. This

landlocked nation sits at the crossroads of Central Asia, the Indian sub-continent, and the Middle East. It is geo-strategically and economically important for a number of reasons. Firstly, Afghanistan is a major geo-strategic hub that conveniently flanks Iran, the former Soviet Union, and China. For most of its history, the geographic area has been a frontier between Iran, India, and China. Later, since its independence from Iran, Afghanistan has served as a buffer state between Iran, Russia and the succeeding USSR, and British-controlled colonial India—later succeeded by the Republic of India and Pakistan. Afghanistan is an ideal location for creating a wedge between the major Eurasian powers and for establishing a permanent military presence for future operations in Eurasia. Secondly, Afghanistan also constitutes a doorway into energy-rich Central Asia, which permits bypassing the territories of Iran, the Russian Federation, and China. This is an important factor because it permits forces from outside the region such as the United States or Britain to use Afghanistan to circumvent these rival regional powers. A pipeline corridor running through Pakistan and Afghanistan from the oil and gas fields of Turkmenistan and Central Asia has been a major project for the United States and its oil corporations for years.

NATO combat missions have largely been concentrated in Southwest and Northwest Afghanistan where a strategic oil and gas pipeline corridor from Central Asia to the Indian Ocean had been projected to run. Prior to September 11, 2001, Washington had been involved in unsuccessful negotiations with the Taliban government with a view to securing this oil and gas route. US oil and gas interests in Afghanistan had a direct bearing on the post-Taliban political setup of Kabul as well as the locations of NATO's combat troops. On December 22, 2001 Hamid Karzai was initially selected to become the interim president of Afghanistan as a result of the lobbying of Union Oil Company of California (UNOCAL). Karzai was not only a former employee of UNOCAL, he had also been collaborating with the Taliban government, in negotiations pertaining to the construction and royalties of a proposed trans-Afghan pipeline running from Turkmenistan to Pakistan. In fact, several UNOCAL officials achieved prominent places in post-Taliban Afghanistan. Zalmay Khalilzad, the US special envoy in both Afghanistan and later Anglo-American occupied Iraq, was also a UNOCAL official.

The NATO offensives in the western half of Afghanistan could be seen as seeking to secure the territory needed for the building of a geo-strategic pipeline from Central Asia to Pakistan through Afghanistan. There even seem to be plans to reconfigure the boundaries of both Afghanistan and Pakistan to facilitate the flow of oil and gas from Central Asia to the shores of the Indian Ocean. Once built, the pipeline corridor and the terminal on the Indian Ocean coastline would be a victory over competing

Russian, Chinese, and Iranian energy interests in the Caspian Basin and Central Asia. This would be similar to the geo-strategic victory that the US won after the opening of the Baku-Tbilisi-Ceyhan (BTC) Oil Terminal, an energy route that bypassed Russia and Iran in bringing Caspian oil to the international market.

Control of Afghanistan is important in deciding the future balance of power in Central Asia and Eurasia, thus whosoever controls Afghanistan has great leverage in the resource-rich Eurasian landmass. Afghanistan constitutes a major area of production of opium, which feeds the illicit narcotics trade out of Afghanistan. This is economically significant since illicit trade in narcotics is classified third in terms of world trade turnover, after oil and the trade in weapons. Its production, however, is not geared to economic benefit to Afghanistan.

The Secret Spoils of War: Afghan Opium

Afghanistan and Colombia, the primary US satellite in South America, are the world's top drug economies based on figures from 2003; drug trafficking amounts to "the third biggest global commodity in [monetary] terms after oil and the arms trade."[15] In 2003, the International Monetary Fund estimated that between $590 billion and $1.5 trillion (US) was laundered annually, representing between 2% and 5% of global GDP, with the majority linked to the illicit drug trade.[16]

Opium and illicit narcotics have played a relatively unknown, yet historic and central, role in world economics and international relations. To understand this and evaluate Afghanistan's role in the drug market we must look back at the history of the opium trade. There were major wars launched because of opium. London and British companies such as the British East India Company (BEIC) which administered and governed India, had shared interests in the trade and trafficking of narcotics. Essentially corporate and government interests in British-ruled India and British colonies were unified and overlapping.

In East Asia and Southeast Asia, opium was an integral part of Western European trade. At its peak in the mid 1880s, opium was one of the most valuable commodities circulating in international trade.[17] British exports of opium out of India had systematically helped weaken Chinese resistance to foreign or colonial powers and also helped balance the enormous trade deficit Britain had with China. The British corporations managing India not only coerced the Chinese government into letting drug addiction run rampant, but also disrupted Indian farmers' traditional economies by forcing them to grow opium. While growing opium had been an irregular practice among farmers in India, the British effectively forced many Indian farmers to become dependent on it for a living. The local economies of many communities of India were systematically driven from food farming and self-subsistence into the cultivation of cash crops for British merchants. Subsistence crops had given farmers some form of autonomy from market forces and guaranteed their survival while cash crops made them dependent on the British and the opium market for survival. Thus British control and exploitation by British companies became entrenched in India.[18]

British-sponsored drug-dealing in Asia was one of the causes of the collapse of the Chinese Empire. Drug addiction was skyrocketing in China, soon forcing the Chinese government to ban opium consumption due to its damaging and destructive effects.

Opium was a major factor in British policy in Asia, with addiction used to exploit Asian nations, populations, and economies. At the same time the revenues from the opium trade supported the Atlantic slave trade tied to the so-called New World's plantation industries. The profits of opium were so significant and lucrative that the British went so far as to declare war on China for encroaching upon its trade in opium.[19] The Chinese Empire reaffirmed its ban on opium imports in 1799, but British companies and merchants merely ignored the ban. The criminalization from opium in China actually worsened the situation by helping to raise its market price.

The situation in China was comparable to the prohibition of alcohol in the United States from 1920 to 1933, except that opium was draining capital from the Chinese economy. By the 1830s, the value of opium exports had outstripped that of international tea exports for the British. In 1838 the death penalty was legally imposed on all drug dealers, traffickers, or smugglers of Chinese citizenship by the Chinese authorities. Even so, the British were exempted from the penalties of the law because the Chinese government did not want to create problems with Britain or have a diplomatic row. By 1839 the Chinese authorities had no choice left other than to enforce the law prohibiting opium imports spearheaded by British companies and merchants which were all fully supported by the British government. China was slipping towards economic disaster as its gold and silver reserves were being used to pay for opium imports, leading to a massive outflow of capital from China to Britain. The Chinese refused to allow further imports and began enforcing the ban, which the British government and European companies had blatantly ignored and violated.[20]

The British declared war on the Chinese Empire on 1839 and sent a naval force supported by British army troops from India into China. China was defeated and in 1841 was forced to sign the unjust Treaty of Nanjing. This led to even further economic exploitation of the Chinese and the Second Opium War. The British fought the Second Opium War using the

Treaty of Nanjing as its justification which led to yet deeper subjugation of China by foreign and colonial powers, including the stationing of foreign troops in the Chinese capital, the ceding of both Hong Kong and Macau, and the loss of Chinese territory. As Lord Palmerston, the British prime minister, noted in reference to the signing of the Treaty of Nanjing to end the First Opium War: "There is no doubt that this event, which will form an epoch in the progress of the civilization of the human races, must be attended with the most important advantages to the commercial interests of England."[21] Such was the importance of the narco-economy to Britain.

Historically, the lucrative opium trade sponsored by the British in Asia created the foundations for the modern global opium and heroin industry as well as for opium farming in present-day Afghanistan, which produces roughly 92% of the global supply of heroin.[22] Opium cultivation was introduced in the Golden Triangle Region (Laos, Myanmar, and Thailand) of Indo-China in Southeast Asia as well as in other areas of Asia. Whole cultures and the economies of nations have historically been warped and changed to appease latent or unseen imperial economic interests. For example, the British coerced Iran into replacing its domestic coffee with British tea. Eventually Iranian society gave up their national drink of coffee for tea from British India simply because of British commercial interests and demands. To this day, while Iranian bistros are called "coffee houses," they primarily serve tea.

The opium trade in Afghanistan is a legacy of both the historic drug trade sponsored by the British and the devastation of Afghanistan during the US-Pakistani initiated Soviet-Afghan War. During the Soviet-Afghan war the large scale commercial cultivation of opium was launched in Afghanistan, supported and protected by Pakistani and US intelligence. This supply was directed towards North American and Western European heroin markets.

The economic principles operative during the Opium Wars are still the same in modern times. Illicit drugs are still a major commodity and an important component of international trade in the black market. Opium from Afghanistan constitutes a large portion of the world's narcotics market, which was estimated by the UN before 9/11 to be worth approximately between $400 to $500 billion (US) annually.[23] In addition to Afghanistan's strategic location, the opium trade remains an extremely lucrative prize for whosoever should control it.

The Proliferation of Afghan Opiates under NATO's Eyes

In 2001, the British government used stopping the cultivation of opium to save British lives as a justification for its invasion of Taliban-controlled Afghanistan. When the US and UK began preparing their invasion, Prime Minister Tony Blair told a political convention that drug trafficking

NATO soldiers walking through an opium poppy field in Afghanistan.

in Afghanistan would be subdued and extinguished: "The arms the Taliban are buying today are paid for with the lives of young British people buying their drugs on British streets. That is another part of their regime that we should seek to destroy."[24] The Anglo-American invasion, however, did not contribute to curtailing the cultivation of opium, quite the opposite.

In economic terms, demand creates supply. The supply and production of opium and heroin has risen since the invasion of Afghanistan in 2001. This has taken place under the Atlantic Alliance's watch. Instead of stopping the massive flow of opiates from Afghanistan, the NATO-led foreign military presence has assisted it. NATO officials have claimed that drug trafficking has been tolerated so as not to incite violence against NATO's soldiers.

However in 2010, Public Intelligence, the international research network aimed at defending the public's rights to access information, had this to say about drug trafficking ties to NATO in Afghanistan:

> In a recent report from Geraldo Rivera which aired in late April on Fox News, a USMC Lt. Col. indicated that US forces encourage the Aghans [*sic*.] to grow different crops, however, out of fear of losing stability poppy cultivation is tolerated and even supported. In November 2009, the Afghan Minister of Counter Narcotics General Khodaidad [...] stated that the majority of drugs are stockpiled in two provinces controlled by troops from the US, the UK, and Canada. He also said that NATO forces are taxing the production of opium in the regions under their control and that foreign troops are earning money from drug production in Afghanistan.[25]

General Khodaidad's clarification about NATO's role was a reaction to an article in *The New York Times* that exposed Hamid Karzai's brother, Ahmed Wali Karzai, as a major drug dealer and a CIA agent, which came at a time of negotiations between both sides about the composition of the Afghan cabinet in Kabul.[26]

The Hindu featured an article by M. K. Bhadrakumar, a prominent former Indian diplomat, addressing the news of NATO's drug taxes:

> It was one thing to be dismissive when the former director general of Pakistan's Inter-Services Intelligence (ISI), General Hamil [*sic*] Gul, alleged that American military aircraft were being used for drug trafficking in Afghanistan. It might also have been expedient to simply ignore the issue when well-informed Russian sources made media comments that US troops were doing roaring business in drug trafficking in Afghanistan running into hundreds of millions of dollars. But Khodaidad is a highly trained professional who knows what he is talking about.
>
> [...]
>
> Therefore, when Khodaidad said on Sunday that the North Atlantic Treaty Organization (NATO) contingents from the US, Britain and Canada are "taxing" the production of opium in the regions under their control, he carried a stern warning on behalf of Karzai. It is a

simple, direct message: don't throw stones while sitting in a glass cage.[27]

It should be dreadfully clear that Atlantic Alliance is clearly an accessory to the trafficking of opium and heroin, and party to criminal activities. For decades the CIA in collaboration with other intelligence agencies, such as the Pakistani ISI, has set up covert operations which support the drug trade. The Pakistani military and its military oligarchs have benefited directly from Afghan opium: "Other than ruling Pakistan directly and indirectly since [Pakistani] independence and controlling its nuclear, defense and foreign policies, the [Pakistani] military remains the country's largest and most profitable business conglomerate."[28] Raoolf Ali Khan, the Pakistani representative to the UN Commission on Narcotics even stated on the record in 1993 that "there is no branch of government [in Pakistan] where drug corruption does not pervade," while the CIA reported in 1994 to the US Congress that heroin had become "the life-blood of the Pakistani economy and political system."[29]

Pakistan, however, is a subordinate player compared to the US and the role of the CIA in the global trafficking of illicit drugs. Peter Dale Scott and Jonathan Marshall summarize this link in their book, *Cocaine Politics, Drugs, Armies and the CIA in Central America*:

> Our conclusion remains that the first target of an effective drug strategy should be Washington itself, and specifically its own connections with corrupt, drug-linked forces in other parts of the world. We argued that Washington's covert operations overseas had been a major factor in generating changes in the overall pattern of drug flows into the United States, and cited the Vietnam-generated heroin epidemic of the 1960s and the Afghan-generated heroin epidemic of the 1980s as analogues of the central concern of this book: the explosion of cocaine trafficking through Central America in the Reagan years, made possible by the administration's covert operation to overthrow the Nicaraguan Sandinistas [vis-à-vis Iran-Contra].[30]

The Nexus of Wall Street, Money Laundering, Drugs, and Weapons

There is more to be said about Afghan opium and why it is important. Drug trafficking is now an instrument of US foreign policy just as it had been for Britain, which also supports the financial interests of Wall Street. Using IMF statistics, it can inferred that money laundering is a significant part of the global economy.[31]

Money laundering is important to maintain the North American and Western European financial sectors. In fact, César Gaviria Trujillo, the former president of Colombia and the former secretary-general of the Organization of American States (OAS), stated when demanding that Washington prevent drug-related money laundering that "[i]f Colombians are the big fish of the drug trade then Americans are the whale." 91% of the billions of US dollars spent on cocaine are deposited in the domestic banking system and help accumulate hard currency for infusion into the US and Canadian economies.[32] In the past, the biggest US banks were estimated to domestically launder an estimated $100 billion (US) annually.[33] The extent of drug money laundered through domestic banks in the United States can be grasped when it is realized that practically every US dollar in domestic circulation literally contains "microscopic traces" of cocaine. This is no mere urban legend, but a verified fact supported by scientists, forensics experts, and the FBI, which signifies the extensive use of cash as a means of payment in drug deals.[34]

Afghanistan forms the starting point of an important trade route within the global black market and the Eurasian drug corridor that includes Albania and the Serbian province of Kosovo as important shipping points. The direct management of Afghanistan by the US and NATO has helped bring the Eurasian drug trade and its main points under the control of Wall Street, completing the circle formed by drug trafficking, money laundering, and illegal arms sales. Within the Eurasian drug corridor there is a two-way stream where illicit drugs flow outwards and arms flow inwards. The biggest benefactor of this process on the geo-political level is the Atlantic Alliance; on the financial level, Wall Street makes the biggest gains from criminal enterprise and conflict.

The Origins and Future of the Taliban

The Taliban are a product of the fighting in Afghanistan and the manipulation of external players in the country's internal affairs. In the first place it has to be acknowledged that the Taliban are a Cold War creation of the CIA, ISI, and Saudi Arabia. The premise that the Soviet invasion of Afghanistan was the antecedent of the extremism and militarism in Afghanistan that could and did create the Taliban is a fallacy. US intelligence operations supporting groups getting ready to oust the Afghan government predate the 1979 Soviet invasion. Extremism in Afghanistan is actually a product of US foreign policy, implemented through the largest intelligence operation ever in the history of the CIA. The Soviet invasion of Afghanistan was engineered by Washington, which helped the Afghan *muhajideen* and eventually gave birth to the Taliban, one of their offshoots twisted and molded in the refugee camps of Pakistan. According to Zbigniew Brzezinski, the United States started the operations to create a civil war in Afghanistan vis-à-vis Pakistan before the Red Army entered Afghanistan on December 24, 1979. During an interview with the *Nouvel Observateur*, Brzezinski admitted the official US directive for the covert support for creating a civil war and opposition to the Afghan government, which was allied to the USSR, was issued on July 3, 1979.[35] This was six months before Soviet troops even entered Afghanistan.

The Taliban had been close US allies since 1996. In that year the Taliban would be catapulted into power in Afghanistan with the direct logistical and military help of the US, Pakistan, and Saudi Arabia. The Taliban's Afghan opponents would even report capturing Pakistani soldiers and volunteers among the Taliban's ranks during the siege of Kabul who could only speak Urdu. What NATO began describing as Taliban fighters were not actually such.

The news coming from Afghanistan was (and remains) highly censored. There are very few independent journalists from NATO countries working there and they all walk a fine line. Other sources of information coming out from Afghanistan are from Iran, Russia, and India, which are highly critical of the Atlantic Alliance; these media openly talk about the high frequency of civilian deaths at the hands of NATO. NATO censorship covers the government-sanctioned media programs of member states and includes training soldiers to act as journalists; this highly limits the amount and shape of information that can leave Afghanistan, because the soldiers fall under military restrictions that prevent them from openly criticizing NATO operations or disclosing anything that can be harmful to the image of the Alliance.[36]

It must be recognized that the insurgency against either the Afghan government or NATO is also in part a resistance movement ongoing in many regions of Afghanistan. In many cases, NATO is strictly targeted. Most of the time the media erroneously or misleadingly call these diverse Afghan movements "the Taliban," simplifying the identity of the enemy for public consumption at home. On the ground in Afghanistan, however, NATO troops identify the Afghan insurgents as Anti-Coalition Militias (ACMs). This title reflects the fact that NATO is fighting a diverse multi-ethnic movement that sees NATO as an occupying foreign military force. The issue of human rights abuses by NATO troops and security contractors or mercenaries has also incited violence among Afghans that has led them to join these movements.[37]

Nor are all the new members of the Taliban in Afghanistan or in the Talibanized areas of Pakistan clones of the old movement:

> The new Taliban in Afghanistan and the Tehrik-e-Taliban
> in Pakistan or the Pakistani Taliban are not like the old
> pre-2001 Taliban. The motivations and origins for the
> latter two groups are different. Most of the new Taliban

in Afghanistan do not share the same ideology as the old Taliban and are fighting against what they see as a foreign invasion of Afghanistan. In regard to the Taliban in Pakistan, in a sense they are the blowback of Pakistani meddling in Afghanistan and a result of the American-led NATO war in Afghanistan. Demands for a united Pashto state are also at play in the formation of the Pakistani Taliban.[38]

The fight against the Taliban served the purpose of entrenching NATO in Afghanistan. As the start of this chapter outlines, the US and its allies had no serious problems with the Taliban, their foreign policy, or their ideology. The US government itself had been silently publishing the text books that were tied to the Taliban's ideology for years.[39] Washington also greatly appreciated the fact that the Taliban kept the Chinese, Iranians, Indians, and Russians out of Afghanistan. It had done everything to help the Taliban rise. On July 12, 2000 the US Congress was even told by California's Republican House Representative Dana Rohrabacher that the US Department of State deliberately only sent humanitarian aid to the Taliban during Afghanistan's internal fighting and that the US government tricked the Taliban's Afghan opponents into disarming while Pakistan was sending arms to the Taliban to rule all Afghanistan.[40] The Taliban were not the enemies of the US, the US merely used them as a justification for its military presence in Central Asia. Since 2006, the US and NATO have tried to broker a deal with the Taliban, enabling them to remain while expanding their attention elsewhere in Eurasia. In the US Senate, Bill Frist in 2006 began calling for the US government to include the Taliban in the Afghan government.[41] In this regard, after long talks involving Qatar, elements of the Taliban have been reported to have "tentatively agreed to open a political office in [Doha] to communicate with the international community [which means the US and NATO]" in 2012.[42]

Afghanistan in an Historical Context: The Opening Salvos of World War III?

The tragic attacks of September 11, 2001 have resulted in more than a decade of perpetual warfare. They were the first drumbeats, or the opening salvos, of a much wider conflict. Was the invasion of Afghanistan the starting battle of a much wider war, comparable to the landing of the Western Allies, specifically the Americans, in North Africa as a bridgehead into Italy and Europe? At the same time as Afghanistan was invaded, NATO has been pushing outward from Europe towards the Eurasian Heartland, similar to the landing of the invading forces of the

Western Allies in France. In this regard it must be asked: was 9/11 the start of the Third World War?

Historically speaking, it should be noted that distinctions between times of war and peace are not always clear cut and conflicts do not always correspond to the dates set and standardized by historians. War was not even declared in many past conflicts, such as in the early 1700s when Augustus II of Saxony-Poland invaded Livonia or when Frederick IV of Denmark invaded the Duchy of Holstein-Gottorp. Also, in many conflicts, attempts were made to cloak or hide the nature of the conflict as a war or an act of aggression. The Romans and other imperial powers regularly engaged in this type of conduct. The subjective nature of historical dating is exemplified by the abstract chronological dates customarily used by historians to note important points in the Second World War and the start of the Cold War.

In Western Europe and North America, the starting date for World War II is considered to be September 1, 1939, when Germany invaded Poland. For the former Czechoslovakia, however, March 16, 1939 (the date Germany invaded Czechoslovakia) was the starting date for the Second World War. In Russia and the former USSR the start date of the Second World War is 1941, the year that the Germans invaded the Soviet Union. Even the end date for World War II differs in Europe, because Germany officially surrendered to the Western Allies (namely the US, UK, and France) on May 8, 1945 and to the Soviet Union on May 9, 1945. The above dates are all situated from an ethnocentric European perspective, which leaves out Asia. The history of World War II starts much earlier for Asia; many consider the start of the Second World War to have been when Japan invaded China in the Second Sino-Japanese War in 1937, two years before 1939. Or even before 1937. Since in 1931 the Chinese and Japanese were in conflict, 1931 too can be seen as the start of World War II. In East Africa, specifically the Ethiopian Empire (Abyssinia), the Second World War started with the Second Italo-Ethiopian War in 1935.

The various dates and events marking the start of the Cold War also vary, because the Cold War's opening salvo(s) are variously viewed. Did the Cold War begin with the 1945 US-Soviet tensions over the occupation of the Korean Peninsula, the Azerbaijan Crisis (1947-1948) arising from the Soviet occupation of the Iranian provinces on the Soviet border, the near wins for the communists in national elections held in France and Italy (1947-1948), the struggle for power between the communists and the non-communists in Czechoslovakia (1947-1948), or the West Berlin Blockade (1948-1949)? Events that took place during the Second World War, such as the Yalta Conference, the Tehran Conference, and the dropping of the atomic bomb on the Japanese in Hiroshima and Nagasaki by President Harry Truman—seen as a warning to the Soviets by American leaders that the US intended to remain supreme in the post-war order—can be considered as the start of the Cold War.

These questions about dates give rise to another point in historiography. The nature of history is seamless and not the arbitrary one unintentionally made out by historians and history textbooks. One set of events leads to another, and onward they flow. The First World War led to the Second World War and the Second World War led to the Cold War, the Cold War has led to the Global War on Terrorism. This is a theme that will re-emerge for readers toward the end of this book as a finishing note. The point herein is that in retrospect, historical dates and events are defined by people in the future and that sometimes people need to stand back to see the larger picture of things. Albeit there are also disadvantages, time gives observers the advantage of seeing things from an altitude that shows events as part of a larger stream or flowing body. The historians of the future may say that World War III started on September 11, 2001 or that the 9/11 attacks were a prelude to World War III.

The Valleys and Mountains of Afghanistan:
Just the Start of the "Long War?"

The Weekly Standard, in the following month after September 11, 2001, ominously went on to outline the broader military campaign that was to unfold in an editorial by Robert Kagan and William Kristol published on October 29, 2001:

> When all is said and done the conflict in Afghanistan
> will be to the war on terrorism what the North Africa
> campaign was to World War II: an essential beginning
> on the path to victory. But to what looms over the
> horizon—a wide-range war in locales from Central
> Asia to the Middle East and, unfortunately, back again
> to the United States—Afghanistan will prove but an
> opening battle.[43]

The Weekly Standard editorial, like a script, went on to clearly state that the multi-front war that was in the works would develop to become or resemble the "Clash of Civilizations" post-Cold-War conflict paradigm outlined by Samuel P. Huntington:

> [T]his war will not end in Afghanistan. It is going to spread
> and engulf a number of countries in conflicts of varying
> intensity. It could well require the use of American
> military power in multiple places simultaneously. It is
> going to resemble the clash of civilizations that everyone

has hoped to avoid. And it is going to put enormous and perhaps unbearable strain on parts of an international coalition that basks in contented consensus.[44]

In 2001, both Robert Kagan and William Kristol were well aware of the conflagration of war in Eurasia. Both men are political insiders in Washington who were aware of what direction US foreign policy would take the US military and NATO. After all, before the time of their writing, Kagan and Kristol were associates of Dick Cheney, Donald Rumsfeld, and Paul Wolfowitz under the umbrella of the political think-tank called the Project for the New American Century (PNAC) that outlined a global military roadmap for just that.

Operation Enduring Freedom, the name for the war in Afghanistan, would branch out to different corners of the globe. From Afghanistan, the US and NATO would march, fly, or sail into Iraq, Somalia, Yemen, Pakistan, and Libya—all countries predominantly inhabited by Muslims. What the scandal-disgraced Belgian, Willem Claes, said as the secretary-general of the Atlantic Alliance, about NATO's adversary becoming Islam after the demise of the communist USSR and Eastern Bloc countries appeared to be turning into a reality. By 2004, NATO had expanded again to include seven new countries: from the former Yugoslavia, Slovenia; from the Baltic, the three post-Soviet republics of Estonia, Latvia, and Lithuania; and Bulgaria, Romania, and Slovakia. Each one of these countries was a troop contributing nation (TCN) to NATO under the PfP program in 24 July 2003. The dates of their deployments in 2003 are directly related to the Anglo-American invasion of Iraq, which forced the US and UK to reposition their military assets from Afghanistan.

Nonetheless all of these new NATO members would promptly contribute more military supplies and personnel to support the efforts of the US in the "long war" once they entered NATO. These former communist states along with the Visegrád Group—that aside from Slovakia includes the Czech Republic, Hungary, and Poland—have acted as what some call blindly loyal US allies and others call bona fide US clients in Taliban-controlled Afghanistan:

> Poland offered an elite command unit, and the Czech Republic an anti-chemical weapons component that had [reportedly] detected traces of nerve gas in the Saudi desert during the Gulf War. Not surprisingly, the more recent NATO allies felt a responsibility to show their fidelity to the [US]. Unlike some of the older allies [that is, the Franco-German Entente and the NATO countries associated with them], they did not attach conditions to

their aid, and conspicuously refrained from interfering in the [Pentagon's] management of the campaign.[45]

Hereto, Bulgaria has about 600 soldiers deployed in Kabul and the NATO regional command covering the Afghan provinces of Badghis, Farah, Ghor, and Herat; Estonia has 154 military personnel posted in Kabul and the province of Helmand; Latvia has 175 troops in Kabul and ISAF Regional Command North, which includes the Afghan provinces of Badakhshan, Baghlan, Balkh, Faryab, Jowzjan, Kunduz, Samangan, Sar-e Pul and Takhar; Lithuania has 247 personnel deployed in Kabul; Romania has a force of 1876 divided between Kabul and the provinces of Zabul in ISAF Regional Command South; Slovakia has a force of 329 divided between Kabul and Kandahar; and Slovenia has 79 military personnel either stationed in Kabul or ISAF Regional Command West.[46]

Afghanistan and the Revamped Atlantic Mandate of Fighting Terrorism

ISAF has become a global army with forces from a multitude of countries forming the largest international military coalition ever known. At the time of this writing, ISAF is constituted by a force of over 130,000 troops deployed throughout NATO-garrisoned Afghanistan. Officially NATO's presence in Afghanistan started as an anti-terrorism operation and has continuously been justified on the basis of an anti-terrorism operation, albeit jargon about stability, statecraft, rule of law, and democracy have been added as justifications. What is important about 9/11 and the war against Afghanistan is that the Atlantic Alliance expanded the basis for fighting terrorism from the 1999 Strategic Concept. Added to the mandates of humanitarian intervention and peacekeeping, fighting terrorism became a central feature of the Atlantic Alliance's self-declared functions and responsibilities. These self-imposed responsibilities have allowed NATO to publicly transform; they have put the Atlantic Alliance on a permanent offensive footing, transforming it from a defensive military body.

When the Washington Treaty was signed in 1949 no one thought that it would be used by the US to commandeer the help of its allies. It was always assumed that the US would be stepping in to protect the other NATO members and not that they would become assets corralled to support an American foreign policy which entailed wars of aggression, but this is exactly what happened after 9/11. In a manner of speaking, the Alliance was effectively enrolled by the US into fighting in the "long war" under the Global War on Terrorism. Operation Enduring Freedom would also expand to the Caribbean, Central America, Georgia, the Horn of Africa, the Sahara Desert, and the Philippines. NATO's first counter-terrorism operations would start in a matter of weeks after 9/11. On

MAP VII: NATO in Afghanistan under ISAF

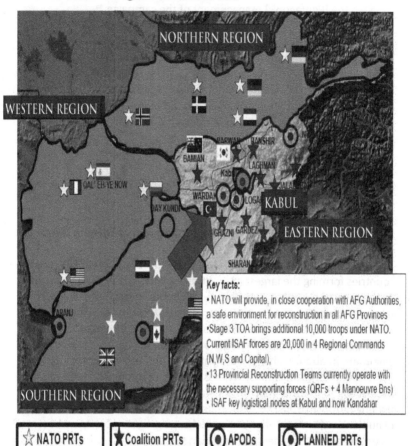

October 4, 2001 the North Atlantic Council agreed on a package of eight measures to support the US. At the request of the US, NATO launched Operation Eagle Assist, its first ever counter-terrorism operation, which ran from mid-October 2001 until mid-May 2002. In the first time that NATO military assets were deployed in support of an Article 5 operation, seven NATO aircraft helped patrol the airspace of the US. The other important operation would be Operation Active Endeavor, which would be started because "the US requested that NATO provide a presence in the Eastern Mediterranean to demonstrate resolve during the crisis."[47] It is important to note that even though the enemy behind 9/11 was undetermined, the US used the opportunity to militarize the Eastern Mediterranean and bring the NATO members onside. This is deeply tied to the geo-political equation in the Levant involving Iran, Israel, Lebanon, Syria, and Palestine.

MAP VIII: NATO in 2004

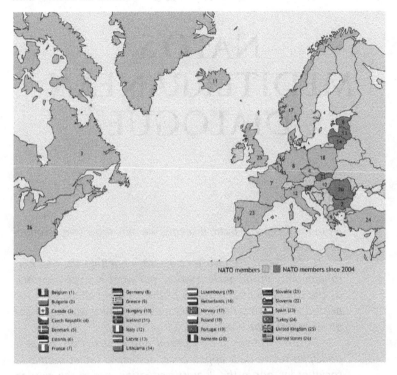

NATO members ☐ ■ NATO members since 2004

Belgium (1)
Bulgaria (2)
Canada (3)
Czech Republic (4)
Denmark (5)
Estonia (6)
France (7)

Germany (8)
Greece (9)
Hungary (10)
Iceland (11)
Italy (12)
Latvia (13)
Lithuania (14)

Luxembourg (15)
Netherlands (16)
Norway (17)
Poland (18)
Portugal (19)
Romania (20)

Slovakia (21)
Slovenia (22)
Spain (23)
Turkey (24)
United Kingdom (25)
United States (26)

CHAPTER 5

NATO'S MEDITERRANEAN DIALOGUE

From the foregoing data, it seems, we may draw two essential conclusions:

1. The Germanic invasions destroyed neither the Mediterranean unity of the ancient world, nor what may be regarded as the truly essential features of the Roman culture as it still existed in the 5th century, at a time when there was no longer an Emperor in the West.

Despite the resulting turmoil and destruction, no new principles made their appearance; neither in the economic or social order, nor in the linguistic situation, nor in the existing institutions. What civilization survived was Mediterranean. It was in the regions by the sea that culture was preserved, and it was from them that the innovations of the age proceeded: monasticism, the conversion of the Anglo-Saxons, the ars Barbarica, etc.

The Orient was the fertilizing factor: Constantinople, the center of the world. In 600 the physiognomy of the world was not different in quality from that which it had revealed in 400.

2. The cause of the break with the tradition of antiquity was the rapid and unexpected advance of Islam. The result of this advance was the final separation of East from West, and the end of the Mediterranean unity.

[...]

The West was blocked and forced to live upon its own resources. For the first time in history the axis of life was shifted northwards from the Mediterranean.

–Henri Pirenne, Belgian historian (1954)

The Pirenne Thesis:
The Importance of the Mediterranean for Western Europe

The Belgian historian Henri Pirenne stipulated that Charlemagne and the Frankish Empire would never have existed if it were not for Arab expansion in the Mediterranean region.[1] Pirenne became known for his thesis that the Germanic tribes, such as the Franks and Goths, that were traditionally credited by historians for the fall of the Western Roman Empire in reality merged with the western half of the Roman Empire and that the economic and institutional templates of Rome continued and stayed intact through this process, while the influence of the East Romans of Byzantium continued. Pirenne's theory challenged the traditional narrative that the invasions of the so-called Germanic barbarians were the reason for the decline of Rome. In most cases Roman traditions and culture were maintained by the emerging Germanic kingdoms. A few observations can be made in support of this aspect of Pierenne's theory. For example, the Franks, who are a Germanic people, gave up their Germanic language and adopted Latin as their language. The Frank dialect of Latin eventually evolved into French over time. The Roman Church also stayed intact as an important societal institution.

To Pirenne, it was clear that the economic framework of the Roman Empire was fixed around the economy and trade related to the Mediterranean Sea. While Western Rome transformed from a politically centralized entity to a network of politically separate kingdoms and states, it did so with the economic framework, fixed on the Mediterranean, staying intact. He theorized that the real decline in the Western Roman entity was brought about by the rapid expansion of the Arabs. A large chunk of the Mediterranean would be incorporated within the vast cosmopolitan realm of the Arabs. This would include the Levant, Egypt, Iberia, Libya, Tunisia, Algeria, Morocco, various Mediterranean islands, and portions of Anatolia or Asia Minor. This would result in the Dark Ages for Western Europe, because the economy of Western Europe was effectively cut off from the rest of the global economy. According to Pirenne, the reason for this was the de-linking or cut in ties between the economies of the bulk of the Mediterranean and Western Europe as a result of Arab expansion. Another factor that should be added to Pirenne's theory about the economic decline of Western Europe after the fall of Rome was that Eastern Rome or Byzantium also diverted its trade or reduced its trade level with Western Europe due to economic realities brought about by the Arab expansion in the Mediterranean. Thus, Western Europe effectively degenerated into a marginalized economic hinterland.

Pirenne's theory goes on to argue that due to its de-linking from the Mediterranean, Western Europe was transformed into a series of low-production farm-based economies, which slowly gave rise to European feudalism. Raw resources were exported outwards with little imports coming into Western Europe, whereas before, items and resources such as valuable metals and Egyptian papyrus would enter Western Europe. The Western European voyages of discovery that take place later in history and give rise to mercantilism can be traced back as a reaction to this period, serving as a means of reversing the de-linking of Western Europe from the Mediterranean and global economies or at least compensating for it. Henri Pirenne's work helps conceptualize the importance of the Mediterranean and its role as a unifier of economies. What's more, it seems that the Pirenne Thesis, which is what this theory about the interplay between the Mediterranean and Western Europe is referred to by scholars, has been ascribed to by EU and Atlanticist leaders. Today, EU leaders see the Mediterranean as an integral part of the EU and control over it as a means of keeping their global footing. The EU has accordingly been working to integrate the entire Mediterranean Basin into the Euro-Atlantic Zone.

Euro-Atlantic Expansion into the Mediterranean Sea and Middle East

While lecturing at Princeton University in 2006, Joschka Fischer the former German Green Party minister of foreign affairs made a profound revelation about the direction of the foreign, security, and defense policy of Germany and France. That direction according to Joschka Fischer was "eastward" with the Middle East and its Eastern Mediterranean waters being named as the new borders of Europe; this region would be part of the new security sphere of the EU and Euro-Atlantic Zone. The former German minister stated that the terrorist bombings in the UK and Spain showed that the Middle East "is truly [Europe's] backyard, and we in the [European Union] must cease our shortsightedness and recognize that."[2] Furthermore, Joschka Fischer warned that the EU needed to shift its attention to the Middle East and Turkey—a member of NATO and one of the "gateways" or "entrances" into the Middle East. As the so-called Arab Spring of 2011 has shown, EU-excluded Turkey's Atlanticist role was to be transformed and reinvigorated as a gendarme in the Middle East and Arab World. *The New York Times* also happened to argue for the expansion of NATO into the Middle East just months after the Anglo-American invasion of Iraq in 2003.[3] By the start of 2004 and through the joint Anglo-American and Franco-German coordination in Lebanon it was clear that France and Germany had agreed or succumbed to act as the bridgeheads of the US in Eurasia. This is what the policies of Angela Merkel and especially Nicolas Sarkozy in Berlin and Paris represent.

The statements of Joschka Fischer reflected a broader attitude within the Franco-German leadership. They were not coincidental remarks or innovative in nature. They reflect well-established objectives and policies that have existed for decades. Fischer's lecture foreshadowed the drive towards the harmonization of Middle Eastern foreign policy between the Franco-German and Anglo-American branches of NATO. What Joschka Fischer would say sealed the rapprochement between both sides that had been developing that led to NATO's Riga Summit that foreshadowed the greater role the EU and NATO would play in US foreign policy and the "long war." *The Daily Princetonian*, Princeton University's newspaper, quoted the former German official as making the following statements: (1) "Europe's security is no longer defined on its [Europe's] eastern borders, but in the Eastern Mediterranean and the Middle East;" and (2) "Turkey should be a security pillar for the European community, and the efforts to derail that relationship are impossibly shortsighted."[4]

Joschka Fischer's statements foreshadowed Nicolas Sarkozy's public campaign in the Mediterranean region.[5] The coinciding of Franco-German policy was also exposed in regard to Turkey; before Nicolas Sarkozy was elected in France, Chancellor Angela Merkel intensified her calls for the inclusion of Turkey within the framework of the EU through a "special relationship," but not as part of the actual EU.[6] What German leaders were telling the Turks was that Turkey would never become a part of the EU, but that they had envisioned a special task for it in the Middle East. The illusions of Ankara's neo-Ottoman policies, which the US has supported in the context of the Arab Spring, are indeed a manifestation of this "special relationship." These German statements also foreshadowed what Nicolas Sarkozy would later propose to the Turks.

Expanding on Fisher's declaration about the EU's new boundaries, NATO too considers the Mediterranean as part of its southern periphery like the Balkans and the Caucasus, which are all areas targeted for Euro-Atlantic expansion. As the EU became more deeply involved in the Mediterranean, Mediterranean issues would increasingly become a part of NATO's agenda.

In 2004 and 2007 EU expansion followed the NATO expansion of the 1990s eastward in the European continent. This expansion took place under Anglo-American pressure. This pattern sets the methodological precedent for what is happening in the Mediterranean Sea. The same NATO-EU template of expansion is also being applied in the Middle East and North Africa. This modus operandi of military-political expansion is also noted by Zbigniew Brzezinski:

> In July [1997] Poland, the Czech Republic, and Hungary
> were officially invited to join NATO. Invitations to

the Baltic [Republics; Lithuania, Latvia, and Estonia], Romania, and Bulgaria soon followed. This expansion made Europe's own expansion logical and unavoidable. With the former European Community having redefined itself as the European Union, Europeans themselves decided that it made no sense to exclude their newly democratic neighbors—already tied through NATO to both the United States and the European Union—from actual [European Union] membership.[7]

Brzezinski's casual rationalization of NATO and EU expansion and his clumsy effort to casually link them through rhetoric as if it all were an unplanned accident that presented a sensible response is just that: a cover story. If this was true then why has NATO member Turkey been denied EU membership since the creation of the European Union? The answer is that NATO and EU expansion were premeditated *Atlanticist* objectives in Eastern Europe.

Firstly, the objective of integrating the Mediterranean into the Euro-Atlantic Zone is reflected by the earlier expansion of NATO in the area through what NATO terms the Mediterranean Dialogue (MD). This NATO project is part of NATO's Mediterranean Initiative. It is modelled on NATO's Partnership for Peace (PfP), which the Atlantic Alliance used by brinkmanship to initially bring the former Warsaw Pact countries into its orbit and then later to transform them into full NATO members. The framework of this relationship creates a de facto extension of NATO. Morocco, Algeria, Mauritania, Tunisia, Egypt, the Hashemite Kingdom of Jordan, and Israel are all members of NATO's Mediterranean Initiative. The only Arab nations in the Mediterranean littoral that were excluded were Libya, Syria, and Lebanon—a situation projected for change. Through this mechanism the Mediterranean Sea has virtually become a NATO lake, almost surrounded entirely by NATO members or de facto NATO members. Bosnia-Herzegovina and Montenegro on the shores of the Adriatic Sea—the north central arm of the Mediterranean—are also controlled by NATO.

Secondly, France's involvement in Libya and the German naval and French land commands over NATO troops on Lebanese soil and off the Lebanese shore are explained by the categorizing of the Franco-German interests for expanding into these regions. It should also be noted that it was in 2001 that the EU, particularly the French, started talking about sending troops under the banner of NATO into the Eastern Mediterranean, specifically Palestine. What is written in the European Security Strategy about the Mediterranean is as follows:

The Mediterranean area generally continues to undergo

serious problems of economic stagnation, social unrest and unresolved conflicts. The European Union's interests require a continued engagement with Mediterranean partners, through more effective economic, security and cultural cooperation in the framework of the Barcelona Process. A broader engagement with the Arab World should also be considered.[8]

What is meant is that a project in the Mediterranean should be engaged as part of a broader engagement of the entire Arab World in economic and socio-political terms, as referenced by the Barcelona Process.

Nicolas Sarkozy and the Union for the Mediterranean

The Mediterranean Dialogue also has a complementary parallel EU program in place called the Euro-Mediterranean Partnership (EUROMED), formerly called the Barcelona Process, which is the basis for the Union for the Mediterranean (UfM), originally called the "Mediterranean Union." This initiative has been spearheaded by France and was officially kicked off by Nicolas Sarkozy on a tour of the Mediterranean that he started in Algeria in early December 2007.[9] The idea of a Mediterranean Union was presented to EU citizens with the election of Nicolas Sarkozy, but this idea is not as new as the mainstream media presents it. Zbigniew Brzezinski acknowledged in 1997 that "France not only seeks a central political role in a unified Europe but also sees itself as the nucleus of a Mediterranean-North African cluster of states that share common concerns."[10]

Something should also be said about the interplay of Anglo-American and Franco-German interests in the Mediterranean. The mechanism and structure established by the extension of the EU into the Mediterranean will determine the level of Anglo-American influence within the Mediterranean littoral. If the EU creates an overlapping mechanism in the Mediterranean where the non-EU nations of the Mediterranean littoral are linked directly only with EU member states on its shores and indirectly with other EU members, then Anglo-American influence will be much weaker than it would be in the case of full integration between the EU and Mediterranean. The former relationship would greatly empower Paris and Berlin within the Mediterranean, while the latter would be more beneficial to Anglo-American interests. Anglo-American control and influence will be maximized if the Mediterranean is wholly amalgamated into the EU.

This process of merging the Mediterranean with the EU, however, could damage the EU and hurt both Anglo-American and

Franco-German interests for different reasons, including demographics, if it is not regulated or executed at a proper pace. If amalgamation is not achieved gradually, the EU could face internal instability. This process is another case where cooperation has been in the interests of both intra-NATO alliances. To ensure a strong Anglo-American role, NATO has been involved and integrated into the framework for a Mediterranean Union.

The role of Turkey as a Mediterranean country is considered pivotal as one of the Union of the Mediterranean backbones. What has been created over the last two decades is an extensive network of relationships and links that will make the whole structure of a Mediterranean Union easy and quick to formalize. The far-reaching economic and military ties between the EU, Turkey, NATO, and Israel are intended to ensure that Tel Aviv is both integrated and normalizes its relations with the Arab World.

The Barcelona Declaration is the foundational block of the Union for the Mediterranean. It was intended to establish an EU-dominated free trade zone in North Africa, the Middle East, and the entire Mediterranean region by 2010. The US Middle East Free Trade Area (MEFTA) is also a parallel to this. The EU's Economic Partnership Agreement (EPA), an aggressive free trade agreement being imposed under economic threats on former Western European colonies, also has similar templates in regards to the ACP States in Africa, the Caribbean, and the Pacific.

The hidden face of neoliberal globalization is exposed through the military-political Atlanticist brinkmanship, which invariably drives an economic objective. In the Mediterranean, there exists a divided, but inter-linked, military and political relationship replicating that which allowed America through NATO to exert its influence in Europe. NATO's Mediterranean Dialogue began in 1994. It was followed in 1995 by the Barcelona Declaration. While the Barcelona Declaration pertains to the economic aspects, NATO's Mediterranean Dialogue represents the underlying military framework. While NATO has already started the military integration of Israel, followed by the nations of North Africa and Jordon, a relationship with the EU serves to integrate these nations gradually through political association and disguise the driving force.

The EU's Role in the Union of the Mediterranean

Franco-German leaders have viewed the mainstay of Europe as their domain, but the French and Germans have had differences of opinion about Europe's peripheries. The French have traditionally looked at North Africa and the Mediterranean as a sphere of influence and the Germans have looked to Eastern Europe and Turkey as a region of economic interest and potential sphere of influence. Europeanists in Berlin and Paris have also looked at cooperation with Russia as a means of balancing Anglo-American influence in Europe. Aside from Turkey, the Germans have also looked at some other core countries in the Middle East, like Iraq and Iran, as part of a region of economic influence. Germany's views on Eastern Europe were a source of uneasiness for Paris. Germany's economic interests in Eastern Europe made it supportive of eastward looking Euro-Atlantic projects, while France saw the entry of the Eastern European states as a weakening of its influence in the EU and as a means for the US to consolidate its strength inside the EU.[11] Since the EU's expansion in Eastern Europe, the Germans have modified their position. In 2009, Germany's government announced that the European Union needed to "consolidate" before any new members were accepted.[12] Unlike on Eastern Europe, however, the position of both countries on the Mediterranean has been more harmonious

The Union of the Mediterranean was unveiled with theatrics and public deceit by EU leaders. Federal Chancellor Angela Merkel publicly claimed that France's idea of a Mediterranean Union threatened the EU and its institutions. German leaders were merely playing a game of on-and-off-again opposition to Paris in regard to the Mediterranean Union. Berlin made a string of critical statements about French actions, but then denied them to create a shroud of confusion among the public. Media reports and Berlin's statements were utterly misleading. Germany was fully involved in the creation of the Mediterranean Union. *The Financial Times* called attention to the fact that Angela Merkel was not really opposed to the Mediterranean Union, but actually wanted Germany and the EU to be fully involved in its creation:

> Angela Merkel, Germany's chancellor, pointedly told France's ruling UMP [*Union pour un Mouvement Populaire*/Union for a Popular Movement] party yesterday that the future stability of the Mediterranean region affected the whole European Union and that all 27 [EU] member states should be involved in the engagement process."[13]

Chancellor Merkel's position was actually that the Barcelona Process of 1995 was too "bureaucratic" and needed to be upgraded with the inclusion of the entire EU. Frau Merkel also emphasized that the Mediterranean was vital for Germany and the northern EU and not just France and the so-called "Club Med" or "Olive Group" countries:

> "Germany wants to assume its responsibilities in the Mediterranean and we want to offer to all [EU] member countries the possibility to participate," she said. "We

should have a reinforced co-operation [between the EU and Mediterranean]. I am convinced that all European countries are interested in this."[14]

Frau Merkel was being disingenuous when she proposed that all the EU should be involved in the formation of the Mediterranean Union, because all its members would be interested. Merkel knew very well that the entire EU was slated from the start to be a part of the process. The issue is not about interest, but about the calculated long-term arrangement of Euro-Atlantic expansion.

All the Mediterranean members of the EU—the neo-colonial "Olive Group"—declared their support for the creation of a Mediterranean Union at a two-day conference that started on January 17, 2008 in Cyprus.[15] The Cypriot Foreign Minister, Eros Kazakou-Marcoullis, speaking on behalf of all the attendees, stated: "We reaffirmed our support to all efforts which have as an objective the strengthening of the cooperation between European and Mediterranean countries and reiterated the importance of the Mediterranean region for the security, stability and prosperity of the European Union."[16] José Luis Rodríguez Zapatero, as the prime minister of Spain at the time, also announced Madrid's support for the creation of a Mediterranean Union and for new migration laws during a meeting with Nicolas Sarkozy.[17] Although it was not tied to the creation of the Mediterranean Union, the drive to establish new migration laws was tied precisely to the anticipated effects of the Mediterranean Union and the influx of migrants that could arrive into the EU from the less developed countries on the southern and eastern shores of the Mediterranean Sea. Italy also signalled its support for the Mediterranean Union and new migration laws in the EU during a tripartite meeting between Zapatero, Sarkozy, and Prodi.[18]

As scepticism, fear, and xenophobia began to put pressure on the EU concerning the Union of the Mediterranean, EU officials made some important omissions. On February 10, 2008 Viviane Reding—at the time sitting in the Office of the EU Commissioner for Information Society and Media—made an important omission on Germany's Deutsche Welle Television as a reaction to scepticism about the Mediterranean Union. Commissioner Reding was told by her interviewer that sceptics in the EU fear that the Mediterranean Union will tear the EU apart. Reding responded that the Mediterranean Union was actually put into place in 1995 through the Barcelona Process and that at the time of the interview—2008—it was merely being fine-tuned: "We already have a Mediterranean Union with the [creation of the] Barcelona Process, where the [European Union] formed a solidarity treaty with the countries of the Southern Mediterranean. The correct action [for the EU] is to build on that."[19]

Union of Inequity: Cheap Labor, Worker Immobility, and Guest Workers

The citizens of the Middle East and North Africa will be treated as second-class and third-class citizens under Euro-Atlantic expansion. The EU is not a union of fair treatment and equity: Eastern European members of the European Union are not only called the "EU-8" and the "EU-8 + 2" but are also legally subordinated within the frameworks of the EU in regard to their relationships with the original fifteen members of the EU, the "EU-15."[20] In many cases gross socio-economic differences have been amplified and remain between Western Europe and Eastern Europe under EU expansion. EU austerity also aggravated this.

The Union of the Mediterranean at its roots is not designed as an equal partnership for all its future members. Under the current framework of the EU it is not in the EU's economic interests to admit Turkey as a full member. States like Germany in the Western European half of the EU benefit from the Turkish cheap migrant labor forces that are causally called "guest workers." If Turkey were to become a full EU member these Turkish workers and Turkey will gain equal rights that the EU does not want to grant them. This would include the right of Turkish workers to be treated in the same manner as nationals of the host countries in every way, including having equal wages and being able to benefit from the host nation's public services. This would also give Turkish workers mobility rights in the EU: free movement, the right to look for other employers (the right of choice), and the right to be accompanied by their families.[21] Upon accession, Turkey would also change the balance of power inside the EU by becoming one of its bigger countries alongside France, Germany, Italy, and the UK.

The same concepts of wage manipulation also apply to the Arab nations of the Southern Mediterranean, like Egypt with its massive pools of labor. The EU has no intention of granting these countries any equal status in a relationship of equal peers. This is why there is a rush to change migration laws in the European Union as the UfM and Mediterranean Dialogue work to integrate the Middle East and North Africa into the Euro-Atlantic Zone. The basis of a "special relationship" or "special partnership" when spoken in the context of Turkey and the EU is very different from that of France and Germany or the US and UK for example. In reality the former is in a subordinate position.

Aside from securing energy supplies and natural resources, another design of the Mediterranean Union is to harness the substantially large work forces in the Southern Mediterranean, while reducing dependency on cheap labor from China and other Asian countries. The Southern Mediterranean is the "near abroad" of the European Union and the establishment of a formal cheap labor market in the Southern

Mediterranean that is deeply tied to the EU in the north would cut geographic distance, wait time, transportation costs, fuel consumption, and dependence on China in regard to products manufactured by cheap labor. To a certain extent, Chinese leverage over the EU would also be dealt a strategic blow. The EU, like the US, is also looking for a means to reduce its dependence on the Chinese before Beijing can be challenged any further over global resources and raw materials. The UfM provides a partial answer to this quest against China and other nations with substantially large populations, such as India and Brazil. Once dependence on the Chinese is reduced then energy supplies to China can be challenged with greater effect and possibly cut.

The underlying economic motives for the UfM explain why the EU started a mad dash to change its migratory laws after Sarkozy announced his plans for Mediterranean integration. The new regulations and laws will touch immigrants, emigrants, migrant workers, tourists, and other visitors. Fingerprinting, scanning, and collecting information on anyone crossing into or outside of the borders of the EU will become standard procedure. This process is also linked to the European Security Strategy, which is the EU replication of the strategic doctrine of the post-9/11 US. The changes to migratory laws are a means to control the free flow of migrant workers from the Southern Mediterranean countries that are expected to gravitate towards the countries of the Northern Mediterranean in search of better wages and jobs as soon as the Mediterranean Union is formalized. A neoliberal paradigm of imparity is being strengthened and reinforced within the Mediterranean Union between capital and labor. Capital will be free to move within the Mediterranean with little regulation, whereas labor forces and individuals from the South Mediterranean will be restricted in their movements and rendered immobile.

Foreigners, including migrant or guest workers, will have to start routinely carrying identity cards and documents on their persons. The European Border Surveillance System (EUROSUR) is being set up to monitor all the EU's different border points using high resolution satellites and unmanned aircraft for migrant movements. Frontex, a border intelligence agency with its headquarters in Poland, was created by the EU to do all the monitoring work. The Warsaw-based agency became operational on October 3, 2005. Additional emphasis has been placed on the EU's borders with Russia and with the EU enclaves of Ceuta and Melilla—frontier points, which include radar detection and sensory systems and an entire network of cameras to monitor migrant movements into the European Union. Both enclaves are tiny Spanish territorial positions in North Africa which Spain gained in 1912 as part of Spanish Morocco and has since refused to return to Morocco even as Madrid demands that the UK return Gibraltar.

The so-called reforms tied to this process are being brought about in the EU under the convenient justification of combating terrorism, illegal migratory movements, and crime. The new EU security measures also threaten and erode the rights guaranteed by UN agreements to asylum seekers trying to attain refugee status. Individuals trying to escape state persecution in North Africa or the Middle East for advocating greater freedom and for labor rights will now be put in a dangerous situation. The European Council on Refugees and Exiles (ECRE) has protested that the sweeping changes in the EU will make it more difficult to stay within the EU for asylum seekers while their requests are being reviewed. A safe haven for movements opposing US and EU allies will be systematically eliminated. Moreover, behind the security and crime fighting agendas sits the real agenda of controlling migratory movements of peoples and wages. The control of labor forces—both domestic and foreign—is the main purpose of the new migratory reforms in the European Union. It is of little wonder that the first joint summit of the Arab League and the EU held in Malta was the scene of not only major free-trade talks, but also major talks on migration control.

The Economics of the Union of the Mediterranean

A process of industrial de-location is also tied to the UfM. It has been underway in the EU for years. EU industries have been relocated to Eastern Europe and other global regions from Western Europe. Under this neoliberal paradigm jobs and industries can gradually be removed from wealthier EU states to Southern Mediterranean nations, where cheap and immobile labor forces will be awaiting. This relationship is analogous to that which occurred in North America during the 1990s when jobs and whole industrial sectors were relocated from Canada and the US to Mexico where cheap labor forces were waiting. In North America this process unfolded under the North American Free Trade Agreement (NAFTA) and resulted in a decline in living standards in all three countries. Costs of living went up, wages experienced a decline, and the resultant gap between the cost of living and wages started to eat away at the middle class.

The wages presently accessible via the cheap labor market in China can also be further lowered by opening a cheap labor market in the EU's "near abroad." This is part of the global "race to the bottom" where regulatory standards in regard to labor and wages are being increasingly dismantled. This process in effect facilitates a state of cannibalism or economic decomposition within the effected labor markets and ultimately brings about a decline in living standards. This is making the much-ballyhooed "creative destruction" of neoliberal capitalism visible as just destruction.

If major cheap labor markets like the Chinese market start to lower their wages to stay competitive with a reconfigured cheap labor market controlled by the EU that would emerge in the Middle East and North, then this will eventually result in much lower wages in other global labor markets. These markets in turn would lower their wages as "a means of staying competitive" while the option of adopting protectionist policies is prevented via the global web of neoliberal free trade agreements and indeed, the spread of corporate production chains over numerous countries. Ultimately there will be worldwide ramifications for lowering global wages that also affect the citizens of the EU, Japan, Australia, New Zealand, and North America whose economies do not exist in isolation from the rest of the world. This is one aspect of the "race to the bottom" and it is part of a cycle that fuels itself into a downward spiral.

With the backdrop of the global economic crises, what is unwinding is a speeded up global leveling of wages. Wage levels within the EU under the onslaught of austerity are experiencing a precipitous decline and being brought downwards. The labor laws protecting the wages and standards of EU citizens are being de-railed too. De-regulation and degeneration are the orders of the day. Before, the "race to the bottom" and these measures were justified by EU officials through neoliberal assertions that wages need to be lowered because of the need for "competitiveness." Now austerity measures are being used as a justification for swifter reform and exploitation, because of the convenience of the global economic crisis.

Aside from exploitation of the work force and surplus labor in the Southern Mediterranean the remaining national assets in these countries, as occurred in Eastern Europe after the end of the Cold War and already visible in Greece, will be privatized further and privately owned. This process will go hand-in-hand with the gradual entrenchment of higher costs of living that will further marginalize local populations, forcing them to sell private property, private assets, or any other means of income out of desperation—decisions that will lock them into a neoliberal-induced state of poverty and helplessness.

The Islamic Union and Turkey

The Union of the Mediterranean, much like the PfP, also prevents other potential blocs from securing a footing in the Mediterranean.[22] The Mediterranean Union serves to challenge the African Union and pan-African integration in North Africa. It also challenges Iranian ideas and proposals about forming an EU-like bloc in the Middle East and North Africa. The Iranians have referred to this project as the "Islamic Union." It is worthy to note that in 2007:

[A]fter Nicholas Sarkozy's trip to Algeria, as part of a
tour to promote the creation of a Mediterranean Union,
an Iranian delegation led by Mahmoud Ahmadinejad
arrived with a counter-proposal for the creation of an
alternative bloc; this was what the Iranians called an
Islamic Union.[23]

The Islamic Union is essentially a rival economic project to the
Mediterranean Union and challenged Euro-Atlantic expansion in both the
Middle East and North Africa. Promises of EU entry to Turkey and "special
relationships" also serve to prevent Ankara from committing to such a
project. Iraq, Iran, Lebanon, Syria and Turkey were all in the process of
establishing several overlapping free-trade agreements and planning on
creating their own Schengen Area—called the *Shamgen* through a fusion
of the Arabic name for Syria and the Levant with the name Shengen—with
a common border and visa-free travel until differences broke out between
Turkey and the rest as a result of the Arab Spring.

The integration project that Turkey was undertaking with Iran
and Syria in the Middle East has effectively been frozen as Ankara with
the encouragement of the Atlanticists has dropped its "zero problems"
policy for neo-Ottomanism. Many Turkish opposition leaders are upset
about this. They see the US, EU, and Israel as the primary beneficiaries
of this. Although Turkey is a NATO ally, it is still a target of the Atlanticists
and their allies in Tel Aviv. This is why the Pentagon and NATO have used
maps outlining a divided Turkey.[24]

The Mediterranean Dialogue and the Individual Cooperation Program

Since the launch of the Mediterranean Dialogue seven states
have joined. Egypt, Israel, Mauritania, Morocco, and Tunisia all joined
in early 1995, while Jordan joined in late 1995. Algeria would join the
Mediterranean Dialogue in 2000. Aside from Algeria, these countries have
all been involved in various operations of the Atlantic Alliance from the
Balkans to NATO-garrisoned Afghanistan. For example, Jordan sent forces
to Afghanistan, helped NATO with the war on the Libyan Arab Jamahiriya,
and has collaborated against Syria with the Atlantic Alliance. Morocco has
participated as a member of KFOR and is an active member of Operation
Active Endeavor. In league with plans for incorporating Spain and the Iberian
Peninsula into NATO's missile shield, the potential for the closing off of the
Mediterranean is taking place with the agreement NATO signed on June 2,
2008 with the Kingdom of Morocco to join Operation Active Endeavor.

From the Mediterranean Dialogue, NATO has fashioned the
Istanbul Cooperation Initiative (ICI). The ICI is the equivalent of the

TABLE 5.1

Mediterranean Dialogue Members*

Country	Full Member of the Union for the Mediterranean	Arab League Member	Entry Date
Algeria	Yes	Yes	14 March 2000
Egypt[†]	Yes	Yes	8 February 1995
Israel[‡]	Yes	No	8 February 1995
Jordan[§]	Yes	Yes	November 1995
Mauritania	Yes	Yes	8 February 1995
Morocco[‖]	Yes	Yes	8 February 1995
Tunisia	Yes	Yes	8 February 1995
Potential New Members in NATO's Mediterranean Dialogue[¶]			
Lebanon	Yes	Yes	-
Libya	No, Observer	Yes	-
Syria	Yes, Suspended[#]	Yes; Suspended	-

* As of February 2012.
† Egypt entered the Individual Cooperation Program (ICP) with NATO on October 9, 2007, intensifying military cooperation with NATO.
‡ Israel entered the Individual Cooperation Program (ICP) with NATO on October 16, 2006, intensifying military cooperation with NATO.
§ Jordan entered the Individual Cooperation Program (ICP) with NATO on April 1, 2009, intensifying military cooperation with NATO.
‖ In practical terms, the Sahrawi Arab Democratic Republic (Western Sahara), which is occupied by Morocco, is included.
¶ The following countries are potential members on the basis that a change in their state policies takes place. When the Mediterranean Initiative was started by NATO, Lebanon and Syria were excluded on the basis of their foreign policy positions. Should regime change take place in Syria and should Lebanon's political map be changed, both Levantine republics would be offered membership in NATO's Mediterranean Dialogue. With the success of regime change Libya is now a strong candidate and its accession into the Mediterranean Dialogue is being talked about.
# Because of Syrian anger over covert and overt support from the EU and NATO for insurgency and opposition movements in its territory, Syria froze all participation in the Union for the Mediterranean (UfM) on June 22, 2011.

Mediterranean Dialogue. Both are essentially the same NATO program, but with different names for different geographic regions. Chapter 6 will discuss NATO's ICI. Moreover, MD countries could in theory be ICI countries too.

Within the framework of the Mediterranean Dialogue there also exists the Individual Cooperation Program (ICP), which upgrades the relationship between the MD state and NATO into full cooperation in many fields; the ICP essentially serves to turn MD countries into de facto members of NATO. Israel was the first MD state to enter the ICP in 2006, joining NATO in patrolling the Red Sea and Eastern Mediterranean Sea in Operation Active Endeavor. Egypt would join in 2007 and Jordan in 2009. In 2006, the Training Cooperation Initiative was also started by NATO to reform and train the armed forces of these MD countries.

Focusing on the Eastern Mediterranean and Red Sea

Both the Mediterranean Sea and the Red Sea (Arabian Gulf) are important transport and trade corridors. NATO's goal of turning the Mediterranean into a lake have almost materialized and its presence in the Red Sea, which through the vitally important Egyptian Suez Canal connects the Mediterranean Sea to the Indian Ocean, has become more or less permanent. The process started as NATO publicly presented itself as readjusting to the post-9/11 reality of international security relations. Within this objective, there was an initial strategic focus on the Eastern Mediterranean and the Red Sea that later spread further out into the world's waters. In October of 2001 NATO produced a blueprint for security operations in the Eastern Mediterranean. This operation was mandated as a part of the Article 5 support being extended to Washington after 9/11. Operation Active Endeavor was initiated on October 9, 2001 as a part of the Global War on Terror on the request of the US that there be a strong NATO presence in the Eastern Mediterranean. Operation Active Endeavor started with a focus on the Eastern Mediterranean and then expanded to the entire Mediterranean. According to the Atlantic Alliance itself:

> The deployment was one of eight measures taken by NATO to support the United States in the wake of the terrorist attacks of 11 September 2001, following the invocation of Article 5 ... for the first time in the Alliance's history.
>
> The deployment started on 6 October and was formally named ... on 26 October 2001. Together with the dispatch of Airborne Warning and Control Systems

(AWACS) aircraft to the United States, it was the first time that NATO assets had been deployed in support of an Article 5 operation.

[...]

Moreover, in March 2003, [it was] expanded to include providing escorts through the Straits of Gibraltar to non-military ships from Alliance member states requesting them.

[...]

One year later, in March 2004, as a result of the success ... in the Eastern Mediterranean, NATO extended its remit to the whole of the Mediterranean.[25]

The Atlantic Alliance began maintaining a permanent out-of-area naval presence off the coasts of Lebanon and Syria and in the Red Sea as it inched deeper towards the Indian Ocean on the basis of fighting maritime terrorism under Operation Active Endeavor. Chapter 8 will discuss the Indian Ocean in much more depth. Anti-piracy responsibilities were also later added to the basis of NATO's naval activities, especially in the waters around the Horn of Africa. The NATO presences in the Eastern Mediterranean benefited Israel and initially put Syria and Lebanon in a tight squeeze, especially after the 2003 invasion of Iraq. Both Arab republics were cut off from Iran and Russia by land and the chances that NATO could have erected a naval barrier through Active Endeavor always existed.

Russian and Iranian Moves in the Mediterranean

Neither Russia nor Iran has been oblivious to NATO's actions in the Eastern Mediterranean. Both have come to look at Operation Active Endeavor suspiciously, albeit Russia and Ukraine have taken part in some of its operations. Both the Iranians and the Russians have refused to allow the Atlantic Alliance to turn the Mediterranean into a NATO lake. Both countries have also worked to improve Syrian defenses since 9/11. In March 2004, the responsibility for US military planning in regard to Lebanon and Syria was transferred from United States European Command to CENTCOM, just before the Cedar Revolution would empower US clients in Beirut and Syrian troops would withdraw from Lebanon. The move by the Pentagon illustrates that the US strategies in Lebanon and Syria were being coordinated with the US strategy in Iraq. In parallel, the Russians began concentrating on entrenching their naval presence in Syria:

Russian military officials have consistently denied reports that Russia is creating a permanent naval base in Tartus, Syria that would give it a Mediterranean outpost and represent a major shift in the regional security balance of the Eastern Mediterranean, the Levant, and the Middle East as a whole. Reports were emerging long before the Israeli attacks on Lebanon that Russia had begun work on deepening the Syrian maritime port of Tartus, used by the Soviet Union and later Russia as a supply point since the Cold War, and widening a channel in Latakia, another Syrian port. Both Tartus and Latakia are significant for both Syria and Russia in that they face the outlet of the Ceyhan end—the receiving end—of the Baku-Tbilisi-Ceyhan oil terminal giving Russia and its partners the ability to disrupt or secure the port and route during the possibility of the eruption of any future war(s) with the United States.

The establishment of this Russian project has been presented as an alternative hub for the Russian Black Sea Fleet, based in the Crimean port of Sevastopol, in the Ukraine, but this seems to be undermined by upgrading and expansion of the Russian naval port of Novorossysk off the eastern margins of the Black Sea. The creation or expansion of naval or military bases off the Syrian coast and Russian coast off the Black Sea seem to imply the future employment of two different forces with different applications for the national and security interests of Russia.[26]

Iran too has begun to expand its naval presence outside of the Persian Gulf and Gulf of Oman. This has included Iranian port calls to Syria starting in 2011. Following a Russian port call, Iranian officials sent a message during a 2012 Iranian port call on Syria:

Iran appeared to have carefully timed the visit of its warships, which have followed the docking earlier at Tartus of the giant Russian aircraft carrier, Admiral Kuznetsov. In Iran, influential law makers were quick off the blocks to suggest that developments in Syria were uniting Tehran and Moscow, with the open ended possibility of other major players occupying the tent.

"The presence of Iran and Russia's flotillas along the Syrian coast has a clear message against [any] possible adventurism [by the US]," said Hossein Ebrahimi, a vice chairman of the Iranian Parliament's national security and foreign policy commission, Fars News Agency reported on Monday. He added: "In case of any U.S. strategic mistake in Syria, there is a possibility that Iran, Russia and a number of other countries will give a crushing response to the U.S."[27]

As long as Syria and Lebanon remain outside of NATO's orbit, the Mediterranean will not be a Euro-Atlantic lake. This is why the Eastern Mediterranean will continue to be a venue of Atlanticist and Eurasianist contention.

MAP IX: The Mediterranean Sea

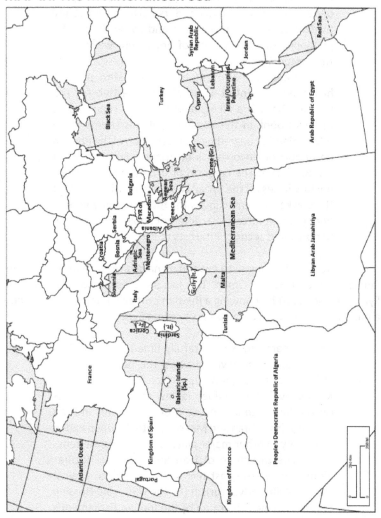

CHAPTER 6

NATO IN THE PERSIAN GULF

THE GULF SECURITY INITIATIVE

But in foreign policy terms as well, the Gulf states have clearly embraced change. They have emerged as true players in their own right, defining their relationships with other actors according to their own strategic interests. And they sometimes have engaged in missions outside their own region, including by participating in NATO-led peacekeeping missions in the Balkans.

As an organisation that has been dealing with multi-national security cooperation for more than half a century, NATO has a wealth of experience to offer to non-NATO countries. Most importantly, over the past decade, we have developed the necessary political and military links with non-NATO countries to make our cooperation very effective. And that is why NATO is now in a far better position to make a tangible contribution to security and stability well beyond its own borders, including here in [the Persian Gulf].

The Istanbul Cooperation Initiative, launched in 2004, is a reflection of these changes. [...] Bahrain chose to join the Initiative early on, together with Kuwait, Qatar and the United Arab Emirates. We hope that the Kingdom of Saudi Arabia and Oman will also join the ICI in the not too distant future.

—NATO Secretary-General Jaap de Hoop Scheffer (2008)

The Istanbul Cooperation Initiative

The North Atlantic Treaty Organization has formally stepped into the Persian Gulf, even though in reality the forces of several NATO nations have been operating there since the Cold War. This has been through the Istanbul Cooperation Initiative (ICI), which stands as another layer of NATO expansion along with the Partnership for Peace and Mediterranean Dialogue programs. The ICI was established at NATO's 2004 summit in Istanbul, Turkey. The summit in Istanbul was remarkable essentially because NATO had in effect formalized its global expansion in addition to its post-Cold War mandate of "global reach." The ICI is an extension of the Mediterranean Dialogue. It works to expand the scope of the Mediterranean Dialogue, especially in the Persian Gulf with the Arab petro-sheikhdoms. The ICI is officially considered by the Atlantic Alliance as a partnership complementing the G8 and, more importantly, the decisions by the US and EU to reform the broader Middle East region. Kuwait would be the first state to join the ICI after talks with NATO in 2004. Bahrain, Qatar, and the United Arab Emirates would all join later in 2005. Along with Saudi Arabia and the Sultanate of Oman, all four of the above sheikhdoms in the ICI form the Gulf Cooperation Council. The Palestinian Authority also began holding "exploratory information" sessions with NATO about both the Mediterranean Dialogue and the ICI in 2005.

The ICI essentially represents an eastern extension of NATO's Mediterranean Dialogue. Furthermore, the presence of NATO in the Persian Gulf through the ICI is part of the broader alliance in the Middle East that is linked to NATO, which includes the Mediterranean Dialogue members Egypt, Israel, and Jordan. Saudi Arabia is also an important partner. This system or chain of alliances is a de facto extension of the Atlantic Alliance.

The Gulf Cooperation Council

The Gulf Cooperation Council (GCC), or formally the Cooperation Council for the Arab States of the Gulf, is formed by some of the closest allies of the US and NATO. These states have individual bilateral security agreements with the US and Britain as well as a covert alliance with Israel. The GCC states have participated in many NATO operations. They helped the US in both its wars against Iraq, respectively in 1991 and 2003; they supported Israel's attacks on Lebanon in 2006; they have launched attacks on Libya with NATO in 2011; and they have helped isolate Syria through their material, diplomatic, and military support for the Syrian National Council (SNC). The GCC states have commandeered the Arab League and used it to isolate and expel both Libya and Syria. These were my observations made about their role against Libya on March 13, 2011:

> What is very striking about these statements and the petro-sheikhdoms' declaration that Qaddafi's regime is not the legal government of Libya is that it is utter

TABLE 6.1

ICI Members and their NATO Participation*

Country	Date Join ICI	Balkans	Afghanistan	Libya	Syria (Covertly)†	Other Nato Activities
Bahrain	Feb. 2005	No	Yes	No	No	Yes
Qatar	Feb. 2005	No	Yes	Yes	Yes	Yes
Kuwait	Dec. 2004	No	Yes	Yes	Unknown	Yes
UAE	June 2005	Yes	Yes	Yes	Unknown‡	Yes

* As of February 2012; current or past involvement in NATO activities includes direct participation in combat, combat support, service (logistical) support, transit rights, and training.

† The internal fighting in Syria is not an official NATO mission; it involves the support of NATO members, such as the US, UK, France, and Turkey, and NATO allies such as Israel, Jordan, and Saudi Arabia.

‡ In late February 2012, the United Arab Emirates started distancing itself from the crisis in Syria and moving towards a publicly neutral position. It also stopped any protests in the UAE supporting or opposing the Syrian regime. There are, however, reports that the UAE is exporting arms to Syria's insurgents (see page 329).

hypocrisy. These condemnations are being made by the same leaders that have used violence and murder against their own populations. These are also the same Arab leaders who use mercenaries and openly and continuously violate human rights and international humanitarian laws themselves.

Saudi Arabia, Oman, Kuwait, and Bahrain all recently used violence against peaceful civilian protesters, in many cases people who were demanding basic human rights like equality or legal recognition. In Bahrain tanks fired at Bahraini protesters in Pearl Square, which is something most of the mainstream media has been trying to hide. Moreover, the GCC ironically has also demanded that "no-fly zones" be established over Libya to protect the civilian population: "The Gulf Cooperation Council demands that the UN Security Council take all necessary measures to protect civilians, including enforcing a no-fly zone."

These autocratic leaders are amongst the greatest hypocrites. They are in no position themselves to speak about any form of legitimacy. Nor are any of these autocrats elected. Under the same principles that they pretend to espouse, they should ask the UN to intervene in their states too. Bear in mind they also spearheaded the movement to suspend Libya from the Arab League in Cairo. These leaders have also pushed the Arab League to support any confrontation against Libya in the form of no-fly zones.[1]

Not only have the GCC sheikhdoms played diplomatic roles against Libya and Syria, they have also played media, military, intelligence, and financial roles in supporting the US and NATO against both Tripoli and Damascus. These states have even bankrolled the fighting against the Syrian Army. Qatar especially has played a key role against both Libya and Syria. In both countries it has mobilized Al Jazeera and its armed forces, intelligence agents, and mercenaries.

The GCC was jointly founded by the leaders of Bahrain, Kuwait, Qatar, Oman, and Saudi Arabia on May 25, 1981. Since then it has developed and maintained its own military force, called the Peninsula Shield Force. The aim of the six GCC states is to integrate with one another as a confederacy that parallels the EU. Their aims are to create a common market in the Persian Gulf, which is slated for gradual amalgamation with the EU and UfM. In this regard the divided European military-political relationship, which is being replicated in the Mediterranean, can also be observed to be at work with variance in the Persian Gulf where NATO and NATO members have military and security agreements with the GCC. In parallel the EU has had a formal relationship with the GCC since 1988. In addition, the Persian Gulf is central to global energy and its prices. It was at one point the core source of hydrocarbon energy supplies for most of the Atlantic Alliance and still is an important source of energy for Turkey and NATO's EU members. The Anglo-American Alliance has deliberately diversified its energy supplies, but still places heavy value over the region to uphold the Alliance and as leverage on the economies of countries like India and China.

US Central Command (CENTCOM) was forged to bind the Persian Gulf to the US, because of the region's vast energy resources. The US Rapid Deployment Force was the antecedent to CENTCOM. It was initially designed to challenge a Soviet push into the Persian Gulf to cut US and NATO energy supplies in the scenario of a major war between the Western Bloc and the Eastern Bloc. The US Rapid Deployment Force was originally a standby large-scale contingent of the US armed forces that was constantly on standby for massive theater-level war anywhere on the globe, with special priority to the Persian Gulf as the energy breadbasket of the Atlantic Alliance.

As a result of the importance of the Persian Gulf, the Carter Doctrine was declared after the USSR intervened militarily inside Afghanistan. On January 23, 1980, President Jimmy Carter stated that the US government would use military force within the Persian Gulf region to defend US economic interests.[2] The new doctrine was deliberately portrayed as a response to Soviet actions, but insofar as eight months later, in September of 1980, the Iraq-Iran War broke out, the Carter Doctrine served in actuality as a warning to the Soviet Union not to get involved in the Iraq-Iran War where the US would be a player. Afghanistan was also conveniently keeping the Soviets busy, giving the US an open hand in the Persian Gulf.

The US and the other members of the Alliance have bases in GCC territory and have used this military infrastructure for the wars in Afghanistan and Iraq. Among these bases is the headquarters of US Naval Forces Central Command and the US Fifth Fleet in Bahrain, the headquarters of US Air Forces Central Command in Qatar, and the French Military Settlement in the UAE. NATO has also remained silent as the GCC countries, especially Bahrain and Saudi Arabia, have suppressed demands for democracy and civil rights. They have even continued to sell arms to the Al-Sauds and Al-Khalifas as they openly repress their citizens. Moreover, the US and NATO use their infrastructure in the GCC states to threaten Iran, now more than ever the regional power of the Persian Gulf.

NATO's "Mutual Defence Clause" used to Control Persian Gulf Energy?

Energy resources are so important for the economies and military forces of the Atlantic Alliance that in 2006 US Senator Richard Lugar called for the Atlantic Alliance to come to the aid of any member of NATO whose energy sources were threatened. Almost all NATO members lack their own energy resources and are highly dependent on foreign energy imports, especially from the former USSR and the Organization of Petroleum Exporting Countries (OPEC). The justification for a military intervention in the name of energy would fall under Article 5 of the Washington Treaty according to Senator Lugar's proposal. His pitch instantaneously received strong support from the Eastern European members of NATO and the EU, which are dependent on the Russian Federation for their energy supplies. Lugar's position is: "[NATO] should recognize that there is little ultimate difference between a member being forced to submit to coercion because of an energy cutoff and a member facing a military blockade or other military demonstration on its borders."[3]

This NATO posture on energy is very important, because Article 5 is the raison d'être of NATO; it construes any attack on one member as an attack on all NATO members. Any interpretation of the Atlantic Alliance's mutual defense clause in regard to energy security would mean that any NATO member whose energy sources are cut off would be able to rely on assistance from the rest of the military alliance. Such a reading could eventually be interpreted to insinuate that the cutting off of energy to any NATO member would be defined as an act of aggression or an act of war. It is no surprise that Russia as a major supplier of coal, gas, and oil was greatly angered and unnerved by the strengthening energy security notion within the Alliance; Russia's state-owned Gazprom has more than 400,000 employees and in 2008 was the fifth largest publicly traded company in the world with a value of $363 billion (US).[4] If such a doctrine were adopted by the Atlantic Alliance, it could be used as a justification for the imposition of economic and political sanctions against Russia and other energy producing countries. Additionally, the clause could provide a mandate for attacking Russia or any other energy exporting country, including Iran, Kazakhstan, Turkmenistan, Angola, Nigeria, Algeria, and Venezuela, with a view to commandeering the energy and natural resources of such countries in the name of maintaining energy security.

In the same time frame as Lugar's statements and NATO's concentration on an energy policy, EU Trade Commissioner Peter Mandelson was stipulating that the EU needed energy security guarantees from Russia and the former USSR. Mandelson released an announcement stating: "Both [Russia and the EU] believe the other is using the energy weapon as an instrument of politics."[5] "Europe wants security of [energy] supply," summarized his demands on behalf of the EU.[6] Because of these statements originating in the Euro-Atlantic Zone, Russia and her allies perceive NATO as planning on commandeering Russian and global energy supplies and natural resources through the threat of force.

If access to energy is the primary concern, however, nowhere seems a more likely place for NATO military action than the Persian Gulf, especially if Iran closes the Strait of Hormuz if it feels threatened enough or if it is attacked by the US. Outside of the mechanisms of the ICI and NATO's public diplomacy conferences, the GCC countries and NATO have had many exchanges and meetings to discuss the topic of Iran. It was at one of these joint GCC and NATO gatherings discussing Iran that Kuwait actually joined the ICI.[7] At a 2006 conference between the two organizations the meeting theme was "Facing Common Challenges."[8] This directly denoted Iran, the powerful northern neighbor of the six GCC state.

It is hard to miss the regional appeal of Iran amongst GCC citizens in Bahrain, Kuwait, the oil-rich Sharqiyah (Eastern) Province of Saudi Arabia, Qatar, and the UAE. In this regard it is not an Iranian invasion that is feared by GCC leaders, but Iranian political and ideological influence. Furthermore, the above conference took place after military drills were held in the Persian Gulf in 2006 by the combined forces of the US, UK, France, Australia, and three GCC members.[9] The war games were not welcomed by Tehran which perceived them as an act of provocation:

> "The message is clear," said William T. Munroe, the American ambassador to Bahrain. "Responsible countries of the world will not stand aside as proliferators circumvent their international obligations. Responsible countries will not hesitate to deny proliferators a safe haven."
>
> American officials insist that the training exercise, planned since January, was not related to tensions over Iran's uranium enrichment activities. Iran said Friday that it had stepped up enrichment in defiance of a Security Council demand to suspend such work.
>
> "This is ultimately important because of where it's happening, when it's happening and why it's happening," said a diplomat observing the exercise, speaking on condition of anonymity because he was not authorized to comment. "Iran and Korea are two main targets, but there are many others of interest to this effort."
>
> Iran warned the exercise's participants on Monday against acts that could destabilize the region. Military officials taking part in the exercise said that Iranian patrol boats came close to coalition ships in

recent days, inspecting their activities and positions.

"We do not consider this exercise appropriate," Muhammad Ali Husseini, the Foreign Ministry spokesman, told reporters on Sunday. United States actions in the region "go in the direction of more adventurism, not of stability and security," he said.

Instead, Iran has proposed that Persian Gulf states form a group, excluding the United States, to maintain security in the region.[10]

First and foremost, NATO members consult on energy developments that could have a security dimension. These consultations can also include partner countries. NATO provides analyses of global energy developments, and it organises workshops on sharing best practices on critical energy infrastructure protection that include other institutions, think tanks and the private sector. The Alliance also implements activities to improve the security of energy infrastructure. NATO's navies provide surveillance of maritime routes and choke points, while NATO's anti-piracy operations help to increase the security of commercial shipping lanes. Energy efficiency among the military is also attracting increasing interest.

In order to more systematically define NATO's role in energy security, the Alliance will intensify its dialogue with other institutions, such as the EU, the International Energy Agency, the OSCE and the Energy Charter, as well as with the private sector. Discussions between the North Atlantic Council with individual partner countries or groups of partners ("28+n") on energy security could also become a more regular part of NATO's political agenda. Upon request, NATO could also set up training and defence reform teams for the protection of critical infrastructure. Such steps would correspond to NATO's core competencies and underline the Allies' determination to regard energy security as part of a comprehensive approach to security.

Above Photo: A NATO pamphlet on energy security.

Creeping towards Iran

NATO has been in a continuous security dialogue with the GCC in pursuit of a more formal and grounded NATO presence in the Persian Gulf and a new security arrangement against Iran and its allies. This is the Gulf Security Initiative, which is now also referred to as the Gulf Security

Dialogue. Aside from the implications of a confrontation with Iran, this cooperation between the GCC and NATO confirms that NATO is preparing to become a global institution and military force.

The US has been building its missile arsenal in the Persian Gulf and transporting large amounts of military hardware and radar systems into the region for years now. Originally, the Pentagon's justifications for the deployment of military hardware into the Persian Gulf were the Gulf War, followed by the Global War on Terrorism. Then the 2003 invasion of Iraq was used as a justification for the US-led militarization of the Persian Gulf. Now, in the last few years up until the present, the new justification has become protecting the GCC allies of the US and NATO against an Iranian ballistic missile threat and keeping the Strait of Hormuz open to the flow of oil exports from the Persian Gulf. It is in this context that Khalifa bin Ahmed Al-Khalifa, the defense minister of Bahrain, stated in 2007: "[GCC countries have] the capability to respond to any attack from neighbouring Iran."[11] He also stated that the GCC would "respond with force" if Tehran blocked the Straits of Hormuz as a result of any US military strikes against Iran.[12] The ICI focus on preventing the proliferation of weapons of mass destruction (WNDs) and on the Proliferation Security Initiative is intended to keep the spotlight on Iran as a dangerous enemy, rather than reflecting any real fears of Iranian nuclear weapons development, which is widely discounted by US intelligence agencies and even the Mossad.

Beside the fact that it is a vital transit point for global energy resources and a strategic chokepoint, two additional issues should be addressed in regard to the Strait of Hormuz and its relationship to Iran. The first concerns the geography of the Strait of Hormuz. The second pertains to the role of Iran in co-managing the strategic strait in accordance with international law and its sovereign national rights. The maritime traffic that goes through the Strait of Hormuz has always been in contact with Iranian naval forces, which are predominantly composed of the Iranian Regular Force Navy and the Iranian Revolutionary Guard Navy. In fact, Iranian naval forces monitor and police the Strait of Hormuz along with the Sultanate of Oman via the Omani enclave of Musandam. More importantly, to transit through the Strait of Hormuz all maritime traffic, including the US Navy, must sail through Iranian territorial waters. Almost all entrances into the Persian Gulf are made through Iranian waters and most exits are through Omani waters. Iran allows foreign ships to use its territorial waters in good faith and on the basis of Part III of the United Nations Convention of the Law of the Sea's maritime transit passage provisions that stipulate that vessels are free to sail through the Strait of Hormuz and similar bodies of water on the basis of speedy and continuous navigation between an open port and the high seas. Although Tehran in custom follows the navigation practices of the Law of the Sea, Tehran is not legally bound by them. Like Washington, Tehran signed this international treaty, but never ratified it.

Due to Tehran's Hormuz card, Washington has been working with the GCC countries to re-route their oil through pipelines bypassing the Strait of Hormuz to channel GCC oil directly to the Indian Ocean, Red Sea, or Mediterranean Sea. Washington has also been pushing Iraq to seek alternative routes in talks with Turkey, Jordan, and Saudi Arabia. Both Israel and Turkey have also been very interested in this strategic project. Ankara has had discussions with Qatar about setting up an oil terminal that would reach Turkey via Iraq. The Turkish government has attempted to get Iraq to link its southern oil fields, like Iraq's northern oil fields, to the transit routes running through Turkey. This is all tied to Turkey's visions of being an energy corridor and important lynchpin of transit. The aims of re-routing oil away from the Persian Gulf would remove an important element of strategic leverage Iran has against Washington and its allies. It would effectively reduce the importance of the Strait of Hormuz. It could very well be a prerequisite to war preparations and a war led by the United States against the Iranians and their allies.

It is within the framework of encroaching on Iran while removing its options that the UAE's Hashan-Fujairah Oil Pipeline is being fostered to bypass the maritime route in the Persian Gulf going through the Strait of Hormuz. The project design was put together in 2006, the contract was issued in 2007, and construction was started in 2008.[13] This pipeline goes straight from Abu Dhabi to the port of Fujairah on the shore of the Gulf of Oman in the Arabian Sea. In other words, it will give oil exports from the UAE direct access to the Indian Ocean. It has been openly presented as a means to ensure energy security by bypassing Hormuz and attempting to avoid the Iranian military. Along with the construction of this pipeline, the erection of a strategic oil reservoir at Fujairah was also envisaged to maintain the flow of oil to the international market should the Persian Gulf be closed off.[14]

Aside from the Petroline (East-West Saudi Pipeline), Saudi Arabia has also been looking at alternative transit routes and examining the ports of its southern neighbours in the Arabian Peninsula, Oman and Yemen. The Yemenite port of Mukalla on the shores of the Gulf of Aden has been of particular interest to Riyadh. In 2007, Israeli sources reported with some fanfare that a pipeline project was in the works that would connect the Saudi oil fields with Fujairah in the UAE, Muscat in Oman, and finally to Mukalla in Yemen. The reopening of the Iraq-Saudi Arabia Pipeline (IPSA), which ironically was built by Saddam Hussein to avoid the Strait of Hormuz and Iran, has also been a subject of discussion for the Saudis with the Iraqi government in Baghdad. If Syria and Lebanon

MAP X

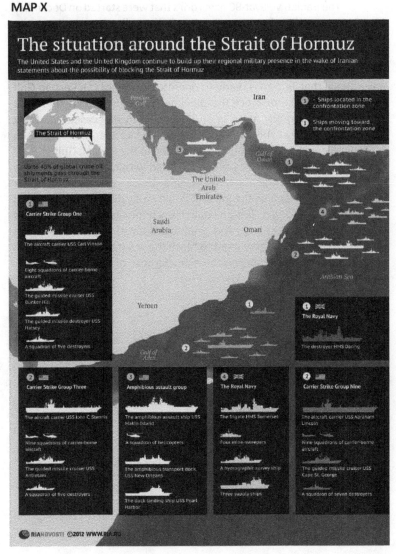

The situation around the Strait of Hormuz

The United States and the United Kingdom continue to build up their regional military presence in the wake of Iranian statements about the possibility of blocking the Strait of Hormuz

The Strait of Hormuz

Up to 40% of global crude oil shipments pass through the Strait of Hormuz.

Iran

Persian Gulf

Gulf of Oman

The United Arab Emirates

Saudi Arabia

Oman

Yemen

Arabian Sea

Gulf of Aden

- Ships located in the confrontation zone
- Ships moving toward the confrontation zone

Carrier Strike Group One

The aircraft carrier USS Carl Vinson

Eight squadrons of carrier-borne aircraft

The guided missile cruiser USS Bunker Hill

The guided missile destroyer USS Halsey

A squadron of five destroyers

The Royal Navy

The destroyer HMS Daring

Carrier Strike Group Three

The aircraft carrier USS John C Stennis

Nine squadrons of carrier-borne aircraft

The guided missile cruiser USS Antietam

A squadron of five destroyers

Amphibious assault group

The amphibious assault ship USS Makin Island

A squadron of helicopters

The amphibious transport dock USS New Orleans

The dock landing ship USS Pearl Harbor

The Royal Navy

The frigate HMS Somerset

Four mine-sweepers

A hydrographic survey ship

Three supply ships

Carrier Strike Group Nine

The aircraft carrier USS Abraham Lincoln

Nine squadrons of carrier-borne aircraft

The guided missile cruiser USS Cape St. George

A squadron of seven destroyers

RIANOVOSTI ©2012 WWW.RIA.RU

were converted into Washington's clients, then the defunct Trans-Arabian Pipeline (Tapline) could also be reactivated, along with other alternative routes going from the Arabian Peninsula to the coast of the Mediterranean Sea via the Levant. Chronologically, this would also fit into Washington's efforts to overrun Lebanon and Syria in an attempt to isolate Iran before any possible showdown with Tehran.

The Iranian Velayat-90 naval drills that were started on December 24, 2011, extending from the Persian Gulf to close proximity to the entrance of the Red Sea in the Gulf of Aden near the shores of Yemen, also took place in the Gulf of Oman facing the coast of Oman and the eastern shores of the United Arab Emirates. Among other things, Velayat-90 was a signal that Tehran is ready to operate outside of the Persian Gulf and can even strike or block the pipelines trying to bypass the Strait of Hormuz. Geography again is on Iran's side in this case. Bypassing the Strait of Hormuz still does not change the fact that most of the oil fields belonging to GCC countries are located in the Persian Gulf or near its shores, which means they are all situated within close proximity to Iran and therefore within Iranian striking distance. As in the case of the Hashan-Fujairah Pipeline, the Iranians could easily disable the flow of oil from the point of origin. Tehran could launch missile and aerial attacks or deploy its ground, sea, air, and amphibious forces into these areas as well. It does not necessarily need to block the Strait of Hormuz; after all preventing the flow of energy is the main purpose of the Iranian threats, not blocking the Strait.

CHAPTER 7

CLAIMING THE POST-SOVIET SPACE

Just as none of us is outside or beyond geography, none of us is completely free from the struggle over geography. That struggle is complex and interesting because it is not only about soldiers and cannons but also about ideas, about forms, about images and imaginings.

—Edward Wadie Saïd (1993)

The End of the USSR and Start of the Commonwealth of Independent States in 1991

On December 8, 1991 the Commonwealth of Independent States (CIS) was born with the signing of the Belavezha Accords or the Creation Agreement of the leaders of the Belarusian Soviet Socialist Republic, the Russian Federal Soviet Socialist Republic, and the Ukrainian Soviet Socialist Republic. Later, Kyrgyzstan, Tajikistan, Turkmenistan, Uzbekistan, Kazakhstan, and Armenia joined the CIS. The leadership of most of the union republics—the leaders of the *troika* (three), Belarus, Russia, and Ukraine; the leaders of the *pyaterka* (five), Kazakhstan, Kyrgyzstan, Tajikistan, Turkmenistan, and Uzbekistan; and also Armenia, the Republic of Azerbaijan, and Moldavia—would gather in Alma-Ata, Kazakhstan, on December 21, 1991 to adopt the Alma-Ata Declaration for dissolving the Soviet Union and establishing the CIS. The nine post-Soviet states assumed membership on the basis of what was supposed to be an equal partnership. It would be the implementation of a "civilized divorce." The only Soviet republics that did not sign the Alma-Ata Protocols were the Republic of Georgia, which had declared independence earlier (April 9, 1991) and did not recognize itself as a union republic, and the three Baltic States, which maintained that they had been occupied states that were never Soviet republics. The dilemmas the body would seek to resolve would include territorial issues, citizenship, currency regulation, division and control of the Soviet military and its assets, and the Soviet nuclear weapons arsenal. On December 26, 1991 the USSR would be formally terminated with the endorsement of one of the chambers of the Supreme Council of the Union of Soviet Socialist Republics.

Since its founding the CIS has functioned much like the British Commonwealth, which was formed as a result of the dissolution of the British Empire. In 1993 the CIS Charter was created and then ratified by all CIS members except for Turkmenistan and Ukraine, which technically makes Ukraine an unofficial member of the CIS. Georgia would also join in 1993. The Baltic States would consistently refuse to join, because of their objectives to re-orient themselves into the Western Bloc and all its institutions and organizations instead of any post-Soviet organizations like the CIS.

The Euro-Atlantic Push into the Post-Soviet Space

With the collapse of the USSR, Euro-Atlantic encroachment into the post-Soviet space began. At first the Russian Federation would be somewhat oblivious to the process, while pursuing its own policies of regional and Euro-Atlantic integration under President Boris Yeltsin. Euro-Atlantic encroachment would take several forms, the most pronounced of which would be when the Baltic States joined the Atlantic Alliance and then the EU in 2004. The other would be the GUAM Organization for Democracy and Economic Development or simply just GUAM (an acronym for Georgia, Ukraine, Azerbaijan, and Moldova).

GUAM was founded in 1997. It has had its name changed three times as a reflection of the geo-politics of the post-Soviet space and the rivalry between Atlanticism and Eurasianism for control over it. The group was formed as a counter-weight to Russian dominance in the CIS. GUAM briefly changed its name GUUAM in 1999, with an extra letter "U" added to its name to represent the Central Asian republic of Uzbekistan. Then, when Uzbekistan left in 2005, as a result of Euro-Atlantic support for a failed color revolution, the organization's name reverted to GUAM. GUAM's members are also all members of the Community of Democratic Choice, which forms a drape from the Baltic to Black Seas around Russia and Belarus.

The Kremlin for a period wanted to utilize the CIS as the major forum to reassert Russian dominance in the post-Soviet space and to pursue regional integration. In this context, Moscow also viewed the CIS as a possible alternative and competitor to the Western Bloc and a barrier to Euro-Atlantic encroachment by NATO and the EU. In many regards the US and the EU have worked to obstruct the CIS and any form of Eurasian integration in the post-Soviet space. Moreover, Russia eventually began to lose interest in the organization as a myriad of other post-Soviet organizations emerged or evolved. Many of these post-Soviet organizations actually sprang forth from agreements, initiatives, or ideas within the Commonwealth of Independent States. The CIS has become a breeding ground for producing structural and regional alternatives in the former Soviet Union. The Collective Security Treaty Organization (CSTO), the Eurasian Economic Community (EurAsEC or EAEC), and the post-Soviet Eurasian customs union were all spawned within the CIS and its bodies.

MAP XI: The Caucasus and Central Asia

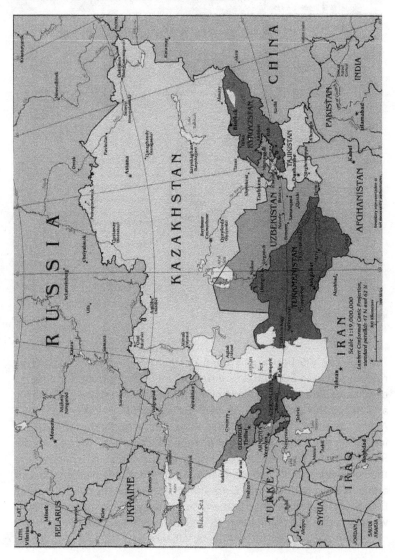

MAP XII

Commonwealth of Independent States

The Commonwealth of Independent States (CIS) is an interstate association of the former republics of the Soviet Union

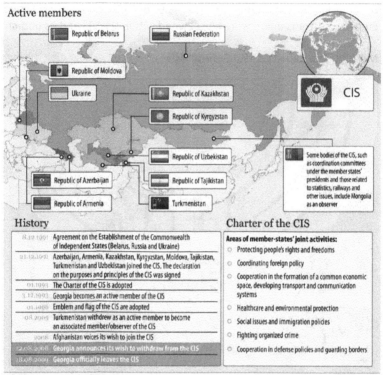

Active members

Republic of Belarus | Russian Federation
Republic of Moldova
Ukraine | Republic of Kazakhstan
Republic of Kyrgyzstan
Republic of Uzbekistan
Republic of Azerbaijan | Republic of Tajikistan
Republic of Armenia | Turkmenistan

CIS

Some bodies of the CIS, such as coordination committees under the member states' presidents and those related to statistics, railways and other issues, include Mongolia as an observer

History

8.12.1991	Agreement on the Establishment of the Commonwealth of Independent States (Belarus, Russia and Ukraine)
21.12.1991	Azerbaijan, Armenia, Kazakhstan, Kyrgyzstan, Moldova, Tajikistan, Turkmenistan and Uzbekistan joined the CIS. The declaration on the purposes and principles of the CIS was signed
01.1993	The Charter of the CIS is adopted
3.12.1993	Georgia becomes an active member of the CIS
01.1996	Emblem and flag of the CIS are adopted
08.2005	Turkmenistan withdrew as an active member to become an associated member/observer of the CIS
2008	Afghanistan voices its wish to join the CIS
12.08.2008	Georgia announces its wish to withdraw from the CIS
18.08.2009	Georgia officially leaves the CIS

Charter of the CIS

Areas of member-states' joint activities:

○ Protecting people's rights and freedoms

○ Coordinating foreign policy

○ Cooperation in the formation of a common economic space, developing transport and communication systems

○ Healthcare and environmental protection

○ Social issues and immigration policies

○ Fighting organized crime

○ Cooperation in defense policies and guarding borders

RIANOVOSTI © 2010   www.rian.ru

The CIS has largely been dormant or ineffective, losing its relevance due to Euro-Atlantic intrusion, internal opposition to Russian dominance, little action or implementation of agreements by its members, and finally the sharpening of divisions among its members after the Anglo-American invasion of Iraq in 2003. This process started with the formation of GUAM in 1997, but divisions became very strong with the Rose Revolution in Georgia and the Orange Revolution in Ukraine where the new governments of Georgia and Ukraine adopted Atlanticist policies and pursued a path towards Euro-Atlantic integration by overtly chasing EU and NATO membership. Cooperation between both states and NATO would deepen to a point where Georgian air defences would eventually become integrated with the Atlantic Alliance and Ukraine would hold discussions about housing NATO's missile shield. The flag of the EU would also heavily be used by these governments alongside their national flags too. While at present Ukraine is no longer in a Euro-Atlantic trajectory, Georgia still chases NATO membership.

The CIS for the most part has been reduced to a shell. In 2005, Turkmenistan downgraded its membership to that of an associate member. In 2008, Georgia announced its withdrawal from the CIS in 2009 as a result of the Russo-Georgian War over South Ossetia. There are, however, alternative and complementary structures now promoting regional integration in the post-Soviet space, the most significant of which are the Collective Security Treaty Organization (CSTO), the Eurasian Union, and the Shanghai Cooperation Organization (SCO).

The Turks and the Iranians also began making bids to increase their influence in the region after the collapse of the USSR by expanding the format of the Economic Cooperation Organization (ECO) to include their kin in the Republic of Azerbaijan and post-Soviet Central Asia. While the ECO remains under Iranian and Turkish leadership, Ankara and Tehran have taken two different approaches in the post-Soviet space in regard to Moscow. Iran still holds on to its influence in Armenia, the Republic of Azerbaijan, Tajikistan, and Turkmenistan, but has also opted to work more closely with Russia in the region. Turkey on the other hand has been more prone to work separately from Russia, with the Turkic Council being an example of Ankara trying to use its linguistic capital to create a regional niche for itself.

The Struggle between "Eurasianist" and "Westernist" Circles in the Kremlin

The narrative for lordship over the post-Soviet space and Eurasia started in many different places and times, but for all intents and purposes, after the collapse of the USSR and the end of the Cold War, the halls of political power in post-Soviet Russia and the Kremlin have played the most crucial roles. One of the reasons that Atlanticism was able to make inroads into the former USSR is that there was an internal struggle among Russian leaders over the direction of their country. Russia faced both Europe and Asia and for a time both Atlanticism and Eurasianism were contending against one another in Russia's policy circles and in the Kremlin. Russia from its re-emergence on December 26, 1991 was swamped with uncertainty. Its elites were faced with the question of succumbing even further to the Atlanticist powers and either becoming their junior partners or vassals. The newly re-emergent Russia also faced all the conditions of economic and social collapse of so-called "failed states."

After the disintegration of the USSR, Western-oriented or Atlanticist policy and Eurasian-oriented policy were in conflict in Russia and other former Soviet republics as their leaders began to search for their places in the post-Cold War international order. Westernist circles in the post-Soviet space were pushing for a strategic alignment with the Atlanticists and Euro-Atlantic integration. They favored a European-oriented policy as well as a push towards the polity of Europe. On the other hand, "Eurasianist" circles were fostering a policy of strategic cooperation with Asian powers as well as cooperation with Europe. This focus was motivated by the dual European and Asian character of the Russian Federation and post-Soviet space. *Euro-Asian* (Eurasian) integration made more sense than Euro-Atlantic integration—meaning the overbearing US and an American-dominated EU—for them. The Eurasianists were also cognizant of the role of the Western Bloc in the economic collapse of Russia—literally its economic Thirdworldization—and its subordination.

The future of the Russian Federation seemed uncertain for a time. After the end of the Cold War, anomie existed throughout much of the country. Privatization was widespread as capitalism was adopted and it appeared that a trajectory towards integration with the Euro-Atlantic Zone would become reality as Russia began to weaken. Boris Yeltsin appeared to be taking Russia down a path towards further disintegration and instability. The NATO war on Yugoslavia over Kosovo and the Chechen War(s), however, appeared to be turning points. With NATO expansion and the realization that the Russian Federation was being targeted by the US, the scales began to tilt in favor of the Eurasianists in Russia. At a November 1999 meeting of the Organization for Security and Cooperation in Europe (OSCE) in Istanbul, Bill Clinton pointed his finger at Yeltsin, demanding he stop the Russian military's campaign to recover the breakaway Caucasian republic of Chechnya, which resulted in Yeltsin leaving the room in protest.[1] If Russia had obeyed Washington's demand to stop the campaign in the Caucasus, it would effectively have resulted in a second defeat for the Russian military in Chechnya and could possibly have created a catalyst for the disintegration of the entire Russian Federation.

Earlier that same year and going into 1998, the drive towards NATO's war over Kosovo was raising tensions between the Atlantic Alliance and the Russians. Russian officials repeatedly warned that the doors were being opened for future NATO intervention against other countries in Europe and for out-of-area NATO wars. Speaking at the Russian Federal Defense Ministry, General Ivashov warned that NATO operations in Yugoslavia would project the Atlantic Alliance's forces towards Russia and its allies and that Russia and other countries could be future targets of NATO military intervention.[2] Despite the saber rattling by Russian generals and military commanders that the Russian Armed Forces might intervene on the side of their Yugoslav friends, the US and NATO continued their march to war against Belgrade. In a veiled threat against the Russian Federation to stand down not just on Yugoslavia but on the Balkans, the US military tested several ballistic missiles from its nuclear submarine, the Henry J. Jackson, during the tensions.[3] It is worth noting that 1999 saw NATO deliberately destroy the Chinese Embassy in Belgrade during the Atlantic Alliance's war with the Federal Republic of Yugoslavia and that the Atlantic Alliance subsequently almost went to war with Russia over control of the Pristina International Airport in Kosovo.[4] As a highpoint of Washington's confidence, US Air Force General Wesley Clark, the supreme military commander of the Atlantic Alliance, ordered a NATO contingent of British and French troops to attack the Russian military unit at the airport.[5] The British and French hesitated, then refused, with British General Michael Jackson saying "I'm not going to start the Third World War for you."[6] Eventually Moscow did back down in Kosovo, but both Russia and China were left with bad aftertastes in their mouths.

For the Kremlin the frictions with the US and NATO over Kosovo and Chechnya were the straws that broke the camel's back. The change in Boris Yeltsin became evident after the clash with Clinton at the OSCE meeting in Istanbul. The next month, President Yeltsin visited the People's Republic of China to cement Sino-Russian strategic ties in the face of Washington's pressure against the Kremlin. Rebuffing Washington's demands on what Moscow saw as a domestic affair, Yeltsin stated: "Yesterday, Clinton permitted himself to put pressure on Russia. It seems he has for a minute, for a second, for half a minute forgotten that Russia has a full arsenal of nuclear weapons. He has forgotten about that."[7] President Yeltsin would also point out that Russia and China were preparing to challenge the unipolar vision of the US for a New World Order: "It has never been the case that he alone dictates to the world how to live, how to work, how to rest and so on. No, and again no. Things will be as we have agreed with Jiang Zemin. We will be saying how to live, not he alone."[8] In short, Yeltsin made it clear that Russia and China would refuse to be dictated to by Washington. President Clinton responded to Yeltsin with a similar veiled threat saying: "I didn't think he'd forgotten that America was a great power when he disagreed with what I did in Kosovo."[9] After these exchanges, illness drove Yeltsin from the presidential office. Before Yeltsin resigned he designated his prime minister, Vladimir Putin, as his presidential successor. Russia under Putin's administration would begin to sort out its internal problems, becoming more and more assertive in the international political arena.

The Eurasianist view and what would eventually be called the Primakov Doctrine would prevail over the Europeanist and Westernist policy cliques in Moscow in parallel to these events. The Primakov Doctrine will also be discussed later on, because of its importance in creating a strategic axis between Beijing, Moscow, and Tehran. The architect of the Primakov Doctrine, Yevgeny Primakov, put all his efforts into having Russia adopt a strategic policy of global multilateralism and toward formulating a Eurasianist strategy as official Kremlin policy. Primakov and the Eurasianists in Moscow knew that the next century would see the rise of China as a global superpower and that the Asia-Pacific region would be the center of the global economy and international affairs.

Eurasianism and Post-Soviet Integration

There is a real and ongoing battle between Atlanticisim and Eurasianism over the post-Soviet space. One of the major prizes is the Caspian Sea Basin and the region of the Caucasus to its west and the region of Central Asia, comprised of Middle Asia and Kazakhstan (*Sredbyaa Azia i Kazakhstan*), to its east. Within this framework, Russia for all intents and purposes has become the main vanguard of Eurasianism and Eurasian integration.

As a first step the Eurasian Economic Community (EurAsEC) emerged from the idea of a CIS customs union put together by Russia, Kazakhstan, and Belarus in 1996. Tajikistan and Kyrgyzstan would later become signatories to the agreement. Together the five republics would form the EurAsEC in 2000. After Uzbekistan realigned itself with Moscow in 2005, it too would join. Belarus and Russia would bilaterally form the ambiguous Commonwealth of Belarus and Russia—later called the Union State—in 1996 too. In 2005, the Central Asian Cooperation Organization (CACO), which was tied to the failed ideas of a Central Asian Union, would also merge into the body with the goal of forming the Common Economic Space or Single Economic Space in coordination with the CIS and the Customs Union of Belarus, Kazakhstan, and Russia. This was a stepping stone towards the formation of the projected Eurasian Union.

Vladimir Putin's article "A New Integration Project for Eurasia: The Future in the Making," published by the Russian newspaper *Izvestia* on October 3, 2011 was not the basis for creating the Eurasian Union. Putin actually announced plans for forming a Eurasian Union while visiting Kazakhstan in 2000, more than a decade before his *Izvestia* article.[10] His proposal was based on various post-Soviet initiatives, including Kazakhstani proposals going back to May 1994.[11] In the same year as the Kazakhstani proposal for forming a Eurasian Union, the CIS signed an agreement to establish a free-trade zone among the members in the future. In 2009, Russia, Belarus, and Kazakhstan all signed an agreement to create a customs union in the post-Soviet space that would pave the way for a single market and one unified economy. The agreement came into force in January 2011, but was unable to be instituted until some disputes were resolved and Moscow, Minsk, and Astana streamlined and standardized their laws.[12] 2012 is to be the effective date.[13] Kyrgyzstan initially said it would examine joining the Eurasian Union, but would not be able too at the start of 2012.[14] By December 2011, the Kyrgyz Republic announced that it would eventually join the Eurasian Union.[15] 2015 is the projected data for the final materialization of the Eurasian Union. Since 2009, Kazakhstan has also proposed that a regional virtual currency called the *yevraz*—which is derived from the Russian word for Eurasia—be adopted by itself and Russia, Belarus, Kyrgyzstan, and Tajikistan.[16]

The media in the Euro-Atlantic Zone quickly projected the idea of a Eurasian Union as a sudden Russian imperial act of hostility, failing to realize that the plans for creating a Eurasian Union had been a long time in the making. Rather than looking at the process and history behind the idea they quickly opted to engage in polemics and attacked Vladimir Putin, who was again the prime minister of Russia at the time. The topic of a Eurasian Union was used to demonize Putin as some type of a neo-Soviet leader trying to re-establish a Stalinist empire to threaten the world. Putin was accused of trying to restart the Cold War and to take Russia back into the past, instead of the future. The hostility that Putin and the Eurasian Union face is due to the fact that the Eurasian Union challenges Euro-Atlantic expansion and its plans to absorb the republics of the former Soviet Union, either through NATO expansion or through the EU's Eastern Partnership. Atlanticists have done whatever they could to prevent any form of Eurasian cohesion, which comes at the cost of Atlanticist plans in the post-Soviet space. In a move to prevent this process, the US has tried to recruit India through an initiative to get it to stake a claim for a sphere of influence in Central Asia. Designated a *New Silk Road* or sometimes Greater Central Asia or Greater South Asia, it is described thus:

> [F]rom Astana to Mumbai, [the entire region] will enjoy expanded trade and transit cooperation. The reintegration of Afghanistan into this region—and into the global economy—can be of tremendous benefit— not just to the Afghani themselves, and not just its neighbors, but to the global economy."[17]

The Eurasian Union, however, has been a process and entity that has been long in the making. It has been an idea that the post-Soviet space has been working to realize, the sum of all processes of regional integration. The process is complemented and encouraged onwards in the military, security, economic, and political fronts by the SCO and CSTO, too. It is a natural course for Russia and the post-Soviet space to take. It will streamline all the agreements and various organizations in the post-Soviet space that were pushing for integration. It is a key for the survival and transformation of the Russian Federation and the other former union republics. It will allow Russia to express its Eurasian characteristics and to look at both Europe and Asia like the Byzantine two-headed eagle that it has inherited as a national symbol. If this integration takes place in the post-Soviet space, then the Russian Federation will secure its footing for the current century as not only a major power, but as the clear leader of what will probably be this century's most important bloc. Even Syria has expressed interest in joining the Eurasian Union.

The coat of arms of the Russian Federation (adopted in 1993) is based on the Byzantine double-headed eagle looking to both the East and the West.

CHAPTER 8

NATO AND THE HIGH SEAS

CONTROL OF STRATEGIC WATERWAYS

Today we are witnessing an almost uncontained hyper use of force—military force—in international relations, force that is plunging the world into an abyss of permanent conflicts. As a result we do not have sufficient strength to find a comprehensive solution to any one of these conflicts. Finding a political settlement also becomes impossible. We are seeing a greater and greater disdain for the basic principles of international law. And independent legal norms are, as a matter of fact, coming increasingly closer to one state's legal system. One state and, of course, first and foremost the United States, has overstepped its national borders in every way.

—Russian President Vladimir Putin (2007)

A Tale of Two Chinas

NATO's modern role in the high seas is tied to the flow of energy and the control of international waterways and strategic chokepoints like the Gulf of Aden and the Bosporus. The Atlantic Alliance likes to portray itself as securing and policing international waters, safeguarding universal interests in a fight against terrorism, smuggling, crime, and illegal weapons proliferation. Critics and adversaries of NATO on the other hand argue that the Atlantic Alliance's actions are nefarious and tied to hegemonic objectives. To a large degree any positive NATO presence in the high seas is overshadowed by the Pentagon's objective of containing the Chinese. Because of this NATO interplay with US policy on China, a good portion of this chapter will be dedicated to China and its "string of pearls" in the Indian Ocean. Thus, we must start with a tale of how two Chinas came about and the geo-strategic importance of Taiwan or Chinese Taipei.

In 1949, the Chinese Communists overran and defeated the military forces of the Kuomintang or Chinese Nationalists in mainland China. Chairperson Mao Zedong would declare the formation of the People's Republic of China on October 1, 1949. Two months later, the Nationalists would evacuate mainland China and land their forces on the island of Taiwan (Formosa) and declare it as their temporary base until they could wrest mainland China away from Mao and the Communists. They declared martial law to suppress what they called the "communist rebellion"—which would last until 1991—and effectively established an authoritarian US-supported dictatorship. Thus two parallel Chinese governments claiming sovereignty over the whole of China came to exist next to each other: Taiwan would effectively take on the mantle of Nationalist China, formally named the Republic of China, while the mainland became the People's Republic of China. While the infamously corrupt Nationalists effectively lost any chances to reclaim the Chinese mainland, the conflict for control of the Taiwan Strait and portions of the South China Sea did not fully end. Fighting broke out and the People's Republic wrested the Dachen Islands away from the Nationalists. Taiwan or "Free China," which is what the Nationalists ironically called their territory to politically distinguish themselves from the People's Republic of China or "Red China," was then recognized as the legitimate government of all China by the US and the Western Bloc.

The fighting between Taiwan and the People's Republic that started in 1954 and resulted in the Dachen Islands falling to Red China in 1955 would lead to the formalization of the US military alliance with Taiwan. The Eisenhower Administration and the regime of Generalissimo Chiang Kai-shek (Jiang Zhongzheng) signed a mutual defense pact in 1954, which put Taiwan under the US nuclear umbrella. Taiwan literally became a US base.

Western Bloc recognition of the Chinese Nationalist government in Taiwan and the Republic of China would wear away in the 1970s as recognition of the People's Republic of China became virtually unavoidable internationally. Via UN Resolution 2758, the UN General Assembly recognized the People's Republic of China as the legitimate government of China on October 25, 1971. The Nationalists were expelled from the UN General Assembly and the People's Republic of China was given the Chinese veto-holding seat at the UN Security Council. Against the backdrop of Sino-Soviet tensions, Henry Kissinger visited the People's Republic to secretly open the door for rapprochement between the US and Red China in 1972 when Richard Nixon would meet Mao in Beijing. On January 1, 1979 the US government formally established diplomatic relations with the People's Republic of China and unilaterally annulled, under Article 10 of the Sino-American Mutual Defense Treaty, its mutual defense pact with Taiwan, which would come to effect on January 1, 1980.

China and East Asia are increasingly becoming the centers of global affairs and economics. More and more, all roads are leading to mainland China. Despite the formal termination of the mutual defense pact between the US and Taiwan, the US and its allies have continued to support Taiwan in multiple ways. This is because Taiwan was and still is part of the US network in Asia for surrounding and containing China militarily. This strategy of containment is nowhere more obvious than how it plays out through Taiwan's naval importance.

Putting a Leash on China:
The Strategic Importance of Maritime Energy Routes

The US retains strong military links with Taiwan because Taiwan provides a logistical hub for military engagement against the People's Republic of China and Chinese energy security. Located between the South China Sea and the East China Sea, Taiwan's geographic position is critically important as it relates to the strategic maritime shipping lanes that transport oil and other resources to China.

Much has been discussed about the important geo-strategic oil routes in Central Asia and about important land corridors, such as the Baku-Tbilisi-Ceyhan (BTC) Oil Terminal, but attention should also be paid to the strategic maritime oil routes and international shipping lanes. As with the US and NATO, energy supplies are closely linked to Chinese national security, development, and military strength. Should China's oil supplies be cut off in the event of a war or, more likely, be delayed, China would be in a very vulnerable position and could potentially be paralyzed and suffocated. A maritime cordon around China would serve such a purpose.

The Strait of Taiwan and the Strait of Malacca are geo-strategically vital to transporting oil and resources to China. Whosoever controls both strategic straits controls the flow of energy to China under the present status quo. It would be a harsh blow to China, should these straits be blocked and the stream of oil tankers heading to China be stopped or delayed, just as it would be a blow to the US and EU should the Strait of Hormuz in the Persian Gulf be blocked by Iran during a conflict. It so happens that the US Navy dominates these shipping lanes. The Pentagon and US Navy also continuously monitor both the Straits of Taiwan and Malacca. Moreover, the US has cultivated a network of military allies around these important waterways in the Indian Ocean. Until China has a secure source of inflowing energy from a route that is not controlled or is overlooked by the United States, it will continue to be vulnerable to the US Navy.

Because of these realities, both Taiwan and Singapore are close allies of the US. Singapore and Taiwan are heavily militarized with a view to exerting military control over these two vital waterways under the scenario of a war between the US and China. In such case, both Singapore and Taiwan, in alliance with the US Navy, have contingency plans to block oil traffic from reaching China. Although the Strait of Malacca lies within the sovereign maritime territory of Malaysia, the rapid militarization of Singapore is aimed at controlling and, if need be, halting the flow of oil tankers through the waters of Malacca. The naval facilities of Singapore are also highly specialized to service warships and submarines and are widely used by the US Navy.

China knows that it is vulnerable to a US-led military attack on its energy supplies. This is why the Chinese have been developing their naval bases and pushing for oil terminals and energy corridors to be built over land routes directly from Central Asia and the Russian Federation to China. Chinese cooperation with Russia, Iran, and the republics of Central Asia serves the purpose of creating a trans-Asian energy corridor that would ensure a continuous flow of energy to China in the event of an US-led naval blockade of the high seas. The discussions that have been underway for years about developing a natural gas pipeline from Iran to Pakistan, India, and China are also part of this Chinese strategy.

The "String of Pearls" and the Militarization of the Indian Ocean

The encirclement of China by the US has two major dimensions. One is the configuring of the structure for an Asian NATO-like alliance against China, which will discussed in Chapter 11, and the other is the militarization of the Indian Ocean and strategic maritime routes. For about a decade the Chinese have been working to secure their energy lifelines by establishing a chain of bases along the strategic maritime energy corridor leading to China. *The Washington Times* has commented: "[The Chinese are] building up military forces and setting up bases along sea lanes from the Middle East to project its power overseas and protect its oil shipments, according to a previously undisclosed internal report prepared for Defense Secretary Donald H. Rumsfeld."[1] The Pentagon on the other hand has done whatever has been in its power to obstruct and prevent China from having a secure energy lifeline. Chinese efforts have been met by a steady US-led naval build-up around the People's Republic of China.

A 2007 report published by the Australian Strategic Policy Institute (ASPI) warned that an Asian arms race was underway. The ASPI report states: "In an arc extending from Pakistan and India through Southeast Asia and up to Japan there is a striking modernization and [military] expansion underway."[2] What's more this process includes an increase in the submarine squadrons navigating the waters of the

Asia-Pacific region. The Chinese have initiated a submarine build-up as an effective means of fighting the US Navy. This is part of Beijing's proactive naval policy aimed at securing the East China Sea, the South China Sea, and the Indian Ocean. These bodies of water all correspond to the international energy maritime route that transports African and Middle Eastern oil to China.

> "China is building strategic relationships along the sea lanes from the Middle East to the South China Sea in ways that suggest defensive and offensive positioning to protect China's energy interests, but also to serve broad security objectives," said the report ["Energy Futures in Asia"] sponsored by the director, Net Assessment, [*sic.*; the director of the Office of Net Assessment (ONA)] who heads Mr. Rumsfeld's office on future-oriented strategies.[3]

The link between the naval build-up and energy security is obvious just from studying the name of the Pentagon's report discussed above: *Energy Futures in Asia*. These naval bases that China is constructing or has already built for the purpose of securing its energy supplies are referred to by the Pentagon as the "string of pearls," because of their geo-strategic importance to the balance of naval power in the Indian Ocean.[4] Chinese naval facilities have been constructed all along this vital maritime corridor. Among them are the naval port of Gwadar in Pakistan, on the shore of the Arabian Sea, and the port of Hambantota on the southern edge of the island of Sri Lanka (Ceylon).[5] Beijing has also worked with Bangladesh and Myanmar (Burma) to secure a naval footing in both countries in league with its geo-strategic objectives in the Indian Ocean.

Myanmar and the Geo-Politics of the Saffron Revolution

Myanmar receives major Chinese military aid and support, because it is an especially important Chinese ally, geo-strategically. The country also has natural gas resources that have been the subject of Sino-Indian rivalry. Geographically, Myanmar sits on the coasts of both the Bay of Bengal and the Andaman Sea (Burma Sea). The Southeast Asian country also directly borders the Chinese province of Yunnan and provides a direct land corridor via car and train to the two mentioned bodies of water through friendly territory for the People's Republic. The naval access that China has from Myanmar to the Bay of Bengal and the Andaman Sea is the main reason that Beijing has been upgrading the transportation infrastructure of Myanmar. China has constructed the port of Kyaukpyu on the Bay of Bengal and expanded the land network connecting Myanmar to Yunnan.[6] What's more China has established listening stations in the Coco Islands and is developing and expanding other Myanma (Burmese) naval bases and military infrastructure.[7]

The Chinese position in Myanmar has given Beijing an important card in securing its access to the high seas. In theory it could relieve or terminate any needs deriving from the threat posed by a closing of both the Strait of Taiwan and the Strait of Malacca by the US and its allies during a conflict. Thus, the Pentagon was anxious when the Chinese navy made their first port call to Myanmar in 2010.[8]

It is because of the importance of Myanmar to China that the US and its allies quickly supported the 2007 protests started by Myanma Buddhist monks against the military junta ruling in Rangoon. The protests became popularly known as the Saffron Revolution and were capitalized on by Washington, which portrayed the protests as a democratic revolution. If Myanmar was not a Chinese ally, Washington's position most probably would have been very different. The US, UK, France, Japan, and their allies spoke out against Rangoon while they and the entire Atlantic Alliance ignored and stayed silent during the popular protests in Georgia against the increasingly authoritarian President Mikheil Saakashvili, because he was an ally of NATO. Just months earlier in January, the US and its allies even tried to pass a UN Security Council resolution against Myanmar, which both China and Russia vetoed.

What the US government and its allies concealed about the nature of the Saffron Revolution in Myanmar with the help of the major media networks was that the protests against the military regime in Rangoon did not erupt as a democracy movement, albeit activists wanting democracy took advantage of the situation to take to the streets, but were sparked by economic grievances, demands that the costs of daily living, from food prices to gasoline, be brought down by the military junta. Nor did the US government and its allies acknowledge that the cost of living in Myanmar had actually risen precipitously because of their own targeted economic sanctions imposed on Myanmar that systematically hurt the ordinary citizens of that Southeast Asian country. As an indicator of the economic basis for the eruption of the Saffron Revolution, the protests subsided after the military junta in Rangoon lowered costs. In 2009, the Karen Human Rights Group monitoring the situation of ethnic Karens in Myanmar even acknowledged this, stating:

> The 2007 protests reached their peak following the dramatic reduction in fuel price subsidies by the State Peace and Development Council (SPDC), Burma's ruling junta, on August 15th 2007 and the subsequent

participation of tens of thousands or Buddhist monks beginning in late August.[9]

Regime change in Rangoon is just one option for Washington to remove Myanmar out of the orbit of China and to end its naval access to the Chinese. The Obama Administration has sought to entice the surrender of Myanmar through rapprochement and encouraging Rangoon to adopt neoliberal economic reforms. The White House also seeks to manipulate Aung San Suu Kyi and the National League for Democracy for US geo-political interests. Since 2010, the military junta formally stopped ruling the country after elections and a civilian government was in place, but the military is still the arbiter of power in Rangoon.

MAP XVI: The String of Pearls: Chinese Naval Bases in the Indian Ocean

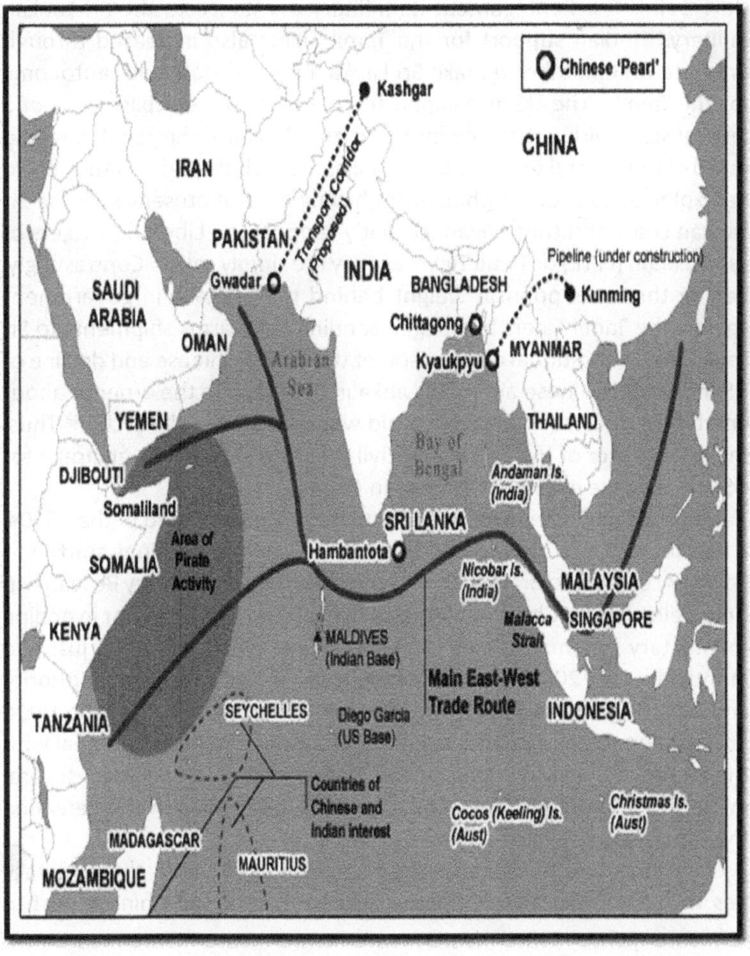

Sri Lanka and the Geo-Politics of the Sri Lankan Civil War

2007 was a milestone year for the Chinese "string of pearls." Not only did the Saffron Revolution erupt in Myanmar, but Sri Lanka firmly entered the orbit of Beijing. On March 12, 2007, Colombo agreed to allow the Chinese to build a massive naval port on its territory, at Hambantota. An agreement on the construction of the port was finalized and signed by the Sri Lankan Port Authority with two Chinese companies, the China Harbor Engineering Company and the Sino Hydo Corporation.[10] The Sri Lankan government's decision was mostly formed on the basis of economic benefits and Chinese support to end the fighting on their island-state.

What followed the deal between Beijing and Colombo in 2007 was the estrangement of Sri Lanka from Washington, plus irritation from New Delhi. The Pentagon cut its military assistance to the Sri Lankan military.[11] Indian support for the Tamil Tigers also increased through pressure on Colombo to make Sri Lanka a federal state with autonomy for the Tamils. The US also supported plans for the establishment of a federal state with autonomy for the Tamils. Because the Tamils covered much of the coastal territory of Sri Lanka, the US believed that they could be exploited to prevent China from having a naval presence off the Sri Lankan coast and thus began to tacitly support the Liberation Tigers of Tamil Ealam (LTTE) or Tamil Tigers as they are simply called. Contrastingly, Beijing threw its political weight behind the Sri Lankan government against the Tamil Tigers and began sending large arms shipments to Sri Lanka. As an additional comparison of the rise of Chinese and decline of US influence, Chinese aid to Sri Lanka in 2008 was in the order of about one billion dollars (US), while US aid was only $7.4 million (US).[12] Thus, the last chapter of the Sri Lankan Civil War in 2009 became an arena for US and Chinese enmity in the Indian Ocean.

While Chinese military ties with Sri Lanka started in the 1990s, it was in 2007 that Chinese and Sri Lankan military relations started to flower. According to Brahma Chellaney of the Centre for Policy Research in New Delhi, India: "China's arms sales [were] the decisive factor in ending the military stalemate [in the Sri Lankan Civil War.]"[13] In April, just one month after the 2007 agreement between the Sri Lankan Port Authority and both the China Harbor Engineering Company and the Sino Hydo Corporation, China signed a major ammunition and ordnance deal with the Sri Lankan military.[14] Beijing also transferred, free of charge, several military jets to the Sri Lankan military, which were decisive in defeating the Tamil Tigers.[15]

Iran and Russia also began to rapidly develop their military ties with Sri Lanka after Colombo agreed to host the Chinese port in

Hambantota. In an AP article titled "US out, enter Russia," published on December 23, 2007, Russian involvement was also addressed:

> In the wake of the United States Senate slashing military assistance to Sri Lanka, the Russian Federation has stepped in to fill the vacuum, sending the first ever top level military delegation to Colombo to discuss military cooperation. A high level Russian military delegation led by [Colonel-General] Vladimir Moltenskoy last week met Defence Secretary Gotabhaya Rajapaksa, Army Commander Sarath Fonseka and Air Force Commander, Roshan Goonathilake and had visited several major military installations in the island. Molpenskoy, a veteran combat General in the Russian Army was formerly the operational commander of the Russian Forces in Chechnya.[16]

In 2007, not only did Moscow, like China, move in to fill the vacuum left by the US government after Sri Lanka agreed to build the Chinese naval port; the Kremlin also sent Colonel-General Vladimir Moltenskoy who oversaw the Russian military campaign against the separatist movement in Chechnya, as a military advisor to Colombo.

The aid of Tehran was also crucial for the Sri Lankan military. *The Island*, a Sri Lankan news source, reported that Iran had literally come to Sri Lanka's rescue by sending several cargo airplanes of equipment to aid the government in the fighting.[17] Before the arrival of a high ranking Iranian military delegation to Sri Lanka in 2009, the same source reported that Iran and Sri Lanka "have over the year developed strategies relating to small [tactical] boat operations."[18] Tehran's aid also included economic support. *The Hindu* on September 21, 2009 published an article partially revealing the depth and importance of the level of help that Sri Lanka had been receiving from Iran alone:

> Iran has extended by another year the four-month interest-free credit facility granted to Sri Lanka after President Mahinda Rajapaksa's visit to Iran in November 2007, state-run Daily News reported on Monday.
>
> It said that consequent to talks with Iranian President Mahmoud Ahmadinejad, the Iranian government granted the facility from January 2008 to August 31.
>
> In 2008, Sri Lanka imported crude oil under this

facility to the tune of $1.05 billion, nearly all of its requirements, easing the pressure on the country's foreign exchange requirements in a year of significance for the government's war with the LTTE [or the Tamil Tigers].

An additional three-month credit package at a concessionary rate of interest was also accommodated in Sri Lanka's favour on September 3 [2009] at a meeting between the representatives of the countries in Tehran.[19]

In this regard, Beijing, Moscow, and Tehran all have cooperation and military agreements with Sri Lanka. The visits of Sri Lankan leaders and military officials to Tehran, Moscow, and Beijing in 2007 and 2008

Above Photo: Iranian military officer (middle) and Russian military officers (front left and front right) seen visiting a Sri Lankan port in February 2012. Sri Lanka is a Chinese ally and a dialogue partner of the SCO.

were all tied to Sri Lankan preparations to militarily disarm the Tamil Tigers with the help of these three countries. China, Russia, and Iran all ultimately helped arm the Sri Lankan military before the last phase of the Sri Lankan Civil War took place to ensure government control over the Sri Lankan coast. Along with Sri Lankan officials, the governments of Iran, Russia, and China all believed that unless the Tamil Tigers were neutralized as a threat, the US and its allies, in possible league with India, could make attempts to overthrow the Sri Lankan government in order to nullify the Sri Lankan naval port agreement with China and remove Sri Lanka from the orbit of Beijing. In this context, they all threw their weight behind Sri Lanka during the fighting in 2009, and in the case of China and Russia, at the UN Security Council as well.

In the same year that the Sri Lankan Civil War ended, 2009, Sri Lanka joined the Shanghai Cooperation Organization, as did Belarus.[20] The entry of Sri Lanka into the SCO as a dialogue partner was announced at the organization's conference in Yekaterinburg that year. At Yekaterinburg, the Sri Lankans thanked the SCO for its collective support against the Tamil Tigers during the civil war. Entry into the SCO puts Sri Lanka publicly underneath the protective umbrella of China and its allies. Although it is not spelled out in Article 14 of the SCO Charter, a dialogue partner can request protection and defensive aid under such a relationship. Dialogue partners are also financially tied to the SCO, which facilitates their integration within the Eurasianist project countering Atlanticism.

Gwadar and Pakistani Baluchistan

The US has also been trying to obstruct any possible means of allowing oil and gas to directly reach China through any trans-Asian oil cooperation aside from the traditional and vulnerable sea routes it patrols. Any trans-Asian energy arrangement, such as the Iran-Pakistan-India (IPI) Friendship Pipeline, is seen as detrimental from the strategic perspective of the Pentagon. The reasons for the destabilization of Pakistan are manifold. As well as being linked to tensions with India and the tensions between Iran and the US, the extension of NATO's attacks into Pakistan from Afghanistan and the rise of militant separatist movements in Pakistan are tied to the enmity between China and the US and the struggle to control the flow of energy.

In regard to strategic energy routes, the Pentagon and NATO see the IPI Friendship Pipeline as a threat or rival energy corridor to the ones they have planned in Eurasia. Islamabad's steadfast refusal to bow to US demands to cancel the pipeline with Iran is directly tied to Chinese geo-strategic interests.[21] As mentioned earlier, there is a strong possibility that China could be included in the pipeline project or that the pipeline could form as an Iran-Pakistan-China pipeline that would bypass India. This is a threat to the US aim of containing China and isolating Iran, respectively, by way of controlling Chinese energy supplies and manipulating the direction of Iranian energy exports.

The Pentagon fears that Islamabad could become a full Chinese client state; this is why it desires a weak and divided Pakistani state. The same is true in regard to Afghanistan where NATO and the Pentagon fear that Iran and China could control Afghanistan through spheres of influence that would see a western zone controlled by Tehran and an eastern zone controlled by Beijing. As testimonial, maps of Pakistan and Afghanistan falling within the geo-political orbit of China have even been produced by strategists and circulated among US and NATO officers. Balkanizing these areas may make it much harder for the area to fall under Chinese and Iranian influence or to turn Pakistan into a modern "pipelineistan." The new and smaller states that could take the places of Afghanistan and Pakistan may ask for the protection of the US and the Atlantic Alliance just as some of the new republics that emerged in the place of Yugoslavia did.

The Pakistani province of Baluchistan figures importantly in this equation. Baluchistan is not only geo-strategically important in regard to Eurasian energy linkages, but is also rich in mineral deposits and energy reserves. In most cases these minerals and energy reserves are all untouched. It would be far easier to procure the mineral and energy recourses of this area from a relatively more lightly populated independent Baluchistan republic that would be happy selling its resources at lower prices. It could also help destabilize the easternmost Iranian provinces, including the province of Sistan-Baluchistan. An independent Pakistani Baluchistan could be at odds with Tehran over territorial claims to Sistan-Baluchistan.

An important question to keep in mind is what role Baluchistan would play in the US project to strategically curtail China in the Indian Ocean. While the military infrastructure of the area is already under the control of the US military, the Chinese hold sway in Gwadar. Speaking of Baluchistan, once again 2007 proves to be an important year for the Chinese "string of pearls." In 2007, with vital Chinese participation, the port at Gwadar became adapted for hosting oceanic traffic. The Chinese give major strategic value to Gwadar, because it is located on the coast of the Arabian Sea at the mouth of the Gulf of Oman (Oman Sea) near China's strategic ally Iran and the energy-rich Persian Gulf. Chinese strategists want to integrate Gwadar with China's Xinjiang Uyghur Autonomous Region like the Karakoram Highway. If this should be done then Chinese energy imports to China can bypass the high seas and further insure Beijing's energy security by insulating China from the

US Navy or any other hostile forces that would try to cut Chinese energy supplies in the scenario of a war. Iran can also directly import to China from Gwadar. The important question for both Beijing and Washington is if an independent Baluchistan would serve or work against Chinese naval interests in Gwadar. By supporting Baluchistan's secession from Pakistan or engineering a Baluchistani-Pakistani conflict the US probably hopes that Beijing would be forced to support Islamabad's efforts to maintain Pakistan's territorial integrity and its own interests. This would alienate Baluchistan from China and maybe result in the loss of Gwadar for the Chinese.

Control of Strategic Waterways, Cordoning the Seas, and NATO's "Global Navy"

Controlling the high seas and trade is an additional line of attack being set up to envelop the Eurasian giants, China and Russia. This is precisely what the Proliferation Security Initiative (PSI), and the establishment of a "global naval force" under the command of the US seeks to accomplish. NATO's Operation Active Endeavor also falls into line with this objective by having the potential to neutralize the Russians in the Mediterranean Sea and prevent Russian naval forces from leaving the Black Sea or entering the Mediterranean Sea from either the Black Sea or through the Strait of Gibraltar. As can be concluded from the lengthy prior discussion, China is in deeper danger from an ocean-based threat than Russia due to the question of energy supplies. The PSI started by the Bush Jr. Administration in 2003, just after the invasion of Iraq, is also a means of controlling the movements of international traffic that can be used to cut energy supplies and natural resources from going to China should a juncture of aggression against the Chinese arrive. Moreover, the subject of North Korean ballistic missile and nuclear weapon proliferation has been capitalized on as a basis for further encircling China in East Asia.

A naval network that has been created by the Atlantic Alliance and NATO partners is beginning to emerge. Over forty countries have participated in NATO's naval patrols and operations in the Arabian Sea and the Indian Ocean.[22] This naval formation is a threat to Chinese energy supplies and international trade going through the Indian Ocean between Africa and Eurasia. Admiral Mike Mullen, while serving in the position of the Chief of US Naval Operations (CNO), stated that the Pentagon sought to establish "a thousand-ship navy" to take charge of international waters.[23] The strategy Admiral Mullen outlined before he sat in the position of the Chairman of the Joint Chiefs of Staff (CJCS) is one that foresees the eventual amalgamation of Atlantic Alliance and NATO allied naval forces in what has been termed by the US Navy as a "global maritime partnership" which "unites navies, coast guards, maritime forces, port operators, commercial shippers and many other government and non-government agencies to address maritime concerns."[24]

The bodies of water where this strategy is coming into play are the Arabian Sea, Gulf of Aden, Mediterranean Sea, Persian Gulf, and Red Sea—essentially the bodies of water surrounding the energy-rich Middle East and East Africa. As a clear illustration of the linkage between the concept of a "global navy" and NATO, Admiral Mullen has cited the existence of a predominantly NATO group of forty-five warships deployed in the Persian Gulf and around the waters of the Middle East as a contingent of this global naval force.[25] In fact, this global naval force is mandated under the combined auspices of NATO and the naval operations wing of CENTCOM. The operations in the waters of the Middle East and in the Arabian Sea include Combined Task Force (CTF) 150 and CTF 152. This NATO naval armada is comprised of three primary CTFs and at least seven supporting naval forces at all times. Among the ships that constitute this multinational fleet are those of the US, UK, Netherlands, France, Germany, Italy, Canada, Turkey, Singapore, South Korea, New Zealand, Japan, and Australia.

CTF 150 operates in the waters of the Gulf of Oman, Gulf of Aden, Red Sea, and the North Arabian Sea, where several French warships are positioned. CTF 152, which includes Italian, French, and German warships, operates in the Persian Gulf and has its operational headquarters in the petro-sheikhdom of Bahrain, like the US Fifth Fleet. In fact it is worth noting that CTF 152 is under the command of the US Navy and CENTCOM, which is why it shares the same headquarters as the US Fifth Fleet. The operations of this NATO-dominated naval force have included Operation Iraqi Freedom in the Persian Gulf and Operation Enduring Freedom off the Horn of Africa. The formation of these large, and relatively unheard of, armadas of warships has been made possible through the Global War on Terror.

The Proliferation Security Initiative:
Controlling International Waters and Movement

Aside from the global naval force being created by the Pentagon and NATO, a strategy has been devised to control international trade, international movement, and international waters. The Proliferation Security Initiative (PSI), under the facade of stopping the smuggling of weapons of mass destruction (WMD) and the systems for their delivery either in whole or by means of components or technology, sets out to control the flow of resources and to control international trade. The initiative was drafted by US Under-Secretary of State for Arms Control and International Security John Bolton, while he was serving in the US

Department of State before his post at the UN and paradoxically outlined the authorization of the open violation of international law to supposedly serve international stability. Under the PSI, the US and its allies can interdict international shipping and take inhibitive action in international waters. The strategy was officially launched on May 31, 2003 by the White House.

Under international law the US Navy or NATO warships are not allowed to board and search foreign merchant ships that they encounter in international waters. Under Part VII (7) of the 1982 UN Convention on the Law of the Sea the US operations are internationally illegal, unless authorized by the home country that the merchant ship originates from. Warships can only board and search or detain ships that are from the same country, unless a bilateral agreement has been signed with another nation granting the right to search merchant ships carrying their flag. In international waters foreign ships can only be searched if polluting near the waters of a naval force's home country or on the reasonable suspicion of piracy. Additionally, in international waters ships owned by a national government have immunity from stops, inspections, and seizures by the vessels of other countries. Under these international guidelines it would be illegal for the US Navy or the British Royal Navy to stop a vessel belonging to the government of Algeria, Argentina, Brazil, China, Cuba, Iran, Malaysia, North Korea, Russia, Syria, Ukraine, or Venezuela in international waters. With US efforts to derail the international waters regime and replace it with the PSI, this would all change. Since its launch the PSI has been used to justify the illegal boarding of North Korean vessels by the US. Many North Korean vessels have been illegally halted and badgered since the initiation of the naval initiative.

The governments of several major Asian nations, inter alia the Chinese, Indian, Indonesian, and Malaysian governments, have openly criticized and questioned the legality of the new operations. China and Iran especially are naturally suspicious of Washington's initiative for international waters and have refused to participate in the PSI. Both Beijing and Tehran see this as a threat to their security. The Chinese particularly see the PSI as a method for the US and its allies to further control international waters and international trade. In 2004, the US tried to use the PSI and the pretext of fighting terrorism to establish a permanent naval presence in the Strait of Malacca:

> Malaysia and Indonesia oppose a proposal by Washington to deploy US marines with high-speed boats to guard the Malacca Straits, one of the world's busiest shipping lanes, against possible terrorist attacks.
>
> [...]
>
> The proposal grows out of the Proliferation Security

Initiative (PSI), a US-led multinational group that cooperates on halting the transfer of nuclear technology by land and sea, including the forced seizure of ships.[26]

Russia, on the other hand, joined the scheme because Moscow is not in the same position as China, whose lifeline is based on maritime traffic and international waters. Moscow wants one foot in the door and one foot outside of the door to be flexible when dealing with the US and NATO in a hostile scenario. Furthermore, the Russia Navy under the scheme can reciprocally halt and board US merchant vessels. Atlanticist strategists, however, want to use a strategy similar to the PSI in the Black Sea to keep Russian ships from heading into the high seas from their ports there. The US government in association with NATO has openly stated that it considers the Black Sea as a potential transit route for WMDs, drugs, and terrorists. This directly denotes Russia and Ukraine. NATO's Operation Active Endeavor in the Mediterranean is already one layer of this. This project prepares the grounds for cutting off the Russians from their allies like Syria, because the only means of travel to Syria for Russia without having to cross non-ally territory—until things settle down in Iraq and a land bridge is available via Iran and Iraq—is through the shipping or maritime routes of the Black Sea and Red Sea that connect with the Mediterranean Sea. What's more, the Atlantic Alliance wants to evict Russia from its naval base in Syria.

The PSI is also clearly fixated on the waters of the Indian and Pacific Oceans surrounding the areas of Eurasia that are not part of the Euro-Atlantic Zone. It is no coincidence that Singapore, Japan, and the South China Sea, all in close proximity to China, have been picked as the main vicinities of the many naval exercises under the banner of this new scheme. The US, Britain, Japan, Australia, Canada, Singapore, France, Italy, and Germany, along with Russia all have taken part in the naval exercises under the PSI. In 2006, the Gulf Cooperation Council began to take part in the exercises with the US and NATO in the Persian Gulf. The PSI is attempting to set a precedent for normalizing the breach of international law through an illegal instrument. The precedent has been set for what could one day lead to assertions of the right to stop Chinese, Iranian, and Russian ships and maritime traffic and trade. It is hard to imagine that these states will accept this and not see it as aggression. This is one of the reasons why Chinese, Iranian, and Russian naval expansions have been underway.

The Militarization of the World's Waterways

The hydrosphere of the world is being militarized from the major river arteries of Europe to all the strategic maritime points of transit. The Gulf Security Initiative between NATO and the Gulf Cooperation Council seeks to also dominate the Persian Gulf and to hem in Iran, while the aims of the PSI are to control all maritime movements and traffic under the guise of international security. NATO vessels are anchored in the Red Sea and the Gulf of Aden; these warships are deployed off the coasts of Somalia, Djibouti, and Yemen as part of NATO's objectives of creating a naval cordon of the seas controlling important strategic waterways. The Indian Ocean is also becoming militarized. These moves by the US and its allies, however, have led to increased Russian and Chinese naval cooperation in the Asia-Pacific region, the naval expansion of Iran into blue or deep waters, and the presence of Chinese, Indian, Iranian, Russian, and Ukrainian warships off the coasts of East Africa. Iranian naval forces are now operating south of the equator and Russia is negotiating for opening naval bases in Cuba, the Seychelles, and Vietnam while taking steps to build Arctic naval bases and establish the superiority of the nuclear capability of its naval fleet.[27]

What these movements and counter-movements amount to are the positioning for dominance on a chessboard of the world's waterways and their marine traffic corridors. Control of these waterways would be vital in a war between the Atlanticisit and Eurasianist camps if a major conflict should erupt between them. In the course of this militarization process the Law of the Sea is being breached and ignored as part of the expansion of a broader extra-territorial legal network dominated and driven by the Atlanticists that is eroding the international legal system of the world.

CHAPTER 9

THE GLOBAL MISSILE SHIELD PROJECT

The policies of the US, since the end of the Cold War, are complicated and vast. They involve intent to dominate and the use of international organizations to advance US economic and geo-political interests. They also include the conversion of NATO into a surrogate military police force for globalization and US world economic domination.
—Ramsey Clark, sixty-sixth US Attorney-General (2000)

Cold War II and Nuclear Primacy:
Moscow's Rollercoaster Ride with Washington

Since September 11, 2001 the relationship between Moscow and Washington has been like a rollercoaster ride. The US has unilaterally left important disarmament agreements and revised its nuclear policy by adopting an aggressive nuclear strike posture. Relations have become tense between Moscow and Washington, then appeared to recover with Barack Obama's "reset," only to worsen again. The post-9/11 relationship between NATO and the Russian Federation has also been tense and described in terms reminiscent of the Cold War. One of the main impetuses for this resumption of Cold War tensions has been the US missile shield project. Russian military leaders began warning the US that it would be the start of a "new arms race" in 2007.[1] Since then, the Russians have consistently proclaimed that the missile defense shield, above all else, is a threat to them and the countries of the former USSR. The idea of a missile shield project is not new. During the Cold War, the idea was inaugurated by Ronald Reagan as part of a grand strategy to deploy missiles, technical facilities, and military bases around the world and in space, which led to the project being called "Star Wars." Since its inauguration the Pentagon has spent billions of dollars in research and development for the project. While the White House and two succeeding US administrations have claimed that the intended purpose of establishing a missile shield is to protect the US and NATO from the threat of hypothetical North Korean or Iranian ballistic missile attacks, the Kremlin regards the missile shield project as a serious threat to its national security. Moscow is adamant about its position and has continuously stated in public that the justifications for the creation of the missile shield are mere pretexts to encircle and neutralize Russia. Russian hostility towards the US missile shield project is based on an understanding of US strategic goals. These goals include the military doctrine of full spectrum dominance, a revamped nuclear first strike policy that now includes the concept of nuclear primacy, and NATO expansion onto the borders of Russia—despite NATO's guarantees that it would not expand beyond the borders of Germany.

US nuclear policy has radically changed since the Cold War. In 2001, the Nuclear Posture Review (NPR) of the United States acknowledged that Russia was the target of possible nuclear attacks by the Pentagon. The 2001 NPR can be recapitulated by the following summary:

> During the Cold War, [the Soviet Union] was the principal nuclear threat to the United States. The demise of the Soviet Union shifted U.S. nuclear weapons planning away from mainly targeting Russia. Nonetheless, Russia remains the only nation that can conceivably destroy the United States because of the size of its nuclear arsenal. Moreover, uncertainty over the future course of Russian foreign policy motivates the United States to keep a massive nuclear weapons reserve force. For these reasons, Russia still occupies a place on the list of potential targets for U.S. nuclear weapons. In addition, the new NPR explicitly lists six other countries as targets: North Korea, Iran, Iraq, Syria, Libya, and China. This nuclear targeting list reflects previous administrations' planning.[2]

Russia is a nuclear target for the Pentagon because it is one of the primary nations capable of militarily challenging the US, but this alone is not what has put Moscow on edge. In 2001, America announced that it would unilaterally withdraw from the Anti-Ballistic Missile (ABM) Treaty, which put legal limitations on the number of US and Russian ballistic missile systems. This was also one of the recommendations of

Dick Cheney and the neoconservative think-tank named the Project for a New American Century (PNAC) in their manuscript *Rebuilding America's Defenses: Strategies, Forces, and Resources For a New Century*. In the PNAC document, published in September 2000, it is categorically stated that America must "DEVELOP AND DEPLOY GLOBAL MISSILE DEFENSES [*sic.*] to defend the American homeland and American allies, and to provide a secure basis for US power projection around the world."[3] The unilateral withdrawal of the United States from the ABM Treaty with Russia was later followed by further announcements of changes in US military doctrine, which was first accentuated by the NPR, and then by the Doctrine for Joint Nuclear Operations (DJNO) and then CONPLAN 8022-02 that made offensive nuclear attacks available options for both pre-emptive and conventional warfare.[4]

In the eyes of Russia the missile shield project is an attempt by the US to establish nuclear primacy by neutralizing any Russian nuclear response and thereby Russia's capabilities to defend itself and its allies. With the missile shield in place Russia would become unable to react to a nuclear first strike by the United States. The Kremlin's nuclear arsenal would virtually become useless, because of the missile shield on its borders. In other words the Pentagon and NATO would eliminate the barrier to nuclear war posed by the deterrent effect of "mutually assured destruction" (MAD), which was present during the Cold War. This would make possible a US nuclear "first strike." During the Cold War the possibility of nuclear retaliation or a "second strike" and MAD were widely seen as the factors that had prevented a global nuclear war between the US and the Soviet Union. US nuclear primacy, however, would change all this.

At the same time, NATO's eastward expansion and the organization's shift from a formerly defensive pact to an interventionist organization have unnerved Russia. The strategic nature of US missile defense, which disturbs nuclear parity between Russia and the US, is further compounded by NATO expansion. Moscow feels threatened by the offensive military characteristics that NATO has adopted since the end of the Cold War, which has taken NATO from intervention in the former Yugoslavia to fighting in Afghanistan and Libya, and both security and training missions in the Middle East and Africa. In this regard, Vladimir Putin's caustic speech on global security should come as no shock. In it Putin accused the US government of pursing the objective of establishing a unipolar world through military might and force:

> Today we are witnessing an almost uncontained
> hyper use of force—military force—in international
> relations, force that is plunging the world into an abyss

of permanent conflicts. As a result we do not have sufficient strength to find a comprehensive solution to any one of these conflicts. Finding a political settlement also becomes impossible.

We are seeing a greater and greater disdain for the basic principles of international law. And independent legal norms are, as a matter of fact, coming increasingly closer to one state's legal system. One state and, of course, first and foremost the United States, has overstepped its national borders in every way.[5]

Putin also alluded to NATO expansion as being targeted against Russia:

I think it is obvious that NATO expansion does not have any relation with the modernisation of [NATO] itself or with ensuring security in Europe. On the contrary, it represents a serious provocation that reduces the level of mutual trust. And we have the right to ask: against whom is this expansion intended? And what happened to the assurances our western partners made after the dissolution of the Warsaw Pact? Where are those declarations today? No one even remembers them. But I will allow myself to remind this audience what was said. I would like to quote the speech of NATO General Secretary Mr Woerner in Brussels on 17 May 1990. He said at the time that: "the fact that we are ready not to place a NATO army outside of German territory gives the Soviet Union a firm security guarantee". Where are these guarantees?[6]

The apprehension of a looming war is very real among many Russians. Indeed it is a fact that the Russian Federation is being simultaneously encircled by NATO, a growing number of military bases, and finally by US and NATO missiles. In many regards, the war with Georgia was seen in Russia as a war against the Pentagon and NATO. The 2008 war between Georgia and Russia in the Caucasus even presents the possibility of a broader war directly involving the US and the Atlantic Alliance. It was even called a proxy war by Russian officials. The Kremlin has stated on several occasions that Mikheil Saakashvili is a US proxy or client.[7] Russian suspicions were further corroborated when the US declared, during Russia's 2008 war with Georgia, that the Caucasus was an area vital to US strategic interests. It is not coincidental that Georgia is one of the fastest militarizing states in the world and one of the largest recipients of US military aid and training. What is most important about the war between Russia and Georgia over South Ossetia is that Russia said it would not have changed its course of action even if Georgia were a member of NATO. This alone demonstrates that the threat of a broader war involving Russia and the US is not unthinkable or a mere illusion.

The so-called "reset button" of the post-9/11 bilateral ties of the US and Russia was a public relations stunt by the Obama Administration, as was the Obama White House's 2009 announcement of a halt to US missile defense plans in Eastern Europe. President Barack Obama's celebrated September 17, 2009 announcement that the US was scrapping the segments of the missile shield that were to be stationed close to Russia's border in the Czech Republic and Poland was misleading. Shortly after Obama's announcement the US launched two experimental missile defense satellites into space from Cape Canaveral in Florida.[8] What Obama actually announced was not the scrapping of the missile shield, but the launching of a much more extensive and effective missile shield under revised plans that will include naval deployments on board Aegis-equipped ships.[9] The deployment of the missile shield has actually been expanded inside and outside Europe by Obama, from Turkey to Spain and from the Mediterranean Sea to the Baltic Sea.

The Kremlin and its allies argue that Iran and North Korea are merely being used as pretexts by the Pentagon and NATO to mask its targeting of Russia. "Our analysis shows that the placing of a radio locating station in the Czech Republic and anti-missile equipment in Poland is a real threat to us," the commander of Russia's space forces, Lieutenant-General Vladimir Popovkin, responded when asked about the missile shield in 2007.[10] The Russian military official also told the press that it was "very doubtful" that the project was aimed at intercepting Iranian ballistic missiles.[11] The response of a Polish official to President Obama's revised plans only substantiates Russian fears. "We were never really threatened by a long-range missile attack from Iran," Slawomir Nowak, a senior government advisor to Poland's Prime Minister Donald Tusk, informed TVP INFO Television shortly after Obama's announcement.[12] To Moscow it became apparent that US strategists and policy makers correlated the deployment of global missile defenses not with an Iranian or North Korean threat, but in the words of the PNAC as a means to "provide a secure basis for US power projection around the world."[13] Just to illustrate how hollow they viewed Obama's pledges about scraping the Pentagon's missile defense plans to be, joint military preparations by Russia and Belarus for bilateral war games to prepare the Russian and Belarusian armed forces for a NATO attack involving a land, sea, and air invasion took place days after.[14]

The New Iron Curtain: A NATO Project from the Start

The missile defense shield was unveiled originally as a US project, but the Atlantic Alliance was involved in it from the beginning. NATO even drafted a missile coordination policy in 2003, the same year as the Anglo-American invasion of Iraq. The draft was ratified by the entire Atlantic Alliance the following year, in 2004. France was also working on its own ballistic missile (SAMP-T) system, while the Dutch, Germans, and the US were jointly developing the integrated Extended Air/Theater Missile systems through Project Optic Windmill.[15]

Records of active NATO missile system proliferation go all the way back to 2005. NATO has been actively working on missile projects such as the Active Layered Theater Ballistic Missile Defense (ALTBMD) program for years. The ALTBMD program was established in 2005 by NATO "after the completion of a two-year feasibility study in which eight NATO nations and various NATO projects cooperatively participated."[16] According to NATO, the focus of the project is to test and integrate NATO's command and control network and individual national missile systems to work inside the Euro-Atlantic Zone and out-of-area.[17] Within NATO, the US, UK, France, Germany, Denmark, Italy, Netherlands, Poland, and Czech Republic are all engaged in missile projects.

De facto NATO members and partners have also been involved in this project. For example, Japan is also funding the deployment of the Patriot PAC-3 and the Aegis Standard Missile-3 (SM-3) and hosts military radar facilities.[18] Israel, India, Australia, Taiwan, Japan, and Ukraine under its Orangist government are all non-NATO states that have also worked with NATO in the Alliance's missile project.

What the missile shield project—henceforth dropping the word "defense" from it altogether—is doing is creating a "new iron curtain." By its nature the project is offensive and a strategic step to end any military balance between the US camp and the major Eurasian powers. This new iron curtain, however, goes far beyond dividing Europe. Eurasia is being marked; a military "ring of fire" is being established around Russia, China, Iran, and their allies.

**"The Ring of Fire" and the Three Theaters
of the Inter-Continental Missile Shield**

The missile shield project is really a triad of predominantly three missile shields that form a global missile shield system surrounding Eurasia. The three theater segments of the missile shield are based in Europe, the Middle East, and East Asia. East Asia includes both Northeast Asia and Southeast Asia. Moreover, there are also overlapping zones that link the triad of missile shields. These are: (1) the Mediterranean, which links Europe and the Middle East; (2) the Indian Ocean, which links the Middle East and East Asia; and (3) North America.

North America acts as the strategic depth of this weapons system and in reality is the system's command center. The system is linked to North American missile defenses over the US, Canada, and Greenland. The North American continent also serves to augment the missile systems in both East Asia and Europe. While Iran has been cited as a justification for a missile shield in Europe, the location of military facilities in Greenland point elsewhere. Geographically, Greenland is not well-located to monitor any possible North Korean or Iranian missile threat. Rather, Greenland is ideal for monitoring any Russian missiles that would travel over the Arctic Circle as the most logical route to North America.

The European segment of the missile shield is primarily aimed at Russia, too. The US and NATO have been eagerly engaging Ukraine and Georgia to house facilities for the missile shield, as well as the Republic of Azerbaijan in the Caucasus; this has angered both Moscow and Tehran. The US and NATO are also looking at deploying the weapons system into the waters of the Black Sea and along the coasts of Bulgaria and Romania. The Middle Eastern portions of the missile shield are being erected in Israel, Turkey, and the Gulf Cooperation Council (GCC) countries of the Persian Gulf, hosted by countries like Saudi Arabia. The missile shield in the Middle East is aimed primarily at Iran and Syria. The establishment of a missile shield in Turkey will also attempt to provide the cover for an Israeli or US attack on Iran. Given this context, many voices in Turkey have been raised in opposition to Turkish participation in the NATO missile shield project. This includes the leader of the People's Voice Party of Turkey who has said that the missile shield project could lead to World War III.[19] The East Asian missile shield is aimed primarily at China under the pretext of being a defensive project against North Korea. It will be adjacent to China's heavily populated eastern provinces and the resource-rich Russian Far East. The work for creating it began in the 1990s when Tokyo and Washington launched a joint missile defense program. This Asiatic missile shield will be roughly located in South Korea, Japan, and Taiwan. Australia has also been working with the US and Japan.

There is also a drive to raise a missile shield in South Asia with India. This effectively means that Eurasia would be encircled by a ring of missile systems. Because of the nature of this Atlanticist project, Russia has been working closely with its allies in Kazakhstan, Belarus, and China on an anti-missile shield system. Iranian military officials have threatened to attack the missile shield in Turkey and denounced the GCC as US and Israeli pawns for housing a missile shield.[20] Like Iran, Russia has also threatened to attack the missile shield.[21] In 2011, there were also reports about the possibility of a combined response to the missile shield by China, Iran, and Russia. It was reported that the former Russian ambassador to NATO, Dmitry Rogozin, would visit Iran and China in 2012 to talk about jointly addressing the missile shield.[22] China has also developed a missile system that can destroy US and NATO satellites with the potential to counter any US space weapons.[23]

The Militarization of Space: From the New Iron Curtain back to Star Wars

The missile shield is not only made of radar facilities, Ground-based Mid-course Defense Segment (GMDS) systems, and Theater High Altitude Area Defense (THAAD) systems, it also has a large mobile naval component that involves ship-based Aegis missiles, airborne laser (ABL) components, and could ultimately lead to the militarization of space with space-based components. The multi-layered global missile shield system is tied into the militarization of space with plans for space-based interceptor (SBI) systems. Currently, the military application of space technology has been limited to spy satellites, communication systems, and the use of GPS.

Despite the differing rhetoric from successive US presidential administrations, the Pentagon and the US government never gave up Star Wars. Brzezinski puts it best when he says:

> As in chess, American global planners must think several moves ahead, anticipating possible countermoves. A sustainable geostrategy must therefore distinguish between the short-run perspective (the next five years), the middle term (up to twenty or so years), and the long run (beyond twenty years). Moreover these phases must be viewed not as watertight compartments but as part of a continuum. The first phase must gradually and consistently lead into the second—indeed, be deliberately pointed toward it—and the second must then lead subsequently into the third.[24]

What Brzezinski means is that US foreign policy works as a continuum and that each successive president continues the work of their predecessor. This process cuts across US party lines and concepts of left-wing and right-wing politics and public input into foreign policy via electoral processes. Democrats and Republicans alike serve the same objectives which are determined and shaped by largely ongoing bureaucracies, but represented publicly under the mirage of different political brands.

On March 23, 1983 Star Wars first came to life as a proposal by President Ronald Reagan called the Strategic Defense Initiative (SDI). SDI was part of the Reagan Administration's vision of a global missile shield based on the ground and in the sea and space. US Space Command (USSPACECOM) was created in 1985 by the Reagan White House as part of this vision. Even Cambridge University's military historian Philip Towle, who has made a supportive argument for the construction of the missile shield, admits that Reagan's proposal and the US missile project would violate the 1967 Outer Space Treaty and the 1972 Anti-Ballistic Missile (ABM) Treaty.[25] Despite this, every preceeding US presidential administration would continue the work towards establishing the missile shield. George H.W. Bush, Sr. would continue the program silently, President Clinton would rename it and assign it to the Ballistic Missile Defense Organization (BMDO), and finally George W. Bush, Jr. would execute the first phase of establishing the ground-based components of this system. Under the Obama Administration this work is continuing and branching out globally on land and at sea.

The involvement of the BMDO, which evolved from an agency that was responsible for the safety of US missile silos into a research and development body, meant one of two things. Firstly, that the military-industrial complex and arms manufacturers were expanding their horizons. Secondly, an agency was officially mandated with the US goal of using its inter-continental ballistic missiles (IBMs) for "theater-level defense," which means the Pentagon not only wanted missiles for defending the US but to develop the capacity to strike different parts, or "theaters," of the world in missile offensives using "hit-to-kill technology." One year after being mandated with SDI, the BMDO jointly launched the Deep Space Program Science Experiment spacecraft with the US National Aeronautics and Space Administration (NASA). In 2002, George W. Bush, Jr. would rename the agency as the Missile Defense Agency. US Space Command would also be merged into United States Strategic Command (USSTRATCOM/STRATCOM) in 2002. Three years later, the Joint Functional Component Command for Space and Global Strike (JFCC SGS) was formed inside STRATCOM. In the same year NATO started work on the ALTBMD.

Critics have said that the missile shield is impractical and will overall prove to be unusable. Even if components of it work during testing, it could fail in real circumstances just like the Patriot missiles defense system did against Iraq in 1991. Other critics point out that the project is meant to bamboozle the state treasury and taxpayers to the benefit of the military-industrial complex and powerful arms manufacturers. The earlier critique has also demobilized the level of opposition to the missile shield. Still more importantly, others critics point out that regardless of its operability, the missile shield will make the world much more unstable by creating an arms race. This of course will also benefit the defense contractors and powerful arms manufacturers in the military-industrial complex. All of these critiques may be correct, but the point should not be lost that if the Russians and their allies did not feel threatened they would not draw the lines in the sand that they have. Nor should it be forgotten that the door has been opened wide for the internationally illegal use of space for military applications.

MAP XIV: The Missile Shield Project

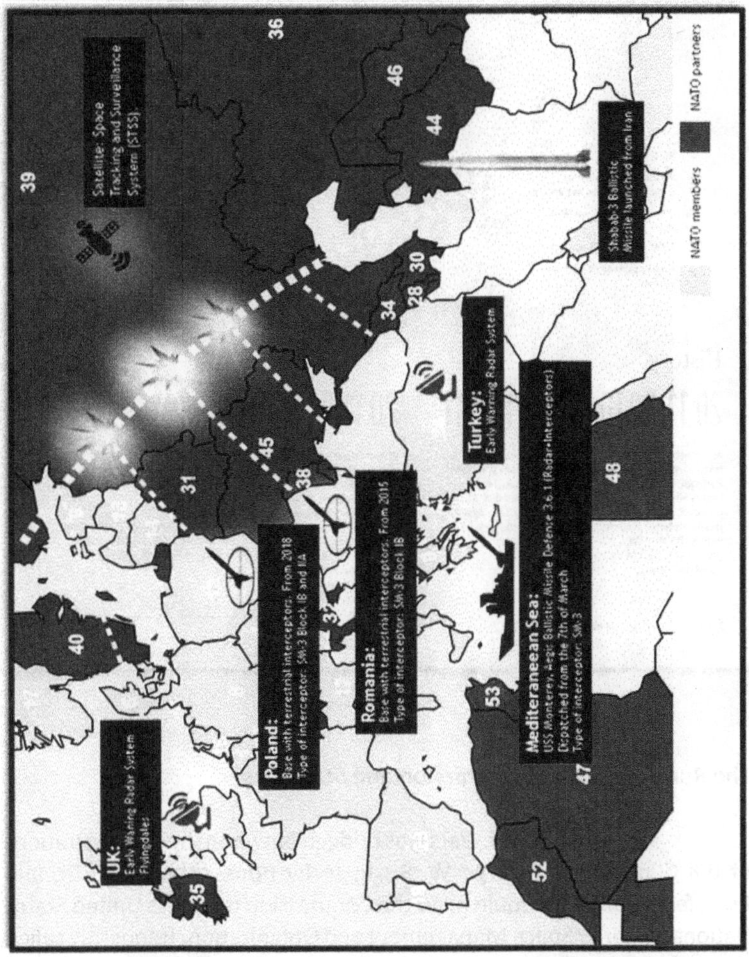

MAP XV

Russia's view of European missile shield

Deployment of a missile defense network in relative proximity to the Russian borders might affect the efficiency of the military application of Russia's strategic nuclear forces

NATO members   Russia

✗ Missile defense systems in the United States and Russia

Planned missile defense systems in Europe

✗ Radar   ✓ SM-3 missiles

✗ Russia's planned strike missile systems

On November 23, 2011, Medvedev outlined optional responses to the deployment of the missile defense system in Europe

Military measures

- Installation of a radar station in the Kaliningrad Region

- Stronger protection of the strategic nuclear facilities

- Equipping missiles with penetration aids

- Possible deployment of strike missile systems in the west and the south of the country. One of such options could be deployment of the Iskander ballistic missile system in the Kaliningrad Region

History

20.11.2010
At a meeting of the NATO-Russia Council in Portugal, President Dmitry Medvedev proposed forming a joint missile defense system with NATO, with its participants becoming equal partners

12.11.2011
After a meeting of U.S. and Russian presidents in Honolulu, Medvedev announced that the two countries have opposing views of the missile defense issue

20.11.2011
At a meeting with military officers of the Southern Military District in Vladikavkaz, the Russian president announced that the response to missile defense deployment plans would be reasonable and sufficient but it would not become an obstacle for further talks with NATO

Diplomatic measures

- Continuing negotiations on missile defense and practical cooperation with the NATO members

- Russia might refuse to continue disarmament in case of any negative developments

- Russia might exercise its right to withdraw from the Strategic Arms Reduction Treaty (START)

RIANOVOSTI ©2011 WWW.RIA.RU

The Rumsfeld Space Commission and Star Wars

The work for Star Wars was bridged between the administrations of Bill Clinton and George W. Bush, Jr. by none other than Donald Rumsfeld. Rumsfeld would head the Commission to Assess United States National Security Space Management and Organization, frequently called the Rumsfeld Space Commission or the Second Rumsfeld Commission. It was established under the Clinton Administration and did its work in 2000.

Rumsfeld would chair the commission from its inception until December 28, 2000, when he would be nominated for secretary of defense. The Space Commission would release its report on January 11, 2001. The report encouraged the US government to militarize space in league with missile defense, which would lead to the announcement of the unilateral withdrawal of the US from the ABM Treaty shortly after on December 13, 2001.[26] The Space Commission's 2001 report starts in an Orwellian fashion claiming that the United States faces the threat of an attack in space and the Pentagon must ensure that the US avoids a "Space Pearl Harbor."[27] Absurdly, the report goes on to pronounce:

> [W]e know from history that every medium—air, land and sea—has seen conflict. Reality indicates that space will be no different. Given this virtual certainty, [US forces] must develop the means both to deter and to defend against hostile acts in and from space. This will require superior space capabilities.[28]

The Space Commission makes no secret that the US must seek the militarization of space as a means of "projecting power" throughout the globe. The report makes this very clear:

> Finally, space offers advantages for basing systems intended to affect air, land and sea operations. Many think of space only as a place for passive collection of images or signals or a switchboard that can quickly pass information back and forth over long distances. It is also possible to project power through and from space in response to events anywhere in the world. Unlike weapons from aircraft, land forces or ships, space missions initiated from earth or space could be carried out with little transit, information or weather delay. Having this capability would give [Washington] a much stronger deterrent and, in a conflict, an extraordinary military advantage.[29]

The "extraordinary military advantage" that the Space Commission casually mentions is the basis for the global missile shield, which is part and parcel of the militarization of space. The ultimate objective is to establish full spectrum dominance by the US over all other countries. What is to guarantee that the space components of the missile shield that the Pentagon wants to develop would only be used to shoot down missiles and not shoot other things?

The aims of Star Wars are very clear to military commanders and leaders throughout the world. Among them is Vishnu Bhagwat. Bhagwat was one of the highest ranking flag officers in the Indian military and the former commander of the Indian Navy; he was dismissed because he refused to blindly follow orders from New Delhi. He has no doubts about the missile shield and Star Wars and what they mean. He has criticized Star Wars as an imperialist project for achieving global hegemony. Speaking about the militarization of space, Bhagwat has written:

> Encouraged by [the Commission to Assess United States National Security Space Management and Organization] which embraced the 'myth of a Space Pearl Harbour' and basing itself on the dubious interpretation that there is no blanket prohibition in [i]nternational law on placing or using weapons in Space, the [Rumsfeld Space Commission] Report also contained the revealing warning that the "US must be cautious of agreements intended for one purpose that when added to [...] treaties or conventions/regulations may have unintended consequences of restricting future activities in space." The US Space Command's Vision Document calls for dominating the Space dimension of military operations to protect US interests and investments. Vision 2020 is for dominating Earth from Space. Its operational concepts are;
> Control of Space.
> Global engagement.
> Full forces integration via information,
> surveillance, reconnaissance (ISR).
> Global partnerships/alliances.
> The US Space Command Vision 2020 document pursues the idea of a Global Area Strike system, of which a key element could be ground based high energy laser capability which bounces off space based mirrors, the placement of Directed Energy Weapons (DEW) and Kinetic Energy Weapons (KEW), soft kill jammers. The 4 yearly Quadrennial Defense Reviews, periodical NSSDs and Nuclear Posture Reviews, the latest of April 2010, are useful reference points for a detailed analysis of clues as to [the] intentions and plans.
> Far more important than any description of the types of weapons and weapon platforms planned for induction in Space, is that the Vision Document

emphasizes "the role of Space IN MANAGING THE GLOBAL ECONOMY....The Globalisation (read neo –imperialism/colonialism) of the world economy will also continue causing a widening gap between the 'haves' and the 'have-nots'.... The view is that by controlling Space and Earth below, the US (meaning the [corporations]) will be able to keep the 'Have-nots' in line."[30]

In 2004, signs of the US drive to militarize space became clearer. NASA transferred its space plane project to the Pentagon. There has been little said or revealed about this spacecraft, Boeing's X-37B. In 2003, NASA said this about the space planes:

As part of the X-37 project, the Boeing Company's Phantom Works division of Huntington Beach, Calif., is developing two vehicles: the X-37 Approach and Landing Test Vehicle and the X-37 Orbital Vehicle. These autonomous space planes, which have no crew, will play a key role in NASA's effort to dramatically reduce the cost of sending humans and payloads into space.[31]

Since the first and second tests of the X-37B, respectively in 2010 and 2011, the US Air Force has consistently insisted that the X-37 program is a purely scientific undertaking and a testing platform for new technologies. Two test flights have been made with the Orbital Test Vehicle One (OTV-1) and Orbital Test Vehicle Two (OTV-2). Aside from these plans there is a general fear that the space planes are being developed as dual civilian and military use technology that are components of an offensive space weaponry system.

Ruling the "International Commons" Militarily: Entering the Theater of the Absurd?

Not only is the Pentagon expanding the dimensions of its military capabilities into space, but it also aims at controlling and enclosing all the international commons. The commons are resources that are held or shared by all and include natural resources such as the air, common grazing grounds, fisheries, and culture.[32] The international commons now includes things such as the South Pole, internet, airwaves, and space. The PNAC outlines this as an aim by saying the Pentagon must: "CONTROL THE NEW 'INTERNATIONAL COMMONS' OF SPACE AND 'CYBERSPACE,' [sic.] and pave the way for the creation of a new military service—[United States] Space Forces—with the mission of space control."[33]

In what appears like a chapter from an outlandish science fiction novel, among these international commons, which include the world's international waters, the weather is something else that the Pentagon has actively been working to control. In 1996 a group of military officers released a report that was based on a study commissioned by the US Air Force about controlling the weather called *Weather as a Force Multiplier: Owning the Weather in 2025.* The 1996 report starts off by stating:

> In 2025, US aerospace forces can "own the weather" by capitalizing on emerging technologies and focusing development of those technologies to war-fighting applications. Such a capability offers the war fighter tools to shape the battlespace in ways never before possible. It provides opportunities to impact operations across the full spectrum of conflict and is pertinent to all possible futures. The purpose of this paper is to outline a strategy for the use of a future weather-modification system to achieve military objectives rather than to provide a detailed technical road map.
>
> A high-risk, high-reward endeavor, weather-modification offers a dilemma not unlike the splitting of the atom. While some segments of society will always be reluctant to examine controversial issues such as weather-modification, the tremendous military capabilities that could result from this field are ignored at our own peril. From enhancing friendly operations or disrupting those of the enemy via small-scale tailoring of natural weather patterns to complete dominance of global communications and counterspace control, weather-modification offers the war fighter a wide-range of possible options to defeat or coerce an adversary.[34]

Like the Space Commission report, the US Air Force's study also speaks in Orwellian terms about the need to militarize and develop weapons because others will do so. Does it cross the mind of these planners that their actions will instead cause militarization and new threats as a reaction? Genuine or otherwise, there is a psychological pattern of paranoia that exhibits itself in all these defense reports. Is this a reflection of their paranoia or the need to create fear in others in order to sell the project? Is this part of it the problem faced by all organizations—develop or die? If there is no next project, no next problem, no next threat, and no next war, then what need is there for them and their agencies or their budgets and staff? The 1996 study concludes:

History also teaches that we cannot afford to be without a weather-modification capability once the technology is developed and used by others. Even if we have no intention of using it, others will. To call upon the atomic weapon analogy again, we need to be able to deter or counter their capability with our own. Therefore, the weather and intelligence communities must keep abreast of the actions of others.

As the preceding chapters have shown, weather-modification is a force multiplier with tremendous power that could be exploited across the full spectrum of war-fighting environments. From enhancing friendly operations or disrupting those of the enemy via small-scale tailoring of natural weather patterns to complete dominance of global communications and counter-space control, weather-modification offers the war fighter a wide-range of possible options to defeat or coerce an adversary. But, while offensive weather modification efforts would certainly be undertaken by US forces with great caution and trepidation, it is clear that we cannot afford to allow an adversary to obtain an exclusive weather-modification capability.[35]

While Star Wars has been developed as a separate Pentagon project from the meteorological research work being conducted by the US military to "own the weather," the two are compartmentalized elements of the same military trend that the US and NATO are globally pursuing: full-spectrum dominance.

CHAPTER 10

NATO
AND AFRICA

As everybody is aware, the AU developed a political roadmap that would have assisted in resolving the political conflict in [Libya]. The AU's plan was completely ignored in favor of bombing Libya by NATO forces. The consequences of actions that were carried out in Libya in the name of the UN Security Council have spilled over into other countries in the region. A problem which was confined to one country, Libya, has now grown to be a regional problem [for Africa].
—South African President Jacob Zuma (2011)

NATO's Involvement in Africa in the New Millennium

The North Atlantic Treaty Organization's 2011 war on Libya is viewed as the epitome of the Alliance's activities in the African continent, but it was in fact merely the visible tip of the iceberg. Trans-Atlantic military operations and involvement inside Africa started years before NATO's war against the Libyan Arab Jamahiriya. Before Libya, Somalia and Sudan were geographic areas of major interest and involvement for the Atlantic Alliance, and even before that, Africa's waters were witnessing NATO naval expansion.

An Overview of NATO's African Operations before the Libyan War

From 2001 onward NATO has expanded its out-of-area operations further away from the Euro-Atlantic Zone, taking on naval missions in the Indian Ocean, which have included the navigating of African waterways by NATO warships. The Pentagon has been a major force behind this, as the establishment of the United States Africa Command (USAFRICOM or AFRICOM) in 2007 as a regional unified combatant command indicates.

Africa has witnessed the gradual expansion of NATO involvement in different forms and shapes. Officially, the process starts in the Mediterranean Sea—the frontier between Africa and the Euro-Atlantic Zone. Yet, as discussed in a previous chapter, NATO's Mediterranean Dialogue (MD) made inroads into North Africa after it was established in 1994 by the North Atlantic Council. Egypt, Mauritania, Morocco, and Tunisia—all African states—would join the Mediterranean Dialogue in 1995 followed lastly by the People's Democratic Republic of Algeria in 2000. A year after Algeria entered the Mediterranean Dialogue, Operation Active Endeavor would be launched by NATO leading to the establishment of a permanent NATO naval presence in the Eastern Mediterranean's waters starting in October 2001, which directly involved the monitoring of African waters and the maritime traffic exiting from the Red Sea into the Mediterranean Sea. Later Operation Active Endeavor would be expanded to encompass the entire Mediterranean; NATO and Moroccan warships would officially begin to jointly monitor the Pillars of Hercules or Strait of Gibraltar, which separate the Kingdom of Morocco in the African continent from the Kingdom of Spain in Europe.

Two years after fighting erupted in Sudan's Darfur region in 2003, the Sudanese would see NATO operations on their soil. This was the start of NATO's first mission on African soil. Khartoum was able to resist NATO's insistence on deploying Bosnia-style peacekeepers on its territory, but had to bitterly accept NATO cooperation with the African Union (AU). Since 2005, NATO's operations in Africa have included training, communications, air surveillance, military transport, and anti-piracy missions in the continent. The AU's forces are increasingly falling under NATO influence.

Just as Operation Active Endeavor branched out from the Eastern Mediterranean to cover the entire Mediterranean, it has further allowed NATO to operate in the South Atlantic, including the Gulf of Guinea. In 2007, a flotilla of NATO warships—Standing NATO Maritime Group One (SNMG1), formerly known as Standing Naval Force Atlantic (STANAVFORLANT)—made a historic voyage around the entire African continent. Overseeing NATO naval deployments in the Red Sea and Arabian Sea, the NATO voyage around Africa was considered by NATO officers as the first *true* out-of-area naval deployment for the Atlantic Alliance.[1] Lieutenant-Commander Angus Topshee, the commanding officer of the Canadian vessel HMCS Toronto deployed with SNMG1, implied that it was a sign of things to come.[2]

In the same year that NATO circumnavigated Africa, it also formally got involved in Somalia. Since June 2007, the Atlantic Alliance has played a supervisory role over the AU in Somalia. This took place against the backdrop of the US-engineered Ethiopian military invasion of

Somalia, which took place in 2006 with direct US participation. The next year, after NATO formally became involved on the ground in Somalia, the Alliance launched Operation Allied Provider. The operation was categorized as both an anti-piracy and a humanitarian mission revolving around Somalia. It also escorted an African Union vessel with AU troops into Somalia. Operation Allied Protector continued the same operations off the Horn of Africa and in the Gulf of Aden in 2009 only to be followed by Operation Ocean Shield.

Moreover, NATO forces have been involved in human intelligence observation missions in Africa. The objective of these missions is to understand how to rally and instigate African societies to destabilize the continent's countries and ouster their governments and leaders, should they prove unreceptive to US and EU interests. These missions have certainly not been limited to Africa, and most probably target all countries outside of the Euro-Atlantic Zone.

NATO's Involvement in Sudan

The Republic of Sudan has been targeted by Atlanticists since its independence. This was first done by London and then carried on by Washington and Tel Aviv. The process started with carving Sudan out of Egypt:

> [T]he balkanization project in Sudan has been going on since the end of British colonial rule in Anglo-Egyptian Sudan. Sudan and Egypt were one country during many different periods. Both Egypt and Sudan were also one country in practice until 1956.
>
> Up until the independence of Sudan, there was a strong movement to keep Egypt and Sudan united as a single Arab state, which was struggling against British interests. London, however, fuelled Sudanese regionalism against Egypt in the same manner that regionalism has been at work in South Sudan against the rest of Sudan. The Egyptian government was depicted in the same way as present-day Khartoum. Egyptians were portrayed as exploiting the Sudanese just as the non-Southern Sudanese have been portrayed as exploiting the South Sudanese.
>
> After the British invasion of Egypt and Sudan, the British also managed to keep their troops stationed in Sudan. Even while working to divide Sudan from Egypt, the British worked to create internal differentiations

between South Sudan and the rest of Sudan. This was done through the Anglo-Egyptian Condominium, from 1899 to 1956, which forced Egypt to share Sudan with Britain after the Mahdist Revolts. Eventually the Egyptian government would refuse to recognize the Anglo-Egyptian Condominium as legal. Cairo continuously asked the British to end their illegal military occupation of Sudan and to stop preventing the re-integration of Egypt and Sudan, but the British refused.

It would be under the presence of British troops that Sudan declared itself independent. This is what led to the emergence of Sudan as a separate Arab and African state from Egypt.[3]

This process of balkanization has continued. Ethnic identity and faith were used to achieve the secession of South Sudan from the rest of the country on July 9, 2011. Despite the fact that all Sudanese are Africans and predominantly black-skinned and the objections of many ethnologists, the conflict has been misleadingly portrayed for popular consumption as a conflict between "Black Africans" and "formerly slaveholding Arabs".

When fighting broke out in Darfur in 2003, NATO was eager to get its boots on the ground. Atlantic Alliance leaders were becoming increasingly vocal about Darfur and major lobbying efforts and public campaigns were underway for military intervention under the pretext of humanitarianism. Hollywood movie actors like George Clooney were recruited to demand an end to "genocide" in Darfur. A NATO intervention similar to that unleashed on Libya in 2011 could very likely have happened to Sudan from approximately 2005 to 2007. Many of the same voices that called for intervention in Libya during 2011 did the exact same thing for Sudan in previous years. From 2004 onward these calls for US and NATO intervention were made under the banner of the "Responsibility to Protect" (R2P) doctrine. In May 2005, Madeline Albright and a group from the Aspen Institute stated:

> The fundamental cause of the humanitarian cata-
> strophe in Darfur is, at best, the failure of the
> government of Sudan to take effective action against
> the militias terrorizing civilians, and at worst, its active
> complicity and support in these activities. Sudan has
> demonstrated that it lacks both the will and capacity
> to protect its own people, and therefore we believe

the international community, consistent with the
emerging international norm of the "Responsibility to
Protect," must act in this glaring case of genocide and
do whatever is necessary to halt the killing and abuse
of innocent civilians.[4]

Via African leaders, the Atlantic Alliance and its leaders did manage
to secure a role for themselves in Sudan in 2005. This was a historic
moment, because NATO officially stepped on African soil. According to
the NATO narrative:

On 26 April 2005, the AU asked NATO to consider the
possibility of providing logistical support to help expand
its peace-support mission in Darfur. In May 2005, the
Chairman of the AU Commission, Mr. Alpha Oumar
Konaré, visited NATO Headquarters—the first ever visit
of an AU official to NATO HQ—to provide details of the
assistance request. The next day, the North Atlantic
Council tasked the Alliance's military authorities to
provide, as a matter of urgency, advice on possible
NATO support.

Following further consultations with the African
Union, the European Union and the United Nations,
in June 2005, NATO formally agreed to provide airlift
support as well as training. The first planes carrying
AU peacekeepers took off on 1 July of the same year.
Training of AU officers started on 1 August and, a few
days later, the North Atlantic Council agreed to assist
in the transport of police to Darfur.[5]

Thus, NATO actively became involved in the AU mission in Darfur
starting on June 1, 2005. 37,000 AU personnel would be transported
by NATO for the Darfur mission from its start until December 31, 2007.
In parallel to NATO's actions in Darfur, the US government managed to
broker the Comprehensive Peace Agreement in South Sudan that would
effectively lead to the division of Sudan.

The Alliance's involvement in Darfur did not start as mere
assistance, though; it started as a NATO "stewardship" of the AU, as
George W. Bush, Jr. referred to it later in 2006. The AU was projected as
incompetent to act on its own and needing the guidance and management
of NATO as a principal—thus also enabling the "stewards" to ensure that
the AU kept "on mission" with Atlanticist interests. NATO's mission in
Sudan took on more than just taxiing soldiers and logistical support; aside

from training, it included the overseeing of the forces of the AU. According to NATO, over 250 African Union Mission in Sudan (AMIS) personnel have been trained by the Atlantic Alliance. Despite having a NATO presence in Darfur, the Atlantic Alliance wanted broader involvement in Sudan and still did not let go of the idea of using R2P. A widely publicized discussion among the Alliance, the EU, and UN led the White House to start demanding NATO do more in Sudan.[6] *The New York Times* reported on February 19, 2006:

> NATO is coming under increasing pressure from the Bush administration to play a much bigger role in Sudan, with President George W. Bush telephoning the NATO secretary general, Jaap de Hoop Scheffer, during the weekend and U.S. senators lobbying NATO to support efforts to stop the war, starvation and abuse of human rights.[7]

The Atlantic Alliance also pushed for further internationalization of the situation in Darfur and for handing the issue over from the African Union to the United Nations. In the words of Lieutenant-Colonel Carpenter, the Pentagon spokesperson at the time, the hope was that "NATO could potentially be a significant leader" in the UN mission, replacing the African Union.[8] Despite the mixed signals about peacekeeping, an attack on Sudan was also foreseen and hinted at in the public discourse that took place about Darfur.[9] "There has to be a consequence for people abusing their fellow citizens," Bush, Jr. would declare, touting the R2P script that the US and its allies, as well as a series of NGOs, were attempting to use against Sudan.[10] NATO military intervention against Sudan, however, was riding on what would happen at UN Headquarters in New York City:

> NATO said it would be placed in an extremely difficult situation if the United Nations agreed to impose a no-flight zone in Darfur that would require the assistance of NATO to enforced [*sic*.].
>
> "Which NATO country would be willing to shoot down a Sudanese plane?" the diplomat said. "Let's see what the UN and Washington asks the alliance."
>
> James Appathurai, a NATO spokesman, said the alliance had not yet been formally asked to play a bigger role in Sudan.
>
> "We will have to see what happens over the coming days," he said Sunday."In the meantime, we are continuing to airlift soldiers from the African Union into

Sudan. We are also involved in training for a mission
that is led by the African Union."[11]

Khartoum was very much alarmed by what NATO leaders were
saying and the increasing talk about no-fly zones, genocide, and R2P. The
Sudanese government vigorously opposed any further role for NATO,
threatening to fight the Atlantic Alliance should it replace African Union
soldiers, and accused NATO's leaders of looking for a pretext to attack
Sudan. The Sudanese government made it clear that it would consider
NATO forces as foreign invaders who were out to plunder Sudan's
national resources. Sudanese Second Vice-President Ali Osman Taha
hailed Lebanon's Hezbollah guerrilla war against Israel and said that
Sudan would follow its model of resistance against NATO.[12] Both China
and Russia also opposed the Atlantic Alliance's plans at the UN Security
Council. A compromise was reached and it was decided that in 2008 the
mission in Darfur would jointly be managed by the UN and AU. Therefore,
the African Union Mission in Sudan (AMIS) ended on December 31, 2007
and was replaced on January 1, 2008 by the mixed police and military
force of the United Nations-African Union Mission in Darfur (UNAMID)
or more commonly called the UN-AU Hybrid Operation in Darfur—the
world's largest peacekeeping operation.[13]

Sudan and the Geo-Politics of Intervention

Sudan stood as the largest country in Africa with a total area
of 967,500 square miles (2,505,813 square kilometers) before South
Sudan's referendum and separation in 2011.[14] The country's immense
geographic size has been matched by a considerable amount of minerals
and other natural resources. Oil, gas, gold, silver, copper, chromium,
iron, mica, silver, uranium, aluminum, tungsten, and zinc are spread
throughout the vast country and mostly unexploited. Sudan's territory
has seen very limited exploration and its mineral wealth has mostly gone
untapped because it is predominantly agrarian with the majority of people
working in the farming and livestock sectors. The US Energy Information
Administration (EIA) noted that in 2009 oil was Sudan's main source of
revenue, comprising more than 90% of Sudan's foreign earnings, up from
EIA's estimate of 70% in 2007.[15] Khartoum's oil exports only started in
1999 and it has the largest oil reserves in sub-Saharan Africa after Angola
and Nigeria.[16] These factors make Sudan a fairly large economic prize.

Because of China's economic and geo-strategic interests,
Russia and China have jointly opposed US, UK, and French efforts to
internationalize the domestic problems of Sudan at the UN Security
Council. Sudanese oil is mostly bought by the China National Petroleum

Corporation (CNPC). Khartoum's energy sector is tied to China through the CNPC. CNPC has the largest stakes in Sudan, followed by Malaysia's Petroliam Nasional Berhad (PETRONAS) and India's Oil and Natural Gas Corporation Limited (ONGC). The European Coalition on Oil in Sudan, a Netherlands-based lobbyist group, reported in 2007:

> CNPC, Petronas and ONGC account for over 90% of Sudan's total output. Not only are these companies important to Sudan, Sudan is also important to them. For each of them, Sudan will be the largest overseas operation in 2007, substantially so for both Petronas and ONGC. And their Sudanese assets are highly profitable. They are not very likely to offer opportunities for newcomers to farm in on their existing assets. They are mostly state-owned and their investment decisions are made at a country level rather than a company level, making them resistant to shareholder activism. While, at a global level, Sudan is a minor oil producing and exporting country, China, India and Malaysia have invested billions of dollars in the country, also outside the oil industry. They consider their relations with the country not only as economic, but also geostrategic and energy-strategic successes that are worth defending.[17]

It should be of little wonder why the US and Atlantic Alliance are so deeply interested in the "security" of Sudan, well outside the Euro-Atlantic Zone. Sudan is being carved up because of its resources and Washington's project to contain the Chinese. This should explain Atlanticist animosity towards Sudan's government. In a break from international norms, the Obama White House even endorsed the division of Sudan before the US-brokered plebiscite on the issue took place.[18] Throughout 2010 members of the Obama Administration continuously met with Sudanese leaders and went to Sudan to make sure that the anticipated referenda would take place. Speaking before the division of Sudan, Konstantin Simonov, the director of the National Energy Security Foundation in Russia, explained:

> US President Obama has promised to recognize the new state in the near future. Other large countries will follow suit. One of the reasons for this policy is the presence of energy resources. US and other large Western companies are interested in getting their hands on them, hence Washington's readiness

to recognize South Sudan. China is traditionally demonstrating its interest, as it has always been a very active player in Africa. In recent years, China has spent a few billion dollars investing in oil and gas extraction in Africa because China is experiencing a growing shortage of energy supplies.[19]

It is due to Sudan's business ties to China that Sudanese leaders have been targeted by the US and EU as human rights violators, while the human rights records of dictators that are US clients in places like Bahrain and Saudi Arabia are ignored. Despite the compromise at the UN and the establishment of the UN-AU Hybrid Operation in Darfur, the Atlanticists kept on pushing for additional intervention in the African country. In 2008, the International Criminal Court accused Sudan's President Omar Al-Bashir of "genocide, crimes against humanity and war crimes in Darfur."[20] The ICC's involvement was mandated in 2005 through UN Security Council Resolution 1593. In regard to the Darfur case, a 2008 ICC press release stated:

> ICC Prosecutor Luis Moreno-Ocampo has presented evidence today showing that Sudanese President, Omar Hassan Ahmad AL BASHIR committed the crimes of genocide, crimes against humanity and war crimes in Darfur.
> Three years after the Security Council requested him to investigate in Darfur, and based on the evidence collected, the Prosecutor has concluded there are reasonable grounds to believe that Omar Hassan Ahmad AL BASHIR bears criminal responsibility in relation to 10 counts of genocide, crimes against humanity and war crimes.
> The Prosecution evidence shows that Al Bashir masterminded and implemented a plan to destroy in substantial part the Fur, Masalit and Zaghawa groups, on account of their ethnicity. Members of the three groups, historically influential in Darfur, were challenging the marginalization of the province; they engaged in a rebellion. AL BASHIR failed to defeat the armed movements, so he went after the people. "His motives were largely political. His alibi was a 'counterinsurgency.' His intent was genocide."[21]

On March 9, 2009 the Pre-Trail Chamber of the ICC issued

a warrant for the arrest of Field Marshal Al-Bashir. Shortly after the warrant was issued, the Speaker of the Iranian Parliament Ali Larijani led an international parliamentary delegation to Khartoum in support of Sudan's embattled president. The arrest warrant was widely snubbed by non-NATO countries as being politically motivated. The African Union, the Arab League, China, India, Iran, Malaysia, Russia, Bolivia, Venezuela, and most of the world's states rejected it or refused to honor it. Nor did Atlantic Alliance leaders fully pursue the matter against President Al-Bashir. The warrant seems to have been simultaneously a pressure tactic to force the Sudanese government to acquiesce to their country's dismantlement and held as a tool for possible intervention in the future.

In varying degrees Khartoum has been forced to acquiesce to Sudanese dismemberment, but there is far more to Sudan's story. For years weapons were funneled into South Sudan and Darfur by NATO powers and Israel. In addition, their Ethiopian and Ugandan allies have played important roles in the siege against Khartoum by supporting two decades of fighting in South Sudan. At the same time, starting in the late-1990s, when oil began being exported, Sudan started implementing the neoliberal reforms imposed by the International Monetary Fund (IMF) and World Bank that have helped amplify the economic dimensions of the grievances in Darfur and South Sudan. While there is a humanitarian crisis in Darfur, the underlying causes of the conflict have been manipulated and distorted. This is intimately related to international economic and strategic interests and not to ethnic cleansing. The US and its allies have had great involvement in the fighting and instability of Sudan just as they were involved in the Angolan Civil War through their support of Apartheidist South Africa, UNITA, and the FLNA against Angola's MPLA. Washington and its allies have assisted in the training, financing, and arming of the militias and forces opposed to the Sudanese government. They lay blame squarely on Khartoum's shoulders for any of the violence in Sudan while they themselves fuel conflict in order to move in.

Israel's Involvement in Sudan

While Israel complains about Iranian arms shipments for the Palestinians going through Sudan, Tel Aviv has a track record of sending weapons to Sudan's opposition groups and separatist movements. According to the American Jewish Committee, Sudan's rebels reached out to Israel in the 1960s.[22] Its account is that "Israel-South Sudan interactions began as early as the late 1960s, when leaders of the Sudanese Peoples Liberation Army, waging an insurrection against the North from the South, and impressed by Israel's victory in the 1967 Six-Day War, reached out to Jerusalem."[23] The American Jewish Committee is actually spelling out a romanticized story, which is contradicted by Israeli sources which say that contacts started a decade earlier and were based on Israel's intent to divide Sudan. According to former Israeli cabinet minister Avi Dichter, Tel Aviv has wanted to balkanize Sudan since the 1950s. In 2008 he told the Israeli Institute for National Security Studies: "Israel had to penetrate the Sudanese arena to exacerbate existing crises and foment new ones."[24] Israeli arms entered Sudan from Ethiopia for years until Eritrea became independent from Ethiopia, which then lost its Red Sea coast, leading to bad relations with the Eritreans. Since then Israeli weapons have been entering South Sudan from Kenya. Israel's allies, the Sudan People's Liberation Movement (SPLM) in South Sudan, helped transfer these arms into Darfur. The Uganda People's Defense Force (UPDF) has also sent arms to both the militias in Darfur and the SPLM. Most of this is also confirmed by Moshe Fergie, a retired Mossad major-general, who categorizes Israeli intervention in Sudan under five phases: (1) the delivery of Israeli humanitarian aid in the 1950s; (2) providing training to Sudanese rebels in Ethiopia in the early-1960s; (3) providing weapons shipments from the mid-1960s up until the 1970s; (4) providing backing for Colonel John Garang de Mabior; (5) and delivering heavy weaponry into Sudan via Kenya and Ethiopia starting in the late-1990s.[25] Israel also had contacts with Sudan's anti-government forces via the US and the NGO sector. The American Jewish Committee, which itself has worked to further Israeli interests in the US and globally, used its Africa Institute to nurture direct connections between the Israeli government and South Sudan.[26]

The ties between Israel and the Sudan People's Liberation Movement are no secret. On March 5, 2008 it was reported that the SPLM had offices in Israel and that the anti-government forces in Darfur had also opened offices earlier.[27] SPLM members and supporters regularly visited Israel. Their leader, Salva Kiir Mayardit, who was also one of Sudan's vice-presidents under the country's power sharing arrangement, had also repeatedly said that South Sudan would recognize Israel when it separated from the rest of Sudan. As part of Khartoum's efforts to facilitate peace in South Sudan, Sudan even removed the Sudanese passport restriction on visiting Israel in late-2009 to appease the SPLM.[28]

After South Sudan's independence, Salva Kiir Mayardit acknowledged Israel's key role in a low-profile visit to Israel on December 19, 2011, stating: "Israel has always supported the South Sudanese people. Without [Israel], we would not have arisen. You struggled alongside us in order to allow the establishment of South Sudan and we are interested in learning from your experience."[29] The SPLM has now opened South Sudan's door to Israel and its allies as foreign investors. One Israeli newspaper had this to say:

There is a "tremendous" amount of money to be made helping the nascent state of South Sudan get off the ground, an Israeli businessman told *The Jerusalem Post* on Monday.

Meir Greiver, 73, said the sky is the limit to the moneymaking potential of the world's youngest country, and founded the South Sudan Development Company, LTD in March [2011] in order to grease the wheels for Israeli businessmen looking to invest in the country.[30]

Israeli businessmen also see South Sudan as an abundant source of cheap labor. To quote Meir Greiver: "[B]ecause the salaries are so very low, I think that many Israeli businessmen who send their manufacturing and textile work to China could do it there instead."[31]

Neoliberal South Sudan: A New NATO Outpost?

The economic exploitation of South Sudan is not in Israeli hands alone. The hotels of Juba, South Sudan's capital city, have been filled by an army of foreigners: "oil analysts, government advisors, workers for charitable organizations and freelance journalists, waiting expectantly, like birth attendants in a delivery room, to see whether the newborn will live or die."[32] What has been taking place, even before South Sudan's independence, is a process of gradual colonization tied to Sudan's overall neoliberal reforms that started in conjunction with its exportation of petroleum. This development has included the arrival of US and EU companies after 2005. Major land grabs by private companies from the US and elsewhere have taken place:

A baseline report on land deals in South Sudan, published by the Norwegian People's Aid (NPA) in March 2011, found that nine percent of the country has been sought or acquired by private interests. The report suggests that the government consider a temporary ban on large-scale land acquisition projects until institutions are better established. In response to the report, Robert Ladu Loki, head of the South Sudan Land Commission, said the investors' contracts will be investigated. Regardless of the kind of development that occurs, there is no doubt that the effects on local communities will be considerable, and that US investors are intimately involved.[33]

These deals are an example of predatory capitalism at work as can be assessed by reading the points of the following land deal:

> The largest land deal in South Sudan to date was negotiated between a Dallas, Texas-based firm, Nile Trading and Development Inc. (NTD) and Mukaya Payam Cooperative in March 2008. The 49-year land lease of 600,000 hectares (with a possibility of 400,000 additional hectares) for 75,000 Sudanese Pounds (equivalent to approximately USD 25,000), allows NTD full rights to exploit all natural resources in the leased land. These include:
>
> - Right to develop, produce and exploit timber/ forestry resources on the leased land, including, without limitation, the harvesting of current tree growth, the planting and harvesting of hardwood trees, and the development of wood-based industries;
> - Right to trade and profit from any resulting carbon credits from timber on the leased land;
> - Right to engage in agricultural activities, including the cultivation of biofuel crops (jatropha plant and palm oil trees);
> - Right to explore, develop, mine, produce and/or exploit petroleum, natural gas, and other hydrocarbon resources for both local and export markets, as well as other minerals, and may also engage in power generation activities on the leased land;
> - Right to sublease any portion or all of the leased land or to sublicense any right to undertake activities on the leased land to third parties.
>
> In addition, the Cooperative agrees to not oppose the undertaking of any such activities by NTD on the leased land and to cooperate with the company in any efforts to obtain more concessions from the government of South Sudan. [34]

In the above deal the Mukaya Payam Cooperative essentially signed away all the rights of the local population and community. The Texas-based company is free to exploit all the land's resources and essentially owns everything. Moreover, the deal was illegal since it was signed before South Sudan became an independent country, but the new SPLM-led government in Juba has been more than happy to accommodate foreign investors. Therefore Juba has endorsed the deal.[35]

These business deals giving away South Sudan's land and resources to foreign companies are actually being made by a minority. This minority, usually tied to the upper echelons of the SPLM and the new governing elite in Juba, has taken advantage of the young country's lack of regulations and lawlessness. The case of the land deal with Nile Trading and Development is a case in point:

> The Agency for Independent Media (AIM), a South Sudanese civil society organization that issued a report on the Nile Trading investment in 2010, asserts that [the Mukaya Payam Cooperative] is a "fictitious cooperative" comprised of "a group of influential natives from Mukaya Payam" who leased the land to Nile Trading without the knowledge of the community." In fact, the three individuals Scopas Loduo Onje, Samuel Tabani Youziel, and Vincent Kujo who are identified as members of the Cooperative are all blood-related.[36]

Even under these conditions the authorities in South Sudan have looked the other way in many cases. The foremost victims of all this are the people of South Sudan who were constantly told that all their woes were completely Khartoum's fault and led astray by racial politics and ethno-nationalism. Since the independence of South Sudan many of its people have realized that they were misled by their leaders. The journalist, Robyn Dixon, describes the situation like this:

> Long marginalized by the Sudanese government in Khartoum, the southern part of the country was one of the most destitute, least developed places on Earth, with just a few miles of paved road. But last year's peaceful secession sparked a surge of hope among South Sudanese. With their own flag, their own government, their own oil, they would build a decent country.
>
> Instead, the government has taken the well-worn path of many other rebels-turned-leaders. Corruption and nepotism are pervasive, public services are negligible, and on a recent visit to Juba there was more evidence of demolition than of reconstruction.[37]

Mixed with capitalist venture in Juba is mayhem and violence. The Republic of South Sudan actually had its birth marked by a series of killings that virtually went unnoticed by the US and NATO:

> The death toll from a cattle raid in an eastern region of
> weeks-old South Sudan rose significantly on Monday
> with the United Nations saying more than 600 people
> had been killed in what was a retaliatory attack that
> has raised fears of ethnic instability on the deeply
> impoverished country.
> [...]
> In a statement, the United Nations said that up to
> 30,000 head of cattle had been stolen and that it was
> investigating the possibility that as many as 200 people
> had been abducted, making it one of the largest attacks
> in recent memory. The statement called for an end to
> the "wanton violence" in the region.[38]

Right after the massacre, Benedict Sannoh, the UN's human
rights chief in South Sudan, was brutally beaten by the South Sudanese
police.[39] Sannoh was beaten after he refused to let the South Sudanese
police check his luggage.[40] In that month there was a clampdown on
human rights organizations or anyone investigating the wave of violence
that had started in South Sudan. Reprisals began and clashes between
the SPLM's militia and other militias took place in different parts of the
country.[41] By the end of 2011, human rights activists in South Sudan
warned that if the fighting between the militias and different tribes
was not stopped, South Sudan could see a genocide take place.[42] All
this time the US, NATO, and the political leaders of the Atlantic Alliance
remained silent—in marked contrast to their vocal positions on Darfur,
a clear indicator that their Atlanticist interests drive NATO's so-called
"humanitarian concerns."

The Obama Administration prepared to dispatch US military
forces into South Sudan in October 2011 when President Obama revealed
that the Pentagon was going to send US combat troops into Uganda to
fight the Lord's Resistance Army and track down its leader, Joseph Kony.[43]
In time, there will be further deployments to South Sudan, the Central
African Republic (CAR), and the Democratic Republic of Congo (Congo-
Brazzaville).[44] The extent of the Pentagon's presence in the area has been
kept under wraps, because large numbers of US personnel and contractors
were already on the ground predating Obama's announcement, numbering
in the thousands. What the US is actually doing is securing an important
future oil hub that extends from South Sudan to the African Great Lakes.

Sailing Africa's Atlantic Coast:
Prelude to South Atlantic Expansion by NATO?

NATO's activities in the waters of Africa and the South Atlantic are viewed with suspicion and anxiety by critics of the Atlantic Alliance. When the voyage of SNMG1 was made, they asked on what grounds NATO gave itself the responsibility of monitoring the African coast and whether NATO members planned to make future claims in the southern waters of Africa and the South Atlantic. In summary, the NATO naval presence was seen as an encroachment by the Alliance.

The Atlantic Alliance is following in the footsteps of the Pentagon in many ways. While NATO had already started operations in Africa's eastern waters, from the coasts of Tanzania and Somalia to the Red Sea, the deployment in the South Atlantic did not go unnoticed in South America by Argentina and Brazil.[45] Since the discovery of large energy reserves in the South Atlantic there have been rising tensions between South America and Atlantic Alliance members. The most noteworthy case is that of the tensions between Argentina and the UK. These South American countries also object to any reference to NATO as the *Atlantic Alliance*, insisting on calling it, as indeed is more accurate, the "North Atlantic Alliance." This is one of the reasons that Venezuelan President Hugo Chavez proposed forming a South Atlantic Treaty Organization (SATO), an alliance mirroring NATO, between Latin American and African countries in 2009.

South Atlantic energy reserves are arguably the motivation for the Pentagon's reactivation of the United States Fourth Fleet in 2008. The US Fourth Fleet had actually been disbanded in 1960. Its area of responsibility was and still is the Caribbean Sea and Latin America's South Atlantic and South Pacific waters. Brazil and other Latin American countries have not reacted favorably to Washington's moves. They do not want NATO in their waters either. In 2009, Brazilian Defense Minister Nelson Jobim complained to Washington about the reactivation of the US Fourth Fleet.[46] This has been followed by more Brazilian protests. In 2010, the government of Brazil openly told NATO to stay in the North Atlantic and not to deploy its warships into the South Atlantic where it had no business.[47]

The Roots of Somalia's Civil War

Before the Atlantic Alliance's presence and operations in Somalia and the Horn of Africa can be discussed, the events that led to the Somalian Civil War must be reviewed. The roots of the internal fighting of 1991 arose from more than just discontent with the military regime in Mogadishu. The legacy of the colonial division of Somalia by the imperialist powers, Britain, France, and Italy—three of the original founding members of NATO in 1949—and Mogadishu's *realpolitik* Cold War alliance with the United States during the Somali Democratic

Republic's Ogaden War with neighboring Ethiopia are two critical factors. These two factors are integrally connected to the chain of events that would result in the spiral of violence in the Horn of Africa and the eventual deployment of NATO forces into the geo-strategically important region. Before the Second World War the Somali people had been divided under the colonial boundaries of Britain, Italy, and France. The Ogaden region had also been ceded to the Abyssinian or Ethiopian Empire in 1897 by the British while southwest Somali lands were incorporated into British-ruled Kenya as the Northern Frontier District, which would later be renamed as the North Eastern Province by the Kenyans. Aside from the Ogaden in Abyssinia or Ethiopia and the Northern Frontier District in Kenya, the names of these different Somali entities were British Somaliland, Italian Somaliland, and French Somaliland. During the Second World War, the British would conquer Italian Somaliland and advance into Italian-occupied Ethiopia in 1941. This would put both Italian Somaliland and the Ogaden under British military control. After the defeat of the Italians, London reluctantly evacuated its army from Ethiopian territory and recognized Ethiopia as a sovereign state. British troops continued to occupy Eritrea and the Ogaden on the grounds that they were not considered territories of the Ethiopian Empire. In 1948, however, Britain returned the Ogaden to Ethiopia. The UN also allowed Italy to administer Italian Somaliland as the UN Trust Territory of Somalia.

As the African colonies of Western Europe started becoming independent, British Somaliland and the UN Trust Territory of Somalia united as Somalia or officially the Somali Republic on July 1, 1960. Paris obstructed the unification of French Somaliland with the other Somali entities, ultimately leaving it in 1977 to become independent as the Republic of Djibouti. The prevention of Somali unity has never been forgotten in the collective memory of most the Somalis, for whom Greater Somalia had long been a vision and an aspiration. Somalia's flag represents this: the five points of the white star represent the Somali people scattered in British Somaliland, Djibouti, Italian Somaliland, the Ogaden in Ethiopia, and Kenya's North Eastern Province.

Pan-Somalism was highly popular at the time of Somalia's birth during the Cold War. This led to support for the Western Somali Liberation Front against Ethiopia by the Somali Democratic Republic, which was formed when Major-General Mohammed Siad Barre and the Supreme Revolutionary Council took over Somalia in a coup on October 21, 1969. The Supreme Revolutionary Council, which would later evolve into the Somali Revolutionary Socialist Party, officially championing national policies formed on the bases of Islam, pan-Somalism, and socialism. They would also align Mogadishu with the Soviets and Eastern Bloc in the Cold War. Herein lies the crux of the matter:

Attempts to achieve greater Somali union with the Somalis of the Ethiopian Ogaden were to involve Somalia in protracted and bitter warfare with Ethiopia for much of the 1970s. Initially the Somali government had been able to count on strong Soviet backing in its war with Ethiopia. But following the overthrow of Emperor Haile Selassie in 1974, the Soviet Union switched sides [in 1977] and poured military aid into the Marxist regime of Brigadier Mengistu Haile Mariam.[48]

Moscow was initially allied to both Ethiopia and Somalia and wanted their differences on the Ogaden resolved, but when Mogadishu refused to let go of its claims the Soviets stopped supporting the Somali Democratic Republic. Many socialist and communist states from Cuba to the People's Democratic Republic of Yemen (South Yemen) began to put their support behind the Ethiopians against Somalia. This included Cuban troops that were dispatched into Ethiopia by Havana to aid Addis Ababa. Major-General Mohammed Siad Barre was furious with the Kremlin and cut his ties with the Soviets. He insisted that Moscow had turned its back on Somalia, because Somalia would not listen to Soviet commands by surrendering its national interests to Ethiopia. His reaction to the Soviet move would be to realign Mogadishu with the United States as a counterweight to Moscow's support for Ethiopia. Hence, inversely, the US was kicked out of Ethiopia in 1977, but in its place began to establish a foothold in Somalia. In the end Mogadishu would lose the war, but its new Cold War alliance with Washington would prove to be much more fatal, with a direct bearing on the future breakdown of the African country.

The US began to arm Somalia in 1978, not to help per se, but as a deliberate tactic to prevent any rapprochement between Moscow and Mogadishu.[49] The US National Security Council also pressured Barre's regime to leave the Ogaden as a means of trying to maintain good relations with the Ethiopians, because "members of the National Security Council, including [the CIA's Ethiopia agent] Paul Henze believed that, in the long term, the United States should not break away from Ethiopia."[50] Neither Ethiopia nor Somalia were ever truly socialist or communist states and Washington believed it could regain its footing in Ethiopia at some point in the future. The fruit of this thinking is very clear today: Addis Ababa is currently one of Washington's most important African allies.

Lost in most accounts of the Somalian Civil War are how the country's economic decline and foreign debt weakened the state, destroyed its institutions, and fostered tribal and regional differences. Instead, the people of Somalia are presented in Orientalist and deeply racist terms as a juvenile people who could not manage their country's affairs and surrendered to their tribal impulses of violence. The Ogaden War hurt both Ethiopia and Somalia economically and disrupted the livelihood of the inhabitants in the border regions of both countries. This, along with the halt to Soviet aid, forced Mogadishu to look to the US and Western Bloc for economic assistance. Their assistance would undo Somalia's social fabrics and traditional economy. As a result of Somalia's realignment with the US and due to its advice, Mogadishu opened its doors to the IMF and World Bank which would impose a neoliberal structural adjustment program on the country. These put an end to important public services and government investment in the public sector and in effect destroyed the foundations of Somalia's economic structure:

> The IMF-World Bank intervention in the early 1980s contributed to exacerbating the crisis of Somali agriculture. The economic reforms undermined the fragile exchange relationship between the "nomadic economy" and the "sedentary economy" – i.e. between pastoralists and small farmers characterized by money transactions as well as traditional barter. A very tight austerity program was imposed on the government largely to release funds required to service Somalia's debt with the Paris Club.[51]

This would reinforce Somalia's dependency on imported foreign grains, which started largely as a result of the war with Ethiopia and draught in the Horn of Africa. The agricultural sector would eventually be destroyed by the foreign aid provided by the US and its allies:

> From the mid-1970s to the mid-1980s, food aid increased fifteen-fold, at the rate of 31 percent per annum. Combined with increased commercial imports, this influx of cheap surplus wheat and rice sold in the domestic market led to the displacement of local producers, as well as to a major shift in food consumption patterns to the detriment of traditional crops (maize and sorghum). The devaluation of the Somali shilling imposed by the IMF in June 1981, was followed by periodic devaluations, leading to hikes in the prices of fuel, fertilizer and farm inputs. The impact on agricultural producers was immediate particularly in rain-fed agriculture, as well as areas of

irrigated farming. Urban purchasing power declined dramatically, government extension programs were curtailed, infrastructure collapsed, the deregulation of the grain market and the influx of "food aid" led to the impoverishment of farming communities.[52]

To add to this, it is important to note that at the same time that the overhead of Somalia's farmers rose due to the increase of costs and the demise of the Somali shilling, the US systematically devastated local farmers by dumping subsidized US grains into Somalia's domestic market: this forced Somalia's farmers to lower their prices to unsustainable figures that made them destitute.[53] Thus, Somalia's farming sector was systematically ruined.

The pastoral cattlemen were also not spared by the devastation of the so-called "economic aid" either. Veterinary services for cattle that were traditionally a free public service provided by the Ministry of Livestock began to become privatized and user fees were introduced. This had devastating effects in Somalia, especially during economically hard times, where half the population were cattle herders. The livestock economy would also collapse.[54] The pastoralists and their traditional exchange economy had deliberately been targeted for elimination by the reforms: "According to the World Bank, 'adjustments' in the size of the herds are, in any event, beneficial because nomadic pastoralists in sub-Saharan Africa are narrowly viewed as a cause of environmental degradation."[55] Australia and Western Europe as creditor countries profited by taking over Mogadishu's traditional export market for beef in the Middle East once Somalia's meat exports fell because of the lack of free veterinary services to maintain cattle health and numbers.[56]

By extension, public health and education programs were destroyed as a result of the IMF and World Bank reforms that began to force Somalia's government to cut back on social services and the public sector to service the country's rising debt. The more Somalia cut back on its vital public services and social programs the weaker the economy became and the higher the debt rose in a vicious cycle. The economy eventually reached a breaking point and Somalia's society fell into turmoil. Added to the corruption of the government, tensions began to rise exponentially until armed opposition groups ousted the regime. The armed militias of the Somali National Movement, Somali Patriotic Movement, Somali Salvation Democratic Front, and United Somali Congress overthrew the government, leading to the eruption of the Somalian Civil War on January 26, 1991—just a few days after the US and its coalition attacked Iraq in the Gulf War.

The Ethiopian-US Invasion of Somalia

Jump about fifteen years forward: 2006 was a critical year in Somalia. Looking back it is clear that the instability in Somalia resulted in the militarization of the Horn of Africa and its waters. The region is of critical strategic importance, because it sits at the mouth of the Red Sea and can be used to control or block all traffic going and leaving the Red Sea, including energy shipments. Is this militarization process the undesired result of instability or was the instability fuelled to justify the militarization process in the Horn of Africa? This is a vital question.

By the end of 2006 it appeared that Somalia was going to be stable once more. The northern regions, Puntland and Somaliland, had virtually been run as relatively peaceful autonomous states. But the south, where the capital is located, had seen continued fighting since 1991. By 2006, however, this was about to change. Many of the warlords had been defeated by the Islamic Courts Union (ICU) and their allies. The ICU united most the southern part of Somalia under its rule and managed to bring law and order to a part of the country that had seen chaos for more than two decades. Peace talks were in the works to unite Somalia. There was high anticipation that a period of relative peace was about to begin in 2007.

But then Ethiopia invaded Somalia on December 20, 2006. The invasion was coordinated with the Pentagon and the US played a direct military role in the fighting as a belligerent through CENTCOM. US planes, ships, intelligence, and small special US ground units all took part in the war against the ICU government of Somalia.[57] To justify the invasion the US invoked the Global War on Terror. At the international level the ICU was portrayed by the US and Ethiopia as an affiliate of Al-Qaeda and as an African version of Afghanistan's Taliban. General John Abizaid, the commander of CENTCOM who was directing the wars in Anglo-American occupied Iraq and NATO-garrisoned Afghanistan, had visited Ethiopia about three weeks earlier to hold a low-profile meeting with Prime Minister Meles Zenawi on December 4, 2006.[58] The two had planned what would become the US-Ethiopian invasion of Somalia.

Soon after the US-Ethiopian war was launched the ICU government of Somalia lost control of the southern portion of the country. The ICU and its allies were forced to wage a guerrilla war against the Ethiopians and US. The Ethiopian military would additionally declare martial law over the southern half of the country during a prolonged stay. Ethiopian soldiers would not leave Somalia until 2009.

In the place of the ICU came the Somali Transitional Federal Government (STFG), a rival group subservient to US and EU edicts, riding into Mogadishu on the backs of Ethiopians tanks. The Somali

Transitional Federal Government and its leaders were immediately accused of collaborating in the dismantlement of Somalia as the clients of the US and other foreign powers by Somalia's parliamentarians and citizens.[59] The Speaker of the Transitional Somali Parliament, Sharif Hassan Sheikh Adan, accused Ethiopia of deliberately sabotaging "any chance of peace in Somalia."[60] He and other parliamentarians who were then taking refuge in Kenya were immediately ordered to leave Kenyan soil by the government in Nairobi.[61] Opposition to the US-Ethiopian invasion, even at the political level, was not tolerated. The expulsion of Somalia's parliamentary leaders from Kenya was tied to the Kenyan government's role in the war and a US-supported plan to send Kenyan troops into Somalia as part of an AU force.

The testimony of Saifa Benaouda about what happened to her during the US-Ethiopian invasion sheds light on how closely the US was calling the shots in East Africa during the war:

> At the Kenyan border, she was detained by soldiers, including three Americans, who had American flag patches on their uniforms, she said. She was then, by turns, imprisoned in Kenya, secretly deported back to Mogadishu, then spirited to Ethiopia, where she was fingerprinted and had her DNA taken by a man who said he was American. She was interrogated by a group of men and women, who she determined by their accents to be Americans and Europeans, she said.[62]

Not only has the instability in Somalia allowed for the region's militarization, it has also opened the doors for a process of neo-colonization, which will be explained in the following section.

The African Union Mission in Somalia: Antecedent to NATO and Neoliberalism

Ethiopia deliberately sabotaged the peace talks in Somalia under US orders, which helped keep Somalia unstable and divided. Moreover, the role of the US-Ethiopian invasion was to open the door for the deployment of African Union troops into Somalia. The Islamic Courts Union had bitterly opposed the entry of any foreign forces inside their country and said that there was no need for them. The ICU government additionally threatened to fight any foreign troops that would step on Somalia's soil, saying they would be seen as an occupation force. The ICU and its allies also accused the African Union of being a surrogate for the US in Africa.

Because of the ICU's opposition, the original January 6, 2005 plans for the AU to put peacekeepers in Somalia under the auspices of the Djibouti-based Intergovernmental Authority on Development (IGAD) never materialized. The name of this peacekeeping force was to be the Intergovernmental Authority on Development Peace Support Mission in Somalia (IGASOM). IGASOM forces were projected to land inside Somalia in March 2005, but the leader of the ICU, Sheikh Hassan Dahir Aweys, warned the forces not to come into his country on March 25, 2005.[63] IGASOM was delayed and all hopes of sending the force faded in May and then died in June 2006 when the ICU took control of Mogadishu.[64] Yet, the AU still persisted in its desire to send a force into Somalia:

> Plans for IGASOM continued, though by July [2006] there were indications of opposition from the ICU, who saw the initiative as a US-backed, western means to curb the growth of [the ICU]. Until December 2006, the UN Security Council had imposed an arms embargo on the group, but the embargo was partially lifted and a mandate for IGASOM issued in December 2006.[65]

With the defeat of the Islamic Courts Union by US and Ethiopian forces, the ground was prepared for AU troops to enter Somalia. On January 19, 2007—a day short of being a month after the US-Ethiopian invasion of Somalia was launched—the African Union's Peace and Security Council created the African Union Mission in Somalia (AMISOM), which replaced and subsumed the IGASOM force that the ICU had prevented from entering Somalia.[66] Burundi, Ghana, Malawi, Nigeria, and Uganda all contributed soldiers to the mission in 2007. Later in 2010, Djibouti and Guinea would join. Kenyan soldiers would operate in Somalia, but would act outside of the AMISOM command structure until 2012.

The IGASOM or AMISOM forces were not ordinary peacekeeping missions. They had specific roles tied to Atlanticist foreign policy objectives in the Horn of Africa. In neoliberal jargon, their mandate was "to create the necessary conditions for reconstruction, reconciliation and the sustainable development of Somalia."[67] In other words, the AMISOM mandate is tied to the neoliberal project for control of Africa's economies. This is the reason that the US and its allies the UK, Germany, Denmark, Japan, Turkey, Australia, South Korea, and Saudi Arabia have financed the AMISOM force.[68] The US, UK, and EU's European Commission have been the largest contributors.[69] From 2007 until 2010 Washington funded about $863 million (US) and the UK about $52 million (US) to the African Union Mission in Somalia.[70] The EU has given 142.5 million euros as of 2012, which includes funding tied to management of natural resources through the EU's Instrument for Stability (IfS).[71] The EU's Somalia Special Support Program, which was started in 2008 to promote development and investment under private enterprise, is also now in force: it is literally a grab for Somalia's resources by foreign investors.

What the US and its allies have done is outsource their neo-colonial projects in Africa to Africans themselves. This is also where the Somali Transitional Federal Government comes into the picture. AU forces were being deployed into Somalia with the primary mission of relocating and protecting the Somali Transitional Federal Government. The group's name should not fool anyone; the Somali Transitional Federal Government was merely a rival faction that had the support of the US and its NATO allies, created in 2004 when two rival groups outside of Somalia agreed to work together, then were literally imposed. It had no real claim of legitimacy over the ICU, which had popular support on the ground in Somalia. While not all the figures in the Somali Transitional Federal Government are corrupt, the agenda for the group has been set by the US and its allies to "reconstruct Somalia's institutions and economy." Those members of the Somali Transitional Federal Government that are not corrupt do not understand or grasp the policies that they will be pursuing with the help of foreign experts.

Again, the exact same pattern is taking place as took place in Sudan, where too, the African Union had opened the door for the military forces from outside of Africa. When the AMISOM force was created at the start of 2007, the AU stipulated that the force would ultimately turn into a UN mission:

> AMISOM shall be deployed for a period of six (6) months, aimed essentially at contributing to the initial stabilization phase in Somalia, with a clear understanding that the mission will evolve to a United Nations operation that will support the long term stabilization and post-conflict reconstruction of Somalia.[72]

But the AMISOM force has not morphed into a mixed UN and AU hybrid force or a "long-term" UN force yet. Instead, it has opened the doors to Atlantic Alliance operations and "NATO stewardship" on Somalia's soil. At this point it should be realized that the military dimensions and socio-economic dimensions of Euro-Atlantic expansion are inseparably tied to one another.

Somalia's Pirates and the Militarization of the Horn of Africa

Piracy in the Horn of Africa and the reasons behind it are grossly misunderstood. There is a strong argument to be made that the piracy problem off the coast of Somalia is a consequence of the militarization of the Horn of Africa and the unchecked behavior of neoliberal capitalist exploitation. *The Daily Telegraph*, a newspaper known to be supportive of neoliberal economics, is worth quoting on the issue of the origins of piracy in the Horn of Africa:

> Maybe we have brought all this on ourselves. Or rather we have preferred to turn a blind eye to those who have ruthlessly, and for many years, exploited the seas off Somalia by the dumping of toxic waste and intensive illegal fishing.
>
> A report for the European Parliament says that dumping has destroyed Somalia's fishing grounds. It names two European companies, one Swiss, one Italian, that signed contracts with warlords to dump 10 million tons of toxic waste into the coastal waters in exchange for £10 million.
>
> The UN reports "a distressingly high incidence of respiratory diseases in Somalia's coastal communities, indicating high levels of radiation".
>
> Our own Department for International Development reckons that Somalia has lost £100 million in revenue because of the depletion of fish stocks through toxic contamination and illegal fishing.
>
> Given this evidence and given that the livelihood of all those Somalis who live by fishing has been destroyed, is it any wonder that they have found another means to survive?
>
> When interviewed by Western reporters, the pirates defend themselves by saying exactly that. They have little to lose and everything to gain.[73]

While the mainstream media has frenziedly reported about the pirates of Somalia, the crimes of large multinational corporations are overlooked. Added to the destruction of the state by the IMF and World Bank structural readjustment programs, the activities of these large multinational corporations in Somalia's waters—where no legal regime has been enforced—have forced many of the inhabitants of Somalia's coastal villages to resort to piracy as an occupation. These activities have destroyed the last remnant of Somalia's traditional economy after small farming and pastoral animal herding: fishing. The traditional fishing economy of Somalia's coast was the smallest component of the traditional economy. It had also served as a form of daily subsistence and commerce. With the collapse of the state and the start of civil war, there was no one to finance and maintain an able bodied maritime force to protect Somalia's waters. Many of the coastguard and navy officers of Somalia's defunct professional maritime services eventually also formed a portion of the pirate fleets as their gang names—such as the Somali Marines and the National Volunteer Coastguard—attest. Left unchecked, Somalia's waters have been illegally exploited by large-scale industrial foreign fishing vessels for more than two decades:

> Ever since a civil war brought down Somalia's last functional government in 1991, the country's 3,330 km (2,000 miles) of coastline—the longest in continental Africa—has been pillaged by foreign vessels. A United Nations report in 2006 said that, in the absence of the country's at one time serviceable coastguard, Somali waters have become the site of an international "free for all," with fishing fleets from around the world illegally plundering Somali stocks and freezing out the country's own rudimentarily-equipped fishermen. According to another U.N. report, an estimated $300 million worth of seafood is stolen from the country's coastline each year. "In any context," says Gustavo Carvalho, a London-based researcher with Global Witness, an environmental NGO, "that is a staggering sum."[74]

These large-scale industrial foreign vessels even had the audacity to attack Somalia's fishermen and bully them in their own waters. As a result, local fisherman began to take arms and form groups to protect themselves in their own waters:

> In the face of this, impoverished Somalis living by the sea have been forced over the years to defend their own fishing expeditions out of ports such as Eyl, Kismayo and Harardhere—all now considered to be pirate dens. Somali fishermen, whose industry was always small-scale, lacked the advanced boats and technologies of their interloping competitors, and also complained of being shot at by foreign fishermen with water cannons and firearms. "The first pirate gangs emerged in the '90s to protect against foreign trawlers," says Peter Lehr, lecturer in terrorism studies at Scotland's University of St. Andrews [...] The waters they sought to

protect, says Lehr, were "an El Dorado for fishing fleets of many nations." A 2006 study published in the journal *Science* predicted that the current rate of commercial fishing would virtually empty the world's oceanic stocks by 2050. Yet, Somalia's seas still offer a particularly fertile patch for tuna, sardines and mackerel, and other lucrative species of seafood, including lobsters and sharks. In other parts of the Indian Ocean region, such as the Persian Gulf, fishermen resort to dynamite and other extreme measures to pull in the kinds of catches that are still in abundance off the Horn of Africa.[75]

According to the East African Seafarers Assistance Program based in Nairobi, piracy emerged from the fisherman's defensive postures leading to ransoms of foreign vessels as compensation. Tsuma Charo of the Kenya-based organization has explained that "illegal trawling has fed the piracy problem."[76] In a 2009 interview with *Time Magazine*, she explained: "In the early days of Somali piracy, those who seized trawlers without licenses could count on a quick ransom payment, since the boat owners and companies backing those vessels didn't want to draw attention to their violation of international maritime law."[77]

Added to the illegal fishing, the waters of the Horn of Africa have become a dumping ground for radioactive and toxic discard matter. A 2005 UN Environmental Program reports states:

> Somalia is one of the many Least Developed Countries that reportedly received countless shipments of illegal nuclear and toxic waste dumped along the coastline. Starting from the early 1980s and continuing into the civil war, the hazardous waste dumped along Somalia's coast comprised uranium radioactive waste, lead, cadmium, mercury, industrial, hospital, chemical, leather treatment and other toxic waste. Most of the waste was simply dumped on the beaches in containers and disposable leaking barrels which ranged from small to big tanks without regard to the health of the local population and any environmentally devastating impacts.
>
> The issue of dumping in Somalia is contentious as it raises both legal and moral questions. First, there is a violation of international treaties in the export of hazardous waste to Somalia. Second, it is ethically questionable to negotiate a hazardous waste disposal

contract with a country in the midst of a protracted civil war and with a factionalized government that could not sustain a functional legal and proper waste management system.[78]

Cyclones and tidal waves like the massive tsunamis caused by the Sumatra-Andaman Earthquake that devastated many of the Indian Ocean's shores in 2004 stir the hazardous toxic and radioactive waste dumped off Somalia's coast and bring it to shore. Unlike earthquakes, tsunamis, draughts, brush fires, and different storm systems such as tornados and tropical cyclones, the effects of toxic and radioactive waste contamination are long-term with devastating effects on crops, fishing, cattle, soil, wildlife, water supplies, and the ecosystem. Local human populations are impacted by the effects of environmental damage, impacted by contaminated and unsafe drinking water, pathological illnesses, contaminated food, loss of livelihood, damage of the traditional economy, lowered fertility rates, increased mortality rates, and an overall lowered quality of life. In Somalia the toxic and radioactive waste has had visible effects on people's lives:

> Contamination from the waste deposits has thus caused health and environmental problems to the surrounding local fishing communities including contamination of groundwater. Many people in these towns have complained of unusual health problems as a result of the tsunami winds blowing towards inland villages. The health problems include acute respiratory infections, dry heavy coughing and mouth bleeding, abdominal haemorrhages, unusual skin chemical reactions, and sudden death after inhaling toxic materials.[79]

One of the causes of the dumping of toxic and radioactive waste in Somalia's waters has been that costs are very low or non-existent. The same UN report says: "It has been estimated that it costs as little as $2.50 per [metric ton] to dump hazardous waste in Africa as opposed to $250 per tonne in Europe."[80]

It can safely be concluded that the piracy phenomenon in the Horn of Africa is the direct result of illegal corporate activity and the sabotage of Somalia's economy by its former US ally. Piracy has been nurtured through neglect. The US and NATO have done very little about the violations of Somalia's waters and international law by large corporations. Instead they have used the piracy problem to justify their naval presence in the waters of the Horn of Africa and as a pretext for militarizing the strategic waterways of the region.

NATO Enters the Horn of Africa

In 2007 the Atlantic Alliance formally started operations in Somalia. These operations started as a "NATO stewardship" over the African Union Mission in Somalia after the US-Ethiopian invasion. The mission started off by providing "strategic airlifts" to the AU and taxiing their soldiers, equipment, and supplies into Somalia. The Atlantic Alliance describes the mission thus:

> NATO has accepted to assist the AU mission in Somalia (AMISOM) by providing strategic airlift and sealift support to AU member states willing to deploy in Somalia under AMISOM. NATO has, for instance, put into practice airlift support from Burundi to Mogadishu and has escorted an AU ship that carried Burundi military equipment for one of the battalions that it had airlifted into Mogadishu.[81]

NATO's operations have since been expanded to include Alliance "strategic sealifts," training, and NATO advisors. These Alliance advisors are called NATO "subject experts," which steer the African Union's policy in Somalia through its Peace Support Operations Division (PSOD).[82]

While NATO was formally involved on the land and air in Somalia, it began to consolidate its presence in the waters off the Horn of Africa through a decision of the North Atlantic Council made on October 9, 2008. Standing NATO Maritime Group Two (SNMG2) was given an expanded mandate from the Eastern Mediterranean into the Gulf of Aden and Arabian Sea. The decision helped facilitate an expanded international maritime position for NATO and complemented the unilateral naval activities of the US Navy that had been in practice off the Horn of Africa. When the North Atlantic Council tasked SNMG2 for the mission off Somalia's coast the force had been in the process of sailing to the Persian Gulf to work with the petro-sheikhdoms of Bahrain, Kuwait, Qatar, and the UAE as part of NATO's Istanbul Cooperation Initiative (ICI).[83] Hence in 2008 Operation Allied Provider was launched to undertake what the Atlantic Alliance called a "counter-piracy" mission that involved policing, maritime surveillance, and escort duties. It also included a request by the Secretariat of the UN to provide security for the vessels of the UN World Food Program sailing through the Gulf of Aden between Somalia and Yemen. While SNMG2 was carrying out its anti-piracy and escorting duties under Allied Protector, the AMISOM forces requested a NATO naval escort for Burundian forces going to Somalia.

The EU also launched a complementary naval operation by the name of Operation Atlanta (EU Naval Force–Atlanta) in December 2008.[84]

The mission and its naval squadron, European Naval Force Somalia, have replicated all of NATO's activities by making patrols to prevent piracy, escorting UN World Food Program ships, and providing support for the AMISOM force. With the acquiescence of the Somali Transitional Federal Government, European Naval Force Somalia's range of operations was extended to include Somalia's sovereign coastal territory and inland waters on March 23, 2012.[85]

In 2009, four events further secured NATO's position in the Horn of Africa. NATO was invited in June 2009 to join the Somalia Contact Group, essentially a body controlled and formed by the US and its NATO allies to normalize external intervention in Somalia.[86] Formed in June 2006 by the US government to build support against the Islamic Courts Union government of Somalia and give the appearance of international legitimacy to the ICU government's Somali Transitional Federal Government rivals, the Somalia Contact Group's members were the US, UK, EU, Italy, Norway, Sweden, and Tanzania. It was the precursor and model for both the Libya Contact Group (Friends of Libya) and the Syria Contact Group (Friends of the Syrian People). The next step by NATO in 2009 would be the Alliance's move to entrench itself in the Gulf of Aden and the Horn of Africa. Operation Ocean Shield commenced on August 17 as a continuation of Allied Protector with a longer term mandate. Finally, the AU requested that NATO conduct strategic sealifts for its Somalia mission. The strategic sealifts were authorized by the North Atlantic Council on September 15, 2009.

The African Union was instrumental in the consolidation of NATO's position and both have collaborated with one another. At sea, the Gulf of Aden is now patrolled constantly by Atlantic Alliance vessels. Operation Ocean Protector is an out-of-area operation that has marked the Indian Ocean as a zone of permanent NATO operations. In military terms, the Indian Ocean is being transformed into an area of responsibility (AOR) by the Alliance.

NATO Enters Libya: From Odyssey Dawn to Unified Protector

The NATO war on Libya is the Atlantic Alliance's most blatant and well-known involvement in Africa. Wesley Clark, NATO's former supreme commander, has testified that Libya—as well as Somalia and Sudan—had been on a list of nations that the Pentagon planned to attack and subjugate, using 9/11 as a pretext.[87] The other Pentagon targets were outside of Africa: Iraq, Lebanon, Syria, and Iran. The image of a military roadmap should be emerging in the minds of readers, which the third portion of this book will deal with.

The stage for the Atlantic Alliance's war on Libya was set by

Barack Obama's 2009 "A New Beginning" speech in Cairo and by the upheavals that would come about through the so-called Arab Spring. Obama's speech was effectively an announcement that the United States was planning to change the structure of the Arab World by supporting the rise of "democracy." This of course was insincere as indicated by the US reactions to the protests in Bahrain, Morocco, Jordan, and Saudi Arabia. Obama had been aware that there was an inter-agency and inter-departmental plan to change the geo-political equation in the Middle East and North Africa before the start of his presidency. His presidential campaign team had actually taken part in meetings with US State Department officials, several corporations, and several key activist groups from the Arab World to talk about the democratization of the Arab countries. The Obama media team even helped train some of these activists. Washington spent the next few years preparing for regime change by working to hijack popular Arab movements and in the cases of Libya and Syria, to fuel insurgencies through groups it had nourished much earlier. In Libya one of these groups would be the Libyan Islamic Fighting Group (LIFG). On the eve of 2011, the Arab Spring would begin in Tunisia. Soon it would hit the giant of the Arab World, Egypt. Not long after, Libya would feel the upheavals inside its borders. At first much of the world thought that what was happening in Libya was a popular and peaceful protest movement, despite the fact that it swiftly escalated into violence without the kind of pro-government mass demonstrations occurring in the adjoining states. An armed insurgency fuelled, aided, and funded by NATO powers and their Gulf Cooperation Council (GCC) allies—who aside from Saudi Arabia and Oman are all Istanbul Cooperation Initiative (ICI) members—was taking place with its epicenter in Benghazi.

Misinformation and rumors ran rampant. The main three were: (1) Colonel Muammar Qaddafi had brought in black-skinned sub-Saharan mercenaries into his country to suppress the Libyan people and their popular demands; (2) Tripoli had dispatched fighter jets to target peaceful protesters; and (3) genocide and massacres were taking place in Benghazi and other major Libyan cities. All of these assertions would turn out to be incorrect, to put it mildly. Gross acts of media deception were at play. The so-called black-skinned sub-Saharan African mercenaries were actually black-skinned Libyans serving in their country's security, police, and military forces. The mainstream media in Atlantic Alliance countries, such as CNN and the BBC, had vilified and painted the black-skinned Libyans as non-Libyan aliens in the most racist of terms. The Libyan jet attacks never happened and NATO leaders would conveniently forget the matter after they militarily intervened and removed Colonel Qaddafi from power after a long and grueling bombing campaign. Anyone with a background as a military pilot can attest to the uselessness and near impossibility of Qaddafi having attempted to use jets for crowd control against protesters. Moreover, the Russian military had satellite images and data that showed no such thing had happened—President Obama and other Atlantic Alliance leaders also had access to satellite imagery and would have been well aware of the lie. Britain and France had actually held war games in November 2010, in which the imaginary enemy "SOUTHLAND" was really Libya; the military assets that both London and Paris had mobilized and put into formation ended up being those used in actuality against Libya.[88] According to the journalist Franco Bechis of the Italian paper *Libero*, the French government had already decided to topple the Libyan government in November 2010.

The US Senate unanimously passed a non-binding resolution urging the UN Security Council to impose a no-fly zone over the Libyans on March 1, 2011.[89] The Italian government quickly repudiated its friendship treaty with Libya, paving the way for its bases to be used by the Atlantic Alliance for the Libyan bombing campaign.[90] Moreover, NATO members had already sent their special forces and private contractors—the real "mercenaries" in this story—inside Libya in February and March to start a NATO regime change operation. The Obama White House would even admit that the CIA was operating on the ground and helping the Libyan insurgents as were dozens of British agents and commandos from MI6, the Special Air Services (SAS) unit, and the Special Boat Services (SBS) units.[91] Foreign fighters began to pour into Libya from the Egyptian border and were ferried in through the Mediterranean. Those who were actually bringing foreign forces into Libya were Qaddafi's accusers: most of the anti-government forces opposed to Qaddafi were comprised of non-Libyans. This is a matter to which I, the author of this book, can personally testify.

I happened to be on the ground in Libya during the war when at least one female negotiator had been allowed to enter the country to negotiate for the retrieval of captured US prisoners, mostly probably US commandos or intelligence agents. I was also told of the presence of French and Qatari soldiers by Libyan volunteers and soldiers who were engaged in combat against what they called "the foreign invasion of our country." After the fall of Tripoli to NATO and anti-government forces, I left Libya in a small ship carrying Reverend Walter Fauntroy, the former representative of the District of Columbia in the US House of Representatives, and three freed Italians with military equipment who had covertly entered Libya to topple the regime before the war began. The three Italians were part of a high priority request by the Italian government to be quickly evacuated to Malta.

The fighting in Libya had been anticipated by the Atlantic Alliance and Atlanticist leaders. One US diplomat was even expelled from Libya just before the violence erupted; against diplomatic norms, the US official had made an authorized secret trip into the Western Mountains in November 2010.[92] Libyan officials maintained that the US official was expelled for coordinating anti-government activities that they later realized were tied to the insurgency.

The massacres that were the basis for UN authorization of no-fly zones were never proved; far from it, the Libyan League for Human Rights (LLHR) making the accusations at the UN Human Rights Council in Geneva was in a total conflict of interest, because its members were key members of the Transitional Council, and lacked credibility. The R2P norm that Madeline Albright and the US State Department had wanted to use against Sudan was at work now against the Jamahiriya. All the usually suspects, so to speak, were clamoring for militarism and intervention—many of whom have long been advocates of global empire. Individuals like Paul Wolfowitz, John McCain, Joseph Lieberman, Elliott Abrams, Leon Wieseltier, John Hannah, Robert Kagan, and William Kristol all called for an attack on Libya. Many of those who supported NATO's past wars in Yugoslavia also got involved, such as the so-called philosopher Bernard-Henri Lévy, who would later publicly claim that it was he who had convinced French President Nicolas Sarkozy to attack Libya. The club of dictators at the Arab League was also used to support the war. On the basis of these lies an undeclared war was started by the US and NATO. France's Sarkozy and the UK's David Cameron took the lead in publicly pushing for war while the Obama Administration pretended that it was reluctant to go to war and was not the main force behind it, perhaps because of Obama's Kenyan heritage, his so-called "peace candidate" credentials, and the strong support for Qaddafi in the African American community. The media and government lies about Libya went unchallenged and permitted the UN Security Council to authorize a no-fly zone on March 17, 2011. This was mandated by UNSC Resolution 1973. Bosnia-Herzegovina, Britain, Colombia, France, Lebanon, Portugal, the US, and the three African countries of Gabon, Nigeria, and South Africa would all vote to pass it; Brazil, China, Germany, India, and Russia would all abstain from voting. NATO quickly took advantage of the resolution to wage an offensive war against Libya.

Almost from the start Tripoli requested that the AU, UN, and EU come to investigate the claims against the Libyan government. Libyan officials even became desperate enough to say NATO could investigate too. Colonel Qaddafi's Jamahiriya government desperately tried to negotiate, but to no avail. At the onset of the fighting Tripoli accepted Venezuela's offers for mediation, which Atlanticist leaders undermined and their Transitional Council allies rejected. In March the Jamahiriya government accepted the AU's ceasefire and reform plan, which was ignored by the US and NATO leaders. The AU repeatedly proposed a ceasefire, the creation of humanitarian corridors, the protection of foreigners, and finally dialogue between both sides in bringing in what it termed democratic reform.[93] Most of the world's governments voiced support for a negotiated settlement in Libya, but this was ignored by the Atlantic Alliance. All requests by Qaddafi and his family for diplomatic negotiations were rejected.[94] Tripoli even accepted African Union offers for mediation spearheaded by South Africa. A massive people's initiative for a reconciliation march across the war zone in Libya was started, which received little press coverage outside of Africa and Latin America.[95] The Jamahiriya government even put together a new constitution.[96] As the war heated up the Jamahiriya allowed the local tribes to establish political order and security in certain areas, so as not to instigate fighting or NATO attacks.[97] Everything Tripoli did to establish peace was stonewalled and obstructed. Even when Jamahiriya officials almost successfully brokered a deal to use their frozen funds to provide humanitarian aid to the Libyan population, their plans were obstructed when France got wind.[98]

The war on Libya officially started with Operation Odyssey Dawn on March 19, 2011. This was the military codename of the offensive launched under the direct command of the Pentagon involving Belgian, British, Canadian, Danish, Dutch, Emirati, French, Italian, Qatari, Norwegian, and Spanish forces. Each one of these countries would have their own codename for Operation Odyssey Dawn. On March 8, NATO began to monitor Libya's airspace with reconnaissance and surveillance flights; on March 10, the Alliance cordoned off Libya's waters, on March 23, NATO imposed a naval embargo around Libya. The North Atlantic Council officially decided to continue the campaign on March 27; this was just a formality, because the Alliance's leaders had decided on going to war earlier. NATO's Operation Unified Protector would start with the start of the NATO naval embargo. The next month the US would officially transfer tactical command of the air campaign to NATO and Operation Odyssey Dawn would officially end on March 31. It would be subsumed into Operation Unified Protector, thereby bringing all those countries which had joined in the offensive under Pentagon command at last under the command of NATO.

NATO's Intended Mission Creep in Libya:
From No-fly Zone to Regime Change

The no fly-zone over Libya resulted in an armed campaign on the ground and in the air. Libyan targets on the ground had to be systematically located, mapped out, and then attacked, which meant that NATO had to have personnel covertly on the ground first before it bombed Libya. This is where the CIA, SAS, and other personnel from the Alliance came into play. The intended mission creep, expanding the aims of the war, began to manifest itself publicly. British Prime Minister David Cameron began facing criticism from the opposition parties and his own party members. Conservative parliamentarians began to openly criticize their leader.[99] MP John Baron criticized Cameron for misleading the British House of Commons, protesting that: "When it was put before the House, the emphasis was very much on humanitarian assistance. This has changed into a mission of regime change [in Libya]."[100]

Inactive and unmanned Libyan naval vessels were among NATO's first targets. Other targets bombed on the first day included civilian structures, including the national mint, where Libyan dinars were issued, and food storage facilities. This helped cause a money shortage and aggravated a food shortage that would come about in the months of June to August. Among other targets were hospitals, medical facilities, residential areas, industrial sites, hotels, the Nasser University campus of Al-Fatah University, a conference hall filled with religious leaders trying to push for national dialogue, water facilities, electricity infrastructure, government buildings, and a bus filled with civilians. Important buildings holding medical records were destroyed too. One such building was a heritage building from the Italian period that hosted the offices of the Down's Syndrome Society, a pre-school, the Libyan Handicapped Women's Foundation, the National Diabetic Research Center, and the Libyan Crippled Children's Foundation.

From the start NATO had planned on regime change in Tripoli. On March 9, one unnamed European diplomat at the UN revealed the true intentions of NATO's leaders: "[We] are talking about military intervention to get rid of one government [in Libya] and putting another one in place [and] [t]his is what it is all about."[101] At least three NATO members—Britain, France, and Italy—would publicly send military advisors to assist the insurgents to topple the government in April.[102] With impunity France even admitted publicly that it was funneling weapons into the Western Mountains to forces hostile to the regime in Tripoli.[103] Qatar's Emir Hamad bin Khalifa Al-Thani also did the same during a CNN interview with Wolf Blitzer. French officials argued that they were sending arms to enable civilians to protect themselves on the basis of what the UN mandated. This was a non-sequitur argument with no legal standing whatsoever, violating the UN mandate in Libya. Weapons shipments were also flown into Benghazi under disguise of humanitarian aid.[104] In other words, NATO collectively breached UNSC Resolution 1970, which was pushed forward by Atlantic Alliance members themselves. NATO even released a video, which it later removed, showing the Canadian vessel HMC Charlottetown allowing offensive weapons to reach the Transitional

Council.[105] The Atlantic Alliance would later claim that it did not breach the embargo. Alliance officials would justify their actions by saying the ship carrying the weapons was allowed to pass, because it was sailing from one Libyan city to another and therefore not bringing weapons into the country.

The Atlantic Alliance's war destroyed Libya's infrastructure and crippled the real economy at a critical period when Libya was emerging as the leading African state. The NATO bombings also killed or maimed large numbers of Libyan civilians. Italian Prime Minister Silvio Berlusconi stated on the record that he was told the war would end when the population of Tripoli revolted against Colonel Qaddafi.[106] This means that the bombings were not intended to end violence or fighting, but rather to punish the Libyan population sufficiently as to instigate them to revolt against their government—surely only a pretext as this kind of notion had already proved unsuccessful in Iraq. At high costs Colonel Qaddafi seemed to have nearly survived the war. Towards August the war began to reach an unsustainable point for the Alliance. NATO put on a brave face saying it could last, but experts began saying the war could only last up until the end of September and the start of October. NATO planes were running out of bombs and many NATO members were running out of steam. Italy was forced to withdraw from the war in late June.[107] Norway also announced that it would withdraw in August 2011.[108] France even accepted what Paris and NATO refused to accept from the start of the conflict, namely to end the war and to stop bombing Libya if both sides in Tripoli and Benghazi started political talks.[109] Alliance attacks became more vicious towards the end of June and the start of August. Fuel supplies and electricity infrastructure were heavily targeted. An even more intense phase of bombings began and NATO forces targeted all the checkpoints protecting Tripoli to open the road to the capital. At the same time the psychological warfare was intensified and the mainstream media began to make false reports about specific locations falling or surrendering, while key figures were secretly being encouraged to defect or surrender. All this began to break the spirit of Tripoli's defenders and fear kicked in, which ultimately allowed the anti-government forces to enter Tripoli in late August.

Qaddafi and his sons relocated to the city of Sirte, the last major stronghold of Jamahiriya forces after the town of Bani Walid surrendered on October 17. Sirte was attacked on September 15 by anti-Jamahiriya forces with NATO air cover and advisors. Three to four major anti-government offensives, which included indiscriminate mortar fire at civilians, would be fended off by Sirte's defenders. NATO did nothing to stop the butchering, except watch. Eventually the beleaguered Libyan city would fall around October 20. NATO jets began to attack the convoys trying to escape Sirte. This clearly had nothing to do with the UN mandate to protect civilians. NATO's insurgent allies then began executing civilians and prisoners in the city. Even Human Rights Watch, which did not take much notice of the Transitional Council's crimes, was forced to make some statements. Among them was a statement about a group of prisoners executed in cold blood before the fall of Sirte:

> "We found 53 decomposing bodies, apparently [Jamahiriya loyalists], at an abandoned hotel in Sirte, and some had their hands bound behind their backs when they were shot," said Peter Bouckaert, emergencies director at Human Rights Watch, who investigated the killings. "This requires the immediate attention of the Libyan authorities to investigate what happened and hold accountable those responsible."
>
> The condition of the bodies suggests the victims were killed approximately one week prior to their discovery, between October 14 and October 19, Human Rights Watch said. The bloodstains on the grass directly below the bodies, bullet holes visible in the ground, and the spent cartridges of AK-47 and FN-1 rifles scattered around the site strongly suggest that some, if not all of the people, were shot and killed in the location where they were discovered, Human Rights Watch said.
>
> All the bodies were in a similar stage of decomposition, suggesting they were killed at the same approximate time. Some of the bodies had their hands tied behind their backs with plastic ties. Others had bandages over serious wounds, suggesting they had been treated for other injuries prior to their deaths.[110]

Since that time reports of widespread human rights violations have emerged from across Libya. Despite the fact that it was internationally listed as a terrorist organization and banned by UN Security Council Committee 1267, the mainstream media also began to talk more openly about the role of the Libyan Islamic Fighting Group in the Libya campaign as an important NATO ally.

Muammar Qaddafi's Execution:
Mob Violence or A Planned Execution?

Soon after the fall of Sirte, it was revealed that Muammar Qaddafi had been captured and summarily executed by a group of anti-government insurgents. Several members of the group would film portions of Qaddafi's last living minutes on their cellular telephones. US Secretary of State Hillary Clinton reacted jubilantly with laughter between interviews. A rolling CBS Network camera caught the moment on tape with Secretary Clinton commenting: "We came, we saw, he died!"—a grim echo of Roman general Julius Caesar's historic comments after he had vanquished Pontiac Shah Pharnaces II: "I came, I saw, I conquered." The killing of Qaddafi and other Jamahiriya figures is a violation of the Geneva Conventions, which explicitly prohibit the summary execution of prisoners of war. While NATO denied any involvement it had been monitoring Qaddafi and following his telephone calls. This may have been the basis for the aerial strikes by US and French aircraft on the loyalist motorcade he was travelling in. Even if, as the Atlantic Alliance maintained, it was not aware that Muammar Qaddafi was travelling in the fleeing convoy, an attack on a fleeing civilian convoy remains a breach of international law and an unjustifiable act.

It seems certain that the US and NATO wanted Qaddafi dead. Many analysts say there were a lot of dirty secrets that needed to be buried with the Libyan leader. His death also eliminated a rallying point for Libya's loyalist forces, speeding a decline to resistance and guaranteeing that a power vacuum would emerge in Libya. The killing was more likely a planned execution insofar as other captured Jamahiriya officials and one of Qaddafi's sons were also killed around the same time, indicating that the killings were coordinated. NATO also had commandos and ground forces present in Sirte at the time. It is additionally known that in many cases the Transitional Council and the anti-government militias had NATO handlers supervising their actions. Vladimir Putin made a very revealing statement on Russian television about the role of the Alliance in the murder:

> All the world saw him being killed, all bloodied. Is
> that democracy? And who did it? Drones, including
> American ones, delivered a strike on his motorcade.
> Then [NATO] commandos, who were not supposed to
> be there, brought in so-called opposition and militants.
> And killed him without trial.[111]

In contrast to Putin's statement, NATO's African allies Ethiopia and Kenya made supportive statements about Qaddafi's death saying it marked the start of a new chapter for Libya. Across Africa there were cautious and muted responses by most leaders in contrast to the anger and shock of their populations. Taking about NATO, Sam Nujoma, the former president of Namibia and leader of SWAPO, warned that the killing of Qaddafi "must serve as a lesson to Africa that foreign aggressors are readying themselves to pounce on the continent."[112] Nujoma's son Utoni, the foreign minister of Namibia, asserted that Africa and the world had watched an extra-judicial execution under the command of NATO.[113]

NATO's War Opens the Doors for Neoliberal Conquest in Libya

The privatization of Libyan national assets, its public sector, and corporations was a latent theme of NATO's war. The Anglo-American financial sectors in Wall Street and Canary Wharf were intimately involved. The Transitional Council established a new Libyan oil corporation and a new national bank, named the Central Bank of Benghazi, from the insurgent stronghold of Benghazi on March 19, 2011, startlingly early in the conflict.[114] The new Benghazi-based oil company and central bank were the first steps at taking over the very lucrative Libyan energy and financial sectors, marking the start of the economic invasion and colonization of Libya and its economy.

While the Central Bank of Benghazi sprang to life under the control of Britain's Hong Kong and Shanghai Banking Corporation (HSBC), the new oil company would fall under the control of Qatar. Oil began to be exported from Cyrenaica under Qatari oversight.[115] The revenues from the insurgents' oil exports were illegally used, violating the Arms Trade Treaty (ATT), to finance weapons purchases. This was casually reported to the public on April 1, 2011:

> A plan to sell rebel-held oil to buy weapons and other supplies has been reached with Qatar, a rebel official said Friday, in another sign of deepening aid for Libya's opposition by the wealthy Gulf state after sending warplanes to help confront [Jamahiriya] forces.
>
> It was not immediately clear when the possible oil sales could begin or how the arms would reach the rebel factions, but any potential revenue stream would be a significant lifeline for the militias and military defectors battling [the Libyan military].[116]

The banking and financial sectors in the NATO countries were supportive of the war, because they could appropriate Libyan investments and holdings. Among them were Goldman Sachs, Société Générale SA, the Carlyle Group, JP Morgan Chase, and Och-Ziff Capital Management Group. Not only have steps for a takeover of Libya's assets and public sector companies been initiated, but a big loan bonanza has begun. A country that was blessed with no international debts was being chained with debts through a loaning scam. The frozen financial assets of Libya were even used to make interest-based loans to the Transitional Council. The European Bank for Reconstruction and Development (EBRD) also cut into the action to make loans to the insurgents under the pretext of furthering democracy.[117] The war and NATO's Transitional Council allies had taken Libya into a debt trap.

The war in Libya had also managed to eliminate a competitor in Africa. The Libyan Minister of International Cooperation, Mohammed Siala, had explained that the US and its major allies in the EU, such as the UK and France, were not happy about Libyan projects to develop Africa locally, which were closing Africa off to them.[118] Libya's actions were conflicting with their strategies of maintaining Africa as an unindustrialized and undeveloped economic periphery and as a provider of raw unmanufactured natural resources. The war also marked an important turning point for the Franco-German Entente with the subordination of France to the US. Germany attempted to resist—knowing the effects control of Libyan oil would have on the euro and the economies of the EU—and to gain control over the spoils of war by proposing that EU peacekeepers take over for NATO in Libya.

NATO and the African Union

The African Union was formed out of the Organization of African Unity (OAU) in 2002. The AU's headquarters are essentially in Ethiopia, insofar as the AU's secretariat, the African Union Commission, is based in Addis Abba. The OAU was formed in 1963 with the goal of uniting a "liberated" Africa during the de-colonization period. For this reason it was at the very least nominally opposed to foreign forces on African soil. The AU appears to have a starkly different policy about foreign troops in Africa.

On the basis of NATO support for the African Union in Sudan from 2005 until 2007, the Atlantic Alliance has turned into a senior partner for the AU. Since NATO and AU collaboration in Sudan, the Alliance has gotten involved in the AU's mission in Somalia. This relationship and tutelage of the AU also involves the European Union and the US specifically at the political, economic, and military levels. Since AU Chairman Alpha Oumar Konaré's 2005 visit to NATO Headquarters in Brussels there have been frequent exchanges between the two sides and relations are handled on the AU side by the Office of the Peace and Security Commission. In March 2007, AU Commissioner for Peace and Security Said Djinnit, an Algerian diplomat whose country is part of NATO's Mediterranean Dialogue, proposed during a visit at NATO Headquarters a wider cooperation between the AU and NATO and sought to engage the Alliance's long-term help in developing the African

Union. The North Atlantic Council then commissioned a NATO study on the African Standby Force (ASF) on September 7, 2007.[119] On the other hand, Libya had been working hard to gain greater influence in the AU by 2010, in line with its other pan-African policies. In mid-February 2011 it was made public that NATO was going to open a liaison office at AU Headquarters in Addis Ababa and was planning on signing a military cooperation accord with the AU—even as one of its members was under the threat of attack by the Alliance.[120] In fact a NATO delegation had been working side by side with the AU's legal department for a good deal of February.[121] This says a lot about the AU as an organization and its leaders. The AU is almost unavoidably subservient to the Atlanticists and their pressure. Its leaders are mostly corrupt figures that quickly give in under pressure.

It is on the basis of these dynamics—and after the war on Libya—that NATO is providing "capacity-building support to [the AU's] long-term peacekeeping capabilities, in particular the African Standby Force."[122] The ASF is of particular importance, because it fits with the contours of the Atlanticist project for Africa. NATO's involvement with the ASF is officially as follows:

> NATO has been providing expert and training support to the African Standby Force (ASF) at the AU's request. Not only does it offer capacity-building support through courses and training events, but it also organizes different forms of support for the operationalization of the ASF all at AU's request.
>
> The ASF, which is intended to be deployed in Africa in times of crisis, is part of the AU's efforts to develop long-term peacekeeping capabilities. ASF represents the AU's vision for a continental, on-call, security apparatus with some similarities to the NATO Response Force.[123]

In 2010, the Norwegians called their embassy in Ethiopia "the informal liaison office of the North Atlantic Treaty Organisation (NATO) to the African Union (AU)."[124] Norway, via its embassy in Ethiopia, plays the special role of organizing diplomatic meetings and being the diplomatic voice of NATO with the AU: "AU requests are communicated via 'Note Verbale' from the AU to the Norwegian Embassy, then via the Joint Force Command (JFC) Lisbon and [Supreme Headquarters Allied Powers Europe] to NATO HQ."[125] The Alliance also has liaison officers who are responsible for the discussions about AU and NATO operations:

The NATO Senior Military Liaison Officer (SMLO) is the primary point of contact for the Alliance's activities with the AU. An SMLO is deployed on a permanent six-month rotational basis in Addis Ababa and is supported by a deputy and an administrative assistant. More specifically, with regard to NATO's support to the AU mission in Somalia, JFC Lisbon—under the overall command of Allied Command Operations—was responsible for the SMLO team operating out of the Ethiopian capital.

This team not only conducts NATO's day-to-day activities, but also serves as the NATO military point of contact with partner countries and regional organisations.[126]

NATO has also quietly guided AU policies in Somalia by advising the AU's Peace and Security Commission and its commissioner. From NATO's own account:

These [NATO] experts offer expertise in areas such as maritime planning, strategic planning, financial planning and monitoring, air movement coordination, logistics, communication and information systems, military manpower management and contingency planning.[127]

What is taking place is that the AU is being turned into an arm of NATO and African governments are handing over control of their forces through NATO and AFRICOM to the Pentagon. These local forces as well as the ASF will be outsourced roles in policing their own continent for the interests of Atlanticists. There already is a consensus among the Atlantic Alliance and bureaucrats at the UN for giving regional organizations such roles. Both Kofi Annan, a former UN secretary-general, and Lloyd Axworthy, a former Canadian foreign minister, were invited to the University of Ottawa for a November 2011 conference on humanitarian intervention named *The Responsibility to Protect—10 Years On: Reflections on its Past, Present and Future*. At the conference both men, who were instrumental in helping put together the Responsibility to Protect (R2P), proposed that regional organizations be given R2P mandates.[128] Under this scheme, on behalf of the EU and US, the AU is set to intervene in Africa and the Arab League is positioned to intervene in Arab countries. This might be wishful thinking, but this appears to be *one* of the roads that the AU and NATO are taking.

From United States Africa Command to NATO Africanus

In 2004, the African Union adopted a Common African Defense and Security Policy (CADSP) that mirrored the EU's Common Security and Defense Policy (CSDP). Since that time Africa's security architecture has begun to be defined more and more by Atlanticist characteristics under what is called the African Peace and Security Architecture (APSA).[129] The African Standby Force is merely one component of this. African security sector reforms and a Continental Early Warning System are also part and parcel of the Atlanticist project in Africa which intends to integrate the continent into the Euro-Atlantic Zone.[130] Even the ASF's policies are jointly formed by the AU and EU.[131]

Washington has a major hand in elaborating African security structures and is openly propagating them through the establishment of United States Africa Command (AFRICOM). AFRICOM is the newest Pentagon unified command, which removed all Africa, except Egypt, from the zone of responsibilities of EUCOM, CENTCOM, and USPACOM. This reveals that the US had devised specific military policies and strategies for Africa. It was authorized in 2006 and became active on October 1, 2008. Under the banner of AFRICOM the Pentagon has begun training and reforming Africa's armies, air forces, intelligence services, and navies. It has also waged war: NATO's war against Libya also involved AFRICOM and was its first war. AFRICOM was responsible for intelligence in the war and the US networks on the ground there and involved in Operation Odyssey Dawn.

Again 9/11 plays an important role in the dynamics of this process. Military and security aid from Washington saw a jump at the expense of US development aid:

> As African-directed aid peaked in 2004, the beneficiaries were either petroleum-exporting countries, such as Nigeria and Angola, or countries that had been enlisted [by the US] to support the [Global War on Terror], such as Egypt, Ethiopia, Kenya and Sudan. [...] The share of official development assistance to Africa in the aftermath of 9/11 significantly declined from about 12.2 per cent in 1990 to 3.8 per cent in 2004. According to UK non-governmental organizations, US military and security-related aid to Africa increased, and countries previously of little importance to the United States acquired new funding as a result of the [Global War on Terror]. Djibouti, for example, received US$31 million for allowing the United States to establish a permanent base there.[132]

9/11 was used to justify the start of a permanent US military presence in Africa that allowed for the deployment of US forces almost anywhere in Africa at short notice, in the name of fighting terrorism. As the US became more involved in Africa, the White House and Pentagon increasingly talked about the expansion of Al-Qaeda franchises in Africa and how the US military must expand into the African continent to address that. Strategic interests like the increasing US obsession with the Gulf of Guinea and African oil supplies are casually brushed over in this narrative. Very little is mentioned about pushing out China, Russia, India, and other economic rivals for the resources of Africa. Instead and as always, US interests in Africa are presented as altruistic ones based on the objective of helping fragile states.

Furthermore, the Pentagon is using AFRICOM to create a NATO-like military structure in Africa. AFRICOM's commander, General Ham, effectively told the US Senate outright that the US was planting the seeds of a future NATO-like military structure in Africa. In General Ham's own words:

> [B]uilding the coalition to address the situation in Libya was greatly facilitated through the benefits of longstanding relationships and inter-operability, in this case through NATO. This is the kind of regional approach to security that US Africa Command seeks to foster on the continent [of Africa]. US Africa Command's priority efforts remain building the security capacity of our African partners. We incorporate regional cooperation and pursuit of inter-operability in all of our programs, activities, and exercises so our African partners are postured to readily form coalitions to address African security challenges as they arise.[133]

Like NATO, Washington is subordinating the African military network that the Pentagon and AFRICOM are constructing. AU forces are now working under direction from the US and NATO. The US is essentially restructuring the African continent like it did Europe after the Second World War. Similar to the function of NATO in Europe, AFRICOM has been used by the US as a means to garrison Africa. Some would call this an occupation.

CHAPTER 11

THE MILITARIZATION OF JAPAN AND THE ASIA-PACIFIC

NATO's agreement to invite Albania and Croatia to become members is a welcome start. So is the somewhat weaker commitment that Ukraine and Georgia will become members of NATO at some point.

But we need to go further. As a rule, when an organization expands, the expansion dilutes its principles. For today's NATO, it is just the opposite. Around the world, there is no shortage of nations who share our values, and are willing to defend them. These include countries like Australia, which sent troops to Iraq; Israel, which has been fighting Islamic terrorism almost since its founding; and Japan, which generally follows a more "Western" policy than most of Western Europe.

—Rupert Murdoch, CEO of News Corporation (2008)

NATO's Partners in the Asia-Pacific Region

Although the Commonwealth of Australia, New Zealand, Singapore, the Republic of Korea (South Korea), Taiwan, the Philippines, and Japan are not formally members of NATO, they are linked through military partnerships, affiliated government agreements, a military network, and bilateral military agreements with the Anglo-American Alliance. Scholars have long argued that Japan and NATO are part of an "interdependent security community."[1] The relationship actually goes beyond this and involves more countries in the Asia-Pacific region. The Atlantic Alliance's interests in the Asia-Pacific region are also registered as far back as at least the 1950s and 1960s.[2] For example, in 1965 during the Vietnam War, "[NATO] Secretary-General Manlio Brosio warned a NATO Parliamentary Conference that a setback of the United States in Southwest Asia would be a defeat for NATO."[3] NATO even had an Expert

Working Group on Southeast Asia dedicated to the Vietnam War and Indo-China, which was viewed as a war serving the interests of the Alliance.[4] Moreover, the Pentagon places great importance on the Asia-Pacific region. According to US Secretary of State Hillary Clinton, the current century is "America's Pacific Century" and its fate will be decided in Asia and not in either NATO-garrisoned Afghanistan or Iraq, now laid to waste.[5] Of the countries listed at the start of this chapter, four—Australia, Japan, New Zealand, and South Korea—are NATO Contact Countries that have formal agreements with the Atlantic Alliance. New Zealand even has an Individual Cooperation Program (ICP) with NATO. These countries in practice form an Asiatic and Pacific branch or extension of NATO. There have been repeated calls for the entry of these countries into the North Atlantic Treaty Organization or for them to form an Asian version of NATO. By extension of US strategy, the creation of a parallel NATO-like sister organization in East Asia and the Pacific Rim is part of the international brinkmanship of creating a unified global military alliance—globalizing NATO and the chain of US alliances. In 2006, Ellen Bork, the deputy executive director of the Project for the New American Century (PNAC), and Gary Schmitt, a resident scholar at the American Enterprise Institute, advocated the creation of a military network in Asia similar to NATO in a text about South Korea. In the article the authors argue:

> Asia's supposed "diversity of interests" generally refers to lingering anger over Japan's wartime aggression and brutality. Certainly, visits to the Yasukuni war shrine by Japanese leaders have hardly helped put those animosities to rest; indeed, they have given Beijing, in particular, a tool to stoke anti-Japanese fires throughout the region. Moreover, when NATO was being built, its core consisted of democracies like Great Britain, France, and West Germany. In contrast, Washington's key Asian allies at the time were more of a mixed lot: defeated Japan and democratic Australia on the one hand, authoritarian South Korea and the Republic of China on the other.
>
> The situation of course has changed since them. A wave of democratization that began in the 1980s swept up the Philippines, South Korea, and Taiwan. Indonesia has joined the democratic club as well.
>
> New security problems have also emerged. In addition to the nuclear and missile threat posed by North Korea, China's economic growth has enabled it to develop a military capacity that now not only

threatens Taiwan but is of growing concern to Japan and East Asia as a whole.

None of these momentous changes is reflected in Asia's multilateral organizations, which downplay the importance of democratic principles and emphasize trade and talk instead. Not surprisingly, Washington's efforts to have these organizations take on security roles are so far largely unproductive. In the meantime, China has begun to assert a regional leadership role which increasingly comes at the expense of the United States.

The objection that Asia's past is an obstacle to updating the region's security arrangements misses the point. In fact, tension between Japan and other countries in the region—especially in light of Tokyo's desire to revise its pacifist constitution and take on a greater role in global security affairs—can be best managed by enmeshing Japan in a multilateral alliance of democracies.

Other problems would also be best solved within such a framework. For example, the incentives and constraints of an alliance structure could help Indonesia to transform its military into a transparent, humane force under civilian control. Much in the manner of NATO (and the European Union of recent years), such an alliance would serve as a magnet to countries that have not yet democratized and could help to prevent backsliding in those that have, be they Thailand or the Philippines.[6]

What is essentially being outlined is that the US must merge all its bilateral or dyadic security ties in the region to form an alliance against the People's Republic of China and its allies in Asia. Moreover, News Corporation CEO and billionaire international media mogul Keith Robert Murdoch in 2008 added his voice to the calls of NATO expansion. Murdoch is one of the most powerful figures in Australia who has used his control of the media to influence politics and policies in Australia and other parts of the world. His position on these types of issues is significant to note, because it reflects more than a personal opinion. In 2008, the Australian media tycoon and owner of Fox News and Sky News called for the inclusion of countries like his native Australia and Japan into an expanded global NATO.[7]

The Militarization of Japan

Japan is deeply linked bilaterally and multilaterally to the US military. The Japanese-US dyad, central to the US strategy in East Asia, came about in 1945. Then under US occupation, Japan was controlled and administered by the Pentagon for a period of several years after the Second World War. In 1951 the Japanese government signed the Japan-US Security Treaty, and then expanded it on January 19, 1960 with another bilateral treaty between Tokyo and Washington, the Treaty of Mutual Security and Cooperation. This committed the US to militarily defend Japan under Article 5, while Japan under Article 6 granted the Pentagon the right to maintain bases on its soil "for the purpose of contributing to the security of Japan and the maintenance of international peace and security in the Far East."[8] The signing of this treaty also was matched by the beginning of what CNN's Special Assignment Unit former reporter Joseph Trento describes as a US-supported Japanese secret nuclear weapons program involving the transfer of US weapons grade plutonium to Japan.[9] Yoichi Shimatsu, the former editor of *Japan Times Weekly*, also concluded this on April 7, 2011 as a result of the Japanese government's secrecy when dealing with the disaster at the Fukushima Daiichi Nuclear Power Plant after the damages caused by an earthquake and subsequent tsunami of March 10, 2011.[10] Since the end of the Cold War, Tokyo has gradually and secretly been militarizing. Its doctrinal posture towards China has been overtly transformed since the end of the Cold War as a result of the Nye Initiative that created the April 1996 Japan-US Joint Security Declaration, which was designed to improve Japanese-US military readiness against Beijing.[11]

Japan, along with Australia and South Korea, is a key part of the global missile shield system and the stationing of US-led rapid military forces, as envisioned during the Reagan Administration. Japan is hosting US military radar facilities that are part of the global missile shield project.[12] Tokyo has actually been one of Washington's oldest partners in the project. In 1999, at a time when NATO had its first round of post-Cold War expansion and was at war with Yugoslavia, the US and Japan already had a missile defense research program.[13] The Japanese government has also funded the deployment of the Patriot PAC-3 and the Aegis Standard Missile-3 (SM-3) in East Asia. Moreover, it has upgraded its Defence Agency into a full-fledged ministry, which constituted a breach of the Japanese Constitution. Starting after the Cold War finished, the Japanese Self-Defense Forces were no longer confined to Japanese territory and began to be deployed abroad by Tokyo in 1992 on the basis of Japan's International Peace Cooperation Law. This has allowed the Japanese Self-Defense Forces to be sent under the auspices of the UN to places like

Angola, Cambodia, Mozambique, El Salvador, East Timor, South Sudan, and NATO-garrisoned Afghanistan. In 2004, Japan also sent troops to Anglo-American occupied Iraq on the basis of a US request; the Japanese deployment was historic, because it involved Japan in an ongoing war and was widely seen as a form of combat support by Tokyo for the US and UK.

The Japanese-US dyad has also begun transforming as the Japanese government has been harmonizing its military policies with those of the US and NATO. One face of the transformation, specifically in relation to NATO, can be summarized thus:

> The US-Japan security dyad constitutes a powerful component of what was originally known as the 'Trilateral Commission' but which has more recently found expression with Japan as a key Pacific contact country in the North Atlantic Treaty Organization (NATO) consultative mechanisms for managing its approaches to contemporary global security.[14]

Ties between Tokyo and the Atlantic Alliance emerged towards the end of the Cold War in the 1990s. NATO explains the history of its ties with Japan as follows:

> A strategic dialogue involving high-level discussions held alternatively in Japan and at NATO Headquarters in Brussels has been ongoing since the early nineties. The initial NATO-Japan exchanges initiated more structured and regular contact. NATO's Secretary General [Jaap de Hoop Scheffer] visited Tokyo in April 2005 and again in December 2007. The then Prime Minister Shinzo Abe also addressed the North Atlantic Council in January 2007. Japanese Foreign Minister Takeaki Matsumoto visited NATO Headquarters on 3 May 2011 and met the Secretary General. In a development that demonstrates the intensification of relations between NATO and Japan in recent years, Japanese officials have also participated in a number of meetings with Allies focusing on peace and security issues of mutual interest, such as North Korea, assistance to Afghanistan, cooperation with Central Asia, missile defence and counter-piracy. Both sides benefit from a regular, informal exchange of views.[15]

The January 2007 visit of Japanese Prime Minister Shinzo Abe to NATO Headquarters in Brussels was a historic moment for both Tokyo and NATO, because it was the first visit by a Japanese government leader to the headquarters of the Atlantic Alliance. Prime Minister Abe also made subsequent visits to the UK and Germany that were tied to his talks with NATO and future weapons development and arms cooperation. What's more, Shinzo Abe's visits to Britain and Germany ensured that he spoke to both the Anglo-American and Franco-German branches of NATO. During Abe's talks with NATO, the Japanese leader pledged that Tokyo would work closely with NATO forces inside Afghanistan. Both sides also discussed the continuation of an EU weapons embargo against the Chinese.[16]

It is clear that the Pentagon's project for the militarization of Japan and the region has been endorsed in Asia on the basis of countering the potential threat of a North Korean missile attack and to contain China's expanding influence. In 2010, the Japanese Self-Defense Forces officially designated China as the new focus of their military planning:

> Japan announced a new defense policy on Friday that will respond to China's rising military might by building more submarines and other mobile forces capable of defending Japan's southernmost islands.
>
> The new National Defense Program Guidelines are the biggest step yet in a decade-long shift away from cold war-era deployments of heavy tank and artillery units on the northern island of Hokkaido—to counter a now-vanished Soviet threat—and toward bolstering Japanese forces in the southern islands around Okinawa, where China's navy has become a growing presence.
>
> The new guidelines also used uncharacteristically strong language to warn of China's rapidly modernizing military, calling it "a matter of concern for the region and the international community." China's growing naval capabilities have been a particular concern in Japan since Beijing and Tokyo clashed diplomatically three months ago over uninhabited islands claimed by both nations but controlled by Japan. The islands are called the Senkaku in Japanese and Diaoyu in Chinese.[17]

Chinese officials have reacted diplomatically for the most part. They have maintained that China's military program is purely defensive and is deliberately being portrayed negatively to justify the encircling of China.[18]

The strategic aim of the US to encircle and contain the Chinese has encouraged the Japanese government to turn its back on its constitutionally required policy of pacifism despite the objections of its citizens. The Japanese government has candidly been in open violation of Article 9 of the Japanese Constitution, which stipulates that Japan cannot have a military force. In this regard, the Japanese government initiated a process to amend the Japanese Constitution, which would pave the way for the formal formation of a military force in Japan and "remove its limits on collective self-defence and on helping allies under attack."[19] Tokyo had already started developing its military capabilities and armed forces. The US, Australia, and NATO have been widely supportive of Tokyo's resolve to militarize Japan.

Australia and the Tightening of the Military Alliance in the Asia-Pacific

Since September 11, 2001 the Japanese government pushed forward with its militarization agenda more openly despite the fact that the majority of Japanese citizens are opposed to the militarization of their country. The "long war" projected by the Americans has necessitated the military mobilization of Japanese support. This is where Australia comes into the picture. Not only has there been a systematic effort to integrate Australia into the polity of Asia, but Canberra and Tokyo began establishing close military cooperation towards the end of the Cold War. This has been part of a process of brinkmanship that can best be described as follows:

> A recent trend in US-Japan security community-building is the incremental or low-key expansion of the dyadic core to include a wider spectrum of strategic partnerships based on commonly held democratic values [that is, shared economic interests and outlooks]. The Australia-Japan-US Trilateral Security Dialogue (TSD) is a case in point.[20]

In 2007, the Japanese government signed a historic security agreement with Australia, its second ever bilateral security treaty.[21] The 2007 pact between Australia and Japan has made Tokyo's military ties with Canberra stronger than its other military ties with any country other than the US. The deal has led to the signing of the Japan-Australia Acquisition and Cross-servicing Agreement (ACSA) on May 19, 2010, which allows for the pooling and sharing of military resources.[22] The term "security" in all these agreements is intentionally used in place of the words "defense" or "military" as a means of hiding the nature of what the treaties represent and indicate: despite what the Japanese public think, their country has never has been the pacifist country it has claimed to be after 1945. The Japanese security treaty with Australia has been the start of deepening security and military links in the Asia-Pacific region that is tightening a net around China. It also serves to keep Japan, which has become economically closer to China, firmly anchored in the orbit of the US through the reinforcement of Australia. Moreover, the triad formed by Australia, Japan, and the US has come to replace and mirror the formation of the Australia, New Zealand, and United States (ANZUS) Security Treaty system of Australasia and Oceania before its fracture into two bilateral agreements in 1984.[23]

Australia has been heavily involved in the militarization of the Asia-Pacific region. Canberra has been one of the staunchest allies of the US and NATO in all their post-2001 wars. Ties are so close that Canberra has an ambassador at NATO Headquarters that sits with the North Atlantic Council on certain issues. Under the coalition government of John W. Howard, formed by a parliamentary coalition of the Australian Liberal and National parties, the Australian armed forces were combatants in the Balkans, Afghanistan, and Iraq. Australian troops have also played combat roles in integrated military operations and missions in Iraq. The Australian Special Forces also actively operate in Southeast Asia: Canberra trains Indonesian troops and the armed forces of Singapore train in Australia. The Australian Navy has ships positioned from the Persian Gulf to the Arabian Sea and Pacific Ocean.

Not only has Australia been a US military partner in Iraq since 2003, it is also a partner in the US missile shield project and, like Japan, has also been a military research partner of the United States.[24] Canberra also plays a key role along with the Australia-Japan-US triad in the Pentagon's policy of encircling the Chinese and their Asian allies. Addressed below more sequentially, the establishment of a US military base near Geraldton has given the US a stronger footing in the Indian Ocean.

The Australian Defense Satellite Communications Station (ADSCS) is located in Kojarena, near Geraldton. The ADSCS is actually under US command. It is an integral part of the ECHELON signal intelligence interceptor system of the Anglo-American Alliance. The Anglo-American spy system was established on the basis of the 1946 signal intelligence agreement signed by the UK and US making Yorkshire's Menwith Hill in Britain the largest intelligence gathering and surveillance facility outside of the US. In 2001, the European Parliament had this to say about the system in an official report discussing US spying in the EU:

> The system known as ECHELON is an interception system which differs from other intelligence systems in that it possesses two features which make it quite unusual:

The first such feature attributed to it is the capacity to carry out quasi-total surveillance. Satellite receiver stations and spy satellites in particular are alleged to give it the ability to intercept any telephone, fax, Internet or e-mail message sent by any individual and thus to inspect its contents.

The second unusual feature of ECHELON is said to be that the system operates worldwide on the basis of cooperation proportionate to their capabilities among several states (the UK, the USA, Canada, Australia and New Zealand), giving it an added value in comparison to national systems: the states participating in ECHELON (UKUSA states) can place their interception systems at each other's disposal, share the cost and make joint use of the resulting information.[25]

The US facility in Geraldton in Western Australia is on the shores of the Indian Ocean south of Indonesia and Malaysia, and facing Africa and the Middle East from afar. The establishment of the US military base follows three years of secret negotiations between Washington and the Australian government.[26] The military base provides an important link for a new network of international military satellites that can be used by the US and its allies to fight wars in the Middle East and Asia.[27] In 2011, in a sign of growing militarization, this agreement was matched with another deal between Canberra and Washington to station US military units in Australia. The agreement was made while President Obama was visiting Prime Minister Julia Gillard, the leader of the Australian Labor Party, indicating consensus across the Australian political spectrum. Beijing reacted quickly, speaking out against the agreement as part of a military alliance being expanded against it in the Asia-Pacific region:

The agreement with Australia amounts to the first long-term expansion of the American military's presence in the Pacific since the end of the Vietnam War. It comes despite budget cuts facing the Pentagon and an increasingly worried reaction from Chinese leaders, who have argued that the United States is seeking to encircle China militarily and economically.

"It may not be quite appropriate to intensify and expand military alliances and may not be in the interest of countries within this region," Liu Weimin, a Foreign Ministry spokesman, said in response to the announcement by Mr. Obama and Prime Minister Julia Gillard of Australia.

In an address to the Australian Parliament on Thursday morning, Mr. Obama said he had "made a deliberate and strategic decision—as a Pacific nation, the United States will play a larger and long-term role in shaping this region and its future."[28]

While Obama and Gillard would try to portray the agreement as being a benign act, one major Chinese newspaper bluntly said:

Apparently, Australia aspires to a situation where it maximizes political and security benefits from its alliance with the US while gaining the greatest economic interests from China. However, Gillard may be ignoring something—their economic cooperation with China does not pose any threat to the US, whereas the Australia-US military alliance serves to counter China.

Australia surely cannot play China for a fool. It is impossible for China to remain detached no matter what Australia does to undermine its security. There is real worry in the Chinese society concerning Australia's acceptance of an increased US military presence. Such psychology will influence the long-term development of the Australia-China relationship.

[...]

But one thing is certain—if Australia uses its military bases to help the US harm Chinese interests, then Australia itself will be caught in the crossfire. Australia should at least prevent things from growing out of control.[29]

Under the terms of the agreement the US Marines would deploy in the Australian port of Darwin, which has been described as "a frontier port and military outpost across the Timor Sea from Indonesia, which will be the center of operations for the coming deployment" by April 2012.[30] Parts of the terms of the agreement are as follows:

The first 200 to 250 Marines will arrive next year, with forces rotating in and out and eventually building up to 2,500, the two leaders said.

The United States will not build new bases on the continent, but will use Australian facilities instead. Mr. Obama said that Marines would rotate through for joint training and exercises with Australians, and the American Air Force would have increased access to airfields in the nation's Northern Territory.[31]

Jumping back to the 2007 agreement between Australia and the US, the early warnings about the restructuring of the region's military equation are coming true.

India and the Strategic Encirclement of China

The Indian Ocean and the Asia-Pacific region are being militarized because of Chinese attempts to ensure the continuous flow and security of their African and Middle Eastern energy supplies. The US mission to prevent China from establishing energy security by encircling it was clarified in a 2008 interview given to the *Voice of America* by Admiral Timothy J. Keating shortly after a new Chinese submarine base was discovered.[32] Admiral Keating, the US flag officer commanding the US forces in East Asia and the Pacific under United States Pacific Command (USPACOM), called the base a threat to US interests—meaning military strength—in the Asia-Pacific Region, and warned that the US would remain the dominant Asian power.

On May 12, 2008, *Agence France-Presse* reported:

China's new underground nuclear submarine base close to vital sea lanes in Southeast Asia has raised US concerns, with experts calling for a shoring up of alliances in the region to check Beijing's growing military clout.

The base's existence on the southern tip of Hainan Island was confirmed for the first time by high resolution satellite images, according to *Jane's Intelligence Review*, a respected defence periodical, this month.

It could hold up to 20 submarines, including a new type of nuclear ballistic missile submarine, and future Chinese aircraft carrier battle groups, posing a challenge to longstanding US military dominance in Asia.

[...]

[Admiral Timothy Keating] said Washington should "tighten" its alliances in Asia to check China's growing military might and develop "interoperability" capabilities among allies such as Japan, South Korea,

Taiwan, the Philippines and Singapore, as well as Indonesia and Malaysia.

James Lyons, an ex-commander of the US Pacific Fleet, said the United States needed to reestablish high-level military ties with the Philippines as part of efforts to enhance US deterrence in the wake of China's naval expansion.

He said "operational tactics" used against the former Soviet Union during the Cold War should be applied against China.

He suggested US leasing a squadron of F-16 fighter jets and navy vessels to the Philippines, where Washington once had naval and air bases, as part of the deterrence strategy.[33]

Without India, using Japan or a whole coalition of other Asian states carries far less weight against China, especially a China allied and supported by Russia. Beijing's territorial disputes in the South China Sea with the Philippines, Indonesia, Taiwan, Vietnam, and Brunei are also being used to motivate the creation of a US-led military front against China.

India is clearly a desired partner in the US geo-strategy for dealing with China and Eurasia in broader terms. The aim of this strategy is to recruit India to form a "Quadrilateral Coalition" with the US, Japan, and Australia to neutralize the Chinese. In 2007, this was the topic of a strategic dialogue between New Delhi and Tokyo.[34] The policy to create the Quadrilateral Coalition, which started in 2006 and was pushed by Japan, had little success.[35]

The tactic of trying to confront China with India is similar to the strategy used by the US in relation to Baghdad and Tehran during the Iraq-Iran War where both Baghdad and Tehran were seen as enemy states by Pentagon strategists and the aim was to get both the Iraqis and Iranians to neutralize one another. The US may be viewing the same scenario as applicable to India and China in case of a war between both sides. The possibility of such a conflict occurring was announced by the Indian military in 2009:

> The Indian military fears a 'Chinese aggression' in less than a decade. A secret exercise, called 'Divine Matrix', by the army's military operations directorate has visualised a war scenario with the nuclear-armed neighbour before 2017.
>
> "A misadventure by China is very much within the realm of possibility with Beijing trying to position

itself as the only power in the region. There will be no nuclear warfare but a short, swift war that could have menacing consequences for India," said an army officer, who was part of the three-day war games that ended on Wednesday.

In the military's assessment, based on a six-month study of various scenarios before the war games, China would rely on information warfare (IW) to bring India down on its knees before launching an offensive.

The war games saw generals raising concerns about the IW battalions of the People's Liberation Army carrying out hacker attacks for military espionage, intelligence collection, paralysing communication systems, compromising airport security, inflicting damage on the banking system and disabling power grids. "We need to spend more on developing information warfare capability," he said.

The war games dispelled the notion that China would take at least one season (one year) for a substantial military build-up across India's northeastern frontiers. "The Tibetan infrastructure has been improved considerably. The PLA can now launch an assault very quickly, without any warning," the officer said.

The military believes that China would have swamped Tibet with sweeping demographic changes in the medium term. For the purposes of Divine Matrix, China would call Dalai Lama for rapprochement and neutralise him. The top brass also brainstormed over India's options in case Pakistan joined the war to [*sic.*; too]. Another apprehension was that Myanmar and Bangladesh would align with China in the future geostrategic environment.[36]

Although China and India have been working to diffuse any tensions and upgrade ties, both sides have contingency plans for the scenario of a war between them.

An Asiatic NATO on the Horizon?

The moves to create a NATO-like sister alliance in the Asia-Pacific region are being justified on the basis of Chinese military expansion coupled with fears of North Korea and even Russia. In 2007, *Reuters* reported:

"Whether or not there is an overt threat, Japan and the so-called 'littoral allies' [meaning countries such as the Philippines, Taiwan, and Singapore] in the region have got to address that," [military analyst Alex Neil] added.

North Korea's nuclear and missile tests last year are a source of worry, and China's shooting down of one of its own satellites with a ballistic missile in January [2007] aroused concern in many capitals.

"We are no longer in an age when either Japan or Australia can rely solely on the United States as an ally," said military analyst Tetsuya Ozeki, who says both China and Russia are set to become equally influential in the region."[37]

In this regard, the US Pacific Fleet is also placing greater strategic importance on the island of Guam than ever before as it deepens its collaboration and military coordination with the Philippines, Australia, Singapore, South Korea, Taiwan, and Japan to militarily tighten the noose around the People's Republic of China.[38] What has been transpiring in the Asia-Pacific region is the taking of aggressive steps to encircle China. What the agreements between Australia and Japan, along with the move by Tokyo to amend the Japanese Constitution, amount to are steps to form an eastern flank in Eurasia against China and Russia through a parallel sister alliance to NATO.

CHAPTER 12

THE DRIVE INTO EURASIA

ENCIRCLING RUSSIA, CHINA AND IRAN

*he·gem·o·ny (hidʒémǝni:) pl. he·gem·o·nies n. leadership
exercised by one state, esp. one in a federation of states [fr. Gk
hegemonia]*

—**The New Lexicon Webster's Dictionary
of the English Language (1987)**

Post-9/11 NATO Expansion

The 9/11 attacks and combating terrorism have been used as
pretexts for the mobilization of unparalleled military might, permitting
the projection of US military strength in far corners of the globe. It has
served to consolidate US power overseas. Anglo-American and NATO
forces could never have invaded Taliban-controlled Afghanistan without
9/11. Nor could they have begun the process of normalizing out-of-area
operations so far from the Euro-Atlantic core that led to NATO missions
in Iraq, Sudan, Somalia, and Libya. Nor could NATO's naval forces have
declared the Eastern Mediterranean, the Red Sea, and the Gulf of Aden
areas of responsibility without assuming a mandate to fight terrorism.

After 9/11, Al-Qaeda was presented to the world by the US
government as an American opponent on a par with the defeated USSR.
In reality Al-Qaeda has been a fictitious bogeyman used as a justification
for US militarism. Al-Qaeda is a one-size-fits-all term used to designate
different assortments of people, some of whom are actually engaged in
anti-imperial struggles from a range of national and religious orientations.
But others designated as Al-Qaeda are actually intelligence operatives or
simply mercenary thugs told to pose as religiously-oriented warriors. In
the former instances, both sides try to use the other while pursuing very
different goals. It is not in the US interest to distinguish between these

266

groups as long as they are struggling against a common target; once the target is defeated, then the anti-imperialist elements are labeled Al-Qaeda as a form of demonization for opposing US interests and destroyed. Michael Scheuer, a Georgetown University professor and the former chief of the CIA's Osama bin Laden unit, would even admit that the Global War on Terror was being fought against a "non-existent enemy." His book *Imperial Hubris*, anonymously published in 2004, contained analysis that was often close to a bin Laden panegyric. On the other hand, in the words of former US foreign secretary Robin Cook, Al-Qaeda is "originally the computer file of the thousands of mujahideen who were recruited and trained with help from the CIA to defeat the [Soviets]."[1]

The Global War on Terror, a subsidiary of Samuel Huntington's "Clash of Civilizations" theory, and NATO expansion are linked through their relationships to US geo-strategy tied to entrenching US primacy in Eurasia. In this context, Western Europe through NATO and the EU forms the primary bridgehead of the United States into Eurasia from its westernmost area, which is part of the Euro-Atlantic Zone. According to Zbigniew Brzezinski:

> [NATO and the EU constitute] America's most important
> global relationship. It is the springboard for U.S. global
> involvement, enabling America to play the decisive
> role of arbiter in Eurasia—the world's central arena
> of power—and it creates a coalition that is globally
> dominant in all key dimensions of power and influence.[2]

The secondary bridgeheads of the US into Eurasia are: Japan and South Korea from the easternmost area of Eurasia in East Asia; the Arabian Peninsula from one of the southern areas of Eurasia; and from NATO-garrisoned Afghanistan. These areas all host US bases. They are essentially the main staging grounds for modern conquest. The US controls a network of three intertwined alliances in these areas, which are complemented by the construction of three branches of the US global missile shield system. These alliances are also formally tied together through ties with NATO. NATO's Mediterranean Dialogue encompasses the Mediterranean Basin and has made inroads into both Africa and the Middle East; the Atlantic Alliance's Istanbul Cooperation Initiative (ICI) ties the Gulf Cooperation Council to NATO and gives the Alliance a footing at the gates of Iran in the Persian Gulf; the Afghanistan-Pakistan-ISAF Tripartite Commission cements a NATO foothold in both NATO-garrisoned Afghanistan and Pakistan; the Partnership for Peace is being used to absorb the countries of the former USSR; and the arrangements with Contact Countries has not only created formal ties with states like Australia, Japan, New Zealand,

South Korea, and Pakistan, it has eliminated geographic boundaries and limitations on NATO. Under NATO the network of US-led alliances in the Middle East and the Asia-Pacific region are consolidated under a global format. In addition to this global military network, NATO and the US are manning the world's international waterways. The high seas, international trade, and maritime traffic are also the focus of a solidifying control regime spearheaded by the US.

The United States is creating a military ring that encircles the Eurasian Heartland. The Nixon Doctrine, which calls for the transformation of US allies into regional arms of the US, is being re-applied. The Atlantic Alliance has become a projection of US power in Europe and the Mediterranean Sea; Australia and Japan are US gendarmes in East Asia and the Asia-Pacific region; and Israel, the GCC, and Turkey are being manipulated in the Middle East. In Africa and Latin America, respectively through countries like Ethiopia and Colombia, the Nixon Doctrine is also being applied with regional gendarmerie. What is different from Nixon's time, however, is that now there is an extensive institutionalized incorporation of these gendarmes into formal security and military structures tied to the US. All these regionalized projections of US influence are also supplemented and harmonized with US military unified combatant commands that create geographic zones of responsibility for the Pentagon's generals and admirals.

What the US has been doing is steadily encircling Russia, Iran, and China. India is also in the firing line. All of these major Eurasian states, as regional powers, constitute challenges to US plans for primacy in Eurasia; Russia being the dominant power in Eastern Europe and the post-Soviet space; Iran being the regional powerhouse in the Persian Gulf and the Middle East; India being South Asia's main power, and China being the dominant power in East Asia. Three strategic Atlanticist fronts are being created in Eurasia: one around China's heavily populated eastern and southern borders; another encompassing Iran and its allies in the Middle East; and the third situated in Eastern Europe looking at Russia's western borders.

The Geography of Encirclement

The Pentagon's unified combatant commands play important roles in the encirclement of the Eurasian Heartland and Russia, Iran, and China. Six of these *geographic* command structures have been made to carve out theater-level areas of responsibility (AOR) for the Pentagon's generals and admirals: US Africa Command (AFRICOM), US Central Command (CENTCOM), US European Command (EUCOM), US Northern Command (NORTHCOM), US Pacific Command (USPACOM), and US Southern Command (SOUTHCOM).[3] EUCOM and USPACOM were created

Table 12.1

NATO and its Global Alliance Network*

NATO Members	Mid-East/ North Africa	Asia-Pacific Allies	Other Allies
Albania	Bahrain	Australia	Azerbaijan Republic of
Belgium	Egypt	Japan	Colombia
Bulgaria	Israel	Korea, Republic of	Finland
Canada	Jordan	New Zealand	Georgia, Republic of
Croatia	Kuwait	Philippines	Kosovo-Serbia
Czech Republic	Libya-Transitional Council	Singapore	Macedonia, FYR of
Denmark	Mauritania	Taiwan	Montenegro
Estonia	Morocco		Pakistan
France	Qatar		Sweden
Germany	Saudi Arabia		
Hungary	United Arab Emirates		
Iceland			
Italy			
Latvia			
Lithuania			
Luxembourg			
Netherlands			
Norway			
Romania			
Slovenia			
Spain			
Turkey			
United Kingdom			
USA			

* Up until February 2012. Excluding allies in sub-Saharan Africa.

in 1947 and are the oldest of these unified commands, signifying the start of US military encroachment into Eurasia from Western Europe and Eastern Asia after the Second World War. It should be noted that the commander of EUCOM is the same US general or admiral that is the supreme commander of NATO. While the position of NATO secretary-general has traditionally been occupied by a Western European, the head of NATO's combined armed forces is always a US general or admiral. On the diplomatic and public fronts the Alliance is represented by a non-American, but this hides or disguises the US dominance of NATO.

Empirically, these unified combatant commands and the strategic fronts they support are aligned with classical Cold War containment doctrine and with its underlying doctrine of strategic incursion, which became visible in the post-Cold War era tied to the master of containment theory Nicholas Spykman's concept of the Eurasian Rimland.[4] Spykman's work builds on Halford Mackinder's calls to create a shatter-belt around the Eurasian Heartland and amidst Germany and Russia from the Baltic to the Aegean Seas. Spykman was one of the figures in the US that aligned containment with incursion—making US defensive strategy effectively strategically *offensive*. Spykman argued that relying on isolationism, based on reliance on the oceans as a protective barrier to invasion, was bound to fail.

> The analysis made by Professor Spykman showed conclusively that this was a dangerous illusion. Against a determined attack launched by a power or group of powers controlling the European mainland, our chances of defending ourselves on this side of the Atlantic were small indeed. Only if the British fleet were in complete control of the Atlantic and Pacific, and if we were able to use the British Isles as an advance base against the continent of Europe, could we be at all sure of our chances of survival.[5]

The Atlantic Alliance and other US military projects in Europe and Asia were meant to prevent any one power from dominating the two sub-units of Eurasia and a means of preventing Eurasian unification through the strategic incursion of the United States:

> The principal lesson is clear. The most important single fact in the American security situation is the question of who controls the rimlands of Europe and Asia. Should these get into the hands of a single power or combination of powers hostile to the United States,

the resulting encirclement would put us in a position of grave peril, regardless of the size of our army and navy. The reality of this threat has been dimly realized in the past; on the two recent occasions when a single power threatened to gain control of the European mainland, we have become involved in a war to stop it. But our efforts have been belated and have been carried out at huge cost to ourselves. Had we been fully conscious of the implications of our geographical location in the world, we might have adopted a foreign policy which would have helped to prevent the threat from arising in the first place.

It is to be expected that there will be some misinterpretation of the implications of this thesis. There will doubtless be some critics who will say that it is not our business to prevent by armed force the unification of Europe or Asia under one power, that such an act would be an undue interference in other people's business.

The best answer to such criticism is to consider the probable situation in Europe and the Far East at the close of this war. The rimlands of Europe will be for the most part in the hands of democracies who will be profoundly concerned to regain their full independence. Any proposal for the unification of Europe would tend to put them in a subordinate position to Germany (regardless of the legal provisions of the arrangement) since Germany, unless broken up into fragments, will still be the biggest nation on the continent.

[...]

Hence there is little basis for apprehension that a security policy based on Professor Spykman's analysis would involve us in an active program of forceful intervention to prevent European or Asiatic unification. What the analysis does emphasize with great clarity is the importance of our taking our rightful part in world affairs as a means of assuring peace in general and our own security in particular.[6]

This line of thinking was clearly built on Makinder's description of an empire-building project under the garments of democratic values. At best it is a form of self-deception and exceptionalism. Offense and aggression are presented as defense and a desire for peace, preventing the unification of other peoples is justified as righteous, and a hegemonic project to dominate others—the continuation of Manifest Destiny—as part of America's "rightful place in the world."

The Rimland is conceived to include the geographic area adjacent to the Eurasian Heartland that is comprised of the western areas of Europe, the Middle East, the Indian sub-continent, Southeast Asia, and East Asia's seaboard. The area in essence forms an enveloping geographic ring around Mackinder's Heartland. In other words, the Rimland surrounds the central or core region(s) of Eurasia; it forms a densely populated oblong that was viewed as a field of containment firstly against the Soviet Union and then against both the Soviets and Maoist China.

From 2000 to 2007 CENTCOM addressed what more or less corresponded to what Brzezinski described as a "large geographic oblong that demarcates the central zone of global instability" which ran all the way from the Balkans and East Africa through the Middle East and Central Asia to Kashmir.[7] This "central zone of global instability" is linked to the central area of the Rimland.

The different geographic regions of Europe and Asia are important, but they are not as pivotal in geo-strategic value as the Middle East and its geographic periphery (including Central Asia). If one scrutinizes a map of Eurasia one will notice that the geographic positioning of Japan or the Korean Peninsula cannot lead to any significant penetration of Eurasia. Indo-China also has limited use. The Russian Federation acts as a barrier to any drive from Eastern Europe that would be meaningless unless Ukraine fell into NATO's orbit and Russia lost its Caucasian republics, which the US has attempted to achieve through the Ukrainian Orangists and support for Caucasian secessionism. Due to political realities India, the giant of the Indian sub-continent, can only be used as a counter-weight to China or to spoil the formation of a Eurasian alliance involving Russia, China, and Iran. Whatever value these geographic areas have in regard to containment theory is lost in regard to US objectives for penetrating into the Heartland, aside from India and Ukraine under the proper circumstances.

The Middle East and CENTCOM play a significant role in the Pentagon's encirclement and penetration strategy. The Middle East or Near East is an abstract geographic concept that has been shifting with geo-strategic, political, and socio-economic changes. The name Middle East, like the Far East, denotes an ethnocentric view of the world with Western Europe as its center; it is a place name that has been fashioned on the basis of proximity to Western Europe. If the relationship were inversed, Western Europe would be called the "Middle West" and North America the "Far West." There were times when academics, map makers, and geographers considered the Balkans to be a part of the Middle East. There is even a current conscientious effort to replace the name Middle East, because of its ethnocentric origins and ties to cultural colonization. In the mind of many North American and European individuals the Middle East is a synonym for the Arab World or for Southwest Asia, but both terms do not correspond. The Middle East includes non-Arab countries like Iran, Turkey, and Cyprus. The term Southwest Asia also excludes Egypt, the European portion of Turkey in Thrace and—depending if you categorize them as part of the region—Albania, Greece, and Libya. The Middle East is defined as a region that embraces the three continents—two if you look at Europe and Asia as Eurasia—Europe, Asia, and Africa; it is a global crossroad and meeting point.

Three important maritime passages and five important bodies of water also are located or embrace the area around the Middle East. Going clockwise the five important bodies of water in this area are the Black Sea, Caspian Sea, Persian Gulf, Red Sea, and the eastern end of the Mediterranean Sea. The region's important maritime passages and straits can be used to manipulate, cut, and control global navigation, international trade, maritime traffic, and energy supplies. These strategic maritime passages or chokepoints are the Suez Canal of Egypt, the Bosporus of Turkey, and the Gate of Tears (Bab Al-Mandeb) located between Djibouti and Yemen at the southern tip of the Red Sea. NATO control over these maritime passages would have grave ramifications for any of its adversaries in regard to trade, naval movements, and energy supplies.

Encircling Russia, Iran, India, and China

What about the states of the Eurasian Heartland? These are the states that US geo-strategy wants to dually prevent from unifying and from dominating Eurasia or its regions. How have they reacted to their strategic encirclement and NATO expansion? Their reactions will be partially described in this chapter, but a great deal more will ultimately be said towards the end of the book involving their counter-alliance against the US and NATO.

The reaction of the Russians has become steadily more and more apprehensive as they realize that they are being encircled by the US and NATO. In February 2007, US Secretary of Defense Robert Gates testified that Russia, along with China, was viewed as a threat by Washington. He stated to members of the US Congress: "In addition to fighting the 'Global War on Terror,' we also face [...] the uncertain paths of China and Russia, which are both pursuing sophisticated military modernization programs."[8] The Russian Foreign Ministry and government immediately demanded an official explanation from the White House for the threatening remarks by Robert Gates. Chief of the Russian Armed Forces General Staff Yuri Baluyevsky warned Russians days later that their country faced even greater military threats than during the Cold War. General Baluyevsky publicly insisted that Russia start to prepare itself against the military threat from NATO.[9] Days apart from the statements of Robert Gates and General Baluyevsky, Vladimir Putin told the elite audience at the Munich Conference on Security Policy in Germany that NATO was targeting his country. It was the first significant Russian statement against the Atlantic Alliance made in front of NATO leaders and a sign that Russia was beginning to feel seriously threatened on its immediate borders.

Both NATO expansion and the missile shield have caused friction with Russia and put the NATO-Russia Council in a state of paralysis. The missile shield was renounced by the Russian military because it would drag Russia "into a new arms race" with the US and NATO.[10] The Russians also adamantly insist, with some reason, that the missile shield is aimed at them and the post-Soviet space. They have looked on angrily as the Atlantic Alliance has courted Georgia and Ukraine. Tensions between the Euro-Atlantic Zone and the Russian Federation reached a new high in 2008 when Russia went to war with Georgia and refused to back down to US and NATO intimidation. The Kremlin and Russian officials have since been agitated by the antagonistic comments of US politicians like John McCain, Sarah Palin, and Mitt Romney that have targeted Russia as a US enemy and threatened regime change. In 2011, Dmitry Medvedev would publicly threaten to attack the missile shield. From a Russian perspective, the Atlantic Alliance is not committed to "peaceful co-existence" or any form of strategic equilibrium.

The Iranians see NATO as no less a threat than their Russian neighbors do. Iran has continuously remained defiant, even in the face of almost complete military encirclement by the US and NATO. Tehran has always had NATO in mind, because it sits on the frontiers of the Euro-Atlantic Zone and shares a border with NATO member Turkey. NATO's ties with Israel have not escaped Iranian officials either. Since 9/11 Tehran's attention has focused more and more on the Atlantic Alliance, given NATO's involvement in Afghanistan; its courtship of the Republic of Azerbaijan; its training mission and advisory role in Iraq; its 2006 intent to deploy peacekeepers to Lebanon; its announcement of the establishment of the missile shield; its war against the Libyan Arab Jamahiriya; and most recently, the threats of a NATO attack against Tehran's Syrian allies.

As the Euro-Atlantic Zone's frontiers began to expand with more out-of-area missions and wars, contact between Tehran and NATO also began. In 2008, a Hungarian plane taking off from Turkey as part of a NATO mission to Afghanistan violated Iranian airspace and was forced to land in Tehran by Iranian jets.[11] In March 2009, Iran and NATO held their first publicly known informal talks in Brussels.[12] NATO Assistant Secretary-General for Political Affairs and Security Policy Martin Erdmann met with an Iranian diplomat to discuss NATO-garrisoned Afghanistan.[13] Two years later, Iranian officials attended the annual session of the NATO Parliamentary Assembly's Mediterranean and Middle East Special Group—which is a supportive structure for NATO's Mediterranean Dialogue and the ICI—for the first time in July 2011 during NATO's war with Libya.[14] Towards the end of 2011, tensions between the US and Iran reached a boiling point. During this period a US spy drone would be taken down by the Iranian military, which prompted NATO officials in Kabul to state that the Lockheed Martin RQ-170 Sentinel spy drone had lost control over NATO-garrisoned Afghanistan.[15] As tensions worsened, Iran threatened to close the Strait of Hormuz, prompting NATO to warn Tehran against such a move in the Persian Gulf.[16]

The encirclement of the Asian giants, India and China, has been mostly a silent affair. NATO has also been evaluating the capacities of both countries and initiated contact with India. Moreover, the US and its allies have sought to use New Delhi against Beijing and have thus kept relations cordial. On the other hand the Chinese have mostly opted to keep silent as East Asia has become militarized. This has begun to change as the Chinese realize that they are the main target of the US and its allies. The US and NATO tensions with Russia and Iran are aimed at reducing two important Chinese allies and energy sources.

In Search of New Justifications for Conflict: Enter Samuel Huntington

With the end of the Cold War, the ideological justifications for conflict faded. The US and NATO could no longer demonize and alienate Russia on the basis of a different ideology. The Russian Federation had adopted capitalism and begun to politically liberalize. The Atlanticists needed new justifications for their pursuit of domination. A regressive paradigm—resembling the fallacious racist constructs of the colonial era used earlier to justify oppression—was adopted, but in a modern format. Ethno-cultural differences were now outlined as the "last phase in the evolution of conflict in the modern world."[17] Intellectual entrepreneur Samuel Huntington became the main spokesperson for this paradigm titled the "Clash of Civilizations," which he summarized in 1993 as follows:

> The great divisions among humankind and the
> dominating source of conflict will be cultural. Nation

states will remain the most powerful actors in world affairs, but the principal conflicts of global politics will occur between nations and groups of different civilizations. The clash of civilizations will dominate global politics. The fault lines between civilizations will be the battle lines of the future.[18]

Now the Russians are demonized because they supposedly belong to another culture and civilization. Huntington's new cultural iron curtain dividing Europe is described thus: "As the ideological division of Europe has disappeared, the cultural division of Europe between Western Christianity, on the one hand, and Orthodox Christianity and Islam, on the other, has reemerged."[19]

Anticipating the absorption by the Western Bloc of most of the Eastern Bloc countries into the Euro-Atlantic Zone, Huntington described the Cold War as a "civil war" within Western Civilization that had ended while the new focal point of global political friction would be between Western and non-Western Civilizations.[20] Firstly, his description of the Cold War as an internal matter for Western Civilization was contradictory, because he categorized the Eastern Bloc as predominately being part of what he problematically called "Slavic-Orthodox Civilization." Secondly, critics can interpret his assessment on Western interaction with non-Western Civilizations as an indicator that the Western Bloc was now turning its attention to conquering other parts of the world just as it did with Eastern Europe and the former USSR.

For Huntington and his supporters the wars of the future were going to be cultural events almost completely based on fixed factors that "are far more fundamental than differences among political ideologies and political regimes."[21] In his own words:

> [C]ultural characteristics and differences are less mutable and hence less easily compromised and resolved than political and economic ones. In the former Soviet Union, communists can become democrats, the rich can become poor and the poor rich, but Russians cannot become Estonians and Azeris cannot become Armenians. In class and ideological conflicts, the key question was "Which side are you on?" and people could and did choose sides and change sides. In conflicts between civilizations, the question is "What are you?" That is a given that cannot be changed.[22]

What Huntington conceptualizes—in what he admittedly says is a political project—is an incredibly dangerous way to look at the world, because it outlines conflict on predominately fixed factors that people cannot change. Therefore individuals or groups become enemies not on the basis of their actions, but on the basis of who they are. In application it is prone to zero-sum political assessments and fails to distinguish between religion and culture, or weigh the interplay between the two.

If it were to be argued that the Cold War conflict related to communism which Huntington is regarding as a Western construct, and that insofar as the USSR was molded by those theories it was operating within that (Western) ideological framework, the counter-argument is that if the system of governance and ideology are the basis for identifying civilizations then so-called Orthodox Civilization countries (e.g., Bulgaria, Romania) are now more Western then ever on the basis of their political systems. Japan, Latin America, China, India, and so on would not be seperate civilizations under his model either.

The "Clash of Civilizations" theory argued that the chief adversaries of Western Civilization are problematically described as Arab-Islamic and Confucian (later called Sinic) Civilizations.[23] Making an appeal to authority by quoting an Indian Muslim, Huntington writes: "The West's 'next confrontation,' observes M. J. Akbar, an Indian Muslim author, 'is definitely going to come from the Muslim world. It is in the sweep of the Islamic nations from the Maghreb to Pakistan that the struggle for a new world order will begin.'"[24] Huntington uses the Nagorno-Karabakh War to also try to prove that religious groups and so-called civilizational groupings stick together—not even knowing that Iran was allied to Orthodox Christian Armenia instead of to the Shiite Muslim Republic of Azerbaijan.

Atlanticism versus Eurasianism

The chess pieces for a colossal geo-strategic project are being put into place and coming together. The ultimate US goal is the encirclement and control of Eurasia through the jackboots of an ever expanding military machine. Resistance has built and brought Russia, China, and Iran into the same camp. The Atlanticist march into Eurasia has given rise to Eurasianism. Russia, China, and Iran have pushed for a united Eurasian front against Washington and its cohorts, which includes hostile governments supported and armed by both the US government and Pentagon.

Atlanticist strategy has focused on dividing the Eurasianist camp. US strategists and analysts have wishfully averred that the Russian Federation will be forced to align with the US against China at a future point; they have hypothesized that the alliance between Beijing and

Moscow is similar to the temporary alliance between the German Third Reich and USSR during the start of the Second World War. In this context, the US has kept separate open channels with both Russia and China in efforts to de-link them from one another. These US efforts are increasingly to no avail.

The 2008 war between Georgia and Russia, the siege against Iran, the tensions between North Korea and South Korea, the revolts in Western China, and the waves of colored revolutions from Lebanon, Central Asia, and Moldova to Southeast Asia are an integral part of this geo-political confrontation. The global dimensions of this militarization process are not limited to Eurasia. From Central and South America to Africa, the Arctic Circle, and the Indian Ocean, the main ingredients for a global conflict are being assembled.

CHAPTER 13

THE EURASIAN COUNTER-ALLIANCES

But if the middle space [Russia and the former Soviet Union] rebuffs the West [the Euro-Atlantic Zone], becomes an assertive single entity, and either gains control over the South [the Greater Middle East] or forms an alliance with the major Eastern actor [China], then America's primacy in Eurasia shrinks dramatically. The same would be the case if the two major Eastern players were somehow to unite. Finally, any ejection of America by its Western partners [the Franco-German Entente] from its perch on the western periphery [Europe] would automatically spell the end of America's participation in the game on the Eurasian chessboard, even though that would probably also mean the eventual subordination of the western extremity to a revived player occupying the middle space [Russia].

—Zbigniew Brzezinski (1997)[1]

The "Anti-Establishmentarianism" of Eurasianism

If the prospects of China becoming a global superpower are real, then the materialization of any solid Eurasian alliance comprised of Russia, Iran, India, and China and augmented by non-Eurasian powers like Brazil would certainly give rise to a "mega power." Such a mega power would dwarf the US demographically, territorially, economically, politically, militarily, and industrially. At best, America would become a secondary power like Germany and Japan presently are in comparison to it. Within this context, the materialization of a strong Eurasian entity has historically been sabotaged, obstructed, and opposed by British and later US strategists in what is best described as an ongoing *Anglo-American geo-strategy* in Eurasia. Historically, London has always worked at preempting the rise of any strong rival power on the Continent (Eurasia). Halford Mackinder, the so-called "father of geo-politics," was not the man who contrived or imagined such an idea, he merely articulated the characteristics of Britain's stratagem much as Machiavelli derived his theories by observing the practice of the Medici. The US now inherits this stratagem, put forward as if it were a font of knowledge for building and retaining power and security. Yet, Isaac Newton's Third Law of Motion states that "for every action there is an equal and opposite reaction." This precept of physics is applicable in the social sciences and the humanities, specifically with reference to social relations and geo-politics. While the Atlanticists have engaged in an ambitious project to assume lordship in Eurasia, their actions have resulted in reactionary counter-measures from Eurasia. Atlanticism has in fact given birth to its antithesis: Eurasianism.

Eurasianism seeks integration in Eurasia as a natural and organic process through such bodies as the Eurasian Union. This is a threat not to Europe but to the US and the Atlanticist project, because it would give rise to a new mega power—a geo-strategic nightmare for the Atlanticists. Eurasian-wide integration running from Lisbon, Paris, Rome, and Berlin through Istanbul, Baghdad, Riyadh, Dushanbe, and Mumbai (Bombay) to Jakarta, Beijing, Vladivostok, and Tokyo would pull the plug on NATO expansion and the "Clash of Civilizations" paradigm being intuitively advocated to justify Atlanticist domination. In this context the deepening cooperation between Russia and other Eurasian states can be called "Halford Mackinder's geo-strategic nightmare." The Russian multilateralist Primakov Doctrine in this sense is a Eurasian rebuttal to Mackinder's admonition about the strategic threat to Britain and to similar maritime or oceanic players, like the US, from a strong Continental actor.

While NATO expands and its partnerships proliferate globally outside the Euro-Atlantic Zone, Eurasianist projects have also begun to oppose and defy NATO expansion and US primacy. A Eurasian-based coalition with a triple entente comprised of China, Russia, and Iran with multiple faces, including the Collective Security Treaty Organization (CSTO) and the Shanghai Cooperation Organization (SCO), has emerged. Latin America and the Caribbean have increasingly begun to challenge US influence and Brazil has partnered with Russia, India, and China under the informal grouping known as the BRIC—followed by South Africa in 2010, creating the BRICS. Russia even proposed the creation of a new collective security agreement in the Persian Gulf that would include Iran and Russia in 2008 as a challenge to the Istanbul Cooperative Initiative in the Persian Gulf.[2]

The Primakov Doctrine and the Emergence of a "Chinese-Russian-Iranian Coalition"

Perhaps it is well-earned that the birth of this anti-establishmentarian phenomenon which opposes Atlanticist domination of the world is none other than post-Soviet Russia, the first and primary target of the Atlanticists. In 1996, Russian decision makers realized that their country was viewed more like a colonial territory to be divided as a spoil of the Cold War than as an equal partner by the Atlanticists. If Russia were to become absorbed into the Euro-Atlantic Zone, it would be as a virtual colony. Since then the Primakov Doctrine—formulated by Yevgeny Primakov the former chairman of the lower house of the Soviet legislature (Soviet of the Union) and the former foreign and prime minister of Russia—began gaining currency in Moscow. Under the Primakov Doctrine the leaders of the Kremlin were primed to establish a strategic alliance with China, India, and Iran. From the seeds of the Primakov Doctrine, a reluctant coalition started to form between China and Russia that would later incorporate Tehran, while New Delhi cordially kept its distance.

Zbigniew Brzezinski made a prefigurative warning against the creation or "emergence of a hostile [Eurasian-based] coalition that could eventually seek to challenge America's primacy."[3] The offensive nature of US strategy is clear in Brzezinski's terminology; he called this potential Eurasian coalition a potential anti-hegemonic alliance or counter-alliance that would be formed on the cornerstone of a "Chinese-Russian-Iranian coalition" with the Chinese at its center of gravity.[4] About China he said:

> In assessing China's future options, one has to consider also the possibility that an economically successful and politically self-confident China—but one which feels excluded from the global system and which decides to become both the advocate and the leader of the deprived states of the world—may decide to pose not only an articulate doctrinal but also a powerful geopolitical challenge to the dominant trilateral world.[5]

Beijing's answer to challenging the global status quo would be the creation of a Chinese-Russian-Iranian coalition:

> For Chinese strategists, confronting the trilateral coalition of America and Europe and Japan, the most effective geopolitical counter might well be to try and fashion a triple alliance of its own, linking China with Iran in the Persian Gulf/Middle East region and with

> Russia in the area of the former Soviet Union [and Eastern Europe].[6]

This Chinese-Russian-Iranian coalition, which Brzezinski calls an "anti-establishmentarian coalition," could become "a potent magnet for other states dissatisfied with the [global] status quo."[7] Hence he warned in 1997 that the "most immediate task [for US officials] is to make certain that no state or combination of states gains the capacity to expel the United States from Eurasia or even to diminish significantly its decisive arbitration role."[8] Since 9/11, however, the opposite has taken place.

China, Iran, and Russia have all increasingly perceived themselves as US and NATO targets—a perception that has in fact been hard to miss. Their mutual fears of encirclement have brought them together. As NATO intervention began in the Balkans, Beijing and Moscow jointly declared in 1996 that they opposed the global imposition of single-state hegemony; this was the same year that Russia and China founded the Shanghai Five, the precursor of the SCO. What can be called an uncodified "Eurasian Charter" hence came into existence when Chinese and Russian leaders declared with several of their allies in 2000 that all nation-states should be treated equally, mutually enjoy security, respect each other's sovereignty, and most importantly not interfere in the internal affairs of one other. These statements were directed towards the Atlanticists in Washington, DC and their cohorts and vassals. As part of this Eurasian Charter, Beijing and Moscow have also called for the establishment of a more equitable economic and political order. It is no accident that when NATO bombarded Yugoslavia in 1999, President Jiang Zemin and President Boris Yeltsin made an anticipated joint declaration at a historic summit in December of 1999 that revealed that China and the Russian Federation would join hands to resist the emerging Atlanticist order and ensure international multipolarity. In July 2000 China and Russia jointly issued statements with Kazakhstan, Kyrgyzstan, and Tajikistan warning that the creation of the missile shield and the contravention of the Anti-Ballistic Missile Treaty by the US would destabilize the international environment and polarize the globe with hostilities.

In 1999, Beijing and Moscow were well aware of what was to come and the direction in which US foreign policy was headed. China and Russia signed the Treaty of Good-Neighborliness and Friendly Cooperation on July 24, 2001—less than two months before 9/11. A softly worded mutual defence pact against the US, NATO, and the US-led Asian military network surrounding China, it went beyond mutual defense and territorial integrity. Article 12 outlined that the Sino-Russian pair would work together to safeguard and maintain a global strategic balance and promote nuclear disarmament—all insinuating a threat from US militarism as a "hyperpower." For almost an entire decade before this, Beijing and Moscow had been working to build one another's trust by acts such as demilitarizing the Sino-Russian border.

Primakov had put special emphasis on strategic coordination with Iran, because of its importance as a geo-strategic pivot and its anti-establishmentarian political nature. Iran also holds a critical place in the national security strategies and interests of Beijing and Moscow:

> The geo-political equation in Eurasia very much hinges on the structure of Iran's political alliances. Were Iran to become an ally of the United States, this would seriously hamper or even destabilize Russia and China. This also pertains to Iran's ethno-cultural, linguistic, economic, religious, and geo-political links to the Caucasus and Central Asia.[9]

Iran is a gateway into Russia and its soft southern underbelly; should Iran align with the US, it would become the greatest conduit of US influence in the Caucasus and Central Asia. China would also become a US hostage if Tehran realigned itself with the US. Chinese energy security would be shattered, because Iran's vast energy reserves would be in the service of the US and energy-rich Central Asia's orbit could change as a result of Iranian realignment. Brzezinski has also acknowledged this:

> [I]t is not in America's interest to perpetuate American-Iranian hostility. Any eventual reconciliation should be based on the recognition of a mutual strategic interest in stabilizing what currently is a very volatile regional environment for Iran. Admittedly, any such reconciliation must be pursued by both sides and is not a favor granted by one to the other. A strong, even religiously motivated but not fanatically anti-Western Iran is in [America's] interest, and ultimately even the Iranian political elite may recognize that reality.[10]

These are the main reasons that China and Russia supported initial UN Security Council resolutions against the Iranians: to maintain the distance between Iran and the US. This created a wider rift between Tehran and Washington.

Iran began to gravitate more closely towards China and Russia after 9/11. It appears that a strategic rapprochement between Tehran and Washington could have even come into fruition from 2001 to 2002.

Iran and the US worked together to oust the Taliban from Kabul and both Lebanon's Hezbollah and Palestine's Hamas, two Arab organizations allied with Tehran, were kept off the US State Department's list of terrorist organizations so as not to complicate relations with Tehran. The Iranians also shared an enthusiasm with the White House for removing Saddam Hussein from power in Iraq; all the major Iraqi players that Washington collaborated with happened to be Iranian allies. But, in his State of the Union address of January 29, 2002, President George W. Bush, Jr. confirmed to the public that the US would also target Tehran; Iran was declared a member of the so-called "Axis of Evil" together with Iraq and North Korea.

The Iranians remained pragmatic up until the 2003 Anglo-American invasion of Iraq. The *Washington Post* provides important insight:

> Just after the lightning takeover of Baghdad by U.S. forces, an unusual two-page document spewed out of a fax machine at the Near East bureau of the State Department. It was a proposal from Iran for a broad dialogue with the United States, and the fax suggested everything was on the table—including full cooperation on nuclear programs, acceptance of Israel and the termination of Iranian support for Palestinian militant groups.[11]

With President Hussein's ouster in 2003, Tehran was one of the first countries to support the new Iraqi political establishment. During the invasion of Iraq, the Pentagon initially attacked the camps of the Iraq-based militia of the People's Mujahedeen Organization or Mujahedeen-e-Khalq (MEK), an Iranian opposition group denounced as a terrorist organization by Tehran. Iranian military jets would also follow suit and strike the Iraqi camps of the MEK in approximately the same window of time. This, however, was as far common interests between Tehran and Washington would proceed. The US would secure the surrender of the MEK and prepare to use them as a tool for covert operations against Iran. The White House, impressed by what it believed were "grand victories" in Afghanistan and Iraq, also ignored the Iranian letter sent via the Swiss government for a "grand bargain." Washington intended to control Iran and its allies in Syria and Lebanon. The Pentagon even formulated an initial war scenario called Theater Iran Near Term (TIRANNT) in July 2003. This was the last US error in a series of events that ensured Iran would join the "Chinese-Russian-Iranian Coalition" that Brzezinski had warned against by saying that "a coalition allying Russia with both China and Iran can develop only if the United States is short-sighted enough to antagonize China and Iran simultaneously."[12]

Uzbekistan and the Post-9/11 Color Revolutions

By April 2005 it appeared that the Atlanticist project in Eurasia was going ahead virtually unchallenged. After 9/11 the doors of Central Asia were swung open for the US and its NATO allies. Washington had managed to finally venture beyond the Eurasian Rimland and penetrate into the Eurasian Heartland. Not only did the Pentagon invade and occupy Afghanistan, but it also attained military posts in post-Soviet Central Asia. The US-led invasion of Iraq had gone ahead and the Franco-German Entente had started intra-NATO rapprochement with the Anglo-American Alliance. A series of Atlanticist-supported color revolutions built on the success of Otpor's US-funded Bulldozer Revolution in the Federal Republic of Yugoslavia in 2000 had also swept across Eurasia in an attempt to transform Russian and Iranian allies into US clients.

The Rose Revolution organized by Kmara—which received training from Serbia's Otpor and the Center for Applied Non Violent Actions and Strategies (CANVAS)—overthrew President Eduard Shevardnadze in Georgia and replaced him with Mikheil Saakashvili and his US advisors in 2003. Saakashvili, a US educated lawyer who had his education financed by the US State Department, would immediately push for Euro-Atlantic integration by calling for Georgia's entry into the EU and NATO. Next the Orange Revolution would take place inside Ukraine from November 2004 to January 2005; as a result Viktor Yushchenko and the Orangists would come into power. In Ukraine the Orangist struggle was painted in the polemics of anti-Russian sentiments. Like Saakashvili, once Yushchenko became president he and Yulia Tymoshenko would push for Euro-Atlantic interrogation and entry into both the EU and NATO. Georgia and Ukraine, like the Republic of Azerbaijan, had already been independently drawing away from Moscow before these color revolutions erupted, but the Rose and Orange Revolutions served to empower Atlanticist ideologues in those states.

In Kyrgyzstan and Lebanon the momentum of Atlanticist success began to slow down. As the Orange Revolution ended, the color revolutions of both Kyrgyzstan and Lebanon would begin in 2005. In Kyrgyzstan the Tulip Revolution would cause President Askar Akayev to flee to Russia and resign, allowing Kurmanbek Bakiyev to take power. In Lebanon, the assassination of Lebanon's former prime minister Rafic Al-Hariri allowed many of Syria's former allies and proxies to turn their backs on Damascus and to form the March 14 Alliance, demanding that Syrian troops leave their bases in Lebanon. Saad, the son of the slain Rafic Al-

Hariri and leader of the March 14 Alliance, accused Syria of being behind the murder, but in 2010 admitted that his accusations were formulated on the basis of political gain. Using bigoted anti-Syrian language similar to that of the anti-Russian polemics of the Ukrainian Orangists, the March 14 Alliance took power in Beirut and tried to de-link Lebanon from Syria and Iran, particularly by targeting Hezbollah. The US believed that with the Tulip and Cedar Revolutions it would gain control of Lebanon and Kyrgyzstan, but it was wrong—as it would be in Ukraine too. Akayev kept the Kyrgyz Republic aligned to Russia and the March 14 Alliance failed to curb Hezbollah and withdraw Lebanon from its alliance with Syria and Iran, which is what the Israeli war against Lebanon in 2006 would try to accomplish—equally to no avail.

The events in Uzbekistan would also deal a major blow to the Atlanticists. The US began courting the authoritarian dictator of Uzbekistan, President Islam Karamov, in the late-1990s. According to Brzezinski, Uzbekistan represented a major obstacle to any renewed Russian control of Central Asia and was virtually invulnerable to Russian pressure. The Uzbek military is also the largest armed force in Central Asia. Because of these reasons, it was important for the Pentagon to secure Uzbekistan as a US and NATO outpost or protectorate in Central Asia. When there was an attempt on President Karamov's life, he suspected the Kremlin because of his independent policy stance and growing ties with the US and NATO. This led Uzbekistan to leave its military alliance with Russia. In 1998, Uzbekistan held war games with NATO troops inside its territory. Karamov was rapidly militarizing his country with US support and receiving generous aid from Washington. That is why Uzbekistan hastily offered a base in Karshi-Khanabad to the Pentagon after 9/11. The honeymoon with Tashkent would end in 2005, because Washington and London contemplated removing Karamov from power through another color revolution. Maybe he was a little too independent or unpredictable as an ally for their comfort and taste. Whatever the case, regime change in Uzbekistan failed.

The tragic events in Andijan on May 13, 2005 marked the breaking point between Uzbekistan and the Atlanticists. The people of Andijan were incited by NGOs from the Euro-Atlantic Zone into confronting the Uzbek authorities, and were met with a heavy security clampdown that resulted in a loss of lives.[13] The event was the nucleus of a revolt and armed groups were also reported to have been involved in clashes with the Uzbek authorities. The Euro-Atlantic media focused on the undeniable human rights violations that took place in Uzbekistan, but failed to mention that the US and UK were held responsible for inciting rebellion in Andijan. M. K. Bhadrakumar, the former Indian ambassador to Uzbekistan, revealed that the Tahrir Party was one of the parties blamed for stirring the crowd in Andijan.[14] The British-based group, whose name would later resurface in Syria in 2011, had used violent tactics.

US gains in post-Soviet Central Asia reversed overnight. Uzbekistan immediately started clamping down on foreign NGOs after the revolt in Andijan, but this would not be the most significant step taken by Karamov's regime. Tashkent would officially leave the NATO-sponsored GUUAM Group, which was established as a counter-balance to Russia in the post-Soviet space, on May 24, 2005. Two months later the US military was unceremoniously ordered to pack up and leave its posts in Uzbekistan within six months from July 29, 2005.[15] The US was literally told that it was no longer welcome in post-Soviet Central Asia. Russia, China, Kazakhstan, Iran, Tajikistan, and Kyrgyzstan all added their voices to the Uzbek demand. By November 2005 the Pentagon cleared its airbase in Uzbekistan. In place of its divorce with the US, Tashkent would restore its membership in the CSTO military alliance with Russia on June 26, 2006.[16] Unlike Uzbekistan, Kyrgyzstan would continue to allow the Pentagon to use Manas Air Base, but with restrictions and in a very uncertain atmosphere. Furthermore, the Kyrgyz government made it clear that Manas could never be used in hostile actions against Iran. By the end of 2005 all of Central Asia's leaders distanced themselves from the US as the Shanghai Cooperation Organization began to shine.

The Collective Security Treaty Organization: A Reincarnation of the Warsaw Pact?

Collective defense in the post-Soviet space has gone through immense changes. After the collapse of the USSR there was a generalized assumption that the Commonwealth of Independent States (CIS) under Russian leadership would continue all the defensive responsibilities of the Soviet Union, at least for a transitional period, for the new republics with the exception of the Baltic States. The CIS Armed Forces was even attached to the Russian Federal Ministry of Defense. Gradually all the members of the CIS started to take their security into their own hands; the collectively shared CIS Armed Forces that had emerged from the Soviet military disappeared and the CIS Council of Defense Ministers came into being. Eventually the CIS would create the mechanisms for the Collective Security Treaty Organization (CSTO).

The CSTO has evolved from being the military wing of the CIS into a separate body independent of the CIS. It was unveiled in 2002, soon after the 2001 invasion of Taliban-controlled Afghanistan. What differentiates the CSTO from the mutual defense arrangements of the CIS under the Collective Security Treaty is that before the creation of the CSTO there was only a treaty-based pledge within the CIS without any of the trappings of a common military institution.

Members of the CSTO—Armenia, Belarus, Kazakhstan, Kyrgyzstan, Russia, Tajikistan, and Uzbekistan—are exclusively located in the post-Soviet space. Aside from Uzbekistan which withdrew from the Collective Security Treaty like the Republic of Azerbaijan and Georgia when it was being courted by the US and NATO, all of these countries had renewed the Collective Security Treaty in 1999 before the CSTO was formed in 2002. After Tashkent's fallout with the US, Uzbekistan would sign the Collective Security Treaty once again and join the CSTO in 2006. While drawing closer to China, Karamov would suspend the CSTO membership of Uzbekistan on June 28, 2012.

The CSTO has been called a reincarnation of the Warsaw Pact and mocked as a mini-NATO. Without Russia the Collective Security Treaty Organization would be nothing, according to its Atlanticist critics, but is NATO any different without the US? The inability of the French and British to proceed against Libya without it is a case in point. Critics have said that the CSTO is actually a string of military relationships centered on the military capabilities of the Russian Federation instead of a cohesive body. In this regard the CSTO has been portrayed as being composed along the lines of Russo-Armenian, Russo-Belarusian, and Russo-Central Asia military coordination and cooperation. In the early days of the CSTO this criticism was accurate, but the CSTO has been evolving. It has been modeled to mirror NATO. Russia and its other members have been working to develop the same capabilities and mechanisms as NATO, including mechanisms for expansion in Eurasia. The prospects of membership for countries like Serbia, Iran, and Ukraine have all been discussed or mentioned publicly.

CSTO Headquarters is located in Moscow where the CSTO Secretariat is based. Three regional headquarters for the military alliance's combined forces also exist: Belarus is home for the regional command for Eastern Europe; Armenia for the regional command for the Caucasus; and Kazakhstan for the regional Central Asia command. A collective standby CSTO force called the Collective Rapid Reaction Forces was created after agreements were reached by all the CSTO members in 2009. This force conducted its first drills on October 25, 2010 in Russia's Urals region of Chelyabinsk. At least eight military units contributed by participating members are at the CSTO's disposal. The CSTO wants to challenge NATO's operations in places like Afghanistan through the UN. At the same time the CSTO has actively been trying to establish a direct relationship with NATO, which the North Atlantic Council has continually declined. CSTO Secretary-General Nikolai Bordyuzha has repeatedly criticized NATO for this, pointing out that while on the one hand NATO says more global security cooperation is needed to address various security problems, on the other, NATO leaders refuse that cooperation when it is offered by the CSTO.

MAP XVI: NATO and the CSTO

TABLE 13.1

Collective Treaty Security Organization Member States*

Country	CIS Member	Eurasian Union Member	CSTO Entry[†]
Current Members			
Armenia	Yes	No	7 October 2002
Belarus	Yes	Yes	7 October 2002
Kazakhstan	Yes	Yes	7 October 2002
Kyrgyzstan	Yes	Interested	7 October 2002
Russia	Yes	Yes	7 October 2002
Tajikistan	Yes	Interested	7 October 2002
Uzbekistan	Yes	No	23 June 2006[‡]
Former Signatories of the Collective Security Treaty (CST)[§]			
Azerbaijan, Republic of	Yes	No	-
Georgia, Republic of	No[ǁ]	No	-
Potential CSTO Candidates [¶]			
Iran	No	No	-
Moldova	Yes	No	-
Mongolia	Observer[#]	No	-
Serbia	No	No	-
Turkmenistan	Associate Member	No	-
Ukraine	De Facto Member	Interested	-

* As of February 2012.

† The funding date can be considered to be the initial signing of the Collective Security Treaty (CST) of the Commonwealth of Independent States (CIS) on May 15, 1992. Aside from the signing of the CSTO Charter (October 7, 2002), the date of September 18, 2003 can also be considered an entry date, because the CSTO Charter would take effect starting on that date.

‡ Uzbekistan was one of the original signatories of the CST, but left in 1999.

§ Both the Republic of Azerbaijan and Georgia withdrew from the CST in 1999.

|| After its war with Russia over South Ossetia, Georgia declared on August 18, 2008 that it would withdraw from the Commonwealth of Independent States (CIS) effective on August 17, 2009.

¶ This includes the former signatories of the CST and states that have been invited by the CSTO Secretariat to join the military alliance.

Mongolia has observer status within specific committees of the Commonwealth of Independent States (CIS).

The CSTO faced its first test in 2010. Kyrgyz President Bakiyev was ousted by his country's opposition and fled to Belarus in April. Questioning the organization's purpose, Minsk demanded that the CSTO intervene against what it called "an unconstitutional coup."[17] Belarus skipped an informal meeting of the CSTO as a sign of protest. But the real basis for Belarusian frustrations was an economic row with Moscow.[18] In June, the CSTO's test came when the interim Kyrgyz president, Roza Otunbayeva, made a hasty request that Russia and the CSTO deploy peacekeepers inside her country after violence followed the April uprising. Not wishing to appear to be replicating the Warsaw Pact interventions in Hungary and Czechoslovakia, Russia and the CSTO rejected the Kyrgyz interim government's request and said that the CSTO was not supposed to deal with domestic issues. Thus, the CSTO enforced its criterion as a mutual defense organization that would only address external threats.

Just as NATO started out as a US security guarantee for Western Europe, the CSTO began as a Russian security guarantee for its sister republics in the post-Soviet space. Unlike NATO, however, the CSTO from the start contained a political, economic, and diplomatic guarantee for the security of Russia by insulating the CSTO's members within the orbit of Moscow. Unlike Washington's motivations for creating NATO, Moscow's motivation to create the CSTO was predominately self-preservation and defensive.

Moscow has prevented Atlanticist attempts to isolate it through the CSTO. It has also insured that a barrier has been raised to NATO expansion into the post-Soviet space by providing an alternative to the Atlantic Alliance.

TEXT BOX

Basic Facts about the Collective Security Treaty Organization

Background

The basis for the creation of the CSTO was provided by the Collective Security Treaty signed on May 15, 1992 by Armenia, Belarus, Georgia, Kazakhstan, Kyrgyzstan, Russia, Tajikistan and Uzbekistan. In 1993 Azerbaijan, Moldova and Ukraine joined the Treaty as observers.

In 1999 Azerbaijan, Georgia and Uzbekistan withdrew from the Collective Security Treaty.

At the Summit of the CIS countries in Chisinau on October 7, 2002 the remaining participants (Armenia, Belarus, Kazakhstan, Kyrgyzstan, Russia and Tajikistan) the Collective Security Treaty Organization (CSTO). On December 26, 2003 the CSTO was registered in the UN as a regional international organization.

On June 23, 2006 Uzbekistan lifted the moratorium on its active participation in the CSTO and became a full member of this Organization.

On October 6, 2007, the 15th CSTO summit took place in Dushanbe (Tajikistan) where the decision was made that the CSTO member states can buy Russian weapons and equipment for their armed forces and special services at Russian domestic prices. The Memorandum on Cooperation between the CSTO and SCO (Shanghai Cooperation Organization) was signed at the summit.

On March 28, 2008 Uzbekistan's Parliament ratified a document formally making it a party to the Collective Security Treaty again.

On June 14, 2009 Moscow hosted the CSTO summit. The main item of the summit agenda was the agreement on creation of Collective Quick Reaction Forces. This agreement was signed by all the CSTO member states except Uzbekistan and Belarus.

In particular Tashkent came out for prohibition of getting Collective Quick Reaction Forces involved in settlement of the CSTO member states conflicts and against the agreement use until the document is ratified by all six countries. Belarus refused to take part in the summit and said that it considered the summit decisions to be illegitimate.

Managing Bodies

The Collective Security Council (CSC) is the CSTO supreme managing body formed by heads of state of the CSTO countries. Between the CSC sessions all the coordination and implementation matters are supervised by the Permanent Council which consists of plenipotentiaries of the member states of the CSTO.

The Council of Ministers of Foreign Affairs (CMFA) and the Council of Ministers of Defense (CMD) are consultative and executive bodies of the CSTO. The CMD comprises the Joint Headquarters, the Committee of Secretaries of Security Councils (CSSC).

The Secretariat is a standing body of the CSTO which is responsible for providing managerial, research and consultative assurance for the CSTO. The Secretariat comprises the Political Cooperation Department, the Military Cooperation Department, the Challenges and Threats Counteraction Department.

Documents

The Collective Security Treaty (CST) signed on May 15, 1992
The CSTO Charter
The Agreement on Legal Status of the Collective Security Treaty
    Organization (CSTO)
The Agreement on Status of Forces and Resources of the
    Collective Security System
The Agreement on General Principles of Military-Technical
    Cooperation between the Member States of the CST

Based on information from the Eurasian Heritage Foundation

TABLE 13.2

Shanghai Cooperation Organization Member States*

Country	CSTO Member	Membership Type	SCO Entry Date
Afghanistan	No	Observer Member	7 June 2012
Belarus	Yes	Dialogue Partner	1 April 2009
China, People's Republic of	No	Full Member	15 June 2001[†]
India	No	Observer Member	5 July 2005
Iran	No	Observer Member	5 July 2005
Kazakhstan	Yes	Full Member	15 June 2001[†]
Kyrgyzstan	Yes	Full Member	15 June 2001 [†]
Mongolia	No	Observer Member	17 June 2004
Pakistan	No	Observer Member	5 July 2005
Russia	Yes	Full Member	15 June 2001[†]
Sri Lanka (Ceylon)	No	Dialogue Partner	1 April 2009
Tajikistan	Yes	Full Member	15 June 2001[†]
Turkey	No	Dialogue Partner	7 June 2012
Uzbekistan	Yes	Full Member	15 June 2001

* As of July 2012; Uzbekistan froze its CSTO membership as of June 28, 2012.

† If the creation date of the Shanghai Five is considered the foundation of the organization, the founding and entry date for these members would be April 26, 1996.

The Shanghai Cooperation Organization:
Proving the "Clash of Civilizations" Wrong

In parallel to the Sino-Russian honeymoon, the Shanghai Cooperation Organization was developed as China and Russia began closing their ranks. The organization was officially established a few months before 9/11 on June 15, 2001; it is the offspring of the Shanghai Five, which as mentioned earlier was founded in 1996. The Shanghai Five—consisting of China, Kazakhstan, Kyrgyzstan, Russia, and Tajikistan—turned into the SCO when Uzbekistan joined the five other members in 2001, making all six full SCO members. Mongolia became the next country to join as the SCO's first observer member in 2004 on the basis of a SCO statute adopted for accepting observers. Without solicitation the US applied for membership too. Washington's request for entry into the SCO was rejected in 2002 as a true illustration of the scope of the SCO's mandate.[19] US entry into the SCO was rejected just as Russia was prevented from entering NATO—because it would neutralized.

Mongolian entry into the SCO, however, was a natural move. Mongolia—one of the world's most isolated countries—is geographically sandwiched between its only two neighbors, China and Russia; from 1924 until the collapse of the USSR it was one of the most obedient Soviet satellites and thereafter a close ally of both China and Russia. Moreover, the US and NATO had begun courting the Mongolians to gain some type of influence or entry into Mongolia due to its strategic position between Russia and China. As part of Ulaanbaatar's "third neighbor" policy to reach out to the outside world—to secure various foreign subsidies—the Mongolians proved receptive and began cooperating with NATO in 2005 by sending a military contingent to Kosovo and then joining ISAF in 2010, resulting in Mongolia officially becoming a NATO Contact Country in 2012.[20] This, however, has not dissociated Mongolia from the SCO or its traditional allies Russia and China.

Iran, India, and Pakistan would enter the SCO in 2005 as observer members. The observer status of Tehran in the SCO in particular is misleading. Iran's observer status is intended to camouflage the nature of trilateral cooperation between Iran, Russia, and China so that the Atlanticists will not be able to demonize the SCO easily. Iran is a de facto member and consults and collaborates in SCO mechanisms regularly; it puts great value on its membership in the SCO and in 2008—when the organization approved an accession mechanism during a meeting in Tajikistan—Tehran applied to become a full member. Until UN sanctions are removed the SCO has said it will not give Iran full membership.[21] Nevertheless, Iran is crucial to the group's objectives. At a 2009 summit in Yekaterinburg, China's President Hu Jintao told Iran's Mahmoud

Ahmadinejad in a revealing gesture that "Tehran and Beijing should help each other to manage global developments in favor of their nations otherwise the same people who are the factors of current international problems will again rule the world."[22]

Belarus and Sri Lanka joined the SCO in 2009 as special SCO dialogue partners. Minsk had been lobbying for full membership or some form of association for years, but Colombo was brought in as a message to the US that Sri Lanka was under the SCO's umbrella. Despite NATO-garrisoned Afghanistan's formal status as a NATO Contact Country and Kabul's subservience to Washington, the SCO has been keen to include it amongst its ranks. In 2009 the SCO and Kabul formed the SCO-Afghanistan Contact Group and in 2012 Afghanistan become an SCO observer. NATO member Turkey would also be granted the status of a dialogue partner at the same time while SCO leaders indirectly warned it about conspiring with the US and its NATO allies against Syria. Furthermore, most of the members of the SCO are members of the Collective Security Treaty Organization, as well as the CIS and several other post-Soviet organizations. The shared membership between the SCO and CSTO creates a major overlap between the two Eurasian organizations and essentially forms a Sino-Russian bloc.

The SCO Charter was created in 2002, using Euro-Atlantic national security jargon, to combat "terrorism, separatism, and extremism." These "three evils," as the SCO calls them, have plagued the SCO's members and a permanent office for overseeing the SCO task of fighting them was established in Tashkent through the Regional Anti-Terrorism Structure (RATS) on June 7, 2002. The Eurasian alliance has earned the nickname of the "NATO of the East," but its functions go far beyond those of NATO. Russia and China actually prefer to stay silent about the SCO's mutual defense characteristics and instead call it an intergovernmental organization working for security and prosperity amongst its members. Key SCO objectives are cooperation in Central Asia, Eurasian integration, and the insulation of China and the post-Soviet space; it serves as a vehicle for Eurasian defense and integration against the trilateral intrusions of the US, the EU, and Japan and the siege of Eurasia from North America, Western Europe, and the Asia-Pacific region. Terrorist activities, separatist movements, and extremist groups in Eurasia are forces that, from the experience of the Chinese and Russians, have for the most part been nurtured, funded, armed, and covertly supported by the US and the triad surrounding the Eurasian Heartland.

The Eurasian Alliances: A Club of Dictators or Much More?

Atlanticists have sneered at both the SCO and CSTO, calling them "clubs for dictators" in contrast to their own NATO "club of democracies." NATO, however, is not synonymous with democracy at all. These criticisms seem to conveniently overlook the fact that NATO had its own dictators as members during the Cold War. NATO members Spain, Portugal, Greece, and Turkey were all dictatorships. NATO's Mediterranean Dialogue and Persian Gulf ICI members are almost all dictatorships; democracy has never been an issue for NATO or its proponents when it comes to these states. Nor have human rights and democracy been an issue in NATO's courtship of the Republic of Azerbaijan under the rule of the Aliyev family. The "clubs for dictators" epithet is a misleading red herring. It is true that the SCO and CSTO include dictatorships, such as Uzbekistan, but these dictatorships are not the sole members in these alliances. The Eurasian alliances include these regimes along with democracies such as Kyrgyzstan, Armenia, and observer member India—dubbed the world's largest democracy by the US and NATO themselves. Proponents of these Eurasian alliances contend that egalitarian political systems will develop among the authoritarian members of the SCO and CSTO in time if they are left alone.

Collectively the SCO and CSTO are actually remarkable for being able to hold such a diverse coalition of countries together (see Table 13.3). These Eurasian alliances bring very diverse societies, cultures, and polities together extending from East Asia and Eastern Europe to the Indian sub-continent, Central Asia, and the Middle East. These countries all have different scripts, languages, geographies, economies, dress codes, diets, political systems, customs, legal traditions, and religions. Together the members of the SCO and CSTO represent over 43% of the entire population of the world, the largest labor forces on the planet, the greatest pool of energy reserves, and about one-fourth of the total land surface area of the Earth. Four of the largest language families of the world—Indo-European, Sino-Tibetan, Dravidian, and Altaic—are all anchored among the grouping. Three of the cradles of civilization where the world's oldest civilizations developed are encompassed by these Eurasian alliances: the Fertile Crescent and Iran; the Yellow River and China; and the Indus Valley and Pakistan and India. Almost all of the SCO's different members—from Russia and Kazakhstan to Iran and India—are ethno-culturally, linguistically, and religiously heterogeneous. Iran is one of the most ethnically diverse members of the SCO with a population composed of Azerbaijanis (Azeris), Armenians, Bakhtari, Baluch, Caspian coastal peoples, Circassians, Georgians, Kurds, Lors, Persians, Talysh, Turkmen, and other groups. Belarus, India, Kazakhstan, Kyrgyzstan, Pakistan, and Sri Lanka are all officially bilingual or multilingual countries. The Russian language is the official language federally in Russia, but many of the constituent republics of the Russian Federation have co-official

TABLE 13.3

Diversity of the Eurasian Alliances*

Country	Main Religion(s)	Main Language(s)	Main Script(s)	Main Ethnic Group(s)
Armenia	Christianity	Armenian	Armenian	Armenian, Kurd
Belarus	Christianity	Belarusian, Russian	Cyrillic	Belarusian, Russian, Polish, Ukrainian
China	Buddhism, Taoism	Mandarin	Chinese	Han
India	Vedicism, Islam	Hindi	Devanagari	Indic groups
Iran	Islam	Persian, Azeri	Arabic	Persian, Azeri, Kurd, Lor, Bakhtari, Arab, Armenian, Turkmen, Georgian, Baluch, Gilaki
Kazakhstan	Islam, Christianity	Kazakh, Russian	Cyrillic	Kazakh, Russian, Ukrainian, Uzbek
Kyrgyzstan	Islam, Christianity	Kyrgyz, Russian	Cyrillic	Kyrgyz, Uzbek, Russian
Mongolia	Buddhism, Islam	Mongolian	Cyrillic	Mongols
Pakistan	Islam	Punjabi, Pashto, Sindhi, Seraiki, Urdu	Arabic	Punjabi, Pashto, Sindhi, Seraiki, Baluch
Russia	Christianity, Islam	Russian, Tartar	Cyrillic	Russian, Tartar, Bashkir, Ukrainian, Chechen, Chuvash, Armenian, Kazakh
Sri Lanka	Buddhism, Vedicism	Sinhalese, Tamil	Sinhala, Tamil	Sinhalese, Tamil
Tajikistan	Islam	Tajik[†]	Cyrillic	Tajik
Uzbekistan	Islam	Uzbek, Tajik[†]	Latin	Uzbek, Tajik

* As of June 1, 2012; excluding both SCO Observer Afghanistan and SCO Dialogue Partner Turkey
† The Tajik language is considered a variant of Persian and is either classified as its own distinct language or a dialect of the modern Persian language.

MAP XVII

Shanghai Cooperation Organization

The Shanghai Cooperation Organization (SCO) is a subregional international organization for mutual protection

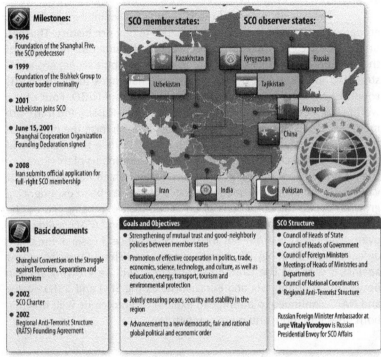

Milestones:

- **1996**
  Foundation of the Shanghai Five, the SCO predecessor

- **1999**
  Foundation of the Bishkek Group to counter border criminality

- **2001**
  Uzbekistan joins SCO

- **June 15, 2001**
  Shanghai Cooperation Organization Founding Declaration signed

- **2008**
  Iran submits official application for full-right SCO membership

SCO member states: Kazakhstan • Kyrgyzstan • Uzbekistan • Tajikistan • China

SCO observer states: Russia • Mongolia • Iran • India • Pakistan

Basic documents

- **2001**
  Shanghai Convention on the Struggle against Terrorism, Separatism and Extremism

- **2002**
  SCO Charter

- **2002**
  Regional Anti-Terrorist Structure (RATS) Founding Agreement

Goals and Objectives

- Strengthening of mutual trust and good-neighborly policies between member states
- Promotion of effective cooperation in politics, trade, economics, science, technology, and culture, as well as education, energy, transport, tourism and environmental protection
- Jointly ensuring peace, security and stability in the region
- Advancement to a new democratic, fair and rational global political and economic order

SCO Structure

- Council of Heads of State
- Council of Heads of Government
- Council of Foreign Ministers
- Meetings of Heads of Ministries and Departments
- Council of National Coordinators
- Regional Anti-Terrorist Structure

Russian Foreign Minister Ambassador at large **Vitaly Vorobyov** is Russian Presidential Envoy for SCO Affairs

languages such as Azeri, Chechen, Ingush, Lezgi, Ossetian, and Tartar. Six of the world's major faiths—Buddhism, Christianity, Islam, Sikhism, Taoism, and Vedicism (Hinduism)—hold sway in the SCO.

There is also a strong argument to be made that the SCO and CSTO represent a barrier to Euro-Atlantic cultural imperialism presently inundating other cultural groups through the neoliberal restructuring of their political and economic systems and ways of living that commodify human life. This is the reality of what Mackinder called the "oceanic freedom" that needed to be exported to the Eurasian Heartland from its peripheries, the intent of which is to justify conquest and colonial projects through the promotion of one group's values and beliefs over other groups. This imposition of an ethnocentric sense of superiority is exactly what the US and NATO have been projecting and the overtones of cultural imperialism have been a consistent part of their wars and expansion.

The eclectic nature of the SCO and CSTO combined makes this grouping of states the most diverse alliance in modern history. Thirteen time zones are encompassed collectively by the different members of the two Eurasian alliances. Their combined geographic scope, economic strength, and industrial output are major challenges to all the NATO countries combined—even with the globalization of NATO. Four of the world's largest economies—by order: China, India, Russia, and Iran—are members of this Eurasian coalition; three of which form the nucleus of the BRICS group with Brazil and South Africa.[23] While the members of the Atlantic Alliance face economic decline, the members of this Eurasian coalition are experiencing growth. Even Iran, which has been under various US-led economic sanctions since 1979, has been experiencing growth despite the conditions of an economic siege being led by the US and EU. Collectively the members of the SCO and CSTO could easily overpower NATO, were it not for the US presence. Russia alone could defeat almost all of NATO's members combined should they go to war against it without the United States. There will be growing friction between the Atlanticists and Eurasianists as the SCO and CSTO evolve and NATO continues to attempt to expand or enforce its will, bringing both sides into more and more competition.

TEXT BOX

A Snapshot of the Shanghai Cooperation Organization in 2008

The SCO was established on the basis of the April 26, 1996 Agreement on Deepening Military Trust in Border Regions—signed on one side by Kazakhstan, Kyrgyzstan, Russia, and Tajikistan and on the other side by China—and the Agreement on the Mutual Reduction of Military Forces in Border Regions, signed on April 24, 1997 by the same countries.

On June 15, 2001, the Declaration of the Shanghai Cooperation Organization was signed in Shanghai. On June 7, 2002, the heads of the SCO member-states signed the SCO Charter elaborating on the organization's purposes, principles, structure and main activities and established it officially in accordance with international law. The SCO Charter came into effect on September 19, 2003.

On August 16, 2007, the Treaty on Long-Term Neighborliness, Friendship and Cooperation creating prerequisites for elevating multi-faceted cooperation on a new level was signed in Bishkek, the capital of Kyrgyzstan.

The Council of SCO Heads of State, the supreme governing body, charts specific priorities and main activities, tackles high-priority issues of the SCO's organization and operation, those pertaining to its cooperation with other countries and international organizations and examines the most important international issues.

The Council of SCO Heads of Government (Prime Ministers) approves the SCO budget and examines and tackles high-priority cooperation issues primarily in the economic area.

The Council of SCO Foreign Ministers prepares meetings of the Council of SCO Heads of State and adopts decisions on holding SCO consultations on international issues.

The Meetings of SCO Ministers and Department Heads examine cooperation issues in specific areas. The SCO has established coordinating mechanisms between foreign-economic and foreign-trade ministers, transport, education, culture, defence and emergencies ministers. There are also Commissions of Senior Officials and Expert Panels.

The judicial, parliamentary, and law enforcement officials meet regularly.

The Council of SCO National Coordinators is responsible for coordinating current SCO activities and facilitating cooperation between ministries and departments of SCO member-states.

The Regional Anti-Terrorism Structure is a permanent body responsible for coordinating cooperation between the concerned SCO agencies under the June 15, 2001 Shanghai Convention on Combating Terrorism, Separatism, and Extremism and other relevant SCO agreements and documents.

The meetings of Security Council Secretaries are an effective coordinating-consultative mechanism of intra-SCO security cooperation and efforts to cope with new threats and challenges.

As of January 2004, the SCO initiated the following permanent administrative bodies, which adopt all resolutions by consensus:

•   SCO Secretariat in Beijing headed by a Secretary-General, the chief SCO executive, appointed by the Council of SCO Heads of State for a period of three years on a rotational basis. The current SCO Secretary-General is Bolat Nurgaliyev of Kazakhstan, appointed on January 1, 2007.

•   Regional Anti-Terrorism Structure's Executive Committee in Tashkent is headed by a Director, appointed by the Council of SCO Heads of State for a period of three years on a rotational basis.

SCO member-states have appointed their Permanent Representatives to the SCO Secretariat in Beijing and the RATS Executive Committee in Tashkent.

In 2004, Mongolia, and in 2005, India, Iran and Pakistan received observer country status with the SCO. Their involvement is regulated by the 2004 Statute on the Status of SCO Observers and the 2006 Regulations for SCO-Observers Cooperation. In 2008, the SCO approved the Regulations for Cooperation Between RATS, States and International Inter-Governmental Organizations with SCO Observer Status.

The August 28, 2008 SCO summit in Dushanbe approved the Statute of SCO Negotiating Partners.

Member-states assume presidency of the SCO for a period of 12 months after a regular SCO summit and until a meeting of the Council of SCO Heads of State on the territory of the presiding state.

The 2007 SCO budget, approved September 15, 2006 by the Council of SCO Heads of Government (Prime Ministers) in Dushanbe, was $3.7 million. The 2006 SCO budget totaled $3.5 billion.

Under the Agreement, Russia and China each contributed 24% of the budget. Kazakhstan, Uzbekistan, Kyrgyzstan and Tajikistan contributed 21%, 15%, 10% and 6%, respectively.

On November 2, 2007, the Council of SCO Heads of Government approved the $3.5 million SCO budget for 2008.

Based on information from the Federal Government of the Russian Federation

CHAPTER 14

NATO AND THE LEVANT

LEBANON AND SYRIA

Israel's diplomatic and security goal ... must be clear: joining NATO and entering the European Union.
—Israeli Minister for Strategic Affairs Avigdor Lieberman (2007)

The Levant: On the Frontiers of the Euro-Atlantic Zone

The Levant is the region of Southwest Asia and the Middle East situated on the coast of the Eastern Mediterranean. Like the geographic term *Middle East*, the name *Levant* is also formed on the geographic orientation of Western Europeans facing the Mediterranean's east. The Arabic name for the area—*Bilad Al-Shams*—roughly corresponds to Greater Syria. The exact boundaries of the region are abstract, but it is roughly formed by an area sandwiched between the Taurus Mountains of Anatolia to its north, the alluvial plains of Iraq to its east, and both Egypt and the Arabian Peninsula to its south. The categorization of Levantine countries, in the geographic sense of the word, is unambiguous. The Lebanese Republic, Palestine/Israel, the Syrian Arab Republic, and the Hashemite Kingdom of Jordan are all considered Levantine. The Turkish province of Hatay, where the city of Alexandretta (Iskenderon) is located, has also traditionally been deemed to be a part of the Levant.

From its ancient Phoenician and Israelite past to the present, the Levant has a rich history as an important juncture for ancient and modern empires and states. Assyria, Hatti, Pharaonic Egypt, Chaldea/Neo-Babylon, Achaemenid Iran, Macedon, Greco-Iranian Seleucia, Hellenistic (Ptolemaic) Egypt, Arsacid (Parthian) Iran, Rome, Byzantium, Sassanid Iran, the Rashidun Caliphate, the Umayyad Caliphate, the Abbasid Caliphate, the Fatimid Caliphate, the Seljuq Empire, the Crusaders, Ayyubid Egypt, the Mongols, Mamluk Egypt, the French First Republic, the Ottoman Empire, the French Third Republic, and Britain have all taken turns in seeing their armies and rule in the Levant.

The State of Israel, a modern Spartan state where the military is intertwined with all aspects of life and is the most important national and societal institution, is an Atlanticist outpost that has been projected by the Anglo-American Alliance onto the Levant. Israel was created by London in 1948 when it was carved out of the British Mandate of Palestine. Mandatory Palestine itself was carved out of the territory of the Ottoman Empire after the Ottomans were defeated by nationalist Arab armies during the Great Arab Revolt exploited by the British and French during the First World War—Arab nationalism was literally exploited as a geo-political weapon of war by the Allies. These Arab forces were promised many things, but most prominently they were told by London and Paris that they would be able to create their own Arab countries if they revolted against the Ottoman government. These promises proved to be lies as the Sykes-Picot Agreement of 1916 proved. Since its creation Israel has continuously been in conflict with the Palestinians and various other Arab populations whose territories it has annexed and continues to occupy. For these reasons Tel Aviv did not join NATO during the Cold War, but Israel has always been a part of the Atlanticist project. The State of Israel has close ties with the EU through an association agreement and Israeli leaders have always considered the Zionist state a cultural extension of Western Europe. Tel Aviv has been a member of the Western European and Others Group (WEOG), an informal regional voting bloc at the UN, since May 2000. Moreover, it is a de facto member of the North Atlantic Treaty Organization. It is also formally a member of the Mediterranean Dialogue and has enhanced military cooperation with the Atlantic Alliance under NATO's Individual Cooperation Program (ICP) which it joined on October 16, 2006. Israeli ships are also members of NATO's Operation Active Endeavor operating in the Mediterranean Sea.

While Israel is the core outpost of NATO in the Levant, NATO also has an entire wing in the region consisting of other countries. Like Tel Aviv, Israel's neighbors Jordan and Egypt joined NATO's Mediterranean Dialogue in 1995. Egypt signed an ICP agreement with NATO in 2007, just a year after Israel signed its ICP agreement. Jordan followed by signing its own ICP agreement in 2009. Aside from their ties to NATO, both the Jordanian and Egyptian military and intelligence establishments are heavily tied to Tel Aviv. Jordan specifically has profound ties to Tel Aviv. Not only do the Jordanian military and intelligence services receive training and direction from Israel, but they act as a regional extension of Israel. NATO member Turkey is also in close proximity to the north of the Levant as are the British in the west from their two militarily administered garrison colonies in the island-state of Cyprus known as the Sovereign Base Areas of Akrotiri and Dhekelia.

The tragic 9/11 attacks were the start of a seismic change for the

Levant. A tectonic shift began pushing the borders of the Euro-Atlantic Zone further into the Middle East from its frontier in the Mediterranean Sea. The first step was the creation of Operation Active Endeavor, which saw NATO permanently deploy itself in the Eastern Mediterranean with a naval armada facing the Levantine coast. Iraq, to the east of the Levant, would fall after the Anglo-American invasion in 2003 that had various forms of NATO involvement. The Levant with NATO's Israeli outpost as a center of influence would become the next Atlanticist target for expansion under the guidelines of the Pentagon's military roadmap to encircle and penetrate Eurasia.

The Pentagon War Plans for Lebanon and Syria

In January 2001, eight months before 9/11, according to Daniel Sobelman, a correspondent for Israel's *Haaretz*, the US government warned Lebanon that the US was planning on going after Hezbollah. Hezbollah had just defeated the Israelis in 2000, forcing Tel Aviv to end its eighteen-year occupation of the southernmost area of Lebanon. The US threats directed at Lebanon were made at the start of the presidential term of George W. Bush, Jr., eight months before the events of September 11, 2001. The Global War on Terror was not a plan drafted after the 9/11 attacks, but had been preconceived by US officials for reigning in the broader Middle East. The blueprints for the Bush Jr. Administration's assaults were actually written under the Clinton Administration. The fight against international terrorism was merely a cover under which these plans were launched targeting the "central" theater of Eurasia—hence the CENTO (Central Treaty Organization) and CENTCOM acronyms—manned by a group of predominately Muslim and Arab state and non-state holdouts and opponents of US influence and penetration. After Afghanistan and Iraq the US and its allies were set on targeting Lebanon and Syria as Wesley Clark, the former supreme commander of NATO, has publicly admitted. In Clark's own words he was told: "[W]e're going to take out seven countries in five years, starting with Iraq, and then Syria, Lebanon, Libya, Somalia, Sudan, and, finishing off, Iran."[1] Another former supreme commander of NATO, Alexander Haig, Jr., would argue for an attack on the Levant, specifically Syria, before Iraq in 2002 and after the invasion of Taliban-controlled Afghanistan.[2] Also in 2002, Pentagon advisor Richard Perle would casually tell a panel of Canadian international affairs experts in a guest appearance on TV Ontario's *Diplomatic Immunity* that after Afghanistan the US was planning to go to war with Iraq, Lebanon, Syria, and Iran.

The Pentagon began preparing for a potential invasion of Syria in 2003 while its tanks were still rolling through Baghdad and other Iraqi cities. The US Congress would also pass the Syria Accountability and

Lebanese Sovereignty Restoration Act to open the door for operations in Syria and Lebanon. *The Guardian* reported on April 15, 2003:

> [US Defense Secretary Rumsfeld ordered] contingency plans for a war on Syria to be reviewed following the fall of Baghdad.
>
> Meanwhile, his undersecretary for policy, Doug Feith, and William Luti, the head of the Pentagon's office of special plans, were asked to put together a briefing paper on the case for war against Syria, outlining its role in supplying weapons to Saddam Hussein, its links with Middle East terrorist groups and its allegedly advanced chemical weapons programme. Mr. Feith and Mr. Luti were both instrumental in persuading the White House to go to war in Iraq.
>
> Mr. Feith and other conservatives now playing important roles in the Bush administration, advised the Israeli government in 1996 that it could "shape its strategic environment... by weakening, containing and even rolling back Syria."[3]

The plans for Pentagon operations against the Syrians were referred to as "phase three" of the Global War on Terror by the White House, which logically meant Afghanistan was the first phase of the war and Iraq the second.[4] Let us pause to analyze the meaning of the White House's terminology and the clear link US officials were making between the wars in Afghanistan and Iraq on the one hand and a potential invasion of Syria on the other. The way the White House linked these countries is an admission that the Global War on Terror is simply a campaign of conquest. If the actual reasons for the invasions were different as seemed to be the case by the official casus belli, how could they be phases in the same war?

Soon after the buzz about US tanks rolling into Damascus began the Iranians would step into the arena. Iranian President Mohammed Khatami visited Lebanon on a landmark visit in May 2003 marking Israel's 2000 defeat in Lebanon, to show Tehran's commitment to all its allies in the Levant. Iranian officials would send repeated messages to the US that Tehran would not tolerate an attack on itself and its Levantine allies, which the Pentagon took seriously. Rear-Admirial Ali Shamkhani, the defense minister of Iran, gave an interview to Al Jazeera in August 2004 that explained why the Pentagon was cautious about launching an attack in the Levant. Shamkhani pointed out that US troops occupying Iran's neighbors did not give Washington the upper hand; on the contrary US and NATO forces would literally become Tehran's prisoners or "hostages" as he put it. He also explained that insofar as Tel Aviv and Washington were working in tandem any attack launched from Israel would not be viewed as an isolated act. Shamkhani warned that Iran could regionally engage the US militarily anywhere: "America is not the only one present in the region. We are present, from Khost to Kandahar in Afghanistan. We are present in the Persian Gulf and we can be present in Iraq."[5] In addition to Iran's capabilities of intervening in Afghanistan and Iraq, Tehran's ballistic missiles—that could reach Israel and all the Pentagon's bases in the Middle East—made Washington suspend its ideas of direct attacks.

Thus the plans for attacking Syria were delayed due to a combination of the international fallout caused by the widely opposed invasion of Iraq, lack of credible pretexts at the time, fears of Iranian intervention, and caution about jeopardizing Israeli security. Iranian officials also said they could halt their oil exports to hurt Israel's NATO allies if an attack on Syria was launched. The system of alliances that tied Beirut and Damascus to Tehran and by extension to Beijing and Moscow did not make an attack on either Lebanon or Syria by the Pentagon and NATO feasible either. Neither the US nor NATO were ready for the consequences of a direct attack. It was felt that Israel, which all along had wanted the US and NATO to conduct the operations, would have to play a role in the invasions. The Pentagon transferred responsibility for Lebanon and Syria from United States European Command (EUCOM) to United States Central Command (CENTCOM) on March 10, 2004—leaving Israel in EUCOM's area of responsibility (AOR) under the watch of NATO's supreme commander. The transfer of Lebanon and Syria was to facilitate common planning against both Levantine republics by the CENTCOM commanders directing the wars in Afghanistan and Iraq. Essentially, a common theater was being created that saw operations against Syria and Lebanon as tied to the wars in NATO-garrisoned Afghanistan and Anglo-American occupied Iraq.

It was decided by the US and its allies that operations to integrate the Levant into the Euro-Atlantic Zone would start from Lebanon, as Richard Perle and the Study Group on a New Israeli Strategy Toward 2000 had suggested in 1996 to Israeli Prime Minister Benjamin Netanyahu. Perle and his collaborators—James Colbert, Charles Fairbanks, Jr., Douglas Feith, Robert Loewenberg, Jonathan Torop, David Wurmser, and Meyrav Wurmser—specify in their *A Clean Break: A New Strategy for Securing the Realm* strategy paper that to defeat Syria the following steps had to be taken: Iraq had to be taken over and balkanized, Syria had to be encircled using "central Iraq" (meaning the Sunni Muslims in Iraq) and its neighbors, a sectarian conflict ignited, and then Lebanon had to be used against Syria. Perle and the Study Group on a New Israeli Strategy Toward 2000 state:

> But Syria enters this conflict with potential weaknesses: Damascus is too preoccupied with dealing with the threatened new regional equation to permit distractions of the Lebanese flank. And Damascus fears that the "natural axis" with Israel on one side, central Iraq and Turkey on the other, and Jordan, in the center would squeeze and detach Syria from the Saudi Peninsula [*sic*.]. For Syria, this could be the prelude to a redrawing of the map of the Middle East which would threaten Syria's territorial integrity.[6]

Perle and company qualify what they mean about using the "Lebanese flank" against Syria: "[Israel must divert] Syria's attention by using Lebanese opposition elements to destabilize Syrian control of Lebanon."[7] The strategy paper—essentially an updated rehash of Israel's Yinon Plan to break up and finlandize the Arab states—would not only be followed in Tel Aviv, but used and supported in Washington when Perle and his fellow collaborators would become members and advisors of the Bush Jr. Administration.

Syria would be surrounded by 2003: NATO member Turkey bordered it to the north; US-led troops were in Anglo-American occupied Iraq to its east; Israel and Jordan, two members of NATO's Mediterranean Dialogue, to its south; and NATO's permanent fleet in the Eastern Mediterranean was sailing the waves to its west. NATO's operations in general had also been shifting eastwards at this time. The conditions for launching a political assault on Syria from the "Lebanese flank" coalesced after Lebanon's former prime minister Rafic Al-Hariri was assassinated on February 14, 2005. This would result in a series of popular protests and counter-protests in Lebanon that opposed or supported Syria and the Lebanese government of Prime Minister Omar Al-Karami. The US State Department's Under-Secretary Paula Dobriansky dubbed the protests against Syria and the Lebanese government the Cedar Revolution. At the same time the US and France began demanding that Syrian troops leave Lebanon and that Hezbollah's guerilla militia fighting Israel from Lebanon's Al-Janub (South) and Nabatiye Governorates disarm. Syrian troops left their barracks in the northern sector of Lebanon, fearing their presence could be used as a pretext by a US-led coalition for launching a war to liberate the Lebanese Republic from what would be portrayed as Syrian occupation *à la* Iraq's occupation of Kuwait.

Map XVIII: NATO Operations in 2006

Together the Cedar Revolution and US-led pressure ultimately empowered the March 14 Alliance in Beirut. This new political alliance partnered the Hariri family's Future Movement—the nucleus of March 14—with Samir Geagea's Lebanese Forces, former president Amine Gemayel's Lebanese Phalange or Kataeb Party, Walid Jumblatt's Progressive Socialist Party, and several independents and smaller proxy parties mostly tied to the Hariri family. Michel Aoun, the former leader of both the Lebanese Armed Forces and a military government in East Beirut that had bitterly fought against the Syrians and a Lebanese civilian government in West Beirut, returned from his exile in France and joined March 14. March 14 leaders capitalized on the resentment that many segments of Lebanese society harbored towards the Syrian regime's control of Lebanon under Hafez Al-Assad. Almost all of March 14's leaders, like the Druze chieftain Walid Jumblatt, had been Syrian clients at one point; most these politicians would effectively transform themselves into

US or Saudi clients overnight. March 14 figures began following the scripts provided to them by the US Embassy in Beirut and without proof started consistently accusing Syria of being behind Hariri's murder—something that his son Saad would later retract and nonchalantly admit had been done on the basis of March 14's "politics."[8] Four Lebanese generals close to the Syrian military would also be detained and arrested on the basis of false witness accounts and March 14's McCarthyite political accusations in 2005. After four years these Lebanese generals—Major-General Jamil Al-Sayyed, Brigadier-General Mustapha Al-Hamdan, Major-General Ali Al-Hajj, and Brigadier-General Raymond Azar—would be freed in 2009 without any charges ever pressed.

The Failure to Remove Hezbollah:
A Prologue to Israel's 2006 War on Lebanon

Despite their initial victories, the March 14 Alliance would fail to transform Lebanon into a full Euro-Atlantic outpost and colony. Hezbollah, the Amal Movement, the Marada Movement, the Popular Nasserite Organization, and a series of Lebanese groups called the March 8 Alliance would refuse to let Lebanon become a Euro-Atlantic protectorate run by the US, France, and Israel. Significantly, by 2006, Lebanon's largest Christian political party, Michel Aoun's Free Patriotic Movement, and a few other Christian groups allied to it had left the March 14 Alliance and joined Hezbollah and the March 8 Alliance. On February 6, 2006, Aoun and Hezbollah Secretary-General Hassan Nasrallah signed a memorandum of understanding in Dahiyeh's Saint Michael's Church between their parties, which even included a formula for the eventual incorporation of Hezbollah into the Lebanese military.

March 14 could not govern Lebanon without the cooperation of Hezbollah and March 8. Although March 14 politicians gained a parliamentary majority in the Lebanese National Assembly and secured the office of the Lebanese prime minister in the Grand Serail for former Citibank and Hariri employee Fouad Siniora in July 2005, the other two main offices of political power in Lebanon remained in the hands of Hezbollah's allies: Emile Lahoud, the Syrian-favored president of Lebanon, would stay in his place at Baabda Palace and refuse to resign; and Nabih Berri, the head of the Amal Movement, would continue to hold the post of Lebanese parliamentary speaker. March 14's parliamentary majority was only formed on the skewed basis of a confessional system of representation; the demographic or popular majority in Lebanon actually supported the March 8 Alliance. Contrary to the democratic principles they claimed to represent, March 14 supporters would snicker and brush these facts aside by saying that the Shiites breed like animals and that Aoun's Free Patriotic Movement's parliamentary coalition did not represent the majority of Christians. Most importantly March 14 politicians could not legally create a governing cabinet without the cooperation of Hezbollah and Amal. Ironically this was due to the same Lebanese confessional political system.

Lebanon's parliament is constitutionally required to have representatives from all of the country's confessional groups and the Lebanese government must have ministerial representation from the major Lebanese confessions in the cabinet on the basis of the National Pact of 1943 and its successor, the Taif Agreement or National Reconciliation Pact of 1989. These ministerial representatives must be: the Maronite Catholics, Greek Orthodox, Mellite Greek Catholics, and Armenian Orthodox from the Christian communities; and the Shiites and Sunnis from the Muslim communities. The Druze (*Al-Muwaḥḥidun*)—considered a Muslim denomination by themselves and under the Lebanese political and legal system—must also be represented in the cabinet. It is through this confessional layout that state offices are assigned and certain positions reserved for specific communities: the presidency and commandership of the Lebanese Armed Forces are to be held by Maronite Catholics; the parliamentary speaker must be a Shia; the prime minister a Sunni; and both the deputy parliamentary speaker and deputy prime minister must be offices held by the Greek Orthodox. This confessional system while reducing the demographic strength of the Shiites as a plurality in Lebanon conversely made Hezbollah and Amal politically indispensable, because of the monopoly they gained through the 2005 elections as the key representatives of the Shia community. The Shiite Muslims and ethnic Armenians unlike other Lebanese communities voted as a relatively unified bloc for the same parties. Prime Minister Siniora and the March 14 leaders had no choice except to include two Hezbollah MPs, two Amal MPs, and one independent MP endorsed by Hezbollah as cabinet ministers in the government seats reserved for the Shiite Muslims. This gave Hezbollah and its political allies an important political veto over the Lebanese government, because should the Shiite ministers resign and walk out of cabinet—as they did alongside Yacoub Sarraf, the Greek Orthodox environment minister, on November 11, 2006—then a constitutional crisis would arise and the Lebanese government would become illegitimate due to its confessional unrepresentativeness.

The political veto that Hezbollah and the March 8 Alliance held in the Lebanese cabinet would prevent many Atlanticist objectives from being adopted and thwarted the removal of Lebanon from the "axis of resistance" or Resistance Bloc that the Mediterranean country formed together with various Palestinian groups, various Iraqi groups, Syria, and Iran. This in turn prevented Lebanon from being turned into an Atlanticist bridgehead against neighboring Syria. Hezbollah and its allies would have to be removed by force to create an Atlanticist "Lebanese flank." March 14 was not strong enough to do this; they did not have the political strength, the popular support, or the physical force needed for the task. Nor could they install their own president into Baabda Palace, because a two-thirds majority was needed in a parliamentary vote. The Lebanese Armed Forces would also refuse any orders from Siniora to fight against Hezbollah should they be asked. Hezbollah was too popular among the Lebanese military and many of the enlistees had come from families in the Shiite Muslim community that supported Hezbollah and its fight against Israel's occupation of Lebanon. Tel Aviv and NATO would have to do the dirty work of removing Hezbollah as both a socio-political and paramilitary force inside Lebanon. NATO—which was officially involved in Iraq and working in the Eastern Mediterranean in addition to its military operations in Afghanistan, the Balkans, the Baltic, and Darfur at this time—would be prepared to intervene in the Levant in 2006, but first it would need Israel to give it a pretext.

NATO's 2006 Plans to Intervene in the Levant

Tel Aviv and the Atlantic Alliance were waiting for a pretext to invade Lebanon and crush Hezbollah in order to establish a NATO garrison and Atlanticist "Lebanese flank." There was also a consensus between the Anglo-American and Franco-German branches of NATO over such an operation. After the fall of Baghdad to US tanks in 2003, French Foreign Minister Dominique René de Villepin began to call for an EU peacekeeping force to be mandated among the Israelis and Palestinians.[9] Calls for an EU force were rebuffed by Israel and the US who proposed instead the Atlantic Alliance or a NATO-dominated force as an alternative.[10] Hence the ideas for sending a NATO force onto the shores of the Eastern Mediterranean had been floating around for several years in NATO capitals before the outbreak of the fighting between Israel, Gaza, and Lebanon in 2006.

In March 2005 the US started delivering the bunker buster bombs that Tel Aviv would use in 2006 against Lebanon.[11] The Pentagon helped the Israelis draw the plans for the war as a "demo for Iran" according to the investigative journalist and Pulitzer Prize winner Seymour Hersh.[12] The US also created the Iran-Syria Planning Group at the start of 2006 to organize operations collectively against the Palestinians, Lebanon, Syria, and Iran. Daniel Halutz, an Israeli air force general, would also be given the rank of *rav aluf* (lieutenant-general)—a position reserved for army generals—on June 1, 2005 to command the entire Israeli military in a historic move that indicated Tel Aviv's decision to place emphasis on a shock and awe air campaign in the upcoming war.

Tel Aviv and NATO began holding close discussions on the Levant and Iran. The German commander of NATO's Airborne Warning and Control System (AWACS) and Control Force arrived in Israel to hold talks in February 2006. Sarah Baxter and Uzi Mahnaimi reported:

> When Major-General Axel Tüttelmann, the head of Nato's Airborne Early Warning and Control Force, showed off an Awacs early warning surveillance plane in Israel a fortnight ago, he caused a flurry of concern back at headquarters in Brussels.
>
> It was not his demonstration that raised eyebrows, but what he said about Nato's possible involvement in any future military strike against Iran. "We would be the first to be called up if the Nato council decided we should be," he said.[13]

Tüttelmann's visit was part of the coordinating of Israel's air defenses by Tel Aviv and the Atlantic Alliance under a scenario that Israel could come under heavy air attacks if the war Tel Aviv planned on launching in the Levant drew in the Iranian military. Moreover, under the claim of preparations against an "Iranian threat," the Israeli military announced it would participate in NATO exercises just before it launched its second invasion of Lebanon.[14] Eight NATO warships visited the Israeli port of Haifa from May 29 until June 14, 2006.[15] One NATO general declared that the visit was meant to familiarize the NATO forces with Israel and ominously added the NATO warships were "maintained at a high state of readiness" and were ready to go wherever the North Atlantic Council ordered them to deploy.[16] The visit was the first time Israeli warships participated as members of an integrated NATO naval force.[17]

Many reports and documents have surfaced that indicate that March 14 figures were actively involved in the preparations for an attack on Lebanon in a bid to see Hezbollah crushed so that they could rule Lebanon without challenge. The most damning reports are those against Elias Al-Murr who was the defense minister of Lebanon during the war. According to Lebanon's *Al-Akbar* newspaper, Al-Murr had advised the US to tell the Israelis to avoid bombing Lebanon's Christian areas so as to keep them indifferent to the attack on their Shiite Muslim compatriots. Al-Murr also pledged that he and the Lebanese government would sequester the Lebanese Armed Forces in its barracks until Tel Aviv won the war and crushed Hezbollah. The Lebanese military was indeed ordered to stand down by Al-Murr and the Lebanese government when Israel finally did attack on July 12, 2006. Embarrassing videos of Lebanese soldiers serving tea inside their barracks to the invading Israelis and reports that members of the March 14 Alliance in East Beirut were celebrating and toasting Israel for attacking Hezbollah would later surface.

The war started after Hezbollah launched one of its raids to capture Israeli soldiers to exchange for the freedom of Lebanese prisoners—or "hostages" as the British MP George Galloway called them during the last days of the war on August 6—that Israel still detained from its previous occupation of Lebanon. The raid near the town of Zarit was not a big surprise for Israel or an uncommon act by Hezbollah. From 2000 up to that point there was continuous border fighting by both sides. Israel was still occupying the Sheeba Farms and the town of Ghajar too, which meant that its withdrawal from Lebanon was incomplete and that Israeli-Lebanese hostilities had not ended. This time, however, Tel Aviv's reaction to Hezbollah's raid was different from all the previous times: a full-fledged war took place. Israel and its supporters argued that Tel Aviv was launching the attack to free its captured soldiers, to put an end to the Hezbollah raids once and for all, and to neutralize the growing threat on its northern flank. The facts would later paint a very different and much more strategic picture involving the entire Levant. Speaking on the first days of the war the Russians frankly let it be known that it was clear to them that Israel was pursuing broader objectives.

The Israeli government used Hezbollah's July 12 raid as an opportunity to launch its second invasion of Lebanon. Israeli reserve units had actually been mobilized weeks before Tel Aviv's soldiers were captured by Hezbollah fighters.[18] It just so happened that the mobilized reserve units that Tel Aviv had called up were indispensable to the 2006 invasion of Lebanon, as the *Jerusalem Post* wrote on the first day of the war.[19] Months later the prime minister of Israel, Ehud Olmert, would testify to the Winograd Commission that the war had been premeditated.[20] In the words of one *Haaretz* report in 2007: "Prime Minister Ehud Olmert told the Winograd Commission that his decision to respond [...] with a broad military operation was made as early as March 2006, four months before last summer's Lebanon war broke out."[21] Olmert's cabinet had been waiting to use a raid by Hezbollah as a pretext to launch a preconceived northward invasion to reoccupy Lebanon at least as far north as the southern end of the Litani River. Correspondingly, Israel had instigated fighting with Hamas and the Palestinians after Israeli commandos illegal entered the Gaza Strip and arrested a Palestinian doctor and another one of his family members on June 24, resulting in the capture of two Israeli soldiers by the Palestinians as retaliation. This was used as the justification for a large-scale Israeli military incursion into Gaza.

Israel's Second Defeat in Lebanon was also a NATO Defeat

Israel's war against Lebanon did not go as US, Israeli, and NATO planners had calculated. The White House and Pentagon had expected Tel Aviv to easily defeat Hezbollah's guerilla fighters. US Secretary of State Condoleezza Rice joyously declared that the war reflected the "birth pangs of a new Middle East." By this she meant that Lebanon and Syria would change orbits and that the Palestinian resistance movements and Iran would become isolated, which would leave the Middle East to be molded and restructured by Washington. Both the US and NATO also planned for the war to expand into Syria and the Atlantic Alliance was keen on establishing some type of so-called "post-conflict" military force in the Levant modeled on NATO's KFOR in Kosovo and ISAF in Afghanistan. General James Jones, the supreme commander of NATO at the time, proclaimed amidst the fighting between Israel and the Lebanese that the Atlantic Alliance was up for the job of stepping into Lebanon.[22] During the initial days of the war Israeli officials and NATO members incessantly talked about how NATO would move into Lebanon after Hezbollah's defeat as if the move had been already determined by the Atlantic Alliance. The Pentagon had actually planned to launch a NATO invasion of Lebanon, which would have included the deployment of the US Marines to fight Hezbollah according to an interview of Alain Pellegrini, the French former military commander of the United Nations Interim Force in Lebanon (UNIFIL), by the Lebanese newspaper *As-Safir*.[23] These NATO invasion plans were also linked to attacking Syria and protecting Israel if the Iranians intervened in the Levant to help Hezbollah and Damascus.

March 14 leaders also thought that their Hezbollah rivals would collapse. Although his government never objected to Hezbollah's previous raids and recognized the mandate given to Hezbollah to fight Israel on the border by preceding governments, Prime Minister Siniora declared that the war was a matter between Hezbollah and Israel and that the Lebanese government was neutral. March 14 had made a gross miscalculation and their role in the war would not stay unknown or go unnoticed by Hezbollah and its allies.

Although Hezbollah's fighters formed the bulk of the resistance and were by far the most disciplined, organized, and well-armed group fighting the Israelis, they were not alone. Various Lebanese fighters, as well as Palestinians, took part in rebuffing the Israeli's ground incursion into Lebanon. Hezbollah would also rain rockets into Israel as a response to the Israelis' bombing campaign. As a result Tel Aviv would intensify its already indiscriminate and brutal attacks on civilian areas throughout Lebanon. From the air the Israelis destroyed a great deal of Lebanon's civilian infrastructure and killed many Lebanese civilians. Tel Aviv also used the opportunity to attack several of the Palestinian refugee camps in Lebanon. The UN and the Red Cross were also attacked by the Israelis. Four UN peacekeepers from Austria, Canada, China, and Finland as well as a UNIFIL staff member and his wife were killed by the Israelis while several peacekeepers were injured.

One of the major aims of the Israeli bombings was to bomb the civilian population into renouncing Hezbollah, but the opposite took place. Lebanese areas that had no ties to Hezbollah whatsoever and even had March 14 supporters were also indiscriminately attacked by Israel, which hoped to create internal pressure and fighting inside Lebanon. Hezbollah and various sources in Lebanon also accused the embassies of the US, UK, France, Germany, and other NATO countries of relaying intelligence reports about Lebanon's internal state for Israel. This included reports about the morale of the Lebanese population. Some of these embassies conducted polls asking the internally displaced refugees fleeing to Beirut if they still supported Hezbollah. Later these allegations would be supported when European agencies were caught secretly coordinating with the Israelis in Lebanon.[24]

Ultimately, Hezbollah defeated Israel on August 14 and decelerated and derailed the Pentagon's war plans in the Middle East. Its victory was a victory for the entire Resistance Bloc against Israel and by extension all NATO. Hezbollah was not only helped by Iran and Syria, but it also received Russian arms and intelligence data gathered through listening posts in Syria jointly operated by Iranian and Russian officers.[25] Iran's Chinese and Russian allies would also help rebuild Lebanon. Both China and Russia sent their forces into Lebanon as a counter-move to NATO at the end of the conflict. The Chinese increased the number of their personnel in the UN's Lebanon force and the Russians sent a force outside of the umbrella of the UN through a bilateral agreement with Beirut to rebuild much of the country's destroyed transport infrastructure. The Kremlin would also deploy air defense systems into the Levant to guard Syria as Russia upgraded its military presence in the Eastern Mediterranean. Ultimately, Israel's second defeat in Lebanon was also a victory for the Russians and Chinese against the Atlantic Alliance.

The Levant and a World War III Scenario

The mainstream media is a vital instrument for inundating society with the views of the most powerful groups and organizations. It helps shape the views and opinions of what the sociologist C. Wright Mills has termed a mass society, one where most members are not involved in expressing their opinions as outputs, but only receiving opinions as instructions and as a form of social programming. In this regard it is important to review what several major media networks in the US started to say about the Israeli attack on Lebanon.

The US media watchdog Media Matters for America observed

that much of the mainstream media was touting that the US was in the midst of a global war just days after Israel began its war with Lebanon. Media Matters for America reported as follows on July 14, 2006:

> Most recently, on the July 13 edition of Fox News' *The O'Reilly Factor*, host Bill O'Reilly said "World War III ... I think we're in it." Similarly, on the July 13 edition of MSNBC's *Tucker*, a graphic read: "On the verge of World War III?" As *Media Matters for America* has noted, CNN Headline News host Glenn Beck began his program on July 12 with a discussion with former CIA officer Robert Baer by saying "we've got World War III to fight," while also warning of the "impending apocalypse." Beck and officer Robert Baer had a similar discussion on July 13, in which Beck said: "I absolutely know that we need to prepare ourselves for World War III. It is here."[26]

It is clear that a World War III scenario was possible in 2006. The Israeli attack on Lebanon could have expanded into Syria. This would have given rise to an Iranian intervention, which would led to the US and NATO entering the war to come to the aid of Tel Aviv as combatants. This could have escalated into a much broader war eventually drawing in the Eurasian alliances linked to Iran.

NATO Covertly Enters Lebanon

As Israel's defeat in 2006 became apparent and Tel Aviv was forced to give up its plans for reaching the Litani River and occupying Lebanon under guise of another so-called "security zone"—like the one Shimon Peres established in 1985 after Israel's 1982 invasion—the speeches about deploying NATO began to die down and then suddenly became mute. Atlanticist leaders became aware that a formal NATO deployment into Lebanon would be too closely identified with the US and Israel, which would never be accepted by the Lebanese. The French and Germans also publicly argued against NATO to exert their own influence in Lebanon, which would have been diluted under a formal NATO mandate. The French would speak to the Iranians while the Germans would talk to both the Iranians and Syrians about the subject. This led to an informal NATO deployment under the banner of a multinational UN peacekeeping force pursuant to UNSC Resolution 1701 that would subsume the older United Nations Interim Force in Lebanon (UNIFIL) that was created in 1978 and under the command of France during the 2006 war.

French and German officials publicly claimed to oppose the

Israeli attack on Lebanon unlike their Anglo-American partners who unapologetically obstructed all international efforts to immediately end the Israeli bombing campaign and invasion of Lebanon. Franco-German statements seemed to be in contrast to a unified position NATO leaders had held to turn Lebanon into a protectorate. They offered a forthcoming force under Franco-German command as an alternative and impartial peacekeeping force. But the plan was to have the Franco-German forces lead the deployment of forces from NATO members into the Levant. The French were supposed to oversee the land operations and the Germans were supposed to oversee naval operations in the Levant.

After the August 14 ceasefire was established troops and sailors from the Atlantic Alliance were deployed onto Lebanese soil and waters under a new and expanded UNIFIL that was no longer a UN observation force like its predecessor. It had distinctly acquired the characteristics of a NATO combat-ready force.[27] France would send 2,000 soldiers to form the nucleus of the most powerful armored force ever dispatched anywhere as part of a UN peacekeeping mission in history.[28] Germany would dispatch as many as 2,400 Germans for the Lebanon mission in the "first German deployment to the Middle East since the end of the Second World War."[29] The Germans would be augmented by the Italians—who were initially commanding the UNIFIL maritime contingent—and other maritime forces from the Netherlands, Spain, Denmark, France, Greece, Turkey, and Bulgaria. Serving under French command the Italians would send their armored reconnaissance and heavily-armed forces specializing in creating beachheads; among them were their army's Serenissima Regiment and their navy's San Marco Regiment. Spanish units would deploy to Tyre (Sur) and the Marjayoun District. Belgium, Britain, Bulgaria, and Turkey would also all contribute land forces. Several of these NATO contingents had also served in Iraq; what their governments, specifically the Italian and Spanish, essentially did is to redeploy these forces from Iraq into Lebanon in an ongoing commitment to the Pentagon.

The Aftermath of Israel's Second Defeat in Lebanon

Relations between the Lebanese March 14 and March 8 groups would start to deteriorate. March 8 bitterly opposed calls for the formation of the Special Tribunal for Lebanon and wanted its seats inside cabinet to be increased—under a "one-third plus one" formula—so as to be more proportionate to its share of seats in the Lebanese National Assembly and as a means of securing an undisputable veto in the government. Tensions boiled when Hezbollah, Amal, and their Christian ally Yacoub Sarraf resigned from the March 14-dominated cabinet in November 2006. A constitutional crisis erupted and large anti-government protests took place in and around Beirut. The divisions played out along sectarian lines with almost all of Lebanon's Shiites unanimously supporting March 8 while most of the Druze and about two-thirds of the Sunnis supported the Hariri family and March 14.

Ironically the US government would try to portray the anti-government protests as "undemocratic" and even pass an executive order on August 2, 2007 to freeze the financial assets of any individual or group deemed to oppose Prime Minister Siniora and his March 14 government.[30] George W. Bush, Jr. said the Lebanese anti-government protesters "constitute an unusual and extraordinary threat to the national security and foreign policy of the United States."[31] The US and its allies also tried to portray the opposition to the March 14-dominated government as being entirely composed of Hezbollah supporters and the Shia. In reality the opposition was extremely diversified. Staunchly secular and pan-Arabist parties such as the Lebanese Community Party, the Lebanese Baath Party, and the Lebanese branch of the Syrian Social Nationalist Party all took part. The Lebanese Islamic Front, the Arab Movement, prominent politicians, several former prime ministers, scholars, and independents from the Sunni community also took part and supported the anti-government protests; among them was Sheikh Yakan who condemned the March 14 government as a US agent spewing sectarian hatred and led a unified outdoor Friday prayer gathering by Shiite and Sunni anti-government forces on December 8, 2006. Lebanon's union leaders and many student associations protested government corruption and economic conditions. The various Christian communities of Lebanon and several Christian political parties and independents, including the Free Patriotic Movement and Marada Movement, made up a very large portion of the protesters. Finally, from the small Druze community the Lebanese Democratic Party of Talal Arslan and the unpopular Wiam Wahhab provided their support to the anti-government protests; fighting even broke out several times inside the Druze community between March 8 and March 14 supporters.

Siniora's government would be called the "Feltman government" by Hezbollah and March 8, because of March 14's constant consultations with Jeffrey Feltman, the US ambassador to Lebanon. Feltman had been a US diplomat in Anglo-American occupied Iraq and in Israel, where he worked for Martin Indyk; the US State Department sent him to Lebanon as part of their focus on dislodging Lebanon from the Resistance Bloc. The role of March 14 in creating the Atlanticist's "Lebanese flank" would become more and more apparent. *Ma'an News Agency* would later report that Prime Minister Siniora actually held secret talks with Ehud Olmert and Prince Bandar bin Sultan Al-Saud, the chair of the Saudi National Security Council, inside Egypt right after the war to find a new way of collectively tackling the March 8 Alliance, Iran, and Syria.[32] Siniora and the March 14 Alliance also pushed for the disarmament of Hezbollah and the weakening of its infrastructure.

March 14 took to importing violent fanatic groups into Lebanon and began to train its own militias as a means of fighting Hezbollah. Seymour Hersh reported in February 2007 that the US had begun working with its Saudi and Jordanian allies to help bring militants into Lebanon to aid the Hariri family and March 14 in a fight against Hezbollah and March 8.[33] Siniora and the Hariris would denounce Hersh's report with outrage, but Hersh would be vindicated three months later as March 14's first option against Hezbollah backfired in May. Their primary fanatic group—called Fatah Al-Islam—got out of control in the Palestinian refugee camp of Nahr Al-Bared in Al-Shamal (North) Governate where they were being housed among 30,000 to 35,000 people. A battle with the Lebanese Army ensued until September. March 14 politicians tried to lay the blame on the Syrians, but the Lebanese military contradicted them by saying that Fatah Al-Islam was not tied to Syria whatsoever. Appallingly, the Palestinian refugees at the camp would also become scapegoats. They would be blamed for "hosting" Fatah Al-Islam and subsequently face vicious reprisals in Lebanon. This malicious treatment would be on top of being used as human shields by Fatah Al-Islam, being caught in the cross-fire of fighting, enduring the malfeasances of the Lebanese Army, and the looting and destruction of their homes and businesses during the course of the fighting. For the first time Lebanon's Sunni Muslim community—which unlike the Christian, Druze, and Shiite Muslim communities had for the most part never mistreated the Palestinians—would also discriminate against them.

After Fatah Al-Islam's defeat, March 14's second option was unleashed during escalating tensions between Siniora and Hezbollah over the discovery of a camera network monitoring the airport in Beirut, March 14's move to remove the brigadier-general responsible for airport security, and Siniora's subsequent attempts to dismantle Hezbollah's Iranian-built security telecommunication network, which was pivotal for winning the recent war against Israel. On May 7, 2008 fighting would break out between March 8 and March 14 militias while most Christians on both sides opted not to get involved. The Lebanese Armed Forces would declare their neutrality. Almost all the fighting would be between the Sunni Tiger militia of the Hariri family's Future Party and March 8's Hezbollah, Amal, and the Syrian Social Nationalist Party. Walid Jumblatt's Progressive Socialist Party and Talal Arslan's Lebanese Democratic Party would wage limited fights amongst the Druze. Hezbollah and its allies routed Hariri's Sunni Tigers and secured Beirut in a lightning takeover on May 9. The offices of the Hariri family were surrounded and their Future Television broadcasting station—rumored to have been used as an espionage center for CIA-led operations—was burned down. Walid Jumblatt was also encircled and forced to surrender. The US, Israel, and Saudi Arabia were horrified and even discussed NATO and GCC intervention among themselves. By May 14 the fighting ended with an unquestionable victory for Hezbollah and its allies. Walid Jumblatt, disillusioned by the weakness of his allies, would also begin to slowly distance himself from March 14, which would result in his formal withdrawal from his alliance with it in 2009. A settlement was reached by both sides through the Doha Accord in Qatar on May 21, which resulted in the formation of a new and enlarged national unity cabinet and the election of General Michel Suleiman as the new consensus president of Lebanon.

The Evasion of a Broader War:
How the Road to Damascus was Blocked in Beirut

Lebanon's sister republic of Syria was one of the main targets of the Israelis and their Atlanticist allies in 2006. The invasion of Lebanon, which Israel called Operation Changing Direction, was supposed to expand into a broader war against the Syrian Arab Republic and the Israelis began talking about an offensive into Syria soon after they began their attack on Lebanon. Tel Aviv justified its plans on the basis that Syria was an arms supplier and depot for Hezbollah as well as a safe haven for the leaders of Hamas and a series of other Palestinian groups fighting Israel.[34] Aside from the Beirut-Damascus Highway, the Israelis had also started to attack Lebanese-Syrian border crossings which had been opened to help over a hundred thousand Lebanese refugees. *The Observer* ominously proclaimed during the first days of the Israeli attacks that "international leaders appeared to be deeply split over how to respond to a crisis that threatens to spill over into a full-scale war involving Syria and Iran as well as Israel, Palestine and Lebanon."[35] What the British newspaper failed to report was that the Pentagon and NATO were in an advanced state of readiness to intervene should Israel not be able to handle an expanded war.

The US and NATO anticipated that Damascus would enter the war against Israel not long after Israeli jets began attacking targets in the Lebanese town of Baalbek—famous for its Roman ruins—near the Syrian border. The Syrians had also braced themselves for a confrontation and mobilized their air and ground units. Damascus threatened to intervene should the Israelis reach the Lebanese-Syrian border.[36] This would leave the nerve center of Syria exposed to Israel. The road to Damascus was through Beirut and all sides seemed to be aware of this. The Lebanese-Syrian border unlike the frontier between Syria and the Israeli-occupied Golan Heights (Syrian Heights) was not heavily fortified. The Syrians feared that Lebanese territory could be used for an invasion in an Israeli equivalent to the Schlieffen Plan in the First World War that saw Germany invade Belgium to bypass the heavily fortified French positions in Alsace-Lorraine. Syrian Information Minister Al-Bilal would articulate Syria's position as this: "What will we do? Stand by with our arms folded? Absolutely not. Without any doubt Syria will intervene in the conflict."[37]

Syria's ambassador to Britain, Sami Al-Khiyami, told Anna Jones in a Sky News interview on August 2 that "Israel has been planning for this [war] for a long time, and the capture of the soldier[s] was only used as a pretext."[38] He revealed that Damascus was aware there was an intent to drag it into the conflict: "Syria is making preparations to defend itself; the idea is that Israel really wants to involve Syria [in the war]."[39] Al-Khiymi also pointed out that Washington was involved in the war plans: "The American administration probably really wants Syria to be involved, but Syria is paying a lot of attention not to be drawn in to this type of conflict."[40] Ambassador Al-Kiyami and his government were right. According to Israeli sources, US officials were furious with the Israeli side for hesitating to attack and extend the war into Syria, which was the main strategic objective of the war.[41] Meyrav Wurmser, wife of Dick Cheney's Middle East advisor and one of the authors of the Israeli strategy paper *A Clean Break* told Israel's *Yedioth Aharonot* in an interview after the war that "the anger [among US officials] is over the fact that Israel did not fight against the Syrians."[42] Wurmser revealed: "Instead of Israel fighting against Hezbollah, many parts of the American administration believe that Israel should have fought against the real enemy, which is Syria and not Hezbollah."[43] The US Senate had even passed a resolution condemning Hamas and Hezbollah and calling for Syria and Iran to be held accountable for their fighting with Israel on July 18. The US was not alone in its demands; France had also been secretly pushing for Israel to attack Syria.[44]

A broader war was evaded for several reasons. Had Hezbollah not been well trained and armed the Israeli army would have reached the banks of the Litani River and the Bekaa Valley, which would have put them on the Lebanese-Syrian border. Hezbollah's thrashing of Israel's advancing Merkava tanks and troops prevented this. Had not Prime Minister Siniora declared the neutrality of the Lebanese government, the war could have seen Syrian entry. Had the Lebanese government declared war on Israel, in response to the Israeli invasion, Syria would have been obligated through two bilateral treaties signed in 1991—the Brotherhood, Cooperation, and Coordination Treaty and the Lebanon-Syria Defense and Security Pact—to directly support Lebanon.

Hezbollah's victory prevented the strategic orbits of Lebanon and Syria from changing, as was the aim of Israel's Operation Changing

Direction, and it helped evade a broader war by halting the Pentagon's military roadmap in Lebanon. The Pentagon had intended for the war to be a demonstration for Tehran, but the tables were reversed. The US, Israel, and NATO realized that if Hezbollah's merely Iranian-supported militia could defeat Israel that Syria and Iran would be exponentially harder enemies to fight. The Lebanese victory also gave a morale boost to the Palestinians in the Gaza Strip and their Hamas government that had come under Israeli attack since June under Operation Summer Rains. If it was not clear before, it was now: the strategic equation in the Middle East had changed in favor of Iran and the Resistance Bloc.

Breaking the Resistance Bloc via Diplomatic Talks with Syria

The new UNIFIL was originally projected to deploy on the Lebanese-Syrian border. German Foreign Minister Frank-Walter Steinmeier, while holding talks during the war with Ehud Olmert, announced that the new UNIFIL mandate "would need to include control of the crossing points from Syria to Lebanon."[45] These demands prompted Syria to repeatedly threaten to close its border with Lebanon on the basis of a threat to its national security and borders by NATO powers.[46] Damascus repeatedly asserted that the US and its allies wanted to turn Lebanon into a forward base against their country.

Syria was an Israeli and NATO target because of the position of the Syrians within the Resistance Bloc. While Iran is the most powerful member of the Resistance Bloc, the central player connecting everyone is the Syrian Arab Republic. Syria acts as the bridge for Iran and Iraq with Lebanon and Palestine. Iranian material support has mostly reached Hezbollah and the Palestinians through Syria. Syria also acts as an Iranian and Russian military outpost in the Eastern Mediterranean with its airspace, naval ports, listening stations, intelligence services, and other military infrastructure at the disposal of Tehran and Moscow. Geographically, Syria is also situated between the three theaters— Palestine, Lebanon, and Iraq—that the US and its allies have been trying to pacify as part of their central front in Eurasia.

The transformation of Syria into a client state would not only help erode the Resistance Bloc, but it would give control over the Levantine energy corridor in the Eastern Mediterranean to Israel and the NATO powers. A direct land bridge would connect Israel and Turkey, and Iran would be cut off from its smaller Levantine allies in Lebanon and Palestine, which would weaken their resistance to Israel. The Mediterranean Sea would become a full NATO lake and a north-south energy transit route in the Levant would fall under Atlanticist control. The Levantine Basin, extending from Gaza to Alexandretta, has several large natural gas reserves that have been the subjects of regional tensions over extraction and ownership rights. Israel has been at odds with both Lebanon and the Palestinians in Gaza over the issue. Both Iran and Russia—the world's two largest proprietors of natural gas—have interests in these natural gas reserves and have been involved in projects to help Lebanon and Syria exploit and develop their gas reserves. With control of Syria or parts of a fractured Syria secured, these natural gas reserves would totally be encompassed by the Atlantic Alliance and the Iranians and Russian would be pushed out.

Additionally, Damascus has been the home of the so-called "Palestinian rejectionists" among whose ranks are Hamas, the Palestinian Islamic Jihad Movement, the Popular Front for the Liberation of Palestine-General Command (PFLP-GC), the Palestinian Revolutionary Communist Party, As-Sa'iqa, and the rejectionist branch of the Palestinian Popular Struggle Front (PPSF/PSF). The Democratic Front for the Liberation of Palestine (DFLP) and the Popular Front for the Liberation of Palestine (PFLP) used to be among their ranks before they left or were expelled. Syria's relationship with these Palestinians ranges from that of outright control over a few to partnership with others. This coalition of Damascus-based Palestinian groups named the Alliance of Palestinian Forces forms a branch of the Resistance Bloc and has been a challenge to Anglo-American and Israeli designs for the Middle East. These Palestinian rejectionists—called the "Palestinian Damascus Ten" in the past—argue that the Palestinians and Arabs have done nothing except appease Israel through bogus and one-sided unjust peace talks controlled by the US. They reject the Oslo Accords and several different agreements as a surrender and betrayal of the Palestinian people and are committed to armed struggle for the liberation of their ancestral homeland. The Palestinian Liberation Organization (PLO) has also been traditionally viewed by these Palestinian groups as a corrupt Israeli and US pawn. For these reasons many Arab capitals have rejected supporting or hosting these Palestinian movements. Nevertheless the lack of broader Arab support has been compensated by the support of Damascus and Tehran, which has made the Palestinian rejectionists committed Syrian and Iranian allies to the point where they have declared that they would fight in any wars targeting Syria and Iran.[47]

Israel's second defeat in Lebanon made US officials scramble in disbelief. The US and Israel had utterly failed to "roll back Syria." As a resulted a new soft power approach towards Damascus was rapidly adopted in the next few months after August 2006. The first result would be that the US and its NATO allies would reverse their decisions to isolate Syrian President Bashar Al-Assad. Washington and Tel Aviv decided to start negotiations with the Syrian regime while Turkish ties with Syria began to deepen in an effort to box in Damascus. Soon diplomats and officials from the US and EU began to scramble to Damascus. Javier Solana, the EU's foreign policy and security chief, would with French approval make what was called a ground breaking March 2007 visit to Damascus where he declared that the EU would begin to diplomatically re-engage Syria.[48] The Baker-Hamilton Commission or the Iraq Study Group (ISG) would also recommend in November 2006 that the US take a new approach towards Damascus and Tehran and seek to co-opt them both through diplomacy and economic reforms. After the Baker-Hamilton Commission's report was made public the US sent its first official to Syria for talks. On the basis of discussing Iraqi refugees the US Department of State sent Assistant Secretary Ellen Sauerbrey to end its diplomatic boycott of Syria in the same month as Solana's visit.[49] US House Speaker Nancy Pelosi and Thomas Lantos, the chairman of the US House Foreign Affairs Committee, would both visit Syria next in April 2007 with a high profile bipartisan delegation of Democrats and Republicans.[50] Turkish Prime Minister Recep Tayyip Erdogan would also visit Bashar Al-Assad in the same month as Pelosi's visit. Erdogan went to discuss the immediate deepening of Syrian-Turkish bilateral trade, security, and energy relations; military cooperation was even discussed prior to his visit by both sides.[51] Atlanticist venues were opened to Syrian officials once again. Syria was even invited to join the Union for the Mediterranean (UfM). Lebanon's March 14 would also make overtures of peace with Syria after May 2008. Walid Jumblatt, Saad Hariri, and various other self-declared Lebanese enemies of Damascus all made trips to Syria.

The aim of all the new diplomacy was to nudge Syria away from Iran and to dissolve the Resistance Bloc through negotiations and enticement. Pelosi and the US delegation pushed President Al-Assad to cut its ties with Iran, Hezbollah, the Iraqi movements opposed to the US, and the Palestinian rejectionists.[52] Thomas Lantos intimated to the Syrians that a few years down the road there would be a new geo-political reality: "Sunni Muslims and not Iran under Mahmoud Ahmadinejad will be in control in the region, and it is to the advantage of Damascus to know which side to be on."[53] Pelosi also acted as one of many Israeli messengers that would arrive in Syria.[54] Ehud Olmert finally announced in April 2008 via Prime Minister Erdogan that Israel would return occupied Syrian territory if Damascus ended its alliance with Iran and left the Resistance Bloc. Despite this diplomatic onslaught being called indirect peace talks, the Syrians were essentially told in the exchanges between them and Tel Aviv: "Join us or face a future war." Syria held out, however, saying its foreign relations were not subject to any peace negotiations. The Iranian-Syrian alliance is the oldest and most tested alliance in the Middle East and a security guarantee for Damascus; there was no way Bashar Al-Assad would end it.

How the NATO Threat to Syria Returned during the Arab Spring

As time passed and Iranian influence began to mushroom in Iraq, the urgency to remove Syria from the Resistance Bloc grew. The US and Israel saw this as a critical move. The Obama Administration made its last diplomatic attempts to win Syria in February 2010.[55] *Reuters* reported the result as follows:

> President Bashar al-Assad and his Iranian counterpart Mahmoud Ahmadinejad signed a bilateral deal to remove travel visas and attended a Muslim ceremony in the Syrian capital.
> Ahmadinejad's visit came a day after Clinton said the United States was asking Syria "to begin to move away from the relationship with Iran," and to stop supporting the Lebanese Shi'ite movement Hezbollah, which is also backed by Iran.
> "We must have understood Clinton wrong because of bad translation or our limited understanding, so we signed the agreement to cancel the visas," Assad said.
> "I find it strange that they (Americans) talk about Middle East stability and peace and the other beautiful principles and call for two countries to move away from each other," he added.
> Ahmadinejad told a joint news conference: "Clinton said we should maintain a distance. I say there is no distance between Iran and Syria."[56]

Adding insult to Washington's injury the Syrians hosted a tripartite summit between President Al-Assad, President Ahmadinejad, and Hezbollah Secretary-General Nasrallah.[57] After this Washington realized that its efforts to de-link Syria from Iran and Hezbollah were in vain. Al-Assad would even confidently tell the Italian newspaper *La Republica* in May that Washington had lost its influence in the Middle East and that his country was in the process of forming a new geo-political alternative with Iran, Russia, and Turkey in the "center of the world."[58] Hence the language of diplomacy began to subside and by 2011 the language of threats returned.

The upheavals of the Arab Spring were used as an opportunity to reactivate plans to attack Syria. NATO returned to the picture as a part of this threat. Turkey cut its ties with Damascus and both Saudi Arabia and Qatar led a campaign to isolate Syria among the Arab countries. This time the excuses for an attack on Syria were based on fighting inside Syria

The Globalization of NATO

between government and anti-government forces, which were being
manipulated and fuelled by the US and its allies to provoke a civil war.
The claims by the US, UK, France, Saudi Arabia, Qatar, Turkey and their
allies—reported by CNN, Fox News, BBC, Sky News, France 24, Al Jazeera,
Al Arabiya, and their other media networks—were that the events in
Syria were nothing short of government massacres of anti-government
protesters. They concealed the role of the US *et al.,* and the fact that their
snipers had been sent in to kill civilians and government forces to ignite
an insurgency. Syrian television would show footage exposing one so-
called activist named Danny Dayem doctoring videos about government
atrocities for CNN, which resulted in Danny appearing on *Anderson Cooper
360°* in March 2012 to announce he had no ties with CNN to counter the
scandal.[59] Danny would not be alone; the British-based Syrian Human
Rights Observatory—which ironically saluted Saudi King Abdullah as a
"democrat"—which would be authoritatively quoted about government
massacres in Syria by Al Jazeera, BBC, CNN, and their ilk, would also be
humiliated for fabricating its information, leading to the organization
claiming that one maverick member was behind it all.

The report of the Arab League's own observers in Syria, which
was brushed aside by the GCC due to the inconvenience of its findings,
even outlined how the insurgent forces had been twisting the facts about
civilian casualties and mostly responsible for the violence. One excerpt
from the report had this to say:

> In Homs, Idlib and Hama, the Observer Mission
> witnessed acts of violence being committed against
> Government forces and civilians that resulted in several
> deaths and injuries. Examples of those acts include
> the bombing of a civilian bus, killing eight persons and
> injuring others, including women and children, and
> the bombing of a train carrying diesel oil. In another
> incident in Homs, a police bus was blown up, killing two
> police officers. A fuel pipeline and some small bridges
> were also bombed.[60]

Arms were sent across Syria's borders by NATO and GCC
members. The Transitional Council in Libya would join the effort to topple
the Syrian regime by sending fighters and arms shipments through the
Lebanese port of Tripoli.[61] What the US and its allies did is unleash the
Salvador option; Washington's so-called "Syrian Free Army" proxies began
systematically massacring civilians in the countryside and detonating
bombs in public places inside Aleppo and Damascus. Turkey provided
access to its territory for the armed groups fighting the Syrian Army and

328

helped arm and train them alongside France, Britain, and other NATO members. On July 4, 2012, about half a year after lifting a five-month arms embargo on Qatar for sending Swiss weapons into Libya, Switzerland even froze all its arms exports to the UAE due to reports that Swiss grenades were being sent to Syria by the Emiratis. British, French, and Turkish operatives and special forces would additionally operate inside Syria and Lebanon. A Turkish jet violating Syrian airspace, in what the Russian Federal Defense Ministry announced was a NATO spy mission, was even shot down on June 22, 2012. Lebanese March 14 MP Jamal Al-Jarrahin, who was responsible for assembling the Hariri family's Sunni Tiger militia that was defeated in May 2008, would also be among those blamed for helping to destabilize Syria.

All the spiritual leaders of Syria's faiths—from Druze Sheikh Al-Aql Hamoud Hennawi and Sunni Grand Mufti Ahmad Badreddin Hassoun to Melkite Patriarch Gregory III Laham, Greek Orthodox Patriarch Ignatius IV, and Syriac Orthodox Patriarch Ignatius Zakka I Iwas—have spoken out against foreign interference in their country, asked Syrians not to be divided, and supported the Syrian government.[62] They have also lamented the role of the foreign media in twisting the facts about who is perpetrating most of the violence. While complaining about the foreign media, Patriarch Gregory has even said that what has been taking place in Syria is not an authentic revolution, but banditry that includes foreign fanatics brought into Syria who are targeting the Christian community.[63] A sectarian card is being played under which the Alawites and Christians are being targeted. Syrian Kurds and peaceful opposition members have been targeted by the Syrian Free Army as well. Supporters of the insurgents also use sectarian chants: "Alawites to the ground and Christians to Lebanon!" This has gotten the attention of the Vatican, the Ecumenical Patriarchate of Constantinople in Istanbul, the Russian Orthodox Church, and Lebanon's Christian communities. Since, 2011, the patriarch of the Maronite Catholic Church in Lebanon has also weighed in on the situation, repeatedly speaking out in support of Damascus and warning against foreign interference—to the anger of Washington and March 14 politicians in Lebanon.[64]

What the US and NATO were trying to do was to pressure Al-Assad to surrender and change orbits or to take over via regime change via a campaign modeled on the takeover of Libya by NATO-controlled fighters. The main US-supported opposition group called the Syrian National Council presented its foreign policy platform as the dissolution of the Resistance Bloc:

> A Syrian government run by the country's main opposition group would cut Damascus's military

relationship to Iran and end arms supplies to Middle
East militant groups such as Hezbollah and Hamas, the
group's leader said, raising the prospect of a dramatic
realignment of powers at the region's core.

Burhan Ghalioun, the president of the Syrian
National Council, said such moves would be part of a
broader Syrian reorientation back into an alliance with
the region's major Arab powers [i.e., the Arab allies
of the US and Israel]. Mr. Ghalioun's comments came
Wednesday, in his first major media interview since he
was made SNC leader in October [2011].[65]

Unlike with Libya, however, Syria's allies presented a barrier to NATO
plans for a direct attack. The Palestinians, Lebanon, and Iraq would
refuse to follow Saudi Arabia and Qatar or their plans to put another Arab
League rubber stamp on a NATO war. Iran would also refuse to abandon
Damascus. China and Russia too would actively step into the scene to
assist Syria with diplomatic, economic, and material help. The SCO and
the BRICS countries would also publicly warn against military intervention.

CHAPTER 15

AMERICA AND NATO AS ROME AND THE PENINSULAR ALLIES

A strong NATO is not only important for Europe but is also critical to American security interests. The United States will not be able to pursue domestic renewal successfully without peace and stability in Europe, a region where [US] geopolitical stake remains paramount. Even excluding Russia, it embodies the largest collection of military power and potential. It is also a key geographical, strategic and logistical link to the Middle East and Persian Gulf areas. NATO members, including the United States, hold six of the seven G7 seats, make up 16 of 22 members of the IMF, and hold three of the five permanent seats at the United Nations.

—NATO Secretary-General Manfred Wörner (1993)

What is the Euro-Atlantic Zone?

The Euro-Atlantic Zone is the combined territory and areas controlled by all the members of the EU and NATO. It is the vicinity of the world where Atlanticism has secured its grip on the political, security, and economic systems. It sprang to life after the Second World War on the basis of forging a permanent bridge between the eastern and western shores of the Atlantic and US permanent engagement in the affairs of Europeans. The Anglo-American and Franco-German branches of NATO are the dominant forces of the Euro-Atlantic Zone and the US is the unquestionable primal state. US influence is paramount on both sides of the Atlantic Ocean, while the collective influence of the UK, France, and Germany on the western side of the Atlantic bears no significant challenge to the US. All Euro-Atlantic architecture is not just affected by Washington, but is governed first and foremost by US behavior. This includes the polity of the European Union; the EU's European Commission in Brussels and the European Council in practice share the influence they have over the EU with Washington, DC.

If the status of the US inside the Euro-Atlantic Zone is of such stature, is the said area a modern day empire controlled by the US? For the most part, discussions about a US empire or US clients and satellites have been discouraged in popular North American culture and mainstream Euro-Atlantic politics. Former associate editor of the magazine *Foreign Policy,* Alan Tonelson, once lectured:

> I am reluctant to use the term *alliance* to describe [the Japanese and NATO] security relationships [with the US] because the sharing of costs and risks in both has been so unequal for so long that the kind of all-for-one and one-for-all implications of the word *alliance* seem to me to be rather inappropriate. What we call allies have really been client states, only they are ruled for the most part by white people, not black or brown people. We tend to shy away from the term *client state* when we talk about states ruled by white people, but in fact, that is exactly what they are.
>
> Specifically, the United States is still using "alliance" policy to prevent Japan and the countries of Western Europe from pursuing their own independent foreign policies.[1]

Tonelson is accurate in saying that the alliance policies of the US have worked to prevent independent action among US allies. His analysis should be taken further and amended to say that US alliance policy has intentionally and systematically worked to turn Washington's allies into clients or satellites. This is what the Gaullists and others in Western Europe were objecting to and fighting against.

What the US has been doing is slowly eroding the independence of its allies. The social, political, legal, and economic institutions of the countries and societies inside the Euro-Atlantic Zone have not only been in the process of standardizing, but they have also become more and more similar to those of the US. The security structures of these states have become more and more integrated with that of the United States: their criminal and airport databases are being networked to those in the US; their security platforms and policies are being reformed to mimic those of the US; and US domination over their security structures is manifest. The elites of various fields, from politics and academia to finance and security, in the Euro-Atlantic Zone are all more and more prone to visit and train in the United States or through US programs in some manner.

On the cultural front Americanization is also strongest in the Euro-Atlantic Zone. All this is much more than the influence of a superpower, because it is actively being pursued by Washington. This is why the Chinese and Russians have consistently complained that the US time and again oversteps its national boundaries and expects other countries to follow its domestic laws and procedures. Countries entering the Euro-Atlantic Zone are all altered under the banners of democratization and the so-called free market; in reality they are transformed into endosymbionts—organisms living within the bodies or cells of larger organisms—which slowly lose their independence and over time become assimilated units of the larger body that absorbed them.

NATO: Continued US Occupation of Post-World War II Europe?

Critics of the Atlantic Alliance have called it the continued post-Second World War occupation of Europe. NATO was formed on the basis of the continued presence of the US military in Western Europe after the Second World War. In East Asia the defense and security ties that the US bilaterally formed with Japan were also formed on the basis of post-Second World War military occupation. That the US military presence was mostly sought in Western Europe did not change what it was and especially what it evolved into. The presence of the US military was also related to consorted efforts to keep the socialists and communists out of power in Western Europe, who would have been elected to government had it not been for Washington's involvement in Europe. Washington saw Western European socialists and communists as much more of a threat than the Soviet Union which was in the process of recovering and rebuilding.

In order to decide whether the US deployment was an occupation, the reason why the US kept its forces in Europe has to be understood and analyzed. US troops were meant to be a final option to forcibly remove any socialist or communist government in the Western Bloc, should they be elected. One incomplete way to analyze the intentions of the US deployment in Europe is to look at US actions once the Eastern Bloc was defeated and the Cold War ended. The US government did not order its forces to leave once the Cold War ended. Was this for defensive reasons even though no threat existed in Western Europe? According to Joseph J. Kruzel, the former deputy assistant secretary of defense for European and NATO policy, the first challenge for the US at the end of the Cold War was to get the idea into everyone's heads that the US had no intention of militarily retiring from Europe. US forces were there to stay. Nor did most of the powerful politicians of NATO countries have any intention of challenging the continued military presence of the

US on their territories, because the Western European elites formed an endosymbiosis with the US elites in a modern and evolving system of empire.

The occupied and colonized can come to accept and adopt the system and ways of their occupiers and colonizers. From Latin America to ancient Gaul (France) and Anatolia this is how new languages, cultures, religions, and different state systems have been adopted and accepted in many societies and new identities formed. It is a part of the constant waltz of history that sees the rejection/resistance and acceptance/surrender—neither one, like all hegemonies ,is ever complete—that gives rise to new peoples. In Western Europe many have come to accept without challenge the primal role of the US over the affairs of their states and give little thought to NATO except as a foundation of their security architecture. They have been raised and socialized with this as a part of their world. In many instances it is not only a normal part of the status quo for them, but also it is *invisible* to them. This is why the post-Cold War continuation of the Atlantic Alliance went mostly unchallenged at the societal level in NATO member states, leaving the US to slowly consolidate its influence in each and every state.

What is going to be explained next is important to note. Towards the end of the Cold War and the demise of the USSR, NATO established a special presidential committee to outline the future decades of the Atlantic Alliance. According to former NATO Parliamentary Assembly president Ton Frinking, the outcome was what is loosely called a "trans-Atlantic bargain" that stressed a continued US military presence in Europe that would be supplemented by the "increased burden relief provided by the European allies through the creation of a viable European pillar" of NATO military power.[2] What this means is that the US now expected the other members of NATO to contribute soldiers, sailors, and airmen like loyal subjects. Intra-NATO relations also changed significantly as the US had consolidated its control over its allies over the decades; Washington had come a long way from the days of the Vietnam War when US Secretary of State Dean Rusk had to plead with NATO allies for support and then "was reduced to pleading with the NATO allies to stop their shipping to North Vietnamese ports."[3]

US Coups in Berlin and Paris?

Zbigniew Brzezinski has continuously stipulated that the ability of the US to project its influence and power in Eurasia relies on its ties to Europe as its main bridgehead. Thus a united Europe would be an essential prerequisite for US domination of Eurasia to proceed. He clarifies that the Franco-German Entente would be a vital partner, because Europe could never be united without Paris and Berlin as its two central players. Here lies the conundrum for Washington: America has needed to insure Franco-German cooperation, without which it can be locked out of continental Europe, but it has also been competing with the Franco-German duo. Years of intra-NATO rivalry between Paris and Washington resurfaced with the strategic opposition of the Franco-German Entente and Russia to the Anglo-American invasion of Iraq where serial tripartite meetings were held by Paris, Berlin, and Moscow. It looked like the US would lose its Eurasian bridgehead, but then there was regime change in Berlin and Paris through the 2005 German federal elections and the 2007 French presidential elections.

In Germany the Christian Democratic Union and its sister-party the Christian Social Union of Bavaria managed to collectively obtain 226 seats in the German Bundestag (Federal Legislature) on September 18, 2005. This was a source of joy for Germany's Anglo-American allies. Though Gerhard Schröder's Social Democrat Party of Germany fell short of winning an absolute majority, it had still secured 222 spots in the Bundestag. Initially, Federal Chancellor Schröder confidently told the German people that he would remain in his position as the leader of the German federal government, because his party had won the most seats. This did not happen though. In last minute inter-party negotiations he was forced to retire to pave the way for the formation of a grand coalition federal government. Schröder effectively surrendered his position to America's "iron lady," Angela Merkel, who would lead a coalition government of the Christian Democratic Union, Christian Social Union of Bavaria, and Schröder's Social Democrats.

The election deadlock was effectively a coup. Schröder's own Social Democrat rivals worked against him and it was clear that a coalition majority could not be formed without Frau Merkel. It resulted in a significant change in the strategic landscape of the EU. Thus a government more favorable to cooperation with the US, that did not want to challenge Washington as far as Schröder would be likely to do, took the helm of the Bundesrepublik.

Panic and anxiety hit Paris as President Jacques Chirac saw himself isolated and put into a position where he too would have to be more accommodating to Washington. Berlin, however, would get its own surprise after the 2007 election of Nicolas Sarkozy in France. While Merkel proved to be pro-US, she was not as subservient as Sarkozy would be. Monsieur Sarkozy—the son of a Magyar (Hungarian) aristocrat who became a refugee in France after Hungary's surrender to the Red Army during the Second World War and a mother who was part Greek and part French—would be accused of being tied to the CIA. A whole set of circumstantial facts led to speculation on his ties to the CIA. One of them would be his step-mother Christine de Ganay's remarriage to Frank George Wisner II, a top ranking US State Department and later Pentagon official who himself was the son of one of the CIA's top ranking officials; Wisner II is widely believed to be a member of the CIA. The other circumstances were that his key presidential staff, advisors, and ministers—from Christine Lagarde to Alain Bauer—would all be Anglophiles linked to the US either through their education, business interests, or previous employment. Regardless of the accusations against Sarkozy, his policies subordinated France to Washington's interest. Under his corrupt presidency France was essentially transformed from an independent ally into a vassal and the Franco-German Entente was greatly undermined.

Following Rome's Path:
The Evolution of NATO into a Military Wing of the US Empire

The United States did not want to have a visible presence during NATO's war against Libya, especially as NATO mobilized for an attack in parallel to Alliance member maneuvers taking place at the UN. The US deliberately let its French and British NATO allies take the public lead in the attacks and tried to distance itself from the war as a reluctant partner. But NATO allies were actually doing the bidding of the US. The cold truth is that NATO members are at Washington's service just as the ancient Latin League towards its latter days was at the service of the city-state of Rome.

The evolution of NATO and other US-led alliances parallel the evolution of the system of alliances led by the Romans in the Italian Peninsula. For the Romans the early alliance they headed seamlessly transformed into their republican empire. NATO is also in the process of evolving in this manner as the military instrument of the modern global empire of the United States.

The Roman Republic's alliance systems started like NATO and the other US-led Cold War alliances. The basis for establishing NATO was a common Soviet threat while the common threat for Rome's early alliance was the Aequi and Volsci tribes. These tribes would take advantage of the fighting between the Romans and Latin League in Latium and mount their own attacks against both sides. This would force the Romans and Latin League to negotiate the *foedus Cassianum* to unite their armies under a new Latin alliance. The alliance facilitated the expansion of Rome in Latium, because Rome by itself would have an equal position and say to all the members of the Latin League combined. This alliance can be compared to NATO, because Rome held a superior standing to all its allies just as the US does to all its NATO allies. Moreover, the Romans formed the bulk of the new alliance's forces by contributing half its soldiers while the rest of the Latin League would collectively provide the other half. This is also similar to the disproportionate contribution of the US to NATO in comparison to that of the other NATO members. The equal standing between the city-state of Rome and the entire Latin League also parallels the relationship of the US and the EU. The US can unilaterally make decisions on its own affecting the entire Euro-Atlantic Zone which the EU has to respect as America's partner, whereas the EU has to form a consensus among its members for its decisions. This automatically places the EU in a disadvantageous position against the US, especially since the US controls several of the EU's members and can effectively prevent consensus.

Under Rome's alliance with the Latin League the two plundered and appropriated land—the basis for wealth in their agrarian societies—which had to be split equally into two shares, one for Rome and the other for all the members of the Latin League. Critics of NATO point out that it has played the role of a tool for plunder through its wars in the former Yugoslavia and Libya where its major powers profited by securing new markets, valuable resources, and reconstruction contracts. Additionally, the Romans never saw themselves as aggressors in any of their expansionist wars just as the US and NATO never admit their roles as aggressors even in the series of wars that were ignited by the launching of their offensives.

Roman power increased under the arrangements of its alliance with the Latin League; the Roman Republic became the arbitrator of Latium, holding authority above all the other Latin city-states and tribes. This is similar to the standing of the US under NATO. Rome by itself could summon the alliance's army, whereas the rest of the Latin League needed to agree collectively before they could summon the common army. Rome enriched itself and grew more powerful on the basis of its disproportionate control of the alliance with the Latin League. The other Latin city-states and tribes would also seek Rome's favor on the basis of its ability to control the alliance and unilaterally summon the common army. Hence other Latin League members further subordinated themselves to Rome as a means of further gain. This internal subordination of allies is similar to the actions of NATO member governments trying to gain favor with the US by subordinating themselves to Washington.

Roman diplomacy was important in creating its empire just as US diplomacy has been in creating the American Empire. The term divide and rule—*divide et impera* in Latin—even comes from the period of Roman alliance-building. The Romans formed a defense pact with the Hernici, who feared the Aequi and Volsci between whose territories they were sandwiched, that isolated and helped eventually defeat the two tribes. The Romans also began to diplomatically exchange the rights of citizenship with the Etruscan city of Caere and the Greek colony of Massilia (modern-day Marseilles) to build a new alliance against the Gallic tribes. These new alliances were formed with partners that the Romans called *socii*. These Roman partners and the NATO allies bear resemblance to each other. *Socii* commanded their own armies and navies, enjoyed some Roman rights, and did not need to pay taxes to Rome, but were required to put their military forces at the disposal of Rome, follow Roman foreign policy, and fight under the supreme command of a Roman general.

Like the Atlantic Alliance and its different categories and layers of cooperation, the Roman alliance system also had different layers. When the Romans began to assimilate members of the Latin League this system would become apparent. The city-state of Tusculum would be the first Latin League member to be assimilated into the Roman Republic. The forced assimilation of Tusculum as a Roman *municipium*—an internally self-administered city with a population bearing obligations as Roman citizens—forced its people to financially contribute to Rome's budget under Roman taxes and contribute men to Rome's defenses and campaigns. This is what the "trans-Atlantic bargain" that former NATO Parliamentary Assembly president Ton Frinking described is. NATO members must contribute each in their own way to the Pentagon's wars but also enjoy voting rights at the North Atlantic Council and a security guarantee under Article 5 of the Washington Treaty.

Under the Roman system, a second class of *municipia* was also created where the people had all the rights and responsibilities of Roman citizenship except the right to help steer the Roman Republic through voting. NATO's second class tier is formed by the Partnership for Peace, the Mediterranean Dialogue, Istanbul Cooperation Initiative, and the Contact Countries which all cooperate and work with NATO, but do not have voting rights at the North Atlantic Council—with a few exceptions— or a security guarantee under Article 5 of the Washington Treaty.[4]

The Romans used diplomacy with their enemies to shape their strategic environment as does the US. While expanding the Roman Republic would arrange a temporary understanding with the Carthaginians on establishing spheres of influence in Italy that prevented Carthage from attacking Roman allies. This move can be compared to the spheres of influence created with Washington's Soviet rival in Europe after the Second World War that kept the USSR at bay while the US entrenched itself in Western Europe. In many cases Rome worked against its own allies just like the US did against France by slowly absorbing its sphere of influence in Africa or against Saddam Hussein and the Taliban after it used them. The Romans made a bilateral alliance with the Samnites that would actually pin down the Samnites while Rome grew stronger.

What the Romans did is wear away their Samnite ally's strength, encircle them, and internally divide them before marching into Samnium and ultimately assimilating it as part of the Roman Republic. Playing the fear of different states against one another was also a Roman tactic. Capua would become a Roman ally out of fear of the Samnites. The US has used these types of tactics in regard to Greece and Turkey. Rome's allies would not be oblivious to this: Hernici and the Latin League tried unsuccessfully to abort their alliances with the Roman Republic after realizing that their alliances with Rome were part of a system of subordination. But the Hernici and Latin League would be unsuccessful and the Romans would force them to renew their alliances under even greater Roman control than before.

It was by means of this system that Rome united and ruled all the Italian Peninsula. Turning Roman allies into citizens at first was perceived negatively, because it removed a community's sovereignty. Once the Latin League was absorbed the different cities and towns were given bilateral treaty rights for interchangeable civil rights with Rome, but banned from sharing them with one another. With time the Romanization of allies was perceived positively, because of the rights and wealth they gained, especially when Rome began its military campaigns outside the Italian Peninsula. Roman allies began to hope to achieve Latin status and eventually be granted Roman citizenship. The Latin allies shared the rights of intermarriage, making legal contracts, and residency with Romans. For the Romans the alliance they headed was an evolving hierarchical system that seamlessly transformed into an empire.

Is the US-led alliance synonymous with empire? It may have not started that way just like initially the Roman alliance with the Latin League did not, but it is going in that direction. Rome's allies were formally considered independent states that joined the Roman Republic in the alliance, but in actuality these allies were subjects of Rome that gradually became absorbed into the Roman Republic. The parallel with what has been taking place with NATO is uncanny. NATO member states pay tribute to the US by signing lucrative defense and arms contracts with US corporations. These members contribute their forces to serve under US command inside of NATO and many of them also contribute to US operations that are formally outside of NATO. Almost all NATO members fall into line with Washington's foreign policy objectives and cannot avoid shaping their policies around those of the United States. Like Rome's allies, they also hope to make gains by serving in US-led wars. Both the Roman and US systems of alliance are forms of subordination. The North Atlantic Council has become an imperial roundtable and NATO and its extensions are part of a modern empire similar to the manner in which the different alliances of Rome led to the formation of its empire.

CHAPTER 16

GLOBAL MILITARIZATION

AT THE DOORS OF WORLD WAR III?

The great wars of history—we have had a world-war about every hundred years for the last four centuries—are the outcome, direct or indirect, of the unequal growth of nations, and that unequal growth is not wholly due to the greater genius and energy of some nations as compared with others; in large measure it is the result of the uneven distribution of fertility and strategical opportunity upon the face of our Globe. In other words, there is in nature no such thing as equality of opportunity for the nations. Unless I wholly misread the facts of geography, I would go further, and say that the grouping of lands and seas, and of fertility and natural pathways, is such as to lead itself to the growth of empires, and in the end of a single World Empire.
—Halford J. Mackinder (1919)

We have a duty to remember that the causes of any war lie above all in the mistakes and miscalculations of peacetime, and that these causes have their roots in an ideology of confrontation and extremism. It is all the more important that we remember this today, because these threats are not becoming fewer but are only transforming and changing their appearance. These new threats, just as under the Third Reich, show the same contempt for human life and the same aspiration to establish an exclusive diktat over the world.
—Russian President Vladimir Putin (2008)

The Hardening Global Lines

While wars have wreaked havoc across the global stage for millennia, modernity offers such unparalleled capacities for communication and destruction that the world may at last be at a point where it is not only possible but crucial to bring that bloody era of human history to a close. But what we see instead is that the world is being increasingly militarized, making it as potentially explosive as a powder keg. The first Cold War never really ended, or at least the mentality behind it never really went away. Nor have the key divisions that were perceived to have existed during the Cold War disappeared; they have been modified, transformed, and repackaged, laying bare the Cold War ideological discourse as a cover for ongoing geo-political ambitions for dominating the map and creating empire. The old battle lines remain—with modifications—between the cardinal oceanic power of the United States and the land powers of Russia and China. The US has played its hand with NATO, showing the world what it would offer it without the Soviet and Eastern Bloc challenge: not peace, not equitable development under the rule of law universally applied, but aggression and imperial expansion leaving a trail of chaos and carnage. In 2011, by the time NATO started its war on Libya it was conducting operations in four continents; three oceans; and multiple countries and bodies of water. These areas of operations included the Atlantic Ocean, the Arctic Ocean, the former Yugoslavia, the Mediterranean Sea, Afghanistan, Pakistan, Iraq, Somalia, Sudan, the Red Sea, the Gulf of Aden, and the Indian Ocean. It is clear that NATO expansion is not just limited to Europe, but is in pursuit of a worldwide capability to expand Washington's empire under a global confederacy.

The system of military alliances is tightening as capital and blocs line up on their respective sides. On one side stand the Atlanticists and their minions and on the other side stand the Eurasianists and their allies. Five of the highest ranking retired military officials from NATO—Jacque Lanxade (France), Klaus Naumann (Germany) Henk van den Breeman (the Netherlands), Peter Inge (UK), and John Shalikashvili (US)—proposed in a 2007 document, *Towards a Grand Strategy for an Uncertain World: Renewing Transatlantic Partnership*, the categorical use of nuclear weapons against rival states and blocs, the globalization of NATO, and the amalgamation of the US, EU, and NATO. The US and NATO have literally authorized themselves to go to war anywhere in the world. The 2010 Strategic Concept of NATO, which was drafted by a committee chaired by Madeleine Albright and vice-chaired by former Royal Dutch Shell CEO Jeroen van der Veer, also asserts the legitimacy of whatever actions NATO members take to secure energy sources as the US and NATO look towards securing all the world's energy hubs. While NATO has been consolidating a global network the Shanghai Cooperation Organization and the Collective Security Treaty Organization have been growing to counter-balance the Alliance. China, Russia, and Iran are in the forefront of what was initially a "coalition of the reluctant" driven

Map XIX: NATO Operations and Missions in 2009

NATO Operations and Missions

Completed NATO operations and missions

1995 - 2004
Bosnia and Herzegovina

2001 - 2003
the former Yugoslav Republic of Macedonia*

Current NATO operations and missions

Jun 1999 –
Kosovo

Oct 2001 –
Monitoring the Mediterranean Sea

Aug 2003 –
Afghanistan

Jun 2004 –
NATO Training Mission in Iraq (NTM-I)

Jun 2005 –
Supporting the African Union

Apr 2008 – Jun 2009
Counter-piracy
Gulf of Aden

Oct 2005 – Feb 2006
Pakistan earthquake relief operation

Oct - Dec 2008
Counter-piracy
Gulf of Aden

* Turkey recognizes the Republic of Macedonia with its constitutional name.

together by mutual fears about Euro-Atlantic expansion that has led to the formation of a loosely-knit Eurasian triple entente. From this Chinese-Russian-Iranian coalition a global anti-establishmentarian counter-alliance has formed against the US and NATO.

Washington has been preparing the global chessboard by entrenching itself in the Eurasian Rimland and guarding pivotal areas that can be used as control points, strategic launch pads, and chokepoints in future military conflicts. In Yemen and its Socotra archipelago the US is setting up a base of power to control the waterway between the Red Sea and Indian Ocean, one of the most vital global maritime routes. A new iron curtain has been created from the Baltic to the Aegean Sea to castrate and contain the European core of Russia and its allies in Eastern Europe. Georgia is being propped up in the Caucasus by the US, NATO, and Israel as a citadel against Russia and Iran. In the Persian Gulf the Alliance is working to incorporate the Gulf Cooperation Council into NATO through the Istanbul Cooperation Initiative. From its bases in Taiwan, South Korea, and Japan the Pentagon is actively pressuring North Korea and China. AFRICOM is being used to huddle the African continent's military forces under US tutelage. In the Western Hemisphere the Pentagon is using Colombia as a bridgehead in a strategy against Venezuela and several of its smaller allies and Haiti is essentially being militarily administered as a US base in the Caribbean Sea. International disarmament has suffered serious setbacks as Washington has walked away from its treaties and legal obligations and Russia and other powers threaten to do the same. The Pentagon also seeks to militarize space. The globe is literally gripped with a series of arenas where the struggle between the US-led alliances and the counter-alliances is taking place. Cyberspace has now become a theater for these rivalries too. The struggles in these fronts vary in shape and dimension, but are all intertwined. The linked nature of all these fronts and their struggles has the potential for destabilizing other parts of the world and escalating into potentially broader conflicts.

The loss of China to Mao and the communists has haunted Washington. The US saw the Chinese as less threatening than the Soviets during the Cold War. This, along with Sino-US collaboration against the USSR, was one of the reasons Washington abandoned its plans to create a Southeast Asian bridgehead against China that was like its Western European bridgehead, with SEATO and a US-controlled ASEAN as equivalents to NATO and the EU. Never did US officials consider that China would become the strategic challenge that it has become. Once the USSR collapsed Washington's attention turned to Beijing. Reportedly, Chairman Deng asserted in 1991 that a "new cold war" had begun between China and the US.[1] Ultimately all roads lead to Beijing in the current century and China is the king piece on the global chessboard on which the US is playing. The globalization of NATO will eventually lead to East Asia and the borders of the Chinese where the US has been waging a shadow war to box China in and checkmate it. For the US, in the words of Zbigniew Brzezinski, "China is unfinished business."[2] There is also a hope among US officials that the alliance between China and Russia is temporary, like the one between Germany and the Soviet Union when they invaded Poland, and that something can be done to play the Eurasian giants against one another.

While the US has lost ground in post-Soviet Central Asia and Iraq, it is still clinging to Afghanistan. Iran, which is entrenching Iraq into its orbit, has been gaining increasing influence in NATO-garrisoned Afghanistan through various economic, political, and cultural projects. The Iranian government has established a Persian-speaking countries forum for Afghanistan, Tajikistan, and Iran as a means to integrate Afghanistan as much as it can into its own orbit and away from the US while preparing the road for a strategic partnership with Kabul. Moscow has also sought to regain influence in Afghanistan. Russia has worked to balance the US and the Afghanistan-Pakistan-ISAF Tripartite Commission through the Afghanistan-Pakistan-Russia-Tajikistan formula and their quadripartite anti-terrorism cooperation agreement. China also looks forward to exerting its influence in Afghanistan and the SCO has given notice that it intends to move into Afghanistan once NATO vacates. This is why the SCO-Afghanistan Contact Group was established in 2009 and Kabul was admitted into the SCO as an observer. The US, however, intends on manipulating India to oppose the Eurasian triple entente and assist Washington in maintaining control over Afghanistan.

Each side in the global struggle is trying to maximize its share of resources and international influence under an evolving so-called system of global governance tied to economic exploitation. These tensions can be felt as Brazil and India demand permanent seats at the UN Security Council and the BRICS demand the reform of international financial institutions through such steps as a redistribution of voting powers inside the International Monetary Fund. In lockstep with these tensions Russia, China, India, Iran, and their allies have been gradually weakening the dollar and trading with one another in their own currencies.[3] The members of the Eurasian Union—Belarus, Kazakhstan, and Russia—and the SCO have all held discussions about instituting regional currencies.

Interception of Russian combat aircraft by NATO fighters has begun since Moscow resumed strategic bomber patrol flights over the international waters of the Arctic, Atlantic and Pacific Oceans by order of Vladimir Putin in August 2007. During patrols over internationally neutral airspace and waterways, Russian jets and ships have been tailed and monitored by NATO warplanes and vessels. On April 9, 2008 four Russian Tupolev Tu-95 strategic bombers and four Il-78 aerial tankers flying near Alaska were intercepted and followed by NATO planes.[4] This was the second such incident in less than a month; on March 19, 2008 two Russian Tupolev Tu-95 strategic bombers were intercepted and followed by F-16 Tornado fighter jets.[5] Russia has sent its planes and strategic nuclear bombers on missions around the world. Cold War flight routes under what are termed "strategic flights" have been resumed. These flights are a military threat to strike rivals in the event of a war and are synonymous with increasing global tensions.

While the total sum of the collective military expenditures of NATO members has not declined, their global share of military spending has (see Chart 19.2). This is alarming, because military and security spending has drastically gone up globally. What this means is that the other non-NATO countries are spending more on their armed forces. The increase in global military spending is a result of an increasing global trend of militarization and the accompanying arms race that Washington is pushing. This militarization process comes with a heavy price. Funds are being reallocated from the civilian sector and public services to the military sector. The only real winners are arms manufacturers. Furthermore, the militarization process has a correlation with the worldwide curtailing of human rights and civil liberties. As militarism and tensions mount, civil liberties and human rights decline in the name of national security agendas.

Moral compasses have long been cast aside and Samuel Huntington's "Clash of Civilizations" paradigm is finding increasing favor as demonization tactics are used to alienate different peoples and justify global confrontation and antagonism, specifically against the Chinese and predominately Muslim societies. Nor will the Atlanticist supporters of empire be pleased until Russia and China are vanquished and balkanized. A world war is not unthinkable under these circumstances. All things have their breaking points under stress and political miscalculations. Nor do the events leading to a new global war necessarily need to be based on a large destructive event that arises all at once. The events leading to a world war could be numerous and the process slow and calculated. 9/11 and the invasion of Taliban-controlled Afghanistan could have been the opening salvos of a world war in which many feel we are already engaged.

The Threat of Nuclear War Makes a Comeback

Nuclear weapons are an overwhelmingly destructive force. They kill the living, poison the land, destroy ecosystems, trigger cancer, contaminate water, and cause unimaginable horrors to future generations by leaving a radioactive legacy for thousands of years that deforms and kills. Only obliteration—as Senator Hillary Clinton indeed threatened during her 2008 campaign to become the Democratic Party nominee for president—can be brought about through the use of these awful devices. In short, nuclear arms are nothing less than satanic. Although nuclear war is far removed from the minds of most of the public, the specter of a nuclear holocaust has not declined since the end of the Cold War. The threat of nuclear war is as strong as it ever was during the Cold War, if not stronger. The public's failure to grasp the threats and risks of a nuclear war allows their national officials and politicians to act in a much more careless and unrestrained manner related to these dreadful weapons.

The 2001 Nuclear Posture Review (NPR) acknowledges that US nuclear weapons have been pointed for use against Iraq, Libya, Syria, Iran, North Korea, China, and Russia. The US, UK, France, and NATO—under Washington's orders—all have refused to commit to a policy of "no first use" for nuclear weapons unlike non-NATO nuclear powers.

The Pentagon's Doctrine for Joint Nuclear Operations allows nuclear weapons to be used by US generals and admirals under a greater variety of circumstances.[6] This includes using nuclear weapons to end a war with a non-nuclear enemy on "terms favorable to the United States and its allies."[7] Flag officers in unified combatant commands, like EUCOM and CENTCOM, are now given authority by the US president to have operational control (OPCON) over nuclear weapons to launch attacks on their own prerogatives.[8] The manual for the Doctrine for Joint Nuclear Operations states: "[G]eographic combatant commanders may be assigned operational control over US Strategic Command nuclear capable forces employed for nuclear operations in support of theater conflicts."[9] Most the world's countries and governments also argue that the US and its NATO allies have violated Articles 1 and 2 of the Non-Proliferation Treaty (NPT), because the Pentagon has maintained a NATO nuclear weapons sharing program and the non-US military hardware of other NATO members has been modified to deliver nuclear weapons. Through its continued construction of nuclear weapons the United States is the chief violator of the NPT and the chief cause for the development of Russian and Chinese nuclear weapons.

The US is not alone in its violation of the NPT either. London began to rearm itself with new Trident nuclear missiles in 2007.[10] British Prime Minister Tony Blair faced a revolt from his own party over the issue, with fierce opposition in the British House of Commons and protests in the streets of London. The British move was a gross breach of the NPT, which stipulates that all nations with nuclear weapons must disarm. France, which makes its nuclear weapons with Germany and is infamous for its nuclear weapons tests in Algeria and Polynesia, has also been forced to follow the Anglo-American lead.

Washington has made it categorically clear that it could attack Iran and North Korea with nukes. The Obama Administration redefined Washington's NPT commitments in April 2010 by declaring that the Pentagon would not honor the NPT's provision which barred a nuclear attack on certain non-nuclear states, meaning Iran and North Korea.[11] Obama's rationale was that both Iran and North Korea were in non-compliance with the NPT *according to the US government*. This was a fallacious claim: in the case of the Iranians, the International Atomic Energy Agency (IAEA) has repeatedly reported that it has not found any evidence that Tehran has a nuclear weapons program and is in breach of the NPT; and in the case of the North Koreans, Pyongyang is not legally bound by the NPT since it cited Article 10 to withdraw from the treaty on April 10, 2003. Tehran subsequently lodged a formal complaint to the UN about Washington's nuclear war threat.[12]

Russia too is rearming itself with nuclear weapons. The Russian Federation has the largest nuclear arsenal in the world and Moscow places special value on it, because it is strongly believed that Russia's nukes are what have stood in the way of US attempts to pummel Russia. From 2006 to 2008 the military budget of Russia has also grown annually by the significant amount of 20%.[13] China too, has been upgrading its military power and bolstering its nuclear weapons arsenal as a result of US threats, leading to roughly a 12% increase in its annual defense budget from 2000 to 2010.[14] According to the Stockholm International Peace Research Institute (SIPRI), China's annual defense expenditures grew from $30 billion (US) in 2000 to almost $120 billion (US) in 2010.[15] Aside from forming a nuclear umbrella over the rest of the CSTO, Moscow has adopted a new nuclear doctrine of pre-emptive nuclear war, including in regional theaters, which came into effect in 2010.[16] Moscow's pre-emptive nuclear attack doctrine is a symmetrical response to the pre-emptive nuclear war doctrines of the US and NATO. Coupled with the adoption of Russia's pre-emptive doctrine, Moscow has also threatened to withdraw from the Intermediate-Range Nuclear Forces (INF) Treaty. In 2007, the head of the Russian Armed Forces General Staff intimated that Russia could withdraw from the INF Treaty in response to US and NATO missile threats.[17] From a strategic military standpoint, Russian threats to withdraw from the INF Treaty mean that the Kremlin wants the ability to be able to target and threaten the continental US with a nuclear strike capability.[18]

Since the end of the Cold War, NATO's nuclear strike posture has become more aggressive. Within NATO and among US allies a consensus has long been established to legitimize and normalize the idea of using nuclear weapons in conventional wars. This consensus also aims to pave the way for pre-emptive nuclear strikes against targets like Russia, China, and Iran. The dangers are exacerbated by the increase in nuclear armed states after the Cold War. The world currently has nine countries with nuclear weapons: Britain, China, France, India, Israel, North Korea, Pakistan, Russia, and the US. When the Soviet Union collapsed Belarus, Kazakhstan, Russia, and Ukraine all inherited the Soviet nuclear arsenal, but the other post-Soviet republics handed their nukes over to post-Soviet Russia. Of the countries that have nuclear weapons: five are permanent members of the UN Security Council, three are full NATO members, one a de facto NATO member, two are full SCO members, and two are SCO observers. With the exception of North Korea, which is a Chinese ally, the so-called "nuclear club" is divided almost evenly into blocs between NATO and the SCO. Hence any conflict between the two blocs could ignite a nuclear war. Even more alarming the US and NATO have always deemed the NPT to be null and void in the scenario of a world war.[19] In essence the NPT is nothing more than a convenient means of holding sway over non-nuclear states and insuring a partial US and NATO nuclear weapons monopoly to insure their dominance over other states; the moment that dominance fades, the US and NATO have no qualms in being unequivocal treaty violators as they themselves have warned.

Enter the Bolivarian Bloc

While the US made some gains in Eurasia after 9/11, the situation was reversed in its own self-declared "back yard." The Bolivarian Republic of Venezuela and its ally Cuba were the first to hold the banners of resistance against US hegemony in Latin America and the Caribbean in the post-Cold War era. Havana under the leadership of Fidel Castro and the Cuban Communist Party had been in effect defying Washington since 1959. With the election of Hugo Chavez in 1998 and the start of his presidency in 1999, Venezuela would open its arms to Cuba and end US attempts to isolate Havana. The bilateral agreements signed by Cuba and Venezuela would form the heart of a new alliance in the Western Hemisphere, originally named the Bolivarian Alternative for the Americas or ALBA (*Alternativa Bolivariana para las Américas*). At the behest of President Chavez this grouping was named after Simon Bolivar, the man who led Venezuela, Bolivia, Peru, Colombia, Ecuador, and Panama to independence in their struggle against the Spanish Empire. Calling this grouping the Bolivarian Bloc is much more suitable.

When Juan Evo Morales, the leader of the Movement for Socialism and an indigenous Aymara farmer, was elected as the new president of Bolivia in 2006 his country quickly joined Cuba and Venezuela in their existing agreements to form the Bolivarian Bloc. From the start Morales was critical of the US like his allies in Caracas and Havana; he declared that Bolivia—which would be renamed the Plurinational State of Bolivia by his government in 2009—had existed under a state of US-supported apartheid that institutionalized the racist oppression of Bolivia's indigenous peoples and that the era of the colonial status quo had ended in Bolivia. Nicaragua would join the Bolivarian Bloc next in 2007 with the return of the Sandinista leader Daniel Ortega to power. Ortega too has been highly critical of the US. The US was actually indicted by the International Court of Justice in 1984 for arming and financing the Contra militias that killed and tortured countless Nicaraguans and mining Nicaragua's harbors as a deliberate tactic to topple Ortega's government during the Cold War—it is of little wonder that many people in Central America believed from the start that the anti-government militants in Libya and Syria were mercenaries controlled by the CIA and Pentagon. Honduras would join ALBA in 2008 and then withdraw in 2009 after a

US-supported military coup removed President José Manuel Zelaya. The Commonwealth of Dominica joined in 2008 followed by Ecuador and both the Caribbean island-states of Antigua-Barbuda and Saint Vincent and the Grenadines in 2009.

The alliance between the Bolivarian Bloc in the Americas and the triple entente in Eurasia is one that is formed by mutual opposition to a US unipolar system. According to the fiery rhetoric of Señor Chavez and his Bolivarian allies their alliance is a common front against the "North American Empire" and its henchmen. For over a decade Venezuela and the Bolivarian Bloc have been busy cementing what they call a "strings of steel" policy to solidify their links with their allies and partners in the Eastern Hemisphere. The Bolivarians have been actively working to reduce US influence in their area by diversifying their trade, using bartering, and gaining control over their national economies. The Bolivarian Bloc has also introduced its own unified regional monetary compensation framework, called the *Sistema Único de Compensación Regional* (SUCRE).[20] The implementation of the SUCRE is a move away from the US dollar that followed similar steps as the euro, being used initially on a virtual basis for trade and eventually as a hard currency. In all these countries the Bolivarian leaders have worked toward removing the local oligarchies allied with the US that have vested interests in keeping their economies dependent on Washington; this has seen Bolivarian leaders in showdowns with powerful cartels, criminal syndicates, and US-backed businessmen. Constitutional reforms have also been central to these battles.

Bolivarian officials have been regular visitors to Russia, Ukraine, Iran, Belarus, China, Namibia, Libya, North Korea, Sudan, Vietnam, Zimbabwe, Algeria, India, Syria, Malaysia, and South Africa. The Bolivarians have opposed NATO's actions in Afghanistan and Libya, refuse to recognize Kosovo, and condemn Israeli aggression against the Palestinians and Lebanon. Their close relationships with China, Russia, and Iran have been a cause of growing worry for the US State Department and Pentagon. Moreover, the Bolivarians have refused to support the sanctions against Iran over its nuclear energy program and fully support Tehran in its altercations with the US. Bolivia, Cuba, Ecuador, Nicaragua, and Venezuela have all vowed to stand by Iran should a conflict erupt between it and the US and Israel. Venezuelan and Iranian leaders consistently promise in their bilateral meetings to oppose US hegemony and to work for an alternative global order. This alliance between Tehran and the Bolivarians has caused US and Israeli officials to make wild accusations that Venezuela and Cuba are either sponsors of terrorism, planning to help Iran make nuclear weapons, Hezbollah bases, or collaborators with Iran planning to launch terrorist attacks on the US.[21]

Venezuela in particular has had many visible rows with Washington where both sides have withdrawn their ambassadors. Chavez even called George W. Bush, Jr. "Satan" in the UN in 2006.[22] His country has also opened its bases up for use by the armed forces of Russia and China and begun to buy its weapons from them instead of from US arms manufacturers. In 2008 two long-range Russian bomber planes were greeted as allied aircraft by Venezuela in a move that upset Washington.[23] The Venezuelans additionally have military cooperation agreements with the Iranians and have even invited them to participate in military exercises between Venezuela and Cuba. Venezuela and the Libyan Arab Jamahiriya ironically also repeatedly called for the creation of a South Atlantic Treaty Organization among African and South American countries to offset any threats by NATO before NATO ousted Muammar Qaddafi.[24]

All the branches of government and power in Washington have viciously attacked the Bolivarian Bloc and its leaders in language that shows that democracy is not the valued political system that US officials claim to espouse. Washington especially loathes losing control over the oil and gas reserves of Venezuela, Ecuador, and Bolivia. The hostile US language has been matched by a series of US covert operations for regime change against the Bolivarian leaders. In the course of these operations US diplomats and embassies have become implicated in supporting violence and force against democratically-elected governments. In 2002, the US supported a failed coup against Chavez by figures in the Venezuelan military.[25] Since 2006 the leadership of Bolivia's energy-rich eastern departments (provinces) of Santa Cruz, Beni, Pando, and Tarija started pushing for autonomy with the help of US funding from the Office of Transition Initiatives of the United States Agency for International Development (USAID). Civil strife began when the mostly non-indigenous leaders of the eastern departments—many of whom have been described by indigenous Bolivians as racist "white supremacists"—started to seize local government buildings, energy facilities, and infrastructure as part of an attempt to separate from Bolivia.[26] The failed US-supported attempts to divide Bolivia were part of an effort by Washington to retain control over Bolivian natural gas. In Honduras, one of the weakest links in the Bolivarian Bloc, a military coup d'état took place under the cloud of a constitutional crisis in 2008. The outcry and clamor against the military coup in Honduras would be so strong that the Obama Administration and Hillary Clinton would pretend publicly that they were opposed to the coup that the US was itself behind.[27] Washington would also support an attempted coup in Ecuador by police units against President Rafael Correa's government in 2010.[28]

The Pentagon has also been arming Colombia and deepening its military ties with Bogota to weaken Caracas and its allies. On October 30, 2009 an agreement was signed by Colombia to permit the Pentagon

TABLE 16.1

The Eurasian Entente and its Global Alliance Network

SCO/CSTO	Resistance Bloc	Bolivarian Bloc	Other Allies
Armenia	Afghan Resistance	Antigua and Barbuda	Abkhazia*
Belarus	Iraq	Bolivia	Algeria
China	Iran	Cuba	Bangladesh
Kazakhstan	Lebanon	Dominica	Brazil
Kyrgyzstan	Palestinian Rejectionists	Ecuador	Bhutan
Russia	Syria	Nicaragua	Eritrea
Tajikistan		St. Vincent and Grenadines	India
Uzbekistan		Venezuela	Korea, Democratic People's Republic
			Nagorno-Karabakh Republic*
			Nepal
			Moldova (including Transnistria)
			Mongolia
			Myanmar (Burma)
			Namibia
			Nepal
			Republika Srpska†
			Serbia
			Sudan
			South Ossetia*
			Sri Lanka
			Turkmenistan
			Ukraine
			Zimbabwe

* Abkhazia and South Ossetia are breakaway republics that are autonomous units of the Republic of Georgia. The Nagorno-Karabakh Republic is also a breakaway republic that has seceded from the Republic of Azerbaijan.

† Republika Srpska which means Serbian Republic in English, is one of the two political sub-units of Bosnia.

to use its military bases. US-garrisoned Haiti also serves the broader hemispheric agenda of the US to challenge the Bolivarian Bloc using the westernmost ridge of the island of Hispaniola. Looking at the map and the militarization of Haiti it is unambiguous that the US plans to use Haiti, like Colombia and Curaçao, as a hub for military and intelligence operations against the Bolivarian Bloc.

MAP XX: The Bolivarian Bloc

NATO Versus the CSTO and SCO

Both the CSTO and SCO are challenges to the domination of the US and NATO in Eurasia. Both organizations have objectives of growing and preventing NATO's membership and operational expansion inside Eurasia. The two Eurasian alliances have also gained ground and influence at the expense of the US and its allies. The SCO and CSTO have cultivated de facto ties with Turkmenistan and Ukraine. After the death of President Saparmurat Niyazov—the Turkmenbashi—in late 2006 his successor, President Berdymukhammedov, brought Turkmenistan closer to the Eurasianists and Turkmenistani officials began to participate in SCO meetings and events. Turkmenistan has effectively walked away from its constitutionally imposed neutralist policy. After the 2010 election victory of Viktor Yanukovych in Ukraine, the same thing has happened. Moscow even invited Kiev to join the CSTO as a full member in 2010, which the Ukrainians declined on the basis of their officially neutralist stance.[29] The Ukrainian government declined joining merely to avoid strengthening the Orangist forces and polarizing Ukraine further on the basis of anti-Russian polemics. In reality Ukraine has been militarily cooperating with Belarus, Russia, and Kazakhstan at the bilateral and multilateral levels. What Ukraine's government has actually done is shut the doors to NATO instead. Ukrainian Foreign Minister Kostyantyn Hryshchenko, commenting on Kiev's decision not to join the CSTO, publicly stated that his country would never join NATO and this decision should open the door for cooperation and partnership with Russia.[30] Kiev is a CSTO partner in all but name.

Both the SCO and the CSTO have plans to challenge the US and NATO in Afghanistan and NATO's UN peacekeeping mandates. The Kremlin has called for both the CSTO and SCO to become involved in NATO-garrisoned Afghanistan as a challenge to NATO's "stabilization monopoly."[31] In July 2007, the CSTO proposed that the SCO and CSTO collaborate together there.[32] Tied to this is the CSTO's push at the UN level for peacekeeping accreditation to counter NATO's monopoly in Afghanistan and other places. In March 2010 the CSTO and the UN signed a cooperation agreement similar to the one secretly signed by UN Secretary-General Ban Ki-moon and NATO on October 9, 2008.[33]

Both the CSTO and the SCO cover much of the same space in Eurasia and have overlapping memberships (see Table 13.2). The two Eurasian organizations complement one another and may indeed merge when the time is right in the future. The relationship between these two organizations parallels that between the EU and NATO and the development of the CSTO and SCO may one day even be compared to that of the Western European Union and NATO. It should come as no surprise that both Eurasian organizations signed a military cooperation agreement in 2007, which effectively makes China a de facto member of the CSTO and creates a unified Sino-Russian military bloc running from the Yellow Sea and Central Asia to Eastern Europe and the Arctic Circle.[34] In 2008, the secretaries-general of the CSTO and SCO, retired Russian general Nikolai Bordyuzha and the Kazakhstani diplomat Bolat Nurgaliyev, met at CSTO Headquarters in Moscow for follow-ups after their CSTO-SCO cooperation agreement was made in Tajikistan. Since the agreement CSTO officials have been regularly attending SCO summits and meetings like their counterparts from the CIS and EurAsEC.

Both the CSTO and SCO are still fledgling alliances. Their collective defense budgets are substantially smaller than the collective defense budgets of all the NATO states, which account for about 65% of global military spending (see Chart 16.1). Despite the fact that their military budgets have been increased (see Chart 16.2), the largest military powers of the SCO and their partners still only constitute a fraction of all global military expenditures (See Chart 16.3). The military expenditures of the US are much higher than the collective military expenditures of all the members of both these Eurasian alliances and all the world's non-NATO countries combined.

CHART 16.1

2011 Break Down of the Share of World Military Expenditures Amongst NATO States

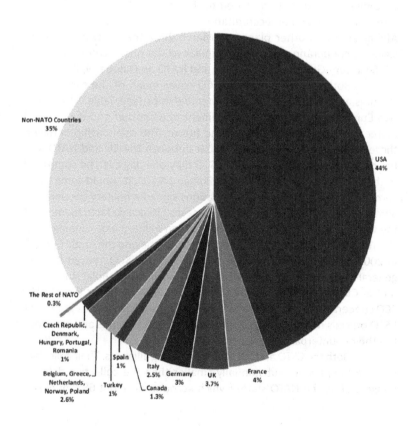

CHART 16.2

Military Expenditures: NATO versus the World

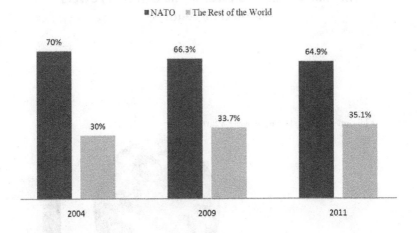

■ NATO   ■ The Rest of the World

The Dangers of a Broader War Igniting from Caucasia

The Caucasus or Caucasia stands at the crossroads of Eurasia as a strategically important region. It is sandwiched between the Caspian and Black Seas and, from north to south, is formed by two Russian federal districts (portions of the Southern Federal District and the entire North Caucasian Federal District), Georgia, the Republic of Azerbaijan, Armenia, the northeastern part of Turkey, and the northern provinces of Iran. Like the Ural Mountains, the Caucasus forms the politically defined borders between Europe and Asia. The region itself, which can also be considered a geographic and cultural northern extension of the Middle East, is divided into two sub-regions: the North and South Caucasus. The North Caucasus exclusively consists of the Russian Federation's Caucasian constituent republics of Adyghea, Chechnya, Dagestan, Ingushetia, Kabardino-Balkaria, Karachay-Cherkessia, Krasnodar Krai, North Ossetia-Alania, and Stavropol Krai. The South Caucasus consists of Georgia, the Republic of Azerbaijan, and Armenia in their entireties; part of the Turkish province of Erzurum and all the Turkish provinces of Ardahan, Artvin, Igdir, and Kars, which were annexed from Georgia and Armenia by the Turks under the 1921 Treaty of Kars; and the Iranian provinces of Ardebil, East Azerbaijan, Gilan, and West Azerbaijan. The region is ethno-linguistically diverse, inhabited by Altaic, Caucasian, and Indo-European speakers. The Altaic speakers are predominately represented by the Azerbaijanis (Azeris) who are descendents of Lezgic and Iranic peoples that became

CHART 16.3

The Military Expenditures of the Eurasian Powers and their Allies

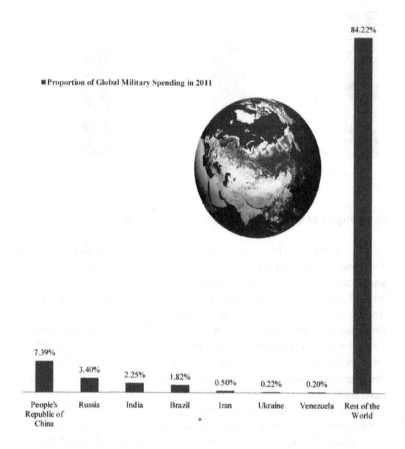

■ Proportion of Global Military Spending in 2011

							84.22%
7.39%	3.40%	2.25%	1.82%	0.50%	0.22%	0.20%	
People's Republic of China	Russia	India	Brazil	Iran	Ukraine	Venezuela	Rest of the World

Turkophones. The ethnic Caucasians consist of a list of peoples, which includes the Abkhazians, Avars, Georgians, Laks, Svans, Nakhs—including the Chechens and Ingush—and different Circassians. Amongst the Indo-European speakers are the more established Armenian and Iranic speakers—Kurds, Ossetians, Persians, Talysh, and Tats—and the Slavic Russians that migrated with Russian expansion. A Pontiac Greek minority has also lived in the region since ancient times.

The region is also divided between Christians and Muslims. Armenia and Georgia are actually the first and third oldest Christian countries in terms of official state adoption. Most Armenians belong to the older Oriental Orthodox (Non-Chalcedonian) branch of Orthodox Christianity while the region's other Christians belong to the dominant Eastern Orthodox branch. The Georgians and Russians are mostly Eastern Orthodox Christians as are at least two-thirds of the Ossetians. About one-third of the Ossetians are Muslims. Georgia has a sizable Muslim population; aside from ethnic Georgian Muslims, the southeast, southwest, and northwest regions of Georgia have significant Muslim populations amongst the Adjarans, Azeris, and Abkhazians. Almost all the ethnic groups in Dagestan are predominately Muslim, with the majority being Sunnites. Almost all the Azeris are Shiite while the majority of Balkars, Circassians, Chechens, Ingush, Karachays, and Kurds are Sunni Muslims. The region also has a sizeable Jewish minority.

Historically, the Caucasus has been contested by Iran, Russia, and the Ottoman Empire as a border region. It is presently important due to the Caspian Basin's energy resources and the corridor it provides into Central Asia. It also provides a strategically important land bridge between Russia and Iran. Since the demise of the USSR the ethno-linguistically diverse area has been the scene of a series of struggles between the local republics, internal actors, and external forces. These conflicts include those between: the Republic of Azerbaijan and breakaway Nagorno-Karabakh; Georgia and breakaway South Ossetia; Georgia and breakaway Abkhazia; Russia and the separatist movements of the North Caucasus, specifically in Chechnya and Dagestan; Armenia and the Republic of Azerbaijan; Armenia and Turkey; and Georgia and Russia. These conflicts have been frozen, but left mostly unsettled. The US has sought to capitalize by manipulating these tensions to form alliances against Moscow. This is part of a US strategy to ally with indigenous players that want to counter-balance larger regional powers.

Washington has sought influence in the region as a means of battling both Russia and Iran. US encroachment has led to Moscow-Tbilisi, Tbilisi-Yerevan, Baku-Tehran, and Baku-Moscow tensions. These tensions and Baku-Yerevan tensions over Nagorno-Karabakh have formed and sustained a strategic regional axis comprised of Russia, Armenia, and Iran. The Moscow-Yerevan-Tehran Axis is naturally opposed to the US, Georgia, and the Republic of Azerbaijan, as well as Turkey on the western flank of the region.

Tensions between Tbilisi and Moscow resulted in the outbreak of a war and the Russian invasion of Georgia in 2008. The Kremlin was aware that the government in Tbilisi was planning to launch military operations to regain control over its breakaway territories and had begun its own preparations to fend them off. Russia began violating Georgian airspace to conduct reconnaissance missions while the Georgian press continuously talked about a coming war.[35] *Rezonansi*, one of Georgia's top newspapers, had front-page headlines about the imminent dangers of a war: "Will war in Abkhazia begin tomorrow?"[36] A month before the war started, Moscow, without giving any notification to Georgia or the CIS, deployed 500 Russian troops into the southern Tkvarchel region of Abkhazia under the banner of a CIS peacekeeping mission, which raised its contingent to 2,542 personnel.[37] Before this the Russians had shot down a Georgian spy drone violating the moratorium on acts of aggression between Georgia and Abkhazia by flying over Abkhazian territory on April 20, 2008.[38] In a move that was one step short of official recognition, Moscow ended its agreement to sanction the Autonomous Republic of Abkhazia and officially began communicating with it to bolster the Abkhazians in the coming war.[39] The Kremlin openly accused Georgia of mobilizing troops to attack Abkhazia, whereas the Georgian government accused Russia of planning to annex Abkhazia and South Ossetia.[40] President Saakashvili publicly acknowledged how close a war was on May 8, 2008.[41] Sergei Shamba, the foreign minister of Abkhazia, asked Russia to sign a formal defense agreement on the same day.[42] Meanwhile the US prepared to support a Georgian attack on South Ossetia. On May 7, 2008 the US House of Representatives passed a resolution that condemned Russia for its "provocative and dangerous statements and actions" in Georgia, and the EU followed suit with similar condemnations of Moscow.[43]

The Institute for War and Peace Reporting (IWPR), a Dutch, UK, and US NGO network chaired by David Bell—the former head of London's *Financial Times*—and funded by the British government, EU, US Department of State, USAID, and several other questionable sources, documented Russia's preparations for the coming war. What is very telling about the war preparations was the secret deployment of Russian anti-tank missiles into Abkhazia. The IWPR gives an important account of this:

> Georgian security forces have again had a confrontation with Russian peacekeepers on the border with Abkhazia, leading to a tense telephone conversation between the two presidents [of Georgia and Russia]. The detention of a Russian army truck by Georgian police appears to be part of a war of nerves over the disputed territory of Abkhazia. Tbilisi claims the Russians are engaged in annexing Abkhazia and insists their peacekeeping forces must be disbanded, while Moscow says the troops are operating under an international mandate and are providing vital security for the Abkhaz. Georgian television channels showed pictures of local police stopping a truck carrying Russian peacekeepers near the village of Rukhi on June 17. They reported that it was carrying weapons illegally through the conflict zone, close to the administrative border

TABLE 16.2

Global Peacekeeping Operations in 2010*		
Organization	Number of Operations	Number of Personnel
NATO	3	140, 354
United Nations	20	103, 404
African Union	1	7999
European Union	12	4606
Ad hoc coalitions	6	3754
Commonwealth of Independent States	1	1452
Economic Community of Central African States	1	880
Organization for Security and Cooperation in Europe	7	363
Organization of American States	1	30
Total	**52**	**262, 842**

Based on figure and date from the Stockholm International Peace Research Institute (SIPRI) 2011 Yearbook.

with Abkhazia. The four soldiers on board the vehicle were released after seven hours in detention. On June 19, the truck was handed back but the Georgians said they were holding onto 20 anti-tank missiles pending an investigation. The Georgians said that the Russians had not asked permission to transport the missiles as they were required to do under the terms that govern the peacekeeping presence. Colonel Vladimir Rogozin, commander of the southern zone of the peacekeeping operation—which comes under the mandate of the Commonwealth of Independent States, CIS, but is entirely manned by Russian troops—said he had simply failed to inform the Georgians about the arms shipment in time. "They were normal weapons permitted by our mandate, and I don't understand why the Georgians detained our soldiers," said Rogozin.[44]

The anti-tank missiles were intended for use against Georgian tanks and deliberately not announced as part of Moscow's war preparations to launch a second front in Abkhazia once Georgia would start the war to forcefully regain control over South Ossetia. It is unlikely that the Georgians could have known about the deployment of Russian anti-tank missiles without intelligence reports from the US or NATO.

The 2008 war between Georgia and South Ossetia was a proxy war just like the 2006 Israeli war against Lebanon. Sergey A. Markov, a co-chair of the National Strategic Council of Russia, has described the war as a US attack on Russia. The war received significant public attention from the US and NATO unlike most previous Caucasian conflicts. Under Washington's patronage Georgia had become one of the fastest militarizing states in the world after the Rose Revolution. Saakashvili had also contributed up to two thousand soldiers for Washington's war in Iraq. His administration evidently thought the US would come to their aid militarily if Georgia could not defeat the combined forces of Russia and South Ossetia. Soon after the war the US and NATO made several revealing moves about their intentions in the Caucasus. Despite the fact that Georgia was not a NATO member, the Atlantic Alliance began to quickly integrate the Georgian air defenses with NATO's own air defense systems.[45] Tbilisi and the Pentagon would reveal that they planned on constructing US military bases in Georgia, which would be threats to both Russia and Iran.[46] Finally, it was revealed that during the war the Russian military took the opportunity to attack Georgian bases that were planned for use in future US, NATO, and Israeli operations against Iran.[47]

To counter Georgian militarization and NATO's agenda for the Caucasus, the Kremlin has beefed up its fortifications and units in the North Caucasus and expanded its military presence in Armenia. In August 2010, Russia and Armenia signed a bilateral military agreement that committed Moscow to protecting Armenia and insuring Armenian security.[48] The old mandate of Russia's forces in Armenia was to provide security for the Armenian-Turkish and Armenian-Iranian borders, but the new agreement removes these restrictions by allowing Moscow to freely use its bases in Armenia for any Russian operations, which could include fighting Georgia and intervention into the Middle East to assist Syria or Iran. Russian support of Abkhazia and South Ossetia in effect has protected Russia too from NATO encroachment on its southern borders and prevented NATO from strategically creating a wedge between Russia and Iran in the Caucasus. Because the Atlantic Alliance cannot accept new members unless all their internal disputes are settled and their boundaries fixed, Georgia has been obstructed from joining NATO due to Russia's support for Abkhazia and South Ossetia. Despite the setbacks for the US and NATO and the frozen regional conflicts, continued plans to encircle Russia and Iran, and NATO encroachment in the Caucasus are still a dangerous mix that can ignite a broader future war.

The Arctic Front: Controlling Future Energy Reserves

The Caucasus is not the only flashpoint that could ignite a broader conflict. Tense rivalries between the Russians and NATO have emerged in the Arctic Circle over claims to the North Pole's vast energy resources. China has also put its weight behind its Russian allies in the hope of benefiting from Arctic resources. Except for Russia, all the nations laying claim to the Arctic's resources are NATO members. These countries—Canada, Denmark, Norway, and the US—in combination have far less Arctic territory than Russia and therefore lesser claims. Sweden, Finland, and NATO member Iceland have stayed relatively passive. The US, Canada, and Denmark have all refused to recognize Russia's territorial claims.

Because of the new Arctic rivalry, the Arctic Circle is being further militarized by both NATO and Russia. NATO countries claim in Orwellian terms that they are working for Arctic peace through regional militarization and the improvement of their combat capabilities and northern military infrastructure. Militarization of the region, however, makes conflict more, not less, likely. There may be a fear in the US that in a global scenario the Arctic could be used as a quick invasion route by China and Russia. That said, this entire process comes at the expense of the historically marginalized indigenous peoples of the Arctic as more outsider claims are being laid on their lands and they are pressured and encouraged to surrender their land ownership claims and to give up what is left of their traditional economic activities to work for the corporations and construction companies exploiting the Arctic.

The battle over the Arctic is well underway. The NATO agenda for control of the region started as early as 2006 when Norway invited NATO and the non-NATO Nordic countries to take part in its Cold Response war games. Canada, which has continuously held Arctic exercises to demonstrate its sovereignty in the Arctic, invited the armed forces of the US and Denmark in 2010 to begin participating in its war games.[49] According to a Canadian military press release the drills were intended "to strengthen preparedness, increase interoperability and exercise a collective response to emerging challenges in the Arctic."[50] Aside from conflict with Russia there is no other situation that could be seen as an emerging challenge that warrants a collective military response by Canada and its US and Danish NATO allies. The US has been mainly pushing Canada forward against Russia, because Canada is the strongest Arctic challenger in terms of territorial size to Russia and both Ottawa and Moscow have claimed the Lomonosov Ridge as an extension of their continental shelves. Washington wants to exploit Canada to tap the energy resources of the Arctic—as it already does with Albertan energy—and for this reason has been streamlining its Arctic policies with those of Ottawa. Prime Minister Steven Harper and the Canadian federal government have diplomatically threatened Moscow to stand down in its Arctic claims: "Canada will maintain control of our Arctic lands and waters and will respond when others [i.e., Russia] take actions that affect our national interests."[51] Ottawa's three Arctic priorities are: (1) demarcating the Arctic; (2) gaining world recognition of Canadian control over the Lomonosov Ridge as an extension of Canada's continental shelf; and (3) creating an "Arctic security regime" in the name of "Arctic governance and emergency measures."[52]

Armageddon and the Middle East

In the Middle East the lines of global rivalry have been drawn in the sand. As has been mentioned in this book in several instances, the front in the Middle East is central to the US strategy in Eurasia. The 9/11 attacks were pivotal at enabling the US to initiate its campaign to control the *broader* Middle East—from North Africa to Central Asia—on its march towards the gates of Beijing. While China is the final goal, it may be in the Middle East that a conflict between the Atlanticist and Eurasianist camps will be lit. The dangers of a catastrophic war igniting from the Middle East exist due to US efforts to neutralize Iran and the Resistance Bloc to ensure the pliancy of what Condoleezza Rice called the "new Middle East." The chapter discussing NATO and the Levant should have made this very clear.

The Iranian nuclear energy program has been politicized by the US, UK, Israel, and their allies as a pretext for threatening Iran as part of the Atlanticist efforts to impose their control over the region. Israeli Minister of Intelligence and Atomic Energy Daniel Meridor stated on the record that the Iranian nuclear program was a mere pretext; what is at stake is the global standing of the US and the balance of power in international relations.[53] What Meridor was saying is that the course of events involving Iran will decide the fate of Washington's empire. The Chinese and Russians will be crippled if Iran and the Middle East fall under the total control of the US and NATO. The stage would be set for a new phase of the Anglo-American "long war." This is the reason why China, Russia, the CSTO, and the SCO have all warned against any attacks on Iran and are opposed to any form of US-led military intervention against either Iran or Syria. India and Brazil have also voiced their strong opposition to US-led wars in the Middle East, knowing full well that the world would be dragged into the abyss.

The voices of Tehran's allies warning against war amplified in 2006 after Pentagon war plans geared up, when it became clear to the US and its allies that Iran would not submit during negotiations with the UK, France, and Germany. The SCO made its warnings in 2006 against any US or NATO attack against Tehran. The Pentagon's reaction would be to launch drills named Vigilant Shield 07 simulating a nuclear world war where the US would target Iran, Russia, China, and North Korea under the codenames Irmingham, Ruebek, Churya, and Nemazee.[54] On behalf of the CSTO, Secretary-General Bordyuzha warned the US government in 2007 not to consider an aggressive move on Iran, making clear, as had the SCO, that there would be major global consequences from an attack on Iran. Military officials from Russia and China added their voices to the chorus. Iran's Armenian allies also warned against war, saying they could not remain neutral if Iran was attacked. Venezuela warned the US that it would take measures to help Iran. During his visit to Tehran in 2007, Vladimir Putin himself would diplomatically warn that Russia and the post-Soviet republics would not accept an attack on Iran due to their national security interests, resulting in George W. Bush, Jr. quickly running to a White House podium to warn that "World War III" could erupt over Iran.[55]

The upheavals of the Arab Spring in 2011 presented an opportunity for the US and NATO to press onward with their military roadmap. The Russians and Chinese began warning Washington once more against attacking Iran. Konstantin Kosachev, the chair of the Committee for International Affairs in the Russian Duma, warned that Russia opposed any attack on its Iranian neighbors. Dmitry Rogozin, who had just freshly been appointed Russian deputy prime minister, declared in no uncertain terms that any attempted military intervention against Iran would be a threat to Russian national security.[56] Earlier in August, Rogozin, while serving as the Russian ambassador to NATO, stated that Syria and Yemen could be attacked by the US and NATO as "stepping stones" to confronting Iran.[57] As recently as May 2012, Dmitry Medvedev has warned the US and NATO in no uncertain terms that military intervention in the sovereign affairs of other states, such as Iran and Syria, may lead to outright nuclear war.[58] In China similar declarations have also been made. Chinese Rear-Admiral Zhang Zhaozhong, a director at the National Defense University of the People's Republic of China, was less diplomatic in his words. Zhazhong warned that Beijing would not hesitate to go to war against the US in support of China's Iranian allies. Any retaliation from Iran's allies in the CSTO and SCO will directly turn the Caucasus, Europe, Central Asia, the Indian Ocean, East Asia, and the Pacific Ocean into military fronts.

As has been explained, the US and Atlantic Alliance intend as policy to use pre-emptive nuclear strikes, to disregard the NPT, and to use nuclear weapons in a global war scenario. If Iran should be attacked then such a global war scenario would very likely materialize contrary to most wargame projections made public which play out a war scenario limited to the Middle East. The next question is: would the US and Atlantic Alliance launch pre-emptive nuclear strikes on Russia and China when they attack Iran? Would these attacks on Russia and China need to be simultaneous with an attack on Iran in order to be pre-emptive? What about the Russians: would they wait or launch pre-emptive nuclear strikes if they believe that a Pentagon attack against Iran was near or that Russia would be attacked too? China, like India and North Korea, has a "no first use" nuclear policy and will not launch a nuclear attack unless it is attacked first, but Russia does not. What if both sides avoided using nuclear weapons, but one was about to lose the war? In such a case, would the US and NATO launch nuclear strikes to attempt to ensure a Pyrrhic victory? It is the policy of the US and NATO to use nuclear weapons when overwhelmed or as a means to guarantee their victory.

The risk of nuclear war also exists in regard to military operations against Iran. The Pentagon and Tel Aviv have seriously contemplated using nuclear weapons against the Iranians. The political groundwork, the military procedures, the dissemination of disinformation, and the media work have all been underway for years. Iran is not a weak nation; it has one of the strongest armed forces in the world. In 2009, Iranian military power started being reviewed under the same annual assessments that the US reserves for Chinese military expansion.[59] Despite Tel Aviv's psychological warfare and the propaganda portraying it as a military powerhouse, Israel is incapable of waging and winning a conventional war against Iran. Israeli intelligence and military leaders like Daniel Halutz, Yuval Diskin, Shlomo Brom, Meir Dagan, and Amnon Lipkin-Shahak are aware of this and that is why they have continued to warn their government that a war against Iran would be disastrous for the State of Israel.[60] They are also aware that any attack on Iran would almost instantly ignite a regional war from the Mediterranean Sea to the Chinese border; the Palestinians, Hezbollah, Syria, and Muqtada Al-Sadr's forces in Iraq have all warned that they would not stand by idly in a war against their Iranian ally. The main difference between Israel and Iran is that Tel Aviv has a stockpile of nuclear weapons. The only way for Tel Aviv to guarantee an Israeli victory against Iran would be to launch a pre-emptive all-out nuclear attack on Iran, but even its capabilities to execute this are doubtful. Israeli strategists are well aware that should they unilaterally try to launch a nuclear strike that they too would be damaged and at best gain a Pyrrhic victory. This is why Benjamin Netanyahu and Ehud Barak want the US to militarily engage Iran for Israel.[61]

Although the US is a far stronger military power than Iran, a

US attack would not be simple either. The US might be able to wreak extensive destruction on Iran, but it could not win a conventional war. General Yuri Baluyevsky, the former chief of the Russian Armed Forces General Staff, said in 2007 that not only would an attack on Iran be a global disaster, but it would be unwinnable for the Pentagon.[62] An attack on Iran would have to be a multilateral venture between Israel, the Anglo-American Alliance, and NATO with limited goals—which it would not be able to maintain. The Pentagon has no hope of occupying Iran and it will have troubles *conventionally* retaliating against Iranian counter-strikes elsewhere in the Middle East, which will drive US forces out of their most important bases and positions. Again, such a war would lead to the use of nuclear weapons against Iran as the only means to defeat Tehran to the degree that the Pentagon desires. Even Saddam Hussein, who once commanded the most powerful Arab state and military force, was aware of this. In July 25, 1990, in a meeting with April C. Glaspie, the US ambassador in Baghdad, Saddam Hussein stated: "But you know you are not the ones who protected your friends [the Arab petro-sheikdoms] during the war with Iran. I assure you, had the Iranians overrun the region, the American troops would not have stopped them, except by the use of nuclear weapons."[63]

The key to this discussion is the differentiation between a conventional and unconventional war. While the Pentagon could not win a conventional war, it could win an unconventional war involving nuclear strikes—most likely without its desired outcomes. Hence the diabolically unthinkable is no longer a taboo: the use of nuclear weapons once again against another non-nuclear country by Washington. This will be a violation of the NPT and international law, which the US has been trying to normalize through such initiatives as the Obama Administration's redefinition of the NPT. This groundwork also includes the normalization of Israeli nukes. US Defense Secretary Robert Gates stated that Israel has nuclear weapons in 2006, which was soon followed by a conveniently-timed slip of the tongue by Ehud Olmert confirming that his country possessed nuclear weapons.[64] Even Japanese Defense Minister Fumio Kyuma during a speech at Reitaku University in 2007 tried to publicly legitimize the US dropping of atom bombs on Japanese civilians as a means of ending the Second World War.[65] Because of the massive public outrage in Japanese society, Kyuma was subsequently forced to resign as Japan's defense minister.[66] This reflects an effort not only to normalize Israel's nukes but the use of nuclear weapons, themselves. That a Japanese defense minister of all persons should be engaged as a propaganda icon to blur the distinction between nuclear and conventional warfare attests to the growing mindset of the leaders of the defense establishments within the circle of the US and its allies.

Any nuclear attack on Iran will have long-term environmental impacts not only on Iran and all its neighbors, but on countries further from Iran in Europe, the Levant, and South Asia. Should a nuclear attack take place in the Middle East then an all-out nuclear global war will surely follow, if it does not all happen simultaneously. This would lead to the extinction of most life on this planet as we know it.

What, then, has become the place of war? Are we truly facing the possibility of global annihilation? Or are US and NATO wars not only waged against outsiders and peoples of other nations, but also now against the peoples of the US and NATO member states themselves. At this final juncture it is worth quoting George Orwell's *Nineteen Eighty-Four* to summarize the internal functionalism of war in what, in our time, is no longer a futurist projection:

> The war, therefore, if we judge it by standards of previous wars, is merely an imposture. [...] But though it is unreal it is not meaningless. It eats up the surplus of consumable goods, and it helps to preserve the special mental atmosphere that a hierarchical society needs. War, it will be seen, is now a purely internal affair. In the past, the ruling groups of all countries, although they might recognise their common interest and therefore limit the destructiveness of war, did fight against one another, and the victor always plundered the vanquished. In our day they are not fighting against one another at all. The war is waged by each ruling group against its own subjects, and the object of the war is not to make or prevent conquests of territory, but to keep the structure of society intact.[67]

What the US does as a declining empire remains to be seen. What will help decide Washington's actions will be the twists and turns of what may be the last round of the "Great Game"—fuelled by America's lust for global hegemony. What is certain is that the so-called "Great Game" never ended. The "Great Game" has always been part of the "long war" that Halford Mackinder and the Anglo-American elites have talked about as the historical process of establishing a "World-Empire."[68] Only the name has changed. Yesterday it was the "Cold War," the day before it was the "Great War" and today it is the "Global War on Terror." Who knows what it will be called tomorrow—maybe World War III—and where it will lead the world? It may end in the plains of Megiddo and Yathrib as some have long believed.

ENDNOTES

Chapter One

1. Ira L. Straus "Russia in NATO: The Fourth Generation of the Atlantic Alliance" in *NATO and the Challenging World Order: An Appraisal by Scholars and Policymakers,* ed. Kenneth W. Thompson (NYC: University Press of America, 1996), p.139.
2. S. Nelson Drew, "Post-Cold War American Leadership in NATO" in *NATO and the Challenging World Order: An Appraisal by Scholars and Policymakers,* ed. Kenneth W. Thompson (NYC: University Press of America, 1996), p.13.
3. "Outrage at 'old Europe' remarks," *British Broadcasting Corporation News,* January 23, 2003.
4. Lawrence J. Korb, "The Pentagon's Eastern Obsession," *The New York Times,* July 30, 2003.
5. "U.S., Romania, Bulgaria team up for Immediate Response 06," *Army News Service,* August 3, 2006.
6. Yevgeny Kryshkin, "NATO seeks unshared responsibility," *Voice of Russia,* September 16, 2010.

Chapter Two

1. These figures are calculations made on the basis of the 2011 data from the Stockholm International Peace Research Institute (SIPRI) Military Expenditures Database.
2. Carroll Quigley, *Tragedy and Hope: A History of the World in Our Time* (NYC: The Macmillan Company, 1966), p.950.
3. Theodore Draper, "The Phantom Alliance" in *The Atlantic Alliance and its Critics,* eds Robert W. Tucker and Linda Wrigley (NYC: Lehrman Institute Books, 1983), p.5.
4. *Ibid.*
5. Ian Taylor, *The International Relations of Sub-Saharan Africa* (NYC: The Continuum International Publishing Group, 2010), p.66.
6. "France cancels 80% of its Iraqi debt," *Business Wire,* December 22, 2005.
7. US Library of Congress, Congressional Research Service, *U.S. Direct Investment Abroad: Trends and Current Issues,* James K. Jackson CRS Report RS21118 (Washington, DC: Office of Congressional Information and Publishing, February 1, 2011), p.2.
8. *Supra* note 1: SIPRI 2011 Military Expenditures Database.
9. Draper, "Phantom Alliance," *op. cit.,* p.8.
10. Zbigniew Brzezinski, "A Geostrategy for Eurasia" in *Preparing America's Foreign Policy for the 21st Century,* eds. David L. Boren and Edward J. Perkins Jr. (Norman, Oklahoma: University of Oklahoma Press, 1999), p.311.
11. James Arthur Salter, *The United States of Europe and Other Papers,* ed. W. Arnold-Forster (Freeport, NY: Random House, 1966), pp.53-70, pp.120-121.
12. Brzezinski, "A Geostrategy for Eurasia," *op. cit.*
13. European Commission, "The Policy: What is the European Neighbourhood Policy?" : <http://ec.europa.eu/world/enp/policy_en.htm>.
14. *Ibid.*

15. Council of the European Union, *A Secure Europe in a Better World: The Euro-pean Security Strategy* (Brussels: Consilium, December 12, 2003), p.9.

16. *Ibid.*, p.1.

17. Desmond Butler, "E.U., U.S. Agree on Iran, Russia Disputes," *Associated Press*, April 30, 2007; "US and EU agree 'single market,'" *British Broadcasting Corpo-ration News,* April 30, 2007.

18. Zbigniew Brzezinski, *The Grand Chessboard: American Primacy and Its Geo-strategic Imperatives* (NYC: Basic Books, 1997), p.200.

19. Prime Minister's Office (10 Downing Street), "UK-France Summit 2010 Declara-tion on Defence and Security Co-operation," November 2, 2010: <www.num-ber10.gov.uk/news/statements-and-articles/2010/11/uk%E2%80%93france-summit-2010-declaration-on-defence-and-security-co-operation-56519>.

20. EU, *European Security Strategy, op. cit*, p.1.

21. *Ibid.*, p.7.

22. *Ibid.*, pp.7-8.

23. *Ibid.*, p.12.

24. Jaques Lévesque, "Introduction" in *The Future of NATO*: Enlargement, Rus-sia, and European Security, eds. Charles-Philippe David and Jacques Lévesque (Montréal, QC: McGill-Queen's University Press, 1999), p.3.

25. NATO, "What does the Military Cooperation/Outreach mean in practice?" <www.aco.nato.int/resources/10/documents/Milcoop%20page-ACO%20 Webpage_ADCOS%20approved2.pdf>.

26. Joseph J. Kruzel, "Partnership for Peace and the Future of European Security" in *NATO and the Challenging World Order: An Appraisal by Scholars and Poli-cymakers,* ed. Kenneth W. Thompson (NYC: University Press of America, 1996), pp.31-32.

27. Patrick Markey, "Columbia seeks more U.S., European aid," *Reuters*, January 29, 2007.

28. NATO, "Partnership Tools." : <www.nato.int/cps/en/SID-0E586A90-9756A0D9/ natolive/topics_80925.htm>.

29. *Ibid.*

30. Since the fragmentation of the Socialist Federal Republic of Yugoslavia there has been a dispute over the name of Macedonia between Greece and the for-mer Yugoslav Republic (FYR) of Macedonia (also FYROM). The Greeks main-tain that the ancient Macedonians, like Alexander the Great, were a Hellenic (Greek) people and not Slavs like the Slavic Macedonians who migrated into the region in a much later period in history. Greeks refer to the Slavic Mace-donians as Skopjians. This has forced the name of FYROM or the FYR of Mace-donia on the Skopjian state. It is also on the basis of this naming dispute that Greece has also blocked the FYR of Macedonia's accession into the EU and NATO.

31. NATO, *Membership Action Plan (MAP)*, April 24, 1999.

Chapter Three

1. S. Nelson Drew, "Post-Cold War American Leadership in NATO" in *NATO and the Challenging World Order: An Appraisal by Scholars and Policymakers*, ed. Kenneth W. Thompson (NYC: University Press of America, 1996), p.5.

2. Joseph Fitchett, "Paris Says it Joined NATO 'Resistance,'" *International Herald Tribune*, November 13, 1990, p.7.

3. Ed Vulliamy, "Secret agents, freemasons, fascists...and a top-level campaign of political 'destabilisation,'" *The Guardian*, 5 December 1990, p.12.

4.   *Ibid.*

5.   Concluded on the bases of all the research conducted by Alberto Franceschi-
        ni and the investigation of Aldo Moro's murder by the Italian judge Rosario
        Priore.

6 .   Daniele Ganser, "NATO's secret armies linked to terrorism?" *Global Research*,
        December 15, 2004; the article is an International Relations and Security (ISN)
        Network excerpt from Ganser's book *NATO's Secret Armies: Operation GLADIO
        and Terrorism in Western Europe.*

7.   *Ibid.*

8.   Daniele Ganser, *NATO's Secret Armies: Operation GLADIO and Terrorism in
        Western Europe* (NYC: Frank Cass Publishers, 2005), p.14.

9.   *Ibid.*, p.1.

10.   *Ibid.*, p.28.

11.   Malcolm Moore, "US envoy admits role in Aldo Moro killing," *The Daily Tele-
        graph*, March 11, 2008.

12.   *Ibid.*

13.   Philip Willan, "US 'supported anti-left terror in Italy,'" *The Guardian*, June 24,
        2000.

14.   Michel Chossudovsky, *The Globalization of Poverty and the New World Order*,
        2nd ed. (Pincourt, QC: Global Research Publishers, 2003), pp.23-24.

15.   *Ibid.*, pp.259-260.

16.   *Ibid.*, p.260

17.   *Ibid.*, pp.260-261.

18.   See n.30 in Chapter 2 about the titular nomenclature and naming dispute over
        Macedonia.

19.   This does not mean that the Bosnian identity is false or manufactured, because
        Bosnia-Herzegovina has had a distinct historic identity and its own separate
        traditions from Serbia and its other neighbors that are analogues to the dis-
        tinctions between Austria and Germany.

20.   Richard J. Aldrich, "America used Islamists to arm the Bosnian Muslims," *The
        Guardian*, April 22, 2002.

21.   *Ibid.*

22.   *Ibid.*

23.   Edward S. Herman, "Summary and Conclusions" in *The Srebrenica Massacre:
        Evidence, Context, Politics*, Edward S. Herman ed. (Evergreen Park IL: Alphabet
        Soup, 2011), p.278.

24.   Philip Corwin, "Forward" in *The Srebrenica Massacre: Evidence, Context, Poli-
        tics*, Edward S. Herman ed. (Evergreen Park IL: Alphabet Soup, 2011), p.7.

25.   Edward Herman, "U.S. Media Coverage of Srebrenica" in *The Srebrenica Mas-
        sacre: Evidence, Context, Politics*, Edward S. Herman ed. (Evergreen Park IL:
        Alphabet Soup, 2011), p.254.

26.   *Ibid.*, pp.257-258, n.30.

27.   *Ibid.*, p.253.

28 .   Chossudovsky, *The Globalization of Poverty*, *op. cit.*, p.258.

29.   Office of the High Representative and EU Special Representative, *The Mandate
        of the OHR*: <www.ohr.int/ohr-info/gen-info/default.asp?content_id=38612>.

30.   Ibid., All Hr's and Deputy Hr's: <www.ohr.int/ohr-info/hrs-dhrs/>.

31 .   Chossudovsky, *The Globalization of Poverty*, *op. cit.*, pp.258-259.

32.   *Ibid.*

33.   US Senate Republican Policy Committee, "The Kosovo Liberation Army: Does
        Clinton Policy Support Group with Terror, Drug Ties? From Terrorists to Part-
        ners," March 31, 1999.

34 .   Allan Little, "How Nato was sucked into the Kosovo conflict," *The Sunday Tele-graph*, February 27, 2000, p.29.

35.   US Library of Congress, Congressional Research Service, *Kosovo: International Reactions to NATO Air Strikes*, Karen Donfried, CRS Report RL30114 (Washington, DC: Office of Congressional Information and Publishing, April 21, 1999), p.11.

36 .   Jens Holsoe, John Sweeney, and Ed Vulliamy, "Nato bombed Chinese deliberately: Nato hit embassy on purpose," *The Guardian,* October 17, 1999.

37.   Saumya Mitra, ed., *Kosovo: Economic and Social Reforms for Peace and Reconciliation* (Washington, DC: World Bank, 2001), pp.22-23.

38.   *Ibid.*

39.   *Ibid.*

40.   Herman, "Summary and Conclusions," *op. cit.*, p.292.

41.   Alex Roslin, "The Kosovo connection: the KLA and the heroin craze of the 90s," *Montreal Gazette,* November 27, 1999.

42.   *Ibid.*

43.   Malcolm Moore and Harry de Quetteville, "Serb prisoners 'were stripped of their organs in Kosovo war,'" *The Daily Telegraph*, April 11, 2008.

44.   Dick Marty, "Inhuman treatment of people and illicit trafficking in human organs in Kosovo," Council of Europe, December 12, 2010.

45.   United Nations, The International Tribunal for the Prosecution of Persons Responsible for Serious Violations of International Humanitarian Law Committed in the Territory of the Former Yugoslavia since 1991, *International Criminal Issues from the Chief Prosecutor's Visit Meeting with the Director, DOJ, UNMIK* (Reference No.: RP/79(03), October 30, 2003, p.3.

46.   Issues from the Chief Prosecutor's Visit Meeting with the Director, DOJ, UNMIK (Reference No.: RP/79/03), United Nations, October 30, 2003, p.2.

47.   "Kouchner refers to reporter as 'sick, insane,'" B92, March 2, 2010.

48.   Information disclosed in a private conversation about an exchange between an Albanian foreign minister and a Bulgarian diplomat; the Albanian official stated: "First Skopje, and then Sofia will come under Albanian domination." This could be foolhardy talk, but it should be noted that large amounts of land in Bulgaria are also being purchased by Albanian nationals and entities.

49.   Chossudovsky, *The Globalization of Poverty, op. cit.*, pp.291-292.

50.   *Ibid.*, pp.293-295.

51.   NATO, "NATO's role in the former Yugoslav Republic of Macedonia." <www.nato.int/fyrom/#ah>.

52.   Mirka Velinovska, "New Paramilitary Army is Ready in Macedonia!" *Centre for Peace in the Balkans*, June 2, 2000.

53.   Michel Chossudovsky, "Washington Behind Terrorist Assaults In Macedonia," *Global Research*, September 10, 2001.

54.   *Ibid.*

55.   NATO, "NATO's role," *op. cit.*

56.   *Ibid.*

57.   Keith Hartley and Todd Sandler, *The Political Economy of NATO: Past, Present, and the 21st Century* (Cambridge: Cambridge University Press, 1999), pp.40-41.

58.   Lawrence S. Kaplan, *NATO Divided, NATO United: The Evolution of an Alliance* (Westport, CT: Praeger), pp.112-113.

59.   *Ibid.*, p.110.

60.   Drew, "Post-Cold War," *op. cit.*, pp.6-7.

61.   *Ibid.*, p.7.

62.   Douglas K. Bereuter, "The Changing Face of NATO: Partnership for Peace and the Combined Joint Task Force" in *NATO and the Challenging World Order: An Appraisal by Scholars and Policymakers*, ed. Kenneth W. Thompson (NYC: University Press of America, 1996), p.133.

63.   John R. Galvin, "Structures for Security in Europe" in *NATO and the Challenging World Order: An Appraisal by Scholars and Policymakers*, ed. Kenneth W. Thompson (NYC: University Press of America, 1996), p.45.

64.   Hartley and Sandler, *The Political Economy, op. cit.*, p.40.

65.   Galvin, "Structures for Security," *op. cit.*, pp.45-46.

66.   George Bogdanich, "UN Report on Srebrenica – A Distorted Picture of Events" in *The Srebrenica Massacre: Evidence, Context, Politics*, Edward S. Herman ed. (Evergreen Park IL: Alphabet Soup, 2011), p.247.

Chapter Four

1.   It is interesting to note that the Afghan leader Mohammed Ismail Khan, or simply Ismail Khan, made these comments to Radosław Sikorski, when Sikorski was a war correspondent from the UK—where he was give asylum in 1982 as a refugee from communist Poland—working for *The Sunday Telegraph*. When the Taliban were ousted from Herat, Ismail Khan would become its governor and would run the most efficient, organized, and popular regional government in Afghanistan complete with social services. His provincial government would also align itself with Iran and refuse to hand over his province's revenues from the taxes on trade with Iran and Turkmenistan to Hamid Karzai. In 2004, he would be pressured into relinquishing his position as Herat's governor by Kazai's forces, attacking warlords, and NATO. He would instead become the Afghan energy and water management minister. By this time, Sikorski had been elevated to a cabinet minister in Poland. The two would meet several times in Poland and NATO-garrisoned Afghanistan as ministers.

2.   Robert Scheer, "Bush's Faustian Deal With the Taliban," *The Nation*, May 22, 2002.

3.   "N.Y. Rescuers Comb Through Rubble," *Associated Press*, September 12, 2001.

4.   "Taliban Says Bin Laden Denies Role in Attacks," *Reuters*, September 13, 2001.

5.   B. Muralidhar Reddy, "Osama will not be extradited without evidence: Taliban," *The Hindu*, September 12, 2001.

6.   "Taliban 'will try Bin Laden if US provides evidence,'" *The Guardian*, October 5, 2011.

7.   Rory McCarthy, "New offer on Bin Laden: Minister makes secret trip to offer trial in third country," *The Guardian*, October 17, 2001.

8.   Ed Harriman *et al.*, "Threat of US strikes passed to Taliban weeks before NY attack," *The Guardian*, September 22, 2001.

9.   Jim Garamone, "Pre-9-11 Exercise Forecasted First War of 21st Century," *American Forces Press Service*, July 30, 2002.

10.   *Ibid.*

11.   *Ibid.*

12.   *Ibid.*

13.   Carl C. Hodge, "Preface and Acknowledgments" in *NATO for a New Century: Atlanticism and European Security*, ed. Carl C. Hodge (Westport, CT: Praeger, 2002), p.xiv.

14.   *Ibid.*

15.   Michel Chossudovsky, "Who benefits from the Afghan Opium Trade?" *Global Research*, September 21, 2006.

16.   *Ibid.*, citing from Asian Banker, August 15, 2003.

17.   John F. Richards, *Opium and the British Indian Empire: The Royal Commission of 1895 Lecture*, University of Cambridge, May 23 2001.

18.   Thomas Roy, China: *The Awakening Giant,* 2nd ed. (Toronto: McGraw-Hill Ryerson Ltd., 1981), p.24; Roy's work is based on the following: Peter Ward Fay, *The Opium War, 1840-1842: Barbarians in the Celestial Empire in the Early Part of the Nineteenth Century and the War by which They Forced Her Gates Ajar* (Chapel Hill, NC: University of North Carolina Press, 1975).

19.   *Ibid.*, pp.24-25.

20.   *Ibid.*, p.25.

21.   *Ibid.*, pp.15-28.

22.   United Nations Office on Drugs and Crime, *The Opium Economy in Afghanistan: An International Problem* (NYC: United Nations Publication, 2003), p.36.

23.   Chossudovsky, "Who benefits," *op. cit.* Chossodovsky cites Douglas I. Keh, *Drug Money in a Changing World: Economic Reform and Criminal Finance,* Technical Document No. 4 (Vienna: UNODC, 1998), p.4.

24.   Ian Traynor, "Heroin oils Afghan war machine: Taliban mullahs tap feudal state's most profitable natural resource," *The Guardian*, October 22, 2001.

25.   Public Intelligence, "US/NATO Troops Patrolling Opium Poppy Fields in Afghanistan," May 21, 2010.

26.   Dexter Filkins, Mark Mazzetti, and James Risen, "Brother of Afghan Leader Said to Be Paid by C.I.A.," *The New York Times*, October 28, 2009, p.A1.

27.   M. K. Bhadrakumar, "U.S. goofs up the Afghan election," *The Hindu*, November 15, 2009.

28.   Rahul Bedi," Pakistan's military is country's largest business conglomerate," *Indo-Asian News Service*, October 12, 2006.

29.   Asad Ismi, "A U.S.-financed Military Dictatorship: Pakistan has Long, Bloody History as the Terrorist Arm of U.S.," *Canadian Centre for Policy Alternatives Monitor,* June 1, 2002.

30.   Peter Dale Scott and Jonathan Marshall, *Cocaine Politics: Drugs, Armies, and the CIA in Central America* (Berkley, CA: University of California Press, 1998), p.xv.

31.   Transnational Institute (TNI), *The Economic Impact of the Illicit Drug Industry,* November 2005, p.13; citing Financial Action Task Force, Money Laundering, FATF-OECD Policy Brief, July 1999.

32.   Excerpt from Asad Ismi, "Drugs and Corruption in North and South America" in *Report on Canada's Sixth Year in the OAS: Focus on Corruption* (Toronto: Canada-Americas Policy Alternatives, June 1996).

33.   *Ibid.*

34.   *Ibid.*

35.   Zbigniew Brzezinski, "Les révélations d'un ancien conseiller de Carter. 'Oui, la CIA est entrée en Afghanistan avant les Russes...,'" interview by Vincent Jauvert, *Le Nouvel Observateur,* No. 1732, January 15-21 Issue, 1998, p.76.

36.   Bob Bergen, "Military Censorship Hiding in Plain Sight, *The Hamilton Spectator,* October 13, 2006; "Military wants to turn soldiers into 'journalists' to win minds overseas," *Brandon Sun,* September 21, 2006.

37.   Douglas Jehl, "Army Details Scale of Abuse of Prisoners in an Afghan Jail," *The New York Times,* March 12, 2005; "More Images Implicate German Soldiers in Afghanistan," *Der Spiegel,* October 27, 2006; Amnesty International, *Getting Away with murder? The impunity of international forces in Afghanistan*

(London: Amnesty International Publications, 2009); Amnesty International, "Afghanistan: German government must investigate deadly Kunduz airstrikes," October 30, 2009; Steve Chase, "Canada complicit in torture of innocent Afghans, diplomat says," *The Globe and Mail*, November 18, 2009; "All Afghan detainees likely tortured: diplomat," Canadian Broadcasting Corporation News, November 18, 2009; David Martin, "U.S. Soldiers Accused in Afghan Civilian Murders," CBS News, May 20, 2010; Amnesty International, "Afghanistan leak exposes NATO's incoherent civilian casualty policy," July 26, 2010; *Afghans for Peace*, "Afghan Civilians Intentionally Targeted by NATO/ISAF Forces," March 8, 2011.

38.   Mahdi Darius Nazemroaya, "Destabilizing Baluchistan, Fracturing Pakistan: The Triangle of Jundallah, the Taliban, and Sipah-e-Sahaba," *Global Research*, November 2, 2008.

39.   Joe Stephens and David B. Ottaway, "From U.S., the ABC's of Jihad; Violent Soviet-Era Textbooks Complicate Afghan Education Efforts," *The Washington Post*, March 23, 2002, p.A1.

40.   US House International Relations Committee, *Global Terrorism and South Asia*, 106th Congress, 2011, 2nd Session, 12 March 2000.

41.   "Include Taliban in government, says U.S. senator," *Associated Press*, October 3, 2006.

42.   Julian E. Barnes, Dion Nissenbaum, and Habib Khan Totakhil, "Taliban To Open Office for Peace Talks," *The Wall Street Journal,* January 4, 2012, p.A8.

43.   Robert Kagan and William Kristol, "The Gathering Storm," *The Weekly Standard*, October 29, 2001, p.13.

44.   *Ibid.*

45.   Lawrence S. Kaplan, *NATO Divided, NATO United: The Evolution of an Alliance* (Westport, CT: Praeger, 2004), pp.138-139

46.   International Security Assistance Force, "Troop Numbers and Contributions." : <www.isaf.nato.int/troop-numbers-and-contributions/index.php>.

47.   NATO, "NATO's Operations: 1949–Present" (Brussels: 2009), p.5.

Chapter Five

1.   Henri Pirenne, *Mohammed and Charlemagne* (Mineola, NY: Dover Publications, [1954] 2001).

2.   "Fischer warns of a 'blind' Europe on Mideast," *Deutsche Presse-Agentur*, October 25, 2006.

3.   Thomas L. Friedman, "Expanding Club NATO," *The New York Times*, October 26, 2003.

4 .   "Fisher warns," DPA, *op. cit.*

5.   Jill Carroll, "In Algeria, Sarkozy condemns colonialism, pushes Mediterranean Union," *The Christian Science Monitor,* December 5, 2007.

6.   "Merkel calls for progress in Turkey's EU membership talks," *Xinhua News Agency*, April 16, 2007.

7.   Zbigniew Brzezinski, *Second Chance: Three Presidents and the Crisis of American Superpower* (NYC: Basic Books, 2007), pp.106-107.

8.   Council of the European Union, *A Secure Europe in a Better World: The European Security Strategy* (Brussels: Consilium, December 12, 2003), p.8.

9.   Carroll, "In Algeria, Sarkozy," *op. cit.*

10.   Zbigniew Brzezinski, *The Grand Chessboard: American Primacy and Its Geo-*

strategic Imperatives (NYC: Basic Books, 1997), p.42.

11.   Paul Létourneau and Philippe Hérbert, "NATO Enlargement: Germany's Euro-Atlantic Design" in *The Future of NATO: Enlargement, Russia, and European Security,* eds. Charles-Philippe David and Jacques Lévesque (Montréal, QC: McGill-Queen's University Press, 2000), pp.108-118; Marie-Claude Plantin, "NATO Enlargement as an Obstacle to France's European Design" in *The Future of NATO: Enlargement, Russia, and European Security,* eds. Charles-Philippe David and Jacques Lévesque (Montréal, QC: McGill-Queen's University Press, 2000), pp.95-107.

12.   Ulrich Speck, "Is Germany Closing The Door On Further EU Enlargement?" *Radio Free Europe,* March 28, 2009.

13.   Bertrand Benoit and John Thornhill, "Merkel Rebuffs Sarkozy on Mediterranean Union plan," *The Financial Times,* January 31, 2008.

14.   *Ibid.*; Mediterranean members of the EU, such as Greece, Italy, Spain, and Cyprus are called the Olive Group because of the olive tree that is found in all the lands of the Mediterranean, which is analogous to the Mediterranean region from the Iberian Peninsula and the Aegean coast to Egypt and the Levant. Club Med is more of a colloquial expression that is short for Club Mediterranean.

15.   Jiang Yuxia, "FMs of Mediterranean EU states to meet in Cyprus on co-op," *Xinhua News Agency,* January 15, 2008; "Cyprus: EU Mediterranean foreign minister to hold talks on Kosovo, Middle East," *Associated Press,* January 17, 2008.

16.   "Mediterranean EU members back creation of Mediterranean Union," *Xinhua News Agency,* January 18, 2008; the discussion about a security zone in the Mediterranean also corresponds with Joschka Fischer's statements at Princeton in 2006.

17.   "France, Spain close ranks on ETA, Mediterranean Union, migration," *Agence France-Presse,* January 10, 2008.

18.   "Sarkozy: Italy, Spain seek to join forces with France on expelling illegal immigrants," *Associated Press,* January 8, 2008.

19.   Viviane Reding, "February 10, 2008 Interview about the Treaty of Lisbon and the EU," interview by Christian F. Trippe, *Journal,* February 10, 2008.

20.   European Commission, Directorate-General for Employment, Social Affairs and Equal Opportunities. *Do you want to work in another EU Member State?* (Brussels: Office for Official Publications of the European Communities, 2006) pp.9, 27-29; The EU-8 are the nations, aside from Malta and Cyprus, that joined the EU on May 1, 2004: Estonia, Latvia, Lithuania, Poland, the Czech Republic, Slovakia, Hungary, and Slovenia; the EU-8 +2 is a grouping of the EU-8 with the additions of Bulgaria and Romania, which both joined on January 1, 2007.

21.   *Ibid.*, pp.5, 7-9, 11-14, 15-25, 33.

22.   See the sections on the Partnership for Peace (PfP) in Chapter 2.

23.   Mahdi Darius Nazemroaya, "The 'Great Game' - Eurasia and the History of War," *Global Research,* December 3, 2007.

24.   Mahdi Darius Nazemroaya, "Plans for Redrawing the Middle East: The Project for a New Middle East," *Global Research,* November 18, 2006.

25.   NATO, "Operation Active Endeavour." : <www.nato.int/cps/en/natolive/topics_7932.htm>.

26.   Mahdi Darius Nazemroaya, "Russian Base in Syria, a Symmetrical Strategic Move," *Global Research,* July 28, 2006.

27.   Atul Aneja, "New Alliances as Iranian warships leave Syria," *The Hindu,* February 21, 2012.

Chapter Six

1. Mahdi Darius Nazemroaya, "'Operation Libya' – Recognizing the Opposition Government Constitutes a Pretext for Military Intervention," *Global Research*, March 13, 2011.
2 . James Earl Carter, Third State of the Union Address (State of the Union Address, Capitol Hill, Washington, District of Columbia, January 23, 1980).
3. Judy Dempsey, "U.S. senator urges use of NATO defense clause for energy," *International Herald Tribune*, November 28, 2006.
4. Thomas F. Remington, Politics in Russia, 7th ed. (NYC: Pearson, 2012), p.255.
5. Mu Xuequan, "Mandelson: Mistrust between Russia, EU worst since Cold War ends," *Xinhua News Agency*, April 21, 2007.
6. *Ibid.*
7. "Kuwait to sign NATO security agreement during Gulf conference next week," *Kuwait News Agency*, December 6, 2006.
8. *Ibid.*
9. Hassan M. Fattah, "U.S.-Led Exercise in Persian Gulf Sets Sights on Deadliest Weapons," *The New York Times*, October 31, 2006.
10. *Ibid.*
11. "Gulf states 'can respond to attack,'" *Gulf Daily News*, March 19, 2007.
12. *Ibid*.
13. Himendra Mohan Kumar, "Fujairah poised to be become oil export hub," *Gulf News*, June 12, 2011.
14 . *Ibid.*

Chapter Seven

1. Charles Babington, "Clinton and Yeltsin Exchange Barbs Over War in Chechnya," *International Herald Tribune*, November 19, 1999; Lester H. Brune and Richard Dean Burns, *Chronological Relations of U.S. Foreign Relations, Volume 3: 1989-2000*, 2nd ed. (NYC: Routledge, 2003), p.1338.
2. Peter Vincent Pry, *War Scare: Russia and America on the Nuclear Brink* (Westport CT: Praeger, 1999), p.284; as an additional note Pry's work was reviewed by the CIA to insure that no classified information was divulged in his book. In the process the CIA imposed no objections about Pry's casual disclosure that the US was making veiled military threats at the Kremlin over Yugoslavia in 1999.
3. *Ibid.*
4. Jens Holsoe, John Sweeney, and Ed Vulliamy, "Nato bombed Chinese deliberately," *The Guardian*, October 17, 1999; "Singer James Blunt 'prevented World War III,'" *British Broadcasting Corporation News*, November 14, 2010; Sean Michaels, "James Blunt: How I prevented a third world war," *The Guardian*, November 15, 2010; Tom Peck, "How James Blunt saved us from World War 3: Singer questioned US general's order while serving in Balkans," *The Independent*, November 15, 2010; Andrea Magrath "'I stopped World War Three by refusing US orders to destroy Russian forces,' claims James Blunt," *Daily Mail*, November 15, 2010.
5. *Ibid.*; "Confrontation over Pristina airport," *British Broadcasting Corporation News*, March 9, 2000; Douglas Hamilton, "Russia ready for re-match over Kosovo," *Reuters*, February 12, 2008.

6. Robertson's plum job in a warring Nato," *The Guardian*, August 3, 1999; "Confrontation over Pristina," BBC News, *op. cit.*
7. Michael Laris, "In China, Yeltsin Lashes Out at Clinton," *The Washington Post*, December 10, 1999, p.A35.
8. *Ibid.*
9. Sebastian Alison, "Putin Pushes for 'Eurasian Union,'" *Reuters*, October 10, 2000.
10. James Kilner, "Kazakhstan welcomes Putin's Eurasian Union concept," *The Daily Telegraph*, October 6, 2011.
11. "Russia expects CIS countries to create free trade zone by year end" [*sic*], *Russian News and Information Agency*, June 17, 2010.
12. *Ibid.*
13. *Ibid.*
14. Marina Levina, "Kyrgyzstan gives nod to joining Customs Union," *The Times of Central Asia*, December 1, 2011.
15. *Ibid.*
16. Anatoly Medetsky and Nadia Popova, "Kazakhstan Suggests New Currency," *The Moscow Times*, March 12, 2009.
17. Robert D. Hormats, "'New Silk Road' Strategy: What is it? Where is it Headed?" US State Department, September 29, 2011: <www.state.gov/e/rls/rmk/2011/174800.htm>.

Chapter Eight

1. Bill Gertz, "China builds up strategic sea lanes," *The Washington Times*, January 18, 2005.
2. Andrew Davies, *The enemy down below: Anti-submarine warfare in the ADF*, (Barton, Australian Capital Territory: Australian Strategic Policy Institute, February 2007), p.1.
3. Gertz, "China builds up," *op.cit.*
4. Pallavi Aiyar, "India to conduct naval exercises with China," *The Hindu*, April 12, 2007.
5. *Ibid.*
6. Graham Lees, "India and China Compete for Burma's Resources," *World Politics Review*, August 21, 2006.
7. Tony Allison, "Myanmar shows India the road to Southeast Asia," *Asia Times*, February 21, 2001.
8. Ben Arnoldy, "China warships dock in Burma, rattling rival naval power India," *The Christian Science Monitor*, August 30, 2010.
9. Karen Human Rights Group, *Whatever happened to the 2007 protesters?* April 29, 2009, p.1.
10. "Sri Lankan gov't, Chinese companies sign port building agreement," *Xinhua News Agency*, March 13, 2007.
11. "US out, enter Russia," *Associated Press*, December 23, 2007.
12. Jeremy Page, "Chinese billions in Sri Lanka fund battle against Tamil Tigers," *The Times*, May 2, 2009.
13. *Ibid.*
14. *Ibid.*
15. *Ibid.*
16. "US out, enter Russia," AP, *op. cit*

17.   Shamindra Ferdinando, "High level Iranian military delegation due in Colombo," *The Island*, October 9, 2009.
18.   *Ibid.*
19.   B. Muralidhar Reddy, "Iran extends credit facility to Sri Lanka," *The Hindu*, September 21, 2009.
20.   B. Muralidhar Reddy, "SCO dialogue partner status for Sri Lanka," *The Hindu*, July 18, 2009.
21.   Rebecca Conway and Qasim Nauman, "Pakistan to speed up Iran pipeline opposed by U.S.," *Reuters*, September 8, 2011; Khaleeq Kiani, "US stiffens opposition to Pak-Iran gas pipeline project," *Dawn*, September 16, 2011; "Iran-Pakistan gas pipeline to 'ease energy crisis,'" *Russian News and Information Agency*, October 17, 2011.
22.   "Naval chief: U.S. has no plan to attack Iran," *Xinhua News Agency*, April 17, 2007.
23.   Thom Shanker, "U.S. and Britain to Add Ships to Persian Gulf in Signal to Iran," *The New York Times*, December 21, 2006.
24.   *Ibid.*
25.   *Ibid.*
26.   John Burton and Shawn Donnan, "Countries oppose US offer to patrol Malacca," *Financial Times*, April 5, 2004.
27.   "IRGC Commander: Iran's Naval Forces Extend Operation beyond Equatorial Line," *Fars News Agency*, July 28, 2012; Henry Meyer and Anatoly Temkin, "Russia Seeks Naval Bases In Cold War Allies Cuba, Vietnam," *Bloomberg*, July 27, 2012; "Vietnam Ready to Host Russian Maritime Base," *Russian News and Information Agency*, July 27, 2012; "Russia to Set Up Naval Infrastructure in Arctic – Patrushev," *Russian News and Information Agency*, August 6, 2012; Gleb Bryanski, "Russia to get stronger nuclear navy, Putin says," ed. Michael Roddy, *Reuters*, July 30, 2012.

Chapter Nine

1.   "U.S. Anti-missile Shield in Europe May Cause Arms Race–Russian General," *MoscNews*, March 16, 2007.
2.   Charles D. Ferguson, Nuclear Posture Review (Nuclear Threat Initiative, August 2002): <www.nti.org/e_research/e3_15a.html>.
3.   The Project for the New American Century, *Rebuilding America's Defenses: Strategy, Forces, and Resources* (Washington, DC: PNAC, September 2000), p.v.
4.   William Arkin, "Not Just A Last Resort?: A Global Strike Plan, With a Nuclear Option," *The Washington Post*, May 15, 2005.
5.   Vladimir Putin, Speech and the Following Discussion at the Munich Conference on Security Policy (Address, Munich Conference on Security Policy, Munich, Bavaria: February 10, 2007).
6.   *Ibid.*
7.   Ian Traynor, "Putin accuses US of starting Georgia crises as election ploy," *The Guardian*, August 29, 2008.
8.   "US sends 2 missile defense satellites into orbit," *Associated Press*, September 25, 2009.
9.   Ian Sample, "US missile system's track record: test, delays, failed launches, missed targets," *The Guardian*, September 17, 2009.
10.   Vera Kalian, "U.S. anti-missile shield threatens Russia: general," *Reuters*, Janu-

ary 22, 2007.

11. *Ibid.*

12. Gareth Jones, "Poland sees merit in new Obama missile plan: aide," *Reuters*, September 24, 2009.

13. PNAC, *Rebuilding America's Defenses, op. cit.*

14. Lucian Kim, "Russian Paratroopers Stage War Games Simulating NATO Attack," *Bloomberg*, September 27, 2009.

15. John C. Rood, Remarks to the 8th Royal United Services Institute (RUSI) Missile Defense Conference (Address, London, United Kingdom: February 27, 2007).

16. NATO Active Layered Theatre Ballistic Missile Defence Programme Office, "ALT-BMD Programme." <www.tmd.nato.int/Pages/default.aspx>.

17. *Ibid.*

18. Rood, RUSI Remarks, *op. cit.*

19. Serkan Demirtaş, "NATO shield could cause World War III, Turkish party leader says," *Hürriyet Daily News and Economic Review*, November 24, 2010.

20. Ali Akbar Dareini, "Iran Threatens to target NATO missile shield in Turkey if attacked by US or Israel," *Associated Press*, November 26, 2011; Zvi Bar'el, "In Syria crisis, Turkey is caught between Iran and a hard place," *Haaretz*, December 7, 2011; D.Khatinoglu, "Iranian minister names Persian Gulf missile shield an 'American plan,'" *Trends News Agency*, April 4, 2012.

21. Andrew Osborn, "Dmitry Medvedev threatens US over planned missile defence shield," *The Daily Telegraph*, November 23, 2011.

22. "No truth behind Russian-Iran missile shield – NATO envoy," *Russian News and Information Agency*, September 30, 2011; "Russia's NATO envoy to visit China, Iran over missile defense," *Russian News and Information Agency*, November 28, 2011.

23. Edward Cody, Marc Kaufman, and Dafna Linzer, "China Criticized for Anti-Satellite Missile Test," *The Washington Post*, January 19, 2007; Li Xiaokun, "US report claims China shoots down its own satellite," *China Daily*, July 19, 2010.

24. Zbigniew Brzezinski, *The Grand Chessboard: American Primacy and Its Geostrategic Imperatives* (NYC: Basic Books, 1997), p.198.

25. Philip Towle, "Missile Defenses: Implications for NATO," in *NATO for a New Century: Atlanticism and European Security*, ed. Carl C. Hodge (Westport, CT: Praeger, 2002), p.127.

26. Office of the Press Secretary, "ATM Treaty Fact Sheet." White House, December 13, 2001:<http://georgewbush-whitehouse.archives.gov/news/releases/2001/12/20011213-2.html>.

27. United States of America, Commission to Assess United States National Security Space Management and Organization, *Report of the Commission to Assess United States National Security Space Management and Organization* (Washington, DC: January 11, 2001), pp.*viii-ix.*

28. *Ibid.*, p.*x.*

29. *Ibid.*, p.33.

30. Vishnu Bhagwat, "The Weaponization of Space: Corporate Driven Military Unleashes Pre-emptive Wars," *Global Research*, October 17, 2010.

31. NASA, FS-2003-05-65-MSFC, May 2003, p.1.

32. While it is said that true commons cannot be commoditized, there has always been a push to privatize or commercially regulate them as a means of capitalist commoditization and profiteering. To say nothing of the privatization of water, concepts such as a global carbon tax or carbon quota and user fees for bandwidth can also be perceived as a part of this process.

33.   PNAC, *Rebuilding America's Defenses, op.cit.*
34.   Ronald J. Celentano *et al.*, *Weather as a Force Multiplier: Owning the Weather in 2025*, US Air Force, August 1996, p.*vi.*
35.   *Ibid.*, p.35.

Chapter Ten

1.   Angus Topshee, "Circumnavigating Africa A Sign of Things to Come?" *FrontLine Defence*, May 2008.
2.   *Ibid.*
3.   Mahdi Darius Nazemroaya, "The Balkanization of Sudan: The Redrawing of the Middle East and North Africa," *Global Research*, January 16, 2011.
4.   Madeleine Albright, "NATO to Darfur," *The New York Times*, May 26, 2005.
5.   NATO, "Assisting the African Union in Darfur, Sudan." : <www.nato.int/cps/en/natolive/topics_49194.htm>.
6.   David E. Sanger, "Bush Sees Need to Expand Role of NATO in Sudan," *The New York Times*, February 18, 2006.
7.   Judy Dempsey, "Pressure rises over NATO's Darfur role," *The New York Times*, February 19, 2006.
8.   Sanger, "Bush Sees Need," *op. cit.*
9.   Albright, "NATO to Darfur," *op. cit.*
10.   Dempsey, "Pressure rises over," *op. cit.*
11.   *Ibid.*
12.   Mohammed Ali Saeed, "Sudan VP vows resistance to UN peacekeepers," *Agence France-Presse*, September 1, 2006.
13.   United Nation, "UNAMID Background." : <www.un.org/en/peacekeeping/missions/unamid/background.shtml>.
14.   Based on UN data. Moreover, after the division of Sudan the People's Democratic Republic of Algeria became Africa's largest country.
15.   US Energy Information Administration, "Country Analysis Briefs: Sudan," 2009; US Energy Information Administration, "Country Analysis Briefs: Sudan," 2007.
16.   Fedoruk Vladimir, "Sudan: new oil rush begins" *Voice of Russia*, February 8, 2011.
17.   Egbert Wesselink, *Fact Sheet II: The Economy of Sudan's Oil* (Utrecht, Netherlands: European Coalition on Oil in Sudan, October 2007), p.2.
18.   "US says South Sudan independence 'inevitable', warns of 'ticking time bomb,'" *Sudan Tribune*, September 8, 2010; Colum Lynch and Scott Wilson, "Obama exhorts Sudan to proceed with vote on independence in south," *The Washington Post*, September 24, 2010; Tristan McConnell, "Sudan Prepares to Break Apart," *The Nation*, December 16, 2010.
19.   Vladimir, "Sudan: new oil," *op. cit.*
20.   International Criminal Court, "ICC Prosecutor presents case against Sudanese President, Hassan Ahmad AL BASHIR, for genocide, crimes against humanity and war crimes in Darfur," Press Release 341, July 14, 2008.
21.   *Ibid.*
22.   American Jewish Committee, "AJC Applauds Israel-South Sudan Diplomatic Ties," January 30, 2011.
23.   *Ibid.*
24.   Achraf El Bahi, "Story of Israel's hand in Sudan division," *The National*, January 12, 2011.

25. *Ibid.*.; for further reading see Moshe Fergie's book *Israel and the Movement for the Liberation of South Sudan* (Moshe Dayan Center for Middle Eastern and African Studies, 2003).

26. AJC, "AJC Applauds Israel-South," *op. cit.*

27. "Sudan's SPLM reportedly opens an office in Israel – statement," *Sudan Tribune*, March 5, 2008.

28. "Sudan removes Israel travel ban from new passport," *Sudan Tribune*, October 3, 2009.

29. Joshua Spurlock, "South Sudan President Visits Israel," *The Mideast Update*, December 20, 2011.

30. Ben Hartman, "Potential to make money in South Sudan is 'enormous,'" *The Jerusalem Post*, July 11, 2011.

31. *Ibid.*

32. Robyn Dixon, "South Sudan's dreams slipping away already," *Los Angeles Times,* March 22, 2012.

33. Oakland Institute, *Understanding Land Investment Deals in Africa: Nile Trading and Development, Inc. in South Sudan* (Oakland, CA: Oakland Institute, May 2011), p.2; citing *Sudan Catholic Radio Network*, "Land Commission to Investigate Reported Foreign Deals," March 28, 2011.

34. *Ibid.*, p.1.

35. David Deng and Anuradha Mittal, *Understanding Land Investment Deals in Africa. Country Report: South Sudan*, eds. Anuradha Mittal and Frederic Mousseau (Oakland, CA: Oakland Institute, 2011), pp.20-21.

36. *Ibid.*, p.24.

37. Dixon, "South Sudan's dreams," *op. cit.*

38. Josh Kron, "Death Toll Passes 600 From Raid in South Sudan," *The New York Times*, August 22, 2011.

39. Jeffrey Gentleman and Josh Kron, "South Sudan Police Assault U.N. Human Rights Official," *The New York Times*, August 26, 2011.

40. *Ibid.*

41. Ngor Arol Garang, "South Sudan minister describes killings in Fangak as a 'massacre,'" *Sudan Tribune*, February 11, 2011; Jeremy Clarke, "Over 200 dead in south Sudan 'massacre': officials," *Reuters*, February 15, 2011.

42. "Activists warn of 'genocide' in S. Sudan's Jonglei conflict," *Sudan Tribune*, December 16, 2011.

43. "Obama Deploys 100 U.S. Combat Troops to Aid Africa Anti-Insurgency," *Associated Press*, October 14, 2011.

44. *Ibid.*

45. Argentina's policy has evolved since the 1990s when the Argentine government was involved in a dialogue to make Buenos Aires "NATO's South Atlantic Partner." Since that time relations have cordially cooled.

46. "NATO presence in South Atlantic 'inappropriate' says Brazil," *MercoPress*, September 16, 2010.

47. Brazil opposed to NATO role in South Atlantic, *United Press International*, September 16, 2010; "NATO presence in South," *op. cit.*

48. Kevin Shillington, *History of Africa*, revised 2nd ed. (NYC: Macmillan, 2005), p.388.

49. Ioannis Mantzikos, "U. S. foreign policymaking toward Ethiopia and Somalia (1974-1980)" in *African Journal of Political Science and International Relations*, Vol. 4, No. 6 (June 2010): p.246.

50. *Ibid.*, pp.245-246.
51. Michel Chossudovsky *The Globalization of Poverty and the New World Order*, 2nd ed. (Pincourt, QC: Global Research Publishers, 2003), p.95.
52. *Ibid.*, p.96.
53. *Ibid.*, p.98.
54. *Ibid.*, pp.96-97.
55. *Ibid.*, p.97.
56. *Ibid.*
57. Suzanne Goldenberg and Xan Rice, "How the US forged an alliance with Ethiopia over invasion," *The Guardian*, January 13, 2007.
58. *Ibid.*
59. "Ethiopia destroyed Somalia Peace Talks: Speaker," *Garowe Ne*ws, January 13, 2007.
60. *Ibid.*
61. *Ibid.*
62. Raymond Bonner, "Lark to Africa descends into Somali nightmare," *The New York Times*, April 15, 2007.
63. "Somali 'jihad' on foreign troops," *British Broadcasting Corporation News*, March 25, 2005.
64. African Union Mission in Somalia, "AMISOM Background." : <http://amisom-au.org/about/amisom-background/>.
65. *Ibid.*
66. *Ibid.*
67. European Commission, Development and Cooperation–EuropeAid, "AMISOM" March 13, 2012 : <http://ec.europa.eu/europeaid/where/acp/regional-cooperation/peace/peace-support-operations/amisom_en.htm>.
68. Global Humanitarian Assistance, *Somalia: International financing investments* (Wells, UK: February 21, 2012), pp.15-17.
69. *Ibid.*
70. *Ibid.*, p.16.
71. EC, EuropeAid, "AMISOM," *op. cit.*; EU, "Instrument for Stability (IfS) – EU in action." : <http://eeas.europa.eu/ifs/index_en.htm>.
72. AU Peace and Security Council, *Communiqué of the 69th Meeting of the Peace and Security Council*, 69th Meeting, February 19, 2007, PSC/PR/Comm LXIX (2007), p.2.
73. Michael Nicholson, "Spirit of Adventure: Behind the rise of the Somali pirates," *The Daily Telegraph*, February 2, 2011.
74. Ishaan Tharoor, "How Somalia's Fishermen Became Pirates," *Time Magazine*, Saturday, April 18, 2009.
75. *Ibid.*
76. *Ibid.*
77. *Ibid.*
78. UN Environment Programme, After *the Tsunami: Rapid Environmental Assessment* (Nairobi: UN, February 22, 2005), p.134.
79. *Ibid.*
80. *Ibid.*, p.135.
81. NATO, "NATO Assistance to the African Union." : <www.nato.int/cps/en/natolive/topics_8191.htm>.
82. NATO, "Assisting the African Union in Somalia." : <www.nato.int/cps/en/natolive/topics_50099.htm>.

83.   NATO, Allied Command Operation, "Operation Allied Provider." : <www.aco.nato.int/page13984631.aspx>.
84.   European Naval Force, "Mission." : <www.eunavfor.eu/about-us/mission/>.
85.   European Naval Force, "EU Extends Counter Piracy Mission Off Coast of Somalia," March 23, 2012: <www.eunavfor.eu/2012/03/eu-extends-counter-piracy-mission-off-coast-of-somalia/>.
86.   NATO, "NATO Assistance," *op. cit.*
87.   Wesley Clark, "92 Street Y Exclusive Live Interview," interview by Amy Goodman, *Democracy Now!* March 2, 2007.
88.   Air Defence and Air Operation Command, Southern Mistral 11: Assets Deployed, February 15, 2011: <www.southern-mistral.cdaoa.fr/GB/index.php?option=com_content&view=article&id=38&Itemid=104>.
89.   According to Conn Carroll of the *Washington Examiner* the resolution in the US Senate was advertised as a condemnation of the human rights violations in Libya, but had the section about a no-fly zone added secretly last minute.
90.   Nick Squires, "Libya: Italy repudiates friendship treaty, paving way for future military action," *The Daily Telegraph*, February 28, 2011.
91.   Mark Hosenball, "Obama authorizes secret help for Libya rebels," *Reuters*, March 30, 2011.
92.   "Libya orders US diplomat to leave: report," *Reuters*, November 8, 2010.
93.   Simon Denyer and Leila Fadel, "Gaddafi accepts African Union's road map for peace," *The Washington Post*, April 10, 2011; Atul Aneja, "AU begins mediation as Qadhafi forces advance," *The Hindu*, April 11, 2011.
94.   Elle Ide, "Italy recognizes Libyan opposition council," *Associated Press*, April 4, 2011.
95.   Ian Black, "Libya's biggest tribe joins march of reconciliation to Benghazi," *The Guardian*, March 23, 2011.
96.   Maria Golovnina, "Libya pledges constitution but Gaddafi role unclear," *Reuters*, April 10, 2011.
97.   Michael Georgy, "McCain visits rebels, Libya adjusts Misrata tactics," *Reuters*, August 22, 2011.
98.   Solomon Hughes and Kim Sengupta, "Gaddafi regime staked £12bn on secret deal in bid to open peace talks," *The Independent*, June 10, 2011.
99.   "MPs rebel over Libya mission creep as Cameron, Obama and Sarkozy promise to keep bombing until Gaddafi regime is gone," *The Daily Mail*, April 15, 2011.
100.   *Ibid.*
101.   Raf Caset *et al.*, "Ahead of summit, European Union downplays likelihood of no-fly zone over Libya," *Associated Press*, March 9, 2011
102.   "3 Western powers sending military advisors to Libya," *Los Angeles Times*, April 20, 2011.
103.   Louis Charbonneau and Hamuda Hassan, "France defends arms airlift to Libyan rebels," *Reuters*, June 30, 2011.
104.   Confidential discussions with sources from France about weapons shipments to Libya.
105.   "Arms Embargo – NATO Boarding," The NATO Channel (May 24, 2011); Mike Mühlberger was the video's producer and reporter.
106.   Lamine Chikhi *et al.*, "Italy's Berlusconi exposes NATO rifts over Libya," ed. Elizabeth Fullerton, *Reuters*, July 7, 2011.
107.   "Berlusconi Opposes Libya Mission; Rome Cuts Involvement," *Voice of America*, July 7, 2011.

108. "Nato capabilities will be exhausted within 90 days in Libya," *Agence-France Presse*, July 11, 2011.

109. "France backs 'political solutions' in Libya crisis," *Agence-France Presse*, July 11, 2011.

110. Human Rights Watch, "Libya: Apparent Execution of 53 Gaddafi Supporters," October 24, 2011.

111. "Putin dubs McCain 'nuts', says US drones, commandos killed Gaddafi," RT, December 15, 2011.

112. Toivo Ndjebela, "Nujoma condemns Gaddafi killing," *New Era*, October 26, 2011.

113. Catherine Sasman, "Namibia deplores 'assassination,'" *The Namibian*, October 24, 2011.

114. William Varner, "Libyan Rebel Council Forms Oil Company to Replace Qaddafi's," *Bloomberg*, March 22, 2011.

115. "Libyan rebels 'disappointed' by NATO," Al Jazeera, April 5, 2011; Atul Aneja, "Opposition allies mull 'political solution' in Libya," *The Hindu*, April 8, 2011.

116. Brian Murphy and Adam Schreck, "Libyan opposition says it has oil deal with Qatar," *Associated Press*, April 1, 2011.

117. Daryna Krasnolutska and Agnes Lovasz, "North African and Mideast Democracy a Condition for EBRD Loans, Mirow Says," *Bloomberg*, April 21, 2011.

118. Discussion between the author and Libyan Minister for International Cooperation Mohammed Siala that took place in Tripoli during NATO's war with Libya on July 4, 2011.

119. NATO, "NATO Assistance," *op. cit.*

120. Argaw Ashine, "Nato to sign security cooperation pact with AU," *Africa Review*, February 18, 2011.

121. *Ibid.*

122. NATO, "NATO Assistance," *op. cit.*

123. *Ibid.*

124. Royal Norwegian Embassy in Addis Ababa, "'Ambassador' of NATO to the AU," February 22, 2010: <www.norway.org.et/News_and_events/NATO/Ambassador-of-NATO-to-the-AU/>.

125. NATO, "NATO Assistance," *op. cit.*

126. *Ibid.*

127. *Ibid.*

128. Mahdi Darius Nazemroaya, "From Srebrenica and Racak to Benghazi and Homs," *Strategic Cultural Foundation*, March 30, 2012.

129. Magnus Ekengren, "The Challenge of a Broadening Security Agenda for EU Security Sector Reform" in *The Politics of Security Sector Reform: Challenges and Opportunities for the European Union's Global Role*, eds. Magnus Ekengren and Greg Simons (Farnham, UK: Ashgate, 2011), p.113.

130. *Ibid.*

131. *Ibid.*

132. A. Sarjoh Bah and Kwesi Aning, "US Peace Operations Policy in Africa: From ACRI to AFRICOM" in *US Peace Operations Policy: A double-edged sword?* ed. Ian Johnstone (NYC: Routledge, 2009), pp.107-108.

133. US Senate Armed Services Committee, *Testimony on U.S. Transportation Command and U.S. Africa Command in review of the Defense Authorization Request for Fiscal Year 2012 and the Future Years Defense Program*, 112th Congress, 2011, 1st Session, 7 April 2011.

Chapter Eleven

1. Sopong Peou, "Security community-building in the Asia-Pacific" in *Security-Politics in the Asia-Pacific: A Regional-Global Nexus?* ed. William T. Tow (Cambridge, NY: Cambridge University Press, 2009), p.154.

2. Lawrence S. Kaplan, *NATO Divided, NATO United: The Evolution of an Alliance* (Westport, CT: Praeger, 2004), pp.44-50.

3. *Ibid.*, p.46.

4. *Ibid.*, p.45.

5. Hillary Clinton, "America's Pacific Century," *Foreign Policy,* November 2011.

6. Ellen Bork and Gary Schmitt, "A NATO for Asia: Helping South Korea despite itself," *The Weekly Standard*, December 11, 2006.

7. Rupert Murdoch, "Enlarging the Atlantic Alliance," *The Wall Street Journal,* April 22, 2008.

8. Michael J. Green, "Interests, Asymmetries, and Strategic Choices" in *The U.S.-Japan Security Alliance in the 21 Century* (NYC: Council on Foreign Relations, 1998), p.1.

9. Trento's work is part of the ongoing investigation of the Public Education Center's *National Security News Service* that started in 1991. Informed sources from Japan also explained to the Centre for Research on Globalization that the Japanese government was trying to hide the military nature of nuclear operations taking place in Fukushima. This is why Japanese officials were preventing and delaying inspections of the Fukushima Daiichi Nuclear Power Plant after the disaster on March 10, 2011. Major news networks in Japan and across the globe also failed to properly acknowledge the impacts of a second catastrophe at the Fukushima Daini Nuclear Power Plant.

10. Yoichi Shimatzu, "Is Japan's Elite Hiding a Weapons Program Inside Nuclear Plants?" *The 4th Media*, April 7, 2011.

11. Green, "Interests, Asymmetries," *op. cit.*, pp.13-14; Ministry of Foreign Affairs of Japan, *Japan-U.S. Joint Declaration on Security: Alliance for the 21st Century,* April 17, 1996: <www.mofa.go.jp/region/n-america/us/security/security.html>.

12. John C. Rood, Remarks to the 8th Royal United Services Institute (RUSI) Missile Defense Conference (Address, London, United Kingdom: February 27, 2007).

13. "Japan's Cabinet approves joint missile project with US," *Xinhua News Agency* December 24, 2005.

14. Peou, "Security community-building," *op. cit.*

15. NATO, "NATO cooperation with Japan.": <www.nato.int/cps/en/natolive/topics_50336.htm>.

16. Judy Dempsey, "Japanese signal new era in ties with NATO: Abe tells alliance it seeks security role," *International Herald Tribune*, January 12, 2007.

17. Martin Fackler, "Japan Announces Defense Policy to Counter China," *The New York Times*, December 17, 2010, p.A10.

18. *Ibid.*

19. "Japan moves to loosen army's role," *British Broadcasting Corporation News,* April 13, 2007.

20. Sopong Peou, "Security community-building," *op. cit.*, pp.154-155.

21. Isabel Reynolds, "Defence pact in focus as Australian PM visits Japan," Reuters, March 10, 2007.

22. Ministry of Foreign Affairs of Japan, The Signing of the Japan-Australia Acquisition and Cross-servicing Agreement (ACSA), May 19, 2010: <www.mofa.go.jp/announce/announce/2010/5/0519_02.html>.

23. Michael Charles Pugh, *The ANZUS Crisis, Nuclear Visiting and Deterrence* (NYC: Cambridge University Press, 1989), p.40.

24. Rood, *RUSI Remarks, op. cit.*

25. European Parliament, *Report on the existence of a global system for the interception of private and commercial communication (ECHELON Interception System)* Gerard Schmid, 2001/2098 (INI)(Brussels: European Parliament, July 11, 2001), p.23.

26. Brendan Nicholson, "US gets military base in Western Australia," *The Age,* February 15, 2007.

27. *Ibid.*

28. Calms and Wines, "A U.S. Marine Base for Australia Irritates China," *The New York Times*, November 16, 2011.

29. "Australia could be caught in Sino-US crossfire," *The Global Times,* November 16, 2011.

30. Calms and Wines, "A U.S. Marine Base," *op. cit.*

31. *Ibid.*

32. "US Pacific Commander Calls on China Not to Seek 'High-End' Military, Says US Will Remain Dominant Asian Power," *Voice of America*, May 8, 2008.

33. "China's new naval base triggers US concerns," *Agence France-Presse*, May 12, 2008.

34. Indrani Bagchi, "India-Japan strategic talks begin," *The Times of India,* March 23, 2007.

35. Peou, "Security community-building," *op. cit.*, p.155.

36. Rahul Singh, "Indian Army fears China attack by 2017," *The Hindustan Times*, March 26, 2009.

37. Reynolds, "Defence pact in," *op. cit.*

38. Luan Shanglin, "U.S. to stage large-scale war games near Guam," *Xinhua News Agency*, April 11, 2007.

Chapter Twelve

1. Robin Cook, "The struggle against terrorism cannot be won by military means," *The Guardian*, July 8, 2005.

2. Zbigniew Brzezinski, *The Geostrategic Triad: Living with China, Europe, and Russia* (Washington, DC: Center for Strategic and International Studies Press, November 3, 2000), p.29.

3. There are also the *non-geographic* unified combatant commands of US Special Operations Command (SOCOM), US Strategic Command (STRATCOM), and US Transportation Command (USTRANSCOM).

4. Nicholas John Spykman, *The Geography of the Peace*, ed. Helen R. Nicholl (NYC: Harcourt, Bruce and Company, 1944).

5. Frederick Sherwood Dunn, "An Introductory Statement" in *The Geography of the Peace* by Nicholas John Spykman, ed. Helen R. Nicholl (NYC: Harcourt, Bruce and Company, 1944), pp.*ix-x*.

6. *Ibid.*, pp.*x-xi*.

7. Zbigniew Brzezinski, *The Grand Chessboard: American Primacy and Its Geostrategic Imperatives* (NYC: Basic Books, 1997), p.123.

8.   Robert M. Gates, *Posture Statement to the Senate Armed Services Committee* (Testimony, Senate Armed Services Committee, Washington, District of Columbia, February 06, 2007).

9.   "U.S. Anti-Missile Systems in Europe Threatens Russia – General," *MoscNews*, February 9, 2007.

10.   "U.S. Anti-missile Shield in Europe May Cause Arms Race – Russian General, *MoscNews*, March 16, 2007.

11.   Alan Cowell, "Iran Withdraws Claim on U.S. Plane," *The New York Times*, October 7, 2008; "Iran says intruding jet belongs to NATO," *Xinhua News Agency*, October 8, 2008.

12.   "Iran and NATO hold first talks in 30 years," *Agence France-Presse*, March 27, 2009.

13.   *Ibid.*

14.   "Iran attends NATO meeting for the first time," *Tehran Times*, July 5, 2011.

15.   Parisa Hafezi, "U.S. official says no sign Iran shot down drone," *Reuters*, December 4, 2011.

16.   "Nato urges Iran to keep Strait of Hormuz open," *The Daily Telegraph*, January 18, 2012.

17.   Samuel P. Huntington, "The Clash of Civilizations?" in *Foreign Affairs*, Vol. 72, No. 3 (Summer 1993): p.22.

18.   *Ibid.*

19.   *Ibid.*, pp.29-30.

20.   *Ibid.*, p.23.

21.   *Ibid.*, p.25.

22.   *Ibid.*, p.27.

23.   *Ibid.* pp.45-46.

24.   *Ibid.*, p.32.

Chapter Thirteen

1.   Zbigniew Brzezinski, *The Grand Chessboard: American Primacy and Its Geostrategic Imperatives* (NYC: Basic Books, 1997), p.35.

2.   "Russia wants creation of organization for Persian Gulf," *Interfax*, January 29, 2008.

3 .   Brzezinski, *The Grand Chessboard, op. cit.*, p.198.

4.   *Ibid.*, pp.115-116, 170, 205-206.

5.   Zbigniew Brzezinski, *Out of Control: Global Turmoil on the Eve of the 21st Century* (NYC: Charles Scribner's Sons, 1993), p.198.

6.   *Ibid.*

7.   *Ibid.*

8.   Brzezinski, *The Grand Chessboard, op. cit.*, p.198.

9.   Mahdi Darius Nazemroaya, "The Eurasian Triple Entente: Touch Iran in a War, You Will Hear Russia and China," *Strategic Cultural Foundation,* January 22, 2012.

10.   Brzezinski, *The Grand Chessboard, op. cit.*, p.204.

11.   Glenn Kessler, "In 2003, U.S. Spurned Iran's Offer of Dialogue," *The Washington Post,* June 18, 2006, p.A16.

12.   Brzezinski, *The Grand Chessboard, op. cit.*, p.116.

13.   In 2011 a contact from Central Asia in close contact with these NGOs clarified that many of them have been involved almost exclusively in the large-scale

bribery of local officials.

14.   M. K. Bhadrakumar, "The lessons from Ferghana," *Asia Times*, May 18, 2005.

15.   Nick Paton Walsh, "Uzbekistan kicks US out of military base," *The Guardian*, August 1, 2005.

16.   Vladimir Radyuhin, "Uzbekistan rejoins defence pact," *The Hindu*, June 26, 2006.

17.   Andrei Makhovsky, "Belarus leader raps Russia, may snub security summit," Reuters, April 25, 2010.

18.   Dmitry Solovyov, "Belarus-Russia rift widens, Minsk snubs Moscow meet," ed. Janet Lawrence, *Reuters*, June 14, 2009.

19.   Fedoruk Vladimir, "Russia, China don't see US in SCO," *The Voice of Russia*, November 1, 2011.

20 .   NATO, "NATO and Mongolia agree programme of cooperation," March 19, 2012: <www.nato.int/cps/en/natolive/news_85430.htm>.

21.   Wu Jiao and Li Xiaokun, "SCO agrees deal to expand," *China Daily*, June 12, 2010.

22.   "Iran, China Calls For A Long-term Strategy To Expand Bilateral Ties," *Iranian Students News Agency,* June 17, 2009.

23.   Rankings calculated on the basis of GDP (PPP) by the IMF in 2011; China being number two, India number four, Russia number six, and Iran seventeenth. On the Atlanticist side of the equation: nine of the largest other economies of the world are NATO members with the US being the first and another three of the world's largest economies belonging to formal NATO partners in the Asia-Pacific region.

Chapter Fourteen

1.   Wesley Clark, "92 Street Y Exclusive Live Interview," interview by Amy Goodman, *Democracy Now!* March 2, 2007.

2.   Arnaud de Borchgrave, "Haig: Syria should be next target," *United Press International*, January 7, 2002.

3.   Julian Borger *et al.*, "Bush vetoes Syria War," *The Guardian*, April 15, 2003.

4.   Ed Vulliamy, "Syria could be next, warns Washington," *The Observer*, April 13, 2003.

5.   Anthon La Guardia, "Iran wars Israel on pre-emptive strike," *The Daily Telegraph*, August 19, 2004.

6.   Richard Perle *et al.*, *A Clean Break: A New Strategy for Securing the Realm*, Institute for Advanced Strategic and Political Studies, 1996: <www.iasps.org/strat1.htm>.

7.   *Ibid.*

8.   Dominic Evans, "Hariri says was wrong to accuse Syria over killing," ed. Samia Nakhoul, *Reuters*, September 6, 2010.

9.   Caroline Wyatt, "France mulls Mid-East peace force," *British Broadcasting Corporation News*, June 15, 2003; "EU to Consider Peacekeeping Force for Palestinian Territory," *Palestinian Media Center*, June 16, 2003; Steven Everts, "Why Nato should keep the Mideast peace," *Centre for European Reform*, July 29, 2003.

10.   *Ibid.*

11.   "Green light for Iran attack?" *Yedioth Aharonot*, March 13, 2005.

12.   Seymour M. Hersh, "Watching Lebanon," *The New Yorker*, August 21, 2006.

13.   Sarah Baxter and Uzi Mahnaimi, "NATO may help US strikes on Iran," *The Sunday Times*, March 5, 2006.
14.   "Israel tightens NATO ties amid Iran nuke jitters," *Reuters*, May 29, 2006.
15.   Israel Ministry of Foreign Affairs, "Israel Navy to participate in NATO Maritime exercise," May 30, 2006: <www.mfa.gov.il/MFA/Government/Communiques/2006/Israel%20Navy%20to%20participate%20in%20NATO%20maritime%20exercise%2030-May-2006.htm>.
16.   *Ibid.*
17.   *Ibid.*
18.   Yakkov Katz, "Reservists called up for Lebanon strike," *The Jerusalem Post*, July 12, 2006.
19.   *Ibid.*
20.   "PM 'says Israel pre-planned war,'" *British Broadcasting Corporation News*, March 8, 2007.
21.   Aluff Benn, "PM: War planned months in advance," *Haaretz*, March 8, 2007.
22.   Judy Dempsey, "If called to Lebanon, NATO 'could go in,'" *International Herald Tribune*, July 27, 2006.
23.   Hala Najjar, ed. and trans. "Pellegrini Reveals US Attempt to Join July War ... and much More...," tayyar.org, November 2, 2010: <www.tayyar.org>; Also see Pellegrini's *Un été de feu au Liban: 2006, les coulisses d>un conflit annoncé* [*A Summer of Fire in Lebanon: 2006, behind the scenes of the conflict*] (Paris: Economica, 2006).
24.   Jack Khourey, "Report: Lebanese man allegedly spied on behalf of European state," *Haaretz*, February 28, 2007.
25.   Ze'ev Schiff, Syria, "Iran intelligence services aided Hezbollah during war," *Haaretz*, October 3, 2006.
26.   *Media Maters for America,* "Right-wing media divided: Is U.S. now in World War III, IV, or V?" July 14, 2006: <http://mediamatters.org/research/200607140017>.
27.   "Hezbollah shadow over UN Lebanon troops," *British Broadcasting Corporation News,* July 16, 2007.
28.   James Keaten, "French tanks bolster UN force in Lebanon: Powerful armor said to be 'deterrent,'" *Associated Press*, September 13, 2006.
29.   Claudia Rach, German Parliament Approves UN Naval Force for Lebanon, *Bloomberg*, September 20, 2006.
30.   Brian Knowlton, Bush seeks to shore up Lebanon, *The New York Times*, August 2, 2007.
31.   *Ibid.*
32.   "Battle lines are drawn as Israeli allies among Arab regimes meet to coordinate the fight against the Iran-Syria axis," *Ma'an News Agency*, December 21, 2006.
33.   Seymour M. Hersh, "The Redirection," *The New Yorker*, February 25, 2006.
34.   Martin Asser, "All quiet on the Syrian front," *British Broadcasting Corporation News*, July 17, 2006.
35.   Inigo Gilmore, Tracy McVeigh, and, Patrick Wintour, "Children die in convoy attack as Israel widens Lebanon assault," *The Observer*, July 16, 2006.
36.   "Syria to enter conflict if Lebanon invaded: minister," *Agence France-Presse*, July 23, 2006.
37.   *Ibid.*
38.   Sami Al-Khiyami, August 2, 2006 Interview, interview by Anna Jones, Sky News, August 2, 2007.

39.   *Ibid.*
40.   *Ibid.*
41.   Yitzhak Benhorin, "Neocons: We expected Israel to attack Syria," *Yedioth Aha-ronot*, December 16, 2006.
42.   *Ibid.*
43.   *Ibid.*
44.   "Report: France urged Israel to hit Syria," *The Jerusalem Post*, March 18, 2007.
45.   Herb Keinon, "Olmert: EU force on border possible," *The Jerusalem Post*, July 24, 2006.
46.   "Syria threatens to close Lebanon border," *Associated Press*, August 23, 2006.
47.   "Hamas springs to Iran's defence," *Agence France-Presse*, December 17, 2005; "PFLP-GC Leader Warns Israel, U.S. Against Attacking Iran," *Associated Press*, April 28, 2006.
48.   "EU plans to re-engage with Syria," *British Broadcasting Corporation News*, March 9, 2007.
49.   Stephen Kaufman, Syria, "United States Exchange Views on Iraqi Refugees: Talks in Damascus described as 'useful' and 'straightforward,'" US State Department, March 12, 2007.
50.   Hassan M. Fattah, "Pelosi's Delegation Presses Syrian Leader on Militants," *The New York Times*, April 5, 2007, p.A3.
51.   Nawal and A.N. Idlebi, "Syria-Turkey enhance Military Cooperation," *Syrian Arab News Agency*, April 3, 2007.
52.   Fattah, "Pelosi's Delegation," *op. cit.*
53.   Aluf Ben, "Israel seeks to reassure Syria: No summer attack," *Haaretz*, April 3, 2007.
54.   Fattah, "Pelosi's Delegation," *op. cit.*
55.   Howard Schneider, "Iran, Syria mock U.S. policy; Ahmadinejad speaks of Israel's 'annihilation,'" *The Washington Post*, February 26, 2010.
56.   Khaled Yacoub Oweis, "Syria and Iran defy Clinton in show of unity," ed. Mark Trevelyan, *Reuters*, February 25, 2010.
57.   "Hezbollah chief Nasrallah meets Ahmadinejad in Syria," *British Broadcasting Corporation News*, February 26, 2010.
58.   Herb Keion, "Assad: US has lost influence in the ME," *The Jerusalem Post*, May 25, 2010.
59.   Dayem's account to CNN would also contradict his official Twitter account's explanation: "This was camera tricks by the Assad regime helped by Russians."
60.   League of Arab States Observer Mission to Syria, *Report of the Head of the League of Arab States Observer Mission to Syria for the period from 24 December 2011 to 18 January 2012* (Damascus/Cairo: January 27, 2012), p.4.
61.   Ruth Sherlock, "Libya's new rulers offer weapons to Syrian rebels," *The Daily Telegraph*, November 25, 2011; "Three Containers Loaded with Weapons in Lutfallah II Ship," *Syrian Arab News Agency*, April 29, 2012; "Saqr orders arrest of crew on ship carrying weapons to Syria," *The Daily Star*, April 30, 2012.
62.   F. Allafi and M. Eyon, "Patriarch Iwas: Syria will Remain Staunch against all Conspiracies," *Syrian Arab News Agency,* October 4, 2011; Michael Shields, "Syrian Christian archbishop backs Assad - newspaper," ed. Alistair Lyon, *Reuters*, November 11, 2011; F. Allafi and M. Eyon, "Patriarchs Hazim, Iwas, Laham Reject Foreign Interference and Violence," *Syrian Arab News Agency*, December 15, 2011; Bassam Alkantar, "Jumblatt and the Druze of Syria," *Al-Akbar English*, January 26, 2012; "Interview: Syria's anti-colonialism cradle boasts sectarian

unity during unrest," *Xinhua News Agency*, January 29, 2012; Firas Choufi, "Lebanese Druze Clergy to Jumblatt: Not in Our Name," *Al-Akbar English*, March 13, 2012; R. Raslan and Ghossoun, "Archbishop Hanna: Syria Will Be Victorious against Conspiracy," *Syrian Arab News Agency*, April 16, 2012.

63.   "Syria has been reduced to banditry and anarchy, says Gregory III Laham," *Vatican Insider*, May 4, 2012.

64.   "Rai warns of sectarian wars during Paris talks," *The Daily Star*, September 6, 2011; H. Sabbagh, "Patriarch al-Rahi Meets Delegation from Tartous, Calls for Confronting Plots against the East," *Syrian Arab News Agency*, December 27, 2011; Samia Nakhoul *et al.*, "Violence turning Arab Spring into winter," ed. Sophie Hares, *Reuters*, March 4, 2012; "Maronite patriarch's interview on Syria stirs new criticism," *The Daily Star*, March 10, 2012; Nicolas Nassif, "The Maronite Patriarch: Staying the Course One Year After His Election," *Al-Akbar English*, March 29, 2012.

65.   Nour Malas and Jay Solomon, "Syria Would Cut Iran Military Tie, Opposition Head Says," *The Wall Street Journal*, December 2, 2011.

Chapter Fifteen

1.   Alan Tonelson, "NATO, East Asia, and Japan" in *NATO and the Challenging World Order: An Appraisal by Scholars and Policymakers*, ed. Kenneth W. Thompson (NYC: University Press of America, 1996), pp.162-163.

2.   Ton Frinking, "Preface" in *NATO in the 1990s*, ed. Stanley R. Solan (NYC: Pergamo-Brassey's International Defense Publishers, 1989), p.*xi*.

3.   Lawrence S. Kaplan, *NATO Divided, NATO United: The Evolution of an Alliance* (Westport, CT: Praeger, 2004), p.46.

4.   NATO grants its partners seats in the North Atlantic Council when it comes to operations they are contributing in. The NATO Contact Countries Australia and New Zealand set the precedent by gaining places at the North Atlantic Council when it came to discussions about the operations in NATO-garrisoned Afghanistan. NATO's Istanbul Cooperation Initiative partner Qatar likewise had a seat at the North Atlantic Council during the war against Libya. This has also led to the appointment of the first Australian ambassadors to NATO Headquarters in 2012.

Chapter Sixteen

1.   Samuel P. Huntington, "The Clash of Civilizations?" in *Foreign Affairs*, Vol. 72, No. 3 (Summer 1993): p.34.

2.   Zbigniew Brzezinski, *The Geostrategic Triad: Living with China, Europe, and Russia* (Washington, DC: Center for Strategic and International Studies Press, November 3, 2000), p.5.

3.   Mahdi Darius Nazemroaya, "Currency Warfare: What are the Real Targets of the E.U. Oil Embargo against Iran?" *Strategic Culture Foundation*, January 31, 2012.

4.   "NATO fighters again accompany Russian bombers near Alaska," *Russian News and Information Agency*, April 9, 2008.

5.   "NATO fighters scramble again to intercept Russian Bear bombers," *Russian News and Information Agency*, March 19, 2008.

6.   US Department of Defense, *Doctrine for Joint Nuclear Operations* (Washington

DC: Department of Defense, March 15, 2005), p.III2.

7.   *Ibid.*, p.I9

8.   *Ibid.*, pp.*x -xiii*, II2-II3, III2.

9.   *Ibid.*, p.II2.

10.   "New Trident system approved," *The Hindu*, March 16, 2007.

11.   Parisa Hafezi, "Iran, at nuclear conference, hits out at 'bullies,'" *Reuters*, April 17, 2010; Peter Baker and David E. Sanger, "Obama Limits When U.S. Would Use Nuclear Arms," *The New York Times*, April 5, 2010.

12.   "Iran to launch protest with U.N.," *The Hindu*, April 13, 2010.

13.   "Russian defense spending to grow 20% in 2008, to $40 bln," *Russian News and Information Agency*, February 26, 2008.

14.   "China's military rise," *The Economist*, April 7-13, 2012, p.13.

15.   "The dragon's new teeth," *The Economist*, April 7-13, 2012, p.27.

16.   Ilya Kramnik, "Who should fear Russia's new military doctrine," *Russian News and Information Agency*, October 23, 2009.

17.   Vladimir Isachenkov, "Reports: Russia may exit Arms Treaty," *The St. Petersburg Times*, February 15, 2007.

18.   Under the terms of the Intermediate-Range Nuclear Forces (INF) Treaty there are limitations placed on the number of medium-range ballistic missiles Russia can have. In a major war scenario against the US and its allies the Kremlin would be forced to reallocate its nuclear inter-continental ballistic missiles (IBMs) for medium-range nuclear strikes instead of striking the continental US in North America and other long-range targets.

19.   Otried Nassauer, "Nuclear Sharing in NATO: Is it Legal?" *Science for Democratic Action*, May 2001, p.1+.

20.   "ALBA Countries To Establish Common Currency Named Sucre," *Cuban News Agency*, November 29, 2008; Michael Fox, "ALBA Summit Ratifies Regional Currency, Prepares for Trinidad," *Venezuela Analysis*, April 17, 2009; Steven Matter, "Venezuela Pays for First ALBA Trade with Ecuador in New Regional Currency", *Venezuela Analysis*, July 7, 2010.

21.   Chris Kraul and Sebastian Rotella, "Fears of a Hezbollah presence in Venezuela," *Los Angeles Times*, August 27, 2008; "Venezuela feared as Hezbollah base," *United Press International*, August 27, 2008; Roger F. Noriega, "Chávez's Secret Nuclear Program," *Foreign Policy*, October 5, 2010; Capitol Hill Cubans, "Iran-Cuba-Venezuela Coordinate U.S. Attacks," December 8, 2011: <www.capitol-hillcubans.com/2011/12/iran-cuba-venezuela-coordinate-us.html>; "Dangerous lies: US Media Outlet Falsely Accuses Venezuela of Terrorist Plot," *Correo del Orinoco International*, December 16, 2011, p.7; "Factbox: Venezuela's ties with Iran," *Reuters*, January 7, 2012.

22.   "Chavez says Bush 'devil' speech spur of the moment," *Reuters*, Nov 30, 2006.

23.   Simon Romero, "Venezuela: Russian Bombers Arrive for an Exercise," *The New York Times*, September 11, 2008, p.A10.

24.   "Venezuela summit criticises West," *British Broadcasting Corporation News*, September 27, 2009; Steven Bodzin and Daniel Cancel, "Chavez, Qaddafi Seek Africa-South America NATO, Bank," *Bloomberg*, September 27, 2009; "President Chávez is Due in Libya this Saturday," *Tripoli Post*, October 24, 2010.

25.   Ed Vulliamy, "Venezuela coup linked to Bush team," *The Observer*, April 21, 2002; Nil Nikandrov, "US ambassadors to Venezuela: chronology of failure," *Strategic Culture Foundation*, February 12, 2012.

26.   Alex Main, "USAID: The Bone of Contention in U.S.–Bolivia Relations," *Center*

for Economic and Policy Research, June 22, 2010; Sara Shahriari, "Morales Says He Won't Hesitate to Expel USAID From Bolivia, La Razon Says," *Bloomberg*, June 23, 2010.

27.   Mark Weisbrot, "Does the US back the Honduran coup?" *The Guardian*, July 1, 2009; "Bolivian president says U.S. behind Honduras coup," *Russian News and Information Agency*, July 14, 2009; "U.S. military denies role in Honduras coup flight," *Associated Press*, August 16, 2009; Dana Frank, "In Honduras, a Mess Made in the U.S.," *The New York Times*, January 27, 2012, p.A27.

28.   The Canadian journalist Jean-Guy Allard stated in an interview with *Radio Del Sur* that the CIA had been infiltrating the ranks of the Ecuadorian police according a 2008 Ecuadorian government report. The US through its NGO proxies also provided funding to Pachakutik Movement, which is reported to have supported the coup.

29.   "Russia would welcome Ukraine into CSTO post-Soviet security bloc," *Russian News and Information Agency*, May 18, 2010.

30.   "Ukraine passes on joining post-Soviet CSTO bloc - Foreign Ministry," *Russian News and Information Agency*, May 28, 2010.

31.   "Russia is for SCO observing countries cooperation activization," *Kazakhstan Today*, July 9, 2007.

32.   "CSTO proposes to SCO joint effort on post-conflict Afghanistan," *Russian News and Information Agency*, July 31, 2007.

33.   "UN, CSTO sign cooperation agreement," *Russian News and Information Agency*, March 18, 2010; Rodger McDermott, "Moscow Pushes For Formal Cooperation Between UN, CSTO," *Radio Free Europe*, October 16, 2009; "Russia stunned by UN-NATO cooperation deal," *Russian News and Information Agency*, October 9, 2008.

34.   Vladimir Radyuhin, "Defence pact to balance NATO," *The Hindu*, October 7, 2007.

35.   Michael Evans, "Georgia linked to Nato early warning system," *The Times*, September 5, 2008; Dmitry Avaliani, "Georgia: Fears of War with Russia," *Institute for War and Peace Reporting*, May 16, 2008.

36.   *Ibid.*

37.   *Ibid.*; Inal Khasing, "Abkhazia Cleaves Closer to Russia," *Institute for War and Peace Reporting*, May 8, 2008.

38.   Avaliani, "Georgia: Fears of War," *op. cit.*

39.   *Ibid.*

40.   *Ibid.*

41.   *Ibid.*

42.   Khasing, "Abkhazia," *op. cit.*; this article also clarified that *Izvestia*, the Russian newspaper, had misquoted Sergei Shamba over asking Moscow for a Russian military administration to be established in Abkhazia.

43.   Avaliani, "Georgia: Fears of War," *op. cit.*

44.   *Ibid.*

45.   Michael Evans, "Georgia linked to Nato early warning system," *The Times*, September 5, 2008.

46.   "USA to Deploy Army Bases in Georgia To Rearm Nation's Army," *Pravda*, September 24, 2009.

47.   Arnaud de Borchgrave, "Commentary: Israel of the Caucasus," *United Press International*, September 2, 2008.

48.   Mariam Harutunian, "Russia extends military presence in Armenia," *Agence*

France-Presse, August 20, 2010.

49. Department of National Defence, "Minister of National Defence visits Operation Nanook", August 23, 2010: <www.airforce.forces.gc.ca/v2/nr-sp/index-eng.asp?id=10905>.

50. *Ibid.*

51. Department of Foreign Affairs and International Trade, *Statement on Canada's Arctic Foreign Policy* (Ottawa: Government of Canada, 2010), p.2.

52. *Ibid.*, p.3.

53. Herb Keion, "Assad: US has lost influence in the ME," *The Jerusalem Post*, May 25, 2010.

54. William A Arkin, "Russia Supports North Korea in Nuclear War," *The Washington Post*, October 6, 2006.

55. Alex Spillius, "George Bush warns Putin over 'World War III,'" *The Daily Telegraph*, October 18, 2007.

56. Sebastian Moffett, "Russia says would be threatened by Iran military action," ed. Sophie Hares, *Reuters*, February 13, 2012.

57. "NATO plans campaign in Syria, tightens noose around Iran – Rogozin," *Russian News and Information Agency,* August 5, 2011.

58. "Medvedev Warns of 'Full-Blown Wars,'" *Russian News and Information Agency*, May 17, 2012.

59. Viola Gienger, "Iran's Military Power Subject to New U.S. Study Used for China," *Bloomberg*, November 3, 3009.

60. Dan Williams, "Israel general doubts power to hit Iran atom sites," ed. Mark Trevelyan, *Reuters*, February 13, 2010; Amos Harel, "Former Mossad chief: Israeli attack on Iran must be stopped to avert catastrophe," *Haaretz*, Dec.1, 2011; Donald Macintyre and Kim Sengupta, "Israel's military leaders warn against Iran attack," *The Independent*, February 2, 2012; Gareth Porter, "Israeli Experts Mum on Iran Attack to Support Bibi's Bluff," *Inter Press Services*, April 2, 2012; Dan Williams, "Israel ex-spy warns against 'messianic' war on Iran," *Reuters*, April 28, 2012.

61. Jeffrey Heller, "Netanyahu to press U.S. for military threat on Iran," ed. Christopher Wilson, *Reuters*, November 7, 2010.

62. "U.S. could strike Iran but not win: Russian general," *Reuters*, April 3, 2007.

63. "Excerpts From Iraqi Document on Meeting with US Envoy," *The New York Times*, September 22, 1990, p.19; it should be noted that more than one transcript exists from the 1990 meeting of Hussein and Glaspie and the one cited from *The New York Times* was done so out of convenience.

64. "Incoming U.S. Defense Secretary tells Senate panel Israel has nuclear weapons," *Associated Press*, December 9, 2006; Allyn Fisher-Ilan, "Olmert, in Europe, hints Israel has nuclear arms," *Reuters*, December 11, 2006; Philippe Naughton, "Olmert's nuclear slip-up sparks outrage in Israel," *The Times*, December 12, 2006.

65. Christopher Hogg, "Japan gets woman defence minister," *British Broadcasting Corporation News*, July 4, 2007.

66. *Ibid.*

67. George Orwell, *Nineteen Eight-Four* (Toronto: Penguin Books, 2000), p.207.

68. Halford John Mackinder, *Democratic Ideals and Reality* (London, UK: Constables and Company Ltd., 1919), pp.2-3.

FIGURE CREDITS

Business Monitor International – Maps XIII, XX.

European Union – Map II.

Government of the Russian Federation – Illustration in Chapter 7.

Government of the United States of America – Map XVIII; Photo in Chapter 4.

North Atlantic Treaty Organization – Chart 2.1; Diagram 2.1; Maps III, V, VI, VII, VIII, XIX; Photo in Chapter 6.

Romanian Students and Alumni Association in Geopolitics and International Relations – Map XIV.

Russian News and Information Agency (RIA Novosti) – Maps I, X, XII, XV, XVII.

TamilNet – Photo in Chapter 8.

United Nations Cartographic Section – Map IV.

University of Alabama, Cartographic Research Laboratory of the Department of Geography – Map IX

University of Texas in Austin – Map XI.

INDEX

A

Abe, Shinzo: 256-257.
Abkhazia: 65, 99, 351, 356-361.
Abrams, Elliott: 240.
Active Layered Theater Ballistic Missile Defense (ALTBMD): 197, 200.
ALBA (Alternativa Bolivariana para las Américas, see Bolivarian Bloc)
Afghanistan: 16, 18, 19, 27, 50, 54, 55, 56, 98, 114-119, 121-127, 129-132, 147, 155, 157, 173, 185-186, 194, 228, 253, 256, 257, 259, 266, 267, 273, 275, 284, 285, 287, 288, 294, 296, 306-308, 313, 316, 341, 343-344, 345, 349, 351, 353. Afghanistan-Pakistan-ISAF Tripartite Commission: 55, 267, 344. AfPak Theater: 55.
African, Caribbean and Pacific Group of States (ACP Countries): 140.
African Standby Force (ASF): 248, 249-250.
African Union (AU): 19, 49, 146, 208, 209, 210, 212-215, 216, 217, 229-231, 236-237, 240-241, 247-251, 259. African Union Mission in Somalia (AMISOM): 229-231, 236-237. African Union Mission in Sudan (AMIS): 213-214.
AFRICOM (see United States Africa Command) .
Ahmadinejad, Mahmoud: 147, 183, 296, 326, 327.
Airborne Warning and Control System (AWACS): 89, 149-150, 314
Al-Qaeda: 114-115, 228, 251, 266-267.
Albania: 25, 29, 43, 45, 48, 53, 56, 65, 81, 82, 94, 99-105, 125, 252, 269,
273 Great Albania: 103, 105.
Albanian National Army (ANA): 107.
Albright, Madeleine Korbelová: 91, 95, 211, 240, 341.
Algeria: 20, 21, 23, 34, 41, 42, 43, 48, 135, 138, 139, 147, 148, 158, 189, 209, 247, 346, 349, 351.
Alternativa Bolivariana para las Américas/Bolivarian Alternative for the Americas (ALBA) (see Bolivarian Bloc)
American Empire 27, 240, 332-334, 336-339, 341, 345, 349, 362, 366. In comparison to the Roman Empire: 336-339.
American Jewish Committee (AJC): 217-218.
Americanization: 332-333.
Andreotti, Giulio: 68, 70-71.
Anglo-American Alliance: 30-41, 49-51, 73, 84, 98, 110, 116, 117, 136-137, 139-141, 157, 246, 252, 257, 259-260, 266, 279, 285, 305, 313, 325, 331, 335, 346, 362, 365, 366.
Anglo-French Defense and Security Cooperation Treaty: 50.
Annan, Kofi Atta: 249.
Anti-Ballistic Missile Treaty (ABM Treaty): 193-194, 200, 203, 282.
Antigua and Barbuda: 349, 351.
Aoun, Michel: 310, 311, 312.
Arab League: 145, 148, 154, 156, 217, 240, 249, 328, 330. Arab League Monitors in Syria: 328.
Arab Spring: 136, 137, 147, 238, 327, 363.
Arabian Peninsula: 19, 162-163, 267, 304.
Arabian Sea: 162, 179, 186, 187, 188, 209, 236, 259.
Arctic Circle: 191, 198, 278, 353,

361-362.
Arctic Ocean: 191, 341.
Argentina: 189, 223.
Armenia: 26, 28-29, 41, 44, 46, 48, 58, 61, 62, 165, 169, 277, 288, 290, 292, 297, 298, 351, 355-356, 357, 360, 363.
Arms Trade Treaty (ATT): 246.
Article 5 (NATO's Mutual Defense Clause): 16, 18, 20-21, 114, 116, 132, 149-150, 158, 255, 338.
Asian NATO: 178, 253-254, 264-265.
Assad, Bashar: 325-327, 329.
Atlantic Ocean: 17, 20-21, 34, 50, 111, 209, 222-223, 270, 331, 341.
Atlanticism: 30-33, 35-39, 50, 83, 138, 140, 147, 166, 168, 169-170, 172, 173, 185, 190, 191, 212, 215, 216, 222, 230, 248, 249, 250, 275, 277-278, 280, 281, 282, 285, 286, 288, 291, 295, 296, 300, 331, 345, 362.
Australia, Commonwealth of: 13, 14, 27, 31, 55, 56, 146, 159, 178, 188, 190, 197, 198, 227, 230, 252-254, 255, 258-262, 263, 265, 267, 268, 269, 390 (n.4).
Australia, New Zealand, and United States Security Treaty (ANZUS): 259.
Austria: 31, 32, 58, 75, 80, 82, 84, 85, 100, 316.
Azerbaijan, Iranian provinces: 128, 355.
Azerbaijan, Republic of: 26, 29, 41, 44, 46, 48, 58, 61, 62, 99, 165, 166, 169, 198, 269, 274, 277, 285, 288, 290-291, 292, 297, 351, 355, 357.

B

Bahrain: 153, 154, 155, 156, 157, 159, 161, 188, 216, 236, 238, 269.
Baker-Hamilton Commission (see Iraq Study Group)

Baku-Tbilisi-Ceyhan (BTC) Oil Terminal: 119, 151, 177.
Balkans: 18, 24, 27, 29, 38, 41, 43-44, 45, 54, 56, 67, 76, 82, 88, 95, 99, 103-108, 111, 114, 116-117, 137, 147, 153, 171, 259, 272, 273, 282, 313.
Balkanization: 80, 82-85, 86-87, 103, 147, 186, 210-211, 218-219, 229, 281, 308, 329, 337, 345, 350.
Baltic Sea: 24, 166, 196, 270, 342.
Baltic States: 26, 130, 138, 165, 166, 287, 313.
Baluchistan, Iranian province (Sistan and Baluchistan): 186,
Baluchistan, Pakistani province: 185-187.
Baluyevsky, Yury Nikolayevich: 274, 365.
Bangladesh: 179, 264, 351.
Barak, Ehud: 364.
Barre, Mohammed Siad: 224-225.
Bashir, Omar: 216-217.
Bauer, Alain W.M.: 336.
Bay of Bengal: 179-180.
Belarus: 26, 29, 36, 41, 43-44, 46, 48, 58, 62, 165, 166, 172-173, 185, 196, 198, 288, 290, 291, 292-293, 294, 296, 297, 298, 344, 347, 349, 351, 353.
Belgium: 19, 20, 23, 31, 35, 38, 40, 71, 72, 84, 85, 241, 269, 319, 323.
Berlusconi, Silvio: 243.
Bhagwat, Vishnu: 204-205.
bin Laden, Osama: 114-116, 267.
Black Sea: 41-42, 151, 166, 187, 190, 198, 273, 355.
Blair, Anthony (Tony) Charles Lynton: 38, 121, 346.
Bolivia, Plurinational State of: 217, 348-349, 350, 351.
Bolivarian Bloc: 348-352.
Bolton, John Robert: 188.
Bordyuzha, Nikolay Nikolayevich: 288, 353, 363.
Bork, Ellen: 253-254.
Bosnia and Herzegovina: 18, 25, 43,

48, 53, 58, 61, 62, 65, 76, 80-81, 82-93, 94, 96, 98, 104, 110, 113, 138, 209, 240, 351. Bosniaks: 80, 81-82, 84, 86-87, 88-92.

Brazil: 144, 189, 223, 240, 279, 280, 300, 344, 351, 362.

BRIC/BRICS: 280, 300, 330, 344.

British Intelligence: 72-73, 239, 259-260, 317.

Brom, Shlomo: 364.

Brosio, Manlio Giovanni: 252.

Brzezinski, Zbigniew Kazimierz: 17-18, 38-39, 50, 125-126, 137-138, 139, 199, 267, 279, 281-283, 284, 286, 334-335, 343.

Bulgaria: 24-25, 53, 65, 75, 82, 105, 130-131, 138, 198, 269, 277, 319.

Burma (see Myanmar)

Burundi: 230, 236.

Bush, George Herbert Walker: 111, 200.

Bush, George Walker: 37, 50, 200, 202, 212, 213, 284, 306, 350, 363. Administration: 115, 187, 202, 213, 306-307, 309, 320. Doctrine: 50.

C

Cameron, David William Donald: 240.

Canada: 13, 16, 17, 20, 23, 31, 43, 123, 145, 188, 190, 198, 260, 269, 316, 361-362.

Carrington-Cutileiro Plan (see Lisbon Agreement)

Carter, James (Jimmy) Earl : 73, 157. Administration: 39 Doctrine: 157.

Caspian Sea: 119, 172, 273, 355, 357.

Caucasus (Caucasia): 26, 41, 44, 45, 49, 56, 137, 167, 170, 172, 195, 198, 272, 283, 288, 342, 355-357, 360-361, 362.

Cedar Revolution: 150, 286, 309-310.

CENTCOM (see United States Central Command)

Center for Applied Non Violent Actions and Strategies (CANVAS): 285.

Central Asia: 24, 26, 56, 98, 116-119, 127, 129, 166, 167, 169, 172, 173, 177, 178, 257, 272, 278, 283, 285-287, 288, 296, 297, 343, 353, 357, 362, 363. Middle Asia and Kazakhstan (Sredbyaa Azia i Kazakhstan): 172.

Central Intelligence Agency (CIA): 69, 72-74, 88-89, 100, 115, 123-124, 125, 225, 239, 242, 267, 318, 322, 335-336, 348.

Chace, James: 17-18.

Chavez Frías, Hugo Rafael: 223, 348-350.

Chechnya: 170-171, 183, 355, 357.

Cheney, Richard (Dick) Bruce: 130, 194, 323.

China, People's Republic of: 13, 14, 26, 36, 83, 96, 97, 99, 118-121, 127, 128, 143-144, 145-146, 157, 171-172, 175-187, 189-191, 193, 197, 198-199, 214-219, 240, 251, 253-254, 255, 257-259, 260-265, 268, 272, 273, 275, 277-278, 279-285, 287, 288, 294, 295-300, 301-303, 308, 316, 317, 330, 333, 341-344, 345, 346 347, 349, 350, 351, 353, 361, 362-364.

China, Republic of (see Taiwan)

Chinese Taipei (see Taiwan)

Chirac, Jacques René: 24, 49, 335.

Chossudovsky, Michel: 76, 78.

Christianity: 80, 81, 82, 83, 276-277, 298, 311, 312, 314, 319, 320, 321, 329, 335, 356-357 Catholicism: 80, 81, 82, 83, 312, 329. Orthodoxy: 80, 81, 82, 276-277, 329, 356-357..

CitiBank: 311.

Civilizations: 29, 129-130, 134, 267, 275-277, 280, 295-299.

Claes, Willem (Willy) Werner Hubert: 19, 130.

Clark, Wesley Kanne: 171, 237, 306.
Clash of Civilizations Theory: 129-130, 267, 275-277, 280, 295-299, 345.
Clinton, Hillary Diane Rodham: 245, 253, 327, 345, 350.
Clinton, William (Bill) Jefferson: 90-91, 170-171, 200, 202. Administration: 88, 94, 202-203, 306.
Co-existence: 274, 295-299.
Cold War: 16-17, 19-22, 23, 24, 25, 26, 38, 50, 63, 68, 70, 76, 79, 102, 112, 116, 125, 128-129, 146, 151, 153, 169-173, 192-194, 223-225, 255-258, 263, 270, 274, 275-277, 281, 297, 305, 333-334, 336, 341, 343, 344, 345, 347, 348, 366.
Collective Security Treaty (CST): 287-288, 290-291, 292-293.
Collective Security Treaty Organization (CSTO): 167, 169, 174, 280, 287-293, 294, 296-297, 299-300, 341, 347, 351, 352-353, 362-363.
Colonialism: 20, 31, 34, 44, 84, 89-93, 97-99, 118-121, 140, 142, 204-205, 210-211, 219-222, 223-224, 229-231, 246-247, 272-273, 275, 281, 299, 305, 311, 334, 338, 348.
Color Revolutions: 26, 53, 82-83, 150, 166, 168, 285-286, 278, 285-286, 309-311, 360. Bulldozer Revolution: 285. Cedar Revolution: 150, 285-286, 309-311. Rose Revolution: 26, 168, 285, 360. Saffron Revolution: 179-181, 182. Orange Revolution: 26, 168, 285-286. Tulip Revolution: 285-286. Twitter Revolution: 82-83.
Combined Joint Task Forces (CJTFs)/ Combined Task Forces (CTFs): 110, 188.
Commission to Assess United States National Security Space Management and Organization: 202-205.

Common African Defense and Security Policy (CADSP): 250.
Common Economic Space (see Eurasian Union)
Common European Economic Space (CEES): 36, 45.
Common Organization of the Saharan Regions (Organisation Commune des Régions Sahariennes): 34.
Commonwealth of Independent States (CIS): 26, 42, 165-169, 172-173, 287, 290-291, 292, 296, 353, 358, 359.
Contact Countries (CC): 54-56, 253, 256, 267-268, 295, 296, 338, 344
Contact Groups: 237.
Cook, Robert Finlayson: 267.
Cooperation Council for the Arab States of the Gulf (see Gulf Cooperation Council)
Corwin, Philip: 90.
Council of Europe: 51, 101-102.
Croatia: 25, 43, 48, 53, 65, 75-76, 80-81, 82-83, 84, 85, 86-87, 92, 104, 108, 252, 269.
Cuba: 19, 189, 191, 225, 248-250, 251.
Cultural imperialism: 299-300.
Cyberspace: 205, 260, 343.
Czech Republic: 24, 25, 53, 60, 63, 65, 81, 96, 130, 137-138, 196, 269.
Czechoslovakia: 25, 84, 85, 128, 291.

D

Dagan, Meir: 364.
Dayton Accords: 92, 98.
de Gaulle, Charles: 31, 33-36, 37.
de Ganay, Christine: 336.
de Hoop Scheffer, Jakob (Jaap) Gijsbert: 153, 213, 256.
Del Ponte, Carla: 101.
Denmark: 20, 23, 71, 72, 128, 197, 230, 241, 269, 319, 361.
Diskin, Yuval: 364.

Doctrine for Joint Nuclear Operations (DJNO): 194, 346.
Dollar (US) Domination: 36, 125, 344. Petro-dollar: 36.
Djibouti: 191, 224, 230, 250, 273.
Dominica, Commonwealth of: 349, 351.
Dobriansky, Paula Jon: 309.
Drew, Samuel Nelson: 19, 111-112.
Drug Trafficking (see Narcotics trade)
Druze: 310, 312, 320, 321, 329.

E

East China Sea: 117, 179.
Eastern Bloc: 16-17, 22, 24, 29, 51-52, 76, 130, 157, 224, 276, 333, 341.
Eastern Partnership (EaP): 41-42, 44-49, 54, 173.
ECHELON signal intelligence interceptor system: 259-260.
Economic Cooperation Organization (ECO): 169.
Ecuador: 348-350, 351.
Energy: 27, 34, 35, 36, 40, 49, 105, 118-119, 143-144, 151, 157-159, 160, 161-164, 175, 177-179, 180, 183-184, 185-187, 188, 214-216, 217, 219, 220, 221, 222, 223, 228, 246, 247, 251, 255, 262, 273, 275, 283, 297, 308, 324-325, 326, 341, 349, 350, 357, 362 Gas: 34, 118, 158, 178, 179, 185, 214-216, 220, 324-325, 350. NATO policy on energy: 27, 49, 157-159, 150, 188, 223, 341. Nuclear: 35, 40, 324, 249, 255, 362. Routes: 27, 118-119, 151, 161, 162-164, 177-179, 185-186, 222, 228, 273, 324, 357. Security: 27, 49, 143, 151, 157-159, 160, 175, 177-179, 185-187, 222, 228, 251, 262, 273, 275, 283, 341. Supplies: 118, 143, 144, 157-159, 160, 162-164, 177-179, 184-184,

187, 214-216, 251, 262, 275, 297, 308, 357, 362 Oil: 27, 34, 36, 105, 118-119, 151, 158, 159, 161-162, 164, 177-179, 183-184, 185, 214-215, 217, 219, 220, 221, 222, 246, 247, 251, 308, 328, 350.
Ethiopia: 128, 209-210, 217, 218, 224-226, 228-230, 236, 245, 247, 248-249, 250, 268. Invasion of Somalia: 228-230, 236.
Estonia: 24, 25, 26, 53, 65, 130, 131, 138, 269, 276.
Erdogan, Recep Tayyip: 326.
Eritrea: 218, 224, 351.
EUCOM (see United States European Command)
Eurasian Economic Community (EurAsEC/EAEC): 167, 172, 353.
Eurasian Triple Entente (the alliance formed by China, Iran, and Russia): 280, 342, 344.
Eurasian Union: 37, 172.
Eurasianism: 32-33, 35-36, 166, 169-174, 277-278, 279-285.
Euro (€): 36, 40, 41, 97, 247, 349. Competition with the US dollar: 36, 247.
Euro-Atlantic Zone: 17, 20-21, 26, 29-30, 31, 38-39, 41, 43, 44, 45, 48, 50-51, 84-85, 93, 99, 104, 108, 110, 136-139, 141, 142-143, 147, 152, 158, 166-168, 169, 170, 173, 190, 197, 208-209, 210, 215, 250, 266, 267, 274-275, 276, 279, 280, 281, 285, 286, 296, 299, 305-306, 308, 311, 331-334, 337, 341-342. Expansion/integration: 30, 38-39, 41, 43, 44, 45, 48, 50-51, 84-85, 99, 104, 108, 136-139, 141, 142-143, 147, 152, 166-168, 169, 170, 208-209, 231, 250, 267, 274-275, 276, 280, 281, 285, 299, 305-306, 308, 311, 334-335, 341-342.
Euro-Mediterranean Partnership (EUROMED; Barcelona Process): 41, 42, 43, 45, 48, 54, 138-146.

European Border Surveillance System (EUROSUR): 144.
European Economic Community (EEC): 31, 37, 40.
European Naval Force Somalia: 236-237.
European Neighborhood Policy (ENP): 30, 41-49, 54.
European Neighborhood and Partnership Instrument (ENPI): 42-43.
European Security Strategy: 49-50, 138-139, 144.
European Union: 17, 29-33, 35, 36-51, 53, 54, 55, 82-83, 92, 93, 97-99, 102, 104, 105, 108, 136-146, 147, 148, 153, 156-157, 158, 166, 168, 170, 173, 177, 210, 212, 213, 216, 219, 228, 230, 236-237, 240, 247, 249, 250, 254, 257, 259, 267, 285, 296, 300, 304, 305, 313, 325-326, 331-332, 337, 341, 343, 353, 358, 359.
European Union Rule of Law Mission in Kosovo (EULEX): 97-98, 102.

F

Fatah Al-Islam: 321.
Fauntroy, Walter Edward: 239.
Feith, Douglas: 307-308.
Feltman, Jeffery D.: 320.
Finland: 58, 269, 316, 361.
Fischer, Joseph (Joschka) Martin: 136-137.
France: 20-21, 23, 24, 30-39, 40, 43, 49, 50, 54, 55, 71, 73, 85, 103, 112, 128, 135, 136-139, 140-143, 155, 157, 159, 171, 180, 188, 190, 197, 214, 223-224, 239-243, 245, 247, 253, 269, 288, 304-305, 309, 310, 311, 313, 316, 317, 318-319, 323, 326, 328, 329, 331, 334, 335-336, 338, 341, 345-347, 363.
Franco-German Entente: 18, 30-39,
49-51, 98, 114, 130-131, 136-140, 247, 257, 279, 285, 313, 319, 331, 334-336.
Free Patriotic Movement: 311-312, 320.
Free-trade: 50, 140, 145-147, 173.
French Empire: 20, 32, 34, 223-224.
Frontex: 144.
Fukushima: 255.
Future Movement: 310.

G

Gaullism: 33-35, 37, 332.
Galvin, John Rogers: 112-113.
Gates, Robert Michael: 273-274, 365.
Georgia, Republic of: 26, 29, 41, 43, 44, 46, 48, 49, 58, 61, 62, 65, 99, 131, 165, 166, 168-169, 180, 195-196, 198, 252, 269, 274, 278, 285, 288, 290-291, 292, 297, 342, 351, 355-361.
Germany: 21-25, 30-33, 35-39, 40, 43, 49, 50, 67, 71, 74, 75-76, 80, 82, 84-85, 87, 89, 108, 110, 111-112, 116, 128, 136-143, 188, 190, 193, 195, 197, 230, 240, 247, 253, 257, 269, 270-271, 274, 278, 279, 314, 317, 318-319, 323, 324, 331, 334-336, 341, 343, 346, 363. German Democratic Republic (East Germany): 21, 23, 24, 31, 84, 112. Federal Republic of Germany (West Germany): 21-22, 23, 31, 35, 40, 253.
Ghana: 230.
Gladio (see Stay-behinds)
Glaspie, April Catherine: 365.
Global War on Terror: 18, 54, 129-132, 149, 161, 188, 228, 250, 267, 273, 306-307, 366.
Great Game: 366.
Great War (see World War I)
Greece: 21, 23, 29, 63, 71, 96-97, 103, 105, 146, 273, 297, 319, 338, 339, 368 (n.30).

GUAM/GUUAM Organization for Democracy and Economic Development: 166, 168, 287.
Gulf Cooperation Council (GCC): 56, 154-157, 159-164, 190-191, 198, 238, 267-268, 322, 328, 342.
Gulf of Aden: 162, 164, 175, 188, 191, 210, 236-237, 266, 341.
Gulf of Guinea: 209, 251.
Gulf War: 18, 110, 111-113, 130-131, 161, 227.
Gulf of Oman (Oman Sea): 151, 162, 164, 186, 188.
Gwadar: 179, 186-187.

H

Halutz, Daniel: 313, 364.
Hamas (Islamic Resistance Movement): 284, 315, 322, 323, 324, 325, 330.
Hannah, John Peter: 240.
Hariri, Saad: 285-286, 321, 326.
Heroin: 99-100, 105, 121-124.
Hersh, Seymour (Sy) Myron: 313, 321.
Hezbollah: 214, 284, 286, 306, 309, 311-317, 319-324, 326, 327, 330, 349, 364.
Honduras: 3448-349, 350.
Hong Kong and Shanghai Banking Corporation (HSBC): 246.
Horn of Africa: 113, 131, 150, 188, 210, 223-226, 228, 230-237.
Human Rights: 64, 126, 156, 180, 213, 216, 222, 240, 244-245, 286, 297, 328, 345.
Humanitarianism: 19, 43, 94-97, 110, 113, 127, 131, 156, 210-212, 217, 218, 222, 241-242, 249.
Hungary: 24, 25, 53, 65, 75, 82, 85, 96, 130, 137, 269, 291, 335.
Huntington, Samuel Philips: 129, 267, 275-277, 345.
Hussein Abdal-Majid Al-Tikriti, Saddam: 36, 162, 284, 307, 338, 365.

I

Iceland: 20, 23, 42, 269, 361.
Identity Politics, Manipulation, and Allegiances: 80-86, 126, 210-211, 275-277, 311-312, 320, 326, 345, 368 (n.30), 369 (n.19).
India: 67, 96, 117, 118, 119-121, 123, 126, 127, 144, 157, 173, 178, 179, 182, 185-186, 189, 197, 198, 204, 215, 217, 240, 251, 262-264, 268, 272, 275, 277, 279, 280, 281, 286, 294, 295, 297, 298, 300, 303, 344, 347, 349, 351, 362, 364.
Indian Ocean: 118, 149, 150, 162, 175, 177, 178-179, 182, 186, 187, 190, 191, 198, 208, 234, 235, 237, 259-260, 262, 278, 341, 342, 363.
Indian sub-continent (South Asia): 56, 118, 173, 198, 268, 272, 297, 366.
Individual Cooperation Program (ICP): 148, 149, 253, 305.
Individual Partnership Action Plans (IPAP): 60-61.
Individual Partnership and Cooperation Program (IPCP): 60.
Inge, Peter: 341.
Intensified Dialogue: 61, 62, 104.
Intergovernmental Authority on Development Peace Support Mission in Somalia (IGASOM): 230.
International Commons: 205-206, 378 (n.32).
International Criminal Court (ICC): 216-217.
International Monetary Fund (IMF): 42-43, 76-77, 79, 92, 119, 124, 217, 226-227, 232, 331, 344.
International Security Assistance Force (ISAF): 18, 117, 131, 295, 316.
Intra-NATO alliances/divisions (see the Anglo-American Alliance

and Franco-German Entente)
Iran: 26, 29, 88, 94-95, 116, 117,
    118-119, 121, 124, 126, 127, 128,
    132, 141, 146-147, 150-152, 157,
    158, 159-164, 169, 172, 177, 178,
    182-187, 189, 190-191, 193, 196,
    197-199, 217, 237, 263, 267-268,
    272, 273, 274-275, 277-278,
    279-285, 286, 287, 288, 290, 294,
    295-296, 297, 298, 300, 303,
    304, 306-308, 312-314, 316, 317,
    318, 320-325, 326-327, 329-330,
    341-342, 343, 344, 345, 346-347,
    349-350, 351, 355-356, 357,
    360-361, 362-266. Influence in
    the Balkans: 88, 94-95. Nuclear
    Dispute: 161, 346, 362. Relations
    with NATO: 274-275, 280, 314,
    341-342. Strategic Alliance with
    Syria: 150-152, 286, 307-308,
    312-314, 316, 317, 318, 320-325,
    326-327, 329-330, 363-364. Stra-
    tegic Alliances in Latin America:
    349-350.
Iran-Pakistan-India Friendship Pipe-
    line: 185-186.
Iraq: 18-19, 24-25, 35, 36, 38, 41, 49,
    54, 56, 84, 98, 111-113, 117, 118,
    130, 136, 141, 147, 150, 154,
    157, 161, 162, 168, 187, 188,
    190, 193, 197, 200, 227,228, 237,
    243, 252, 253, 256, 259, 263,
    266, 274, 284-285, 304, 306-309,
    312, 313, 319, 320, 324, 326,
    327, 330, 335, 341, 343, 345,
    351, 360, 364, 365.
Iraq Study Group (ISG): 326.
Ireland: 58.
Islam (also see Muslim): 19, 82, 130,
    134, 224, 276-277, 298, 299.
Islamic Courts Union (ICU): 228-231,
    237.
Islamic Union: 146-147.
Islamophobia: 103, 277, 345.
Ismay, Hastings Lionel: 21, 67, 85.
Israel: 14, 27, 29, 31, 41, 42, 45, 48,
    56, 89, 103, 111, 132, 138, 140,

147, 148, 149-151, 154, 155, 162,
    197, 198, 210, 214, 217-219, 252,
    268, 269, 274, 284, 286, 304-309,
    311, 313-319, 320-327, 330, 342,
    347, 349, 360, 362, 364-365.
Istanbul Cooperation Initiative (ICI):
    54, 56, 147, 149, 153-154, 155,
    159, 161, 236, 238, 267, 275,
    297, 338, 342.
Italy: 20, 23, 29, 36, 40, 43, 68-75, 76,
    97, 99, 103, 111, 127, 128, 142,
    143, 188, 190, 197, 223-224, 232,
    237, 239, 241, 243, 269, 319,
    327, 336, 338, 339.
Ivashov, Leonid Grigoryevich: 27,
    170-171.
Izetbegović, Alija: 80, 86, 90-91.

J

Jackson, Michael David: 171.
Japan: 27, 31, 38, 55, 56, 128, 146,
    178, 180, 188, 190, 197, 198,
    230, 252-259, 262-263, 265,
    267, 269, 272, 277, 279, 281,
    296, 332, 333, 343-344, 365.
    Japanese-US Dyad: 38, 255-256,
    257, 258, 262-263, 268, 333.
    International Peace Coopera-
    tion Law: 255-256. Relations
    with NATO: 27, 55, 56, 197, 252-
    254, 256-257, 258, 267. Secret
    Nuclear Weapons Program: 255.
Jintao, Hu: 295-296.
Jobim, Nelson Azevedo: 223.
Jordan, Hashemite Kingdom of: 41,
    43, 48, 138, 147, 148, 149, 154,
    155, 162, 238, 269, 304, 305,
    309, 321.
Jumblatt, Walid: 310-311, 321-322,
    326.

K

Kagan, Robert: 129-130, 240.
Karakoram Highway: 186-187.
Karamov, Islam Abduganiyevich:

286-288.
Karzai, Hamid: 118, 123-124, 371 (n.1).
Kazakhstan: 26, 29, 30, 36, 58, 61, 62, 158, 165, 172-173, 198, 282, 287-288, 290, 292, 294, 295, 297, 298, 301-303, 344, 347, 351, 353.
Kenya: 218, 224, 229-230, 234, 240, 245, 250.
Khalilzad, Zalmay: 118.
Kiir Mayardit, Salva: 218.
Ki-moon, Ban: 253.
Kissinger, Heinz (Henry) Alfred: 73, 176.
Korea, Democratic People's Republic of (North Korea): 187, 189, 193, 196, 198, 253-254, 256, 257, 264-265, 278, 284, 343, 345-346, 347, 349, 363, 364.
Korea, Republic of (South Korea): 31, 55, 56, 188, 198, 230, 252, 253-254, 255, 262, 265, 267-268, 278, 342-343.
Kosachev, Konstantin Iosifovich: 363.
Kosovo and Metohija: 18, 48, 65, 80, 81, 93-103, 104, 105, 106-107, 113, 125, 170-171, 269, 295, 316, 349.
Kosovo Force (KFOR): 98, 106, 107-108, 147, 316.
Kosovo Liberation Army (KLA): 18, 94-97, 98-105, 107. Criminal Activities: 94, 99-103, 105. See the National Liberation Army (NLA) and Albanian National Army (ANA) for the Macedonian branch of the KLA.
Kosovo War: 93-99, 101.
Kouchner, Bernard: 102-103.
Kristol, William: 129-130, 240.
Kurd: 84, 112, 287, 298, 329, 356-357.
Kuwait: 111, 153, 154-156, 159, 236, 269, 309.
Kyrgyzstan: 30, 58, 165, 172, 173, 282, 285-288, 290, 291, 292, 294, 295, 297, 298, 301, 303, 351.
Kyuma, Fumio: 365.

L

Lagarde, Christine Madeleine Odette: 336.
Lantos, Thomas (Tom) Peter: 326.
Lanxade, Jacques: 341.
Larijani, Ali Ardashir: 217.
Latvia: 24, 25, 26, 49, 53, 65, 130, 131, 137-138, 269.
League of Arab States (see Arab League)
Lebanon: 41, 42, 48, 132, 136, 138, 147, 148, 150, 151, 152, 154, 162-163, 214, 237, 240, 274, 278, 284, 285-286, 304, 306-325, 326, 327, 328-329, 330, 349, 351, 360. Membership in the Resistance Bloc: 152, 284, 285-286, 306-308, 312-313, 314, 316, 317, 318, 320-321, 322-324, 325, 327, 330, 351. 2006 war with Israel: 42, 151, 154, 214, 308-309, 313-319, 320-321, 322-324, 325, 360. Political System: 310-313, 319-320
Lebanon-Syria Defense and Security Pact: 323.
Levant (Greater Syria): 132, 135, 147, 148, 151, 163, 304-319, 324, 362, 366.
Lévy, Bernard-Henri: 240.
Lieberman, Joseph Isadore: 240.
Liberation Tigers of Tamil Ealam (LTTE) 182-185.
Libya: 19, 27, 41, 43, 48, 130, 135, 138, 147, 148, 154, 155, 156, 193, 194, 208, 211, 237-248, 250-251, 266, 269, 273, 274, 275, 288, 306, 328-329, 330, 336, 337, 341, 345, 348, 349, 350.
Libyan Islamic Fighting Group (LIFG): 238, 244.
Libyan League for Human Rights (LLHR): 240.
Lipkin-Shahak, Amnon: 364.

Lisbon Agreement: 85-86.
Lithuania: 24, 25, 26, 53, 65, 130, 131, 138-139, 269.
Loewenberg, Robert J.: 308.
Lomonosov Ridge: 362.
Luns, Joseph Marie Antoine Hubert: 35.
Luti, William J.: 307.
Luxembourg: 20, 31, 38, 40, 269.

M

Macedonia, Former Yugoslav Republic of (FYROM): 18, 25, 43, 48, 58, 61, 62, 63, 65, 76, 80, 81, 82, 94, 103, 104, 105, 107, 108, 269, 368 (n.30).
Mackinder, Halford John: 32, 270, 272, 280, 299-300, 340, 360.
Malawi: 230.
Malaysia: 178, 189, 215, 217, 260, 262-263, 349.
March 8 Alliance: 311-312, 319-321.
March 14 Alliance: 285-286, 310-317, 319-322, 326, 329.
Maronite: 312, 329.
Massoud, Ahmad Shah: 116.
Mauritania: 138, 147, 148, 209, 269.
McCain, John Sidney: 240, 274.
Mediterranean Dialogue (MD): 30, 54, 56, 138-140, 143, 147, 148, 149, 154, 209, 247, 267, 275, 297, 305, 309, 338.
Mediterranean Sea: 18, 21, 30, 42-43, 35, 49, 51, 56, 110, 132, 134-152, 157, 162, 163, 187, 188, 190, 196, 198, 209, 236, 239, 266, 267, 268, 273, 305-306, 309, 312, 313, 317, 324, 341, 364.
Mediterranean Union (see Union for the Mediterranean)
Medvedev, Dmitry Anatolyevich: 274, 363.
Membership Action Plan (MAP): 25, 61-65.
Mercenaries: 126, 156, 238, 239, 266, 348.

Merkel, Angela Dorothea: 36, 50, 136-137, 141-142, 335.
Middle East: 14, 24, 39, 49, 56, 85, 98, 111, 118, 129, 136-137, 140-141, 143, 145-147, 151, 154, 178, 179, 188, 194, 197-198, 227, 238, 260, 262, 267-268, 272-273, 275, 279, 281, 297, 304, 306-309, 316, 317, 319, 323, 324, 325, 326, 327, 330, 331, 355, 360, 362, 364-366.
MI6 (Military Intelligence, Section 6; see British Intelligence)
Missile Shield: 27, 147, 168-169, 192, 193-204, 255, 259, 267, 274, 282.
Mitterrand, François Maurice Adrien Marie: 33.
Moldova: 29, 41, 43, 44, 46, 48, 58, 61, 62, 82-85, 166, 278, 290, 292, 351.
Money laundering: 121, 124-125.
Mongolia: 54, 56, 290-291, 294, 295, 298, 303, 351.
Morales Ayma, Juan Evo: 348.
Moro, Aldo: 69, 73-74.
Morocco: 34, 41, 42, 43, 48, 135, 138, 144, 147, 148, 209, 238, 269.
Mossad: 161, 218.
Mujahedeen-e-Khalq (MEK): 284.
Mullen, Michael (Mike) Glenn : 187-188.
Murdoch, Keith Rupert: 252, 254.
Murr, Elias: 314.
Muslim (also see Islam): 19, 80-82, 84-85, 86, 90, 111, 114, 130, 277, 306, 308, 312-313, 314, 321, 326, 327, 345, 356-357. Obama's "A New Beginning" Speech: 237-238. Shia/Shiite: 84-84, 277, 311-314, 320-321, 357. Sunni/Sunnite: 84-85, 308, 312, 320-321, 326, 329, 357.
Myanmar: 121, 179-182, 264, 351.

N

Nagorno-Karabakh: 277, 351, 357.

National Aeronautics and Space Administration (NASA): 200, 205.
National Liberation Army (NLA): 105, 107-108.
Narcotics Trade: 99-100, 105, 119-125, 190.
Nasrallah, Hassan: 312, 327.
NATO Defense Planning Committee: 35, 111.
NATO Parliamentary Assembly (NATO PA): 22, 112, 275, 334, 338.
NATO-Russia Council: 54, 56, 274.
NATO Strategic Concept: 109-110, 131, 341.
NATO Training Mission–Iraq: 18-19, 306, 313.
NATO-Ukraine Commission: 54, 56.
Naumann, Klas: 341.
Netanyahu, Benjamin (Bibi): 308, 364.
Netherlands: 20, 23, 35, 40, 43, 55, 89, 188, 197, 215, 241, 269, 319, 341, 358.
Neoliberalism: 140, 143-146, 181, 217, 219-221, 226, 230-232, 246-247, 299.
New Middle East: 316, 362.
New Zealand: 55, 56, 146, 188, 252-253, 259, 260, 267, 390 (n.4).
Nicaragua: 124, 348-349, 351.
Nigeria: 158, 214, 230, 240.
Nixon, Richard Milhous: 176, 268 Doctrine: 268.
Non-Proliferation Treaty (NPT): 346,-348, 363, 365.
North Atlantic Assembly (see NATO Parliamentary Assembly [NATO PA])
North Atlantic Cooperation Council (NACC): 51, 53, 110.
North Atlantic Council (NAC): 21-22, 24, 30, 35, 52, 61, 63, 96, 111, 114, 131-132, 209, 212, 236-237, 241, 248, 256, 259, 288, 314, 338, 339, 390 (n.4).
North Atlantic Treaty (see Washington Treaty)
North Korea (see Korea, Democratic People's Republic of)
Norway: 20, 23, 42, 72, 237, 243, 248, 269, 361.
Nuclear Club: 347-348.
Nuclear Primacy: 192-194.
Nuclear War: 193-194, 263-264, 345-348, 362-366. No First Use Policy: 345-346, 364. US Simulations of Nuclear War: 363.
Nujoma, Samuel Daniel Shafiishuna: 245-246.
Nujoma, Utoni Daniel: 246.

O

Oceania (geographic term): 251.
Oceania (fictitious term): 32.
Obama, Barack Hussein: 85, 181, 192, 196, 200, 215, 222, 238-240, 260-262, 327, 346, 350, 365. Administration: 85, 181, 196, 200, 215, 222, 238-240, 327, 346, 350, 365.
Ogaden Border Dispute/War: 223-224, 225-226. Region: 224-225, 226.
Ohrid Framework Agreement: 105-106.
Olmert, Ehud: 315, 320, 324, 326, 365.
Oman: 153, 154, 156, 161, 162, 238.
Operation Ace Guard: 111.
Operation Active Endeavor: 18, 132, 147, 149-150, 187, 190, 209, 305, 306.
Operation Allied Force: 93, 97, 110.
Operation Allied Provider: 19, 210, 236.
Operation Allied Protector: 19, 210, 236-237,
Operation Allied Harmony: 108.
Operation Amber Fox: 108.
Operation Atlanta (EU Naval Force–Atlanta): 236-237.
Operation Changing Direction: 322

Operation Deliberate Force: 92.
Operation Deny Flight: 87-89.
Operation Determined Falcon: 94.
Operation Eagle Assist: 132.
Operation Enduring Freedom: 116, 130-131, 188.
Operation Essential Harvest: 107-108.
Operation Mistral: 92.
Operation Noble Eagle: 116.
Operation Ocean Protector: 237.
Operation Ocean Shield: 210, 237.
Operation Odyssey Dawn: 241-242, 250.
Operation Sharp Guard: 87.
Operation Sky Monitor: 87.
Operation Summer Rains: 324.
Operation Unified Protector: 341.
Opium: 119-125.
Organization of African Unity (OAU): 247.
Organization of Petroleum Export-ing Countries (OPEC): 158.
Organization for Security and Co-operation in Europe (OSCE): 30, 51, 64, 107-108, 170-171, 359.
Ortega Saavedra, José Daniel: 348.
Orwell, George: 32, 366.
Otpor: 285.

P

Pacific Ocean: 140, 190, 223, 253, 259-265, 270, 344, 363.
Pakistan: 55, 56, 115-118, 121, 123, 124, 125-127, 130, 178-179, 185-187, 264, 267-268, 269, 277, 294, 295, 297, 298, 303, 341, 344, 347.
Palestine: 132, 138, 217, 304, 305, 313, 315-316, 322, 324-326, 349.
Palestinian Authority: 41, 42, 48, 154, 284.
Palin, Sarah Louise: 274.
Pan-Africanism: 146, 248.
Pan-Europeanism: 31-33, 36-39. 140-141.

Pan-Somalism: 224.
Partners Across the Globe (see Contact Countries)
Partnership for Peace (PfP): 30, 51-54, 56, 58, 60-64, 130, 138, 146, 154, 267, 338.
Pelosi, Nancy Patricia D'Alesandro: 326.
Perle, Richard Norman: 306, 308-309.
Persian Gulf: 56, 111, 151, 153-154, 156-157, 159-164, 177, 186, 188, 190-191, 198, 234, 236, 259, 267, 268, 273, 275, 280, 281, 297, 308, 331, 342.
Piracy: 189, 231-237. Concerning NATO Anti-Piracy Operations: 19, 150, 209-210, 256. Off the Somalian Coast: 210, 231-237.
Pirenne, Henri: 134, 135-136.
Poland: 18, 24, 25, 39, 44, 53, 65, 96, 128, 130, 137-138, 144, 196-197, 343, 371 (n.1).
Portugal: 20, 23, 240, 297.
Post-Soviet Space (former USSR): 26, 29, 41-44, 45, 51-52, 56, 84, 85, 118, 128, 158, 165-174, 192, 263, 267-268, 274, 276, 279, 285-299.
Primakov, Yevgeny Maksimovich: 172, 281, 283. Primakov Doc-trine: 172, 280-281, 283.
Project for the New American Century (PNAC): 130, 194, 196, 205, 253.
Proliferation Security Initiative (PSI): 161, 187-191.
Putin, Vladimir Vladimirovich: 171, 172, 173, 175, 194-195, 245, 274, 340, 344, 363.

Q

Qaddafi, Muammar Mohammed Abu Minyar: 27, 154, 238-241, 243-246, 350. Execution: 244-246.
Qatar: 127, 153-157, 159, 162, 236,

239, 241, 242, 246, 269, 322, 327-328, 329, 330, 390 (n.4).
Quigley, Carroll: 32.

R

Rasmussen, Anders Fogh: 27.
Red Sea (Arabian Gulf): 149-150, 162, 164, 188-191, 209, 218,223, 228, 266, 273, 341-342.
Republika Srpska: 86-88, 92, 351.
Resistance Bloc: 308, 312-313, 317, 320-321, 324-327, 329-330, 351, 362, 364.
Responsibility to Protect (R2P): 211-214, 240, 249.
Rice, Condoleezza: 316, 362.
Robertson, George Islay MacNeill: 35.
Rogozin, Dmitry Olegovich: 199, 363.
Romania: 24-25, 42, 53, 62, 65, 75, 82-85, 109, 130-131, 137-138, 198, 269, 277.
Romney, Willard Mitt: 274.
Rumsfeld, Donald Henry: 24, 37, 130, 178, 179, 202-203, 307.
Rumsfeld Space Commission (see Commission to Assess United States National Security Space Management and Organization)
Rusk, David Dean: 334.
Russian Federal Ministry of Defense: 287-288, 329.
Russian Federation: 17-18, 26-27, 29, 31, 32, 36, 42, 43-46, 48, 49, 51-52, 54, 56, 58, 65, 67, 96, 98-99, 110, 114, 116, 117-119, 123, 126-127, 128, 140-141, 144, 150-152, 158-159, 165-174, 175, 178, 180, 182-185, 187, 189, 190-191, 192-199, 201, 214, 215, 217, 225, 239, 240, 245, 251, 263, 264-265, 268, 270, 272-278, 279-303, 308, 315, 317, 324, 324-325, 329, 330, 331, 333, 335, 340 341-347, 349-350, 351, 353, 355-365.
Eurasianist Policies: 36, 46, 49, 166-174, 277-278, 279-283, 327.
Relations with NATO: 26-27, 51-52, 54, 56, 58, 67, 96, 110, 126, 150, 152, 158-159, 165, 166, 170-171, 192-193, 195-196, 214, 272, 273, 274, 295, 329, 341-342, 344, 361-362. Strategic Alliance with China: 171-172, 178, 180, 182-183, 185, 198-199, 263, 275, 277-278, 279-283, 295-296, 301-302, 341-342, 343, 353.

S

Saakashvili, Mikheil: 26, 65, 189, 195, 285, 358, 360.
Sadr, Muqtada: 264.
Saint Vincent and the Grenadines: 349, 351.
Salter, James Arthur: 38.
Sandinista National Liberation Front: 124, 348.
Santos Calderón, Juan Manuel: 55.
Sarkozy, Nicolas Paul Stéphane: 30, 33, 35-36, 41, 103, 136-137, 139, 142, 144, 147, 240, 335-336.
Saud, Bandar bin Sultan: 320.
Sauerbrey, Ellen: 326.
Saudi Arabia: 112, 125-126, 130, 153-157, 159, 162, 198, 216, 230, 238, 269, 309, 310-311, 320-322, 327-328, 330.
Schmitt, Gary: 253-254.
Schröder, Gerhard Fritz Kurt: 24, 49, 335.
September 11, 2011 Attacks (9/11): 18, 114-116, 118, 121, 127-129, 131-132, 144, 149, 150, 192, 196, 237, 250-251, 258, 266, 274, 282-283, 285-286, 295, 305-306, 345, 348, 362.
Serbia: 18, 29, 43, 48, 53, 58, 61, 62, 75-76, 81, 83, 86, 93-98, 101, 103, 104, 105, 108, 125, 269, 285, 288, 290, 351.
Serravalle, Gerardo: 69.

Shalikashvili, John Malchase David: 341.

Shamkhani, Ali: 307-308.

Shanghai Cooperation Organization (SCO): 169, 174, 184, 280, 282, 287, 292, 294, 295-303, 330, 341, 344, 347, 351, 352-354, 362-363.

Singapore: 177-178, 188, 190, 252, 259, 262-263, 265, 269.

Siniora, Fouad: 42, 311-313, 316, 320-321, 323.

Slovakia: 24, 25, 53, 65, 75, 130-131, 291.

Slovenia: 24, 25, 53, 65, 75-76, 80, 81, 104, 108, 130-131, 269.

Somali Transitional Federal Government: 228-229, 237.

Somalia: 19, 113, 130, 191, 208-210, 223-237, 247, 249, 266, 306, 341.

Somalian Civil War: 223, 225-227.

South Africa: 74, 208, 217, 240, 241, 280, 300, 349.

South America: 55, 119, 223, 278, 350.

South Asia (see Indian sub-continent)

South Atlantic Treaty Organization (SATO): 223, 350.

South China Sea: 14, 176, 177, 179, 190, 263.

South Korea (see Korea, Republic of)

South Ossetia: 65, 99, 169, 196, 291, 351, 357-361.

South Sudan: 85, 210-212, 214, 215-222, 256.

Soviet Bloc (see Eastern Bloc)

Spain: 22, 23, 97, 99, 136, 142, 144, 147, 196, 209, 241, 269, 297, 319, 348.

Spykman, Nicholas John: 270-272.

Srebrenica Massacre: 89-92.

Sri Lanka: 99, 179, 182-185, 294, 296, 297, 298, 351.

Sri Lankan Civil War: 182-185.

Stabilization and Association Process (SAP): 43-45, 48.

Stabilization Force (SFOR): 93.

Standing NATO Maritime Group One (SNMG1): 209, 222-223.

Standing NATO Maritime Group Two (SNMG2): 236.

Star Wars (see Missile Shield)

Stay-Behind Cells: 67-75, 111.

Strait of Hormuz: 159, 161-164, 177, 275.

Strait of Malacca: 177-178, 180, 189-190.

STRATCOM (see United States Strategic Command)

Straus, Ira: 17-18.

Sudan: 19, 85, 99, 208, 209-222, 231, 237, 240, 247, 250, 266, 306, 341, 349, 351.

Sudan People's Liberation Movement (SPLM): 218, 220-222.

Sweden: 27, 44, 58, 107-108, 237, 269, 361.

Switzerland: 29, 58, 100, 101, 232, 284, 329.

Syria: 41, 42, 43, 48, 132, 138, 147, 148, 150-152, 154, 155, 156, 162-163, 174, 189, 190, 193, 198, 237-238, 274, 284-287, 296, 304, 306-330, 345, 348, 349, 351, 360, 362, 363-364. Strategic Alliance with Iran: 150-152, 286, 307-308, 312-314, 316, 317, 318, 320-325, 326-327, 329-330, 363-364. Strategic Alliance with Russia: 150-152, 190, 308, 317, 324-325, 327, 329-330, 360.

Syrian Free Army: 328-329.

Syrian Human Rights Observatory: 328.

Syrian National Council (SNC): 154, 329-330.

T

Taiwan (Formosa): 99, 175-178, 180, 197, 198, 252, 253-254, 263, 265, 269, 342.

Tajikistan: 30, 58, 117, 165, 169, 172, 173, 282, 287-288, 290, 292, 294, 295, 298, 301, 303, 343-344, 351, 353.

Taliban: 18, 114-118, 121-122, 125-127, 130, 228, 266, 284, 287, 306, 338, 345.
Tamil Tigers (see Liberation Tigers of Tamil Ealam)
Tanzania: 223, 237.
Tartus: 150-151.
Thaçi, Hashim: 95-96, 98, 100-101.
Theater Iran Near Term (TIRANNT): 284.
Tibet: 264.
Tito, Josip Broz: 76, 166.
Tonelson, Alan: 332.
Torop, Jonathan: 308.
Trans-Atlantic Bargain: 334, 338.
Trans-Atlantic Rift: 24, 32-38, 50, 334-335.
Transitional Council (Transitional National Council, NTC): 48, 240, 244-247, 328.
Treaty of Good-Neighborliness and Friendly Cooperation: 282-283.
Treaty of Mutual Security and Cooperation: 255.
Tunisia: 34, 41, 42, 48, 135, 138, 147, 148, 209, 238.
Turkey: 18, 21, 23, 29, 35, 39, 58, 68, 89, 98, 99, 103, 111-112, 136-138, 140-141, 143, 146-147, 154, 155, 157, 162, 169, 188, 196, 198, 230, 268, 269, 273, 274, 275, 290, 294, 296, 297, 298, 304, 305, 309, 319, 324, 325-329, 339, 355, 357, 360. Neo-Otto-manism: 137, 147.
Turkmenistan: 58, 118, 158, 165-166, 169, 290, 297, 351, 352-353.
Tüttelmann, Axel: 314.
Tymoshenko, Yulia Volodymyrivna: 61, 285.

U

Uganda: 217-218, 222, 230.
Ukraine: 26, 29, 41-42, 43, 44, 46, 48, 49, 54, 56, 58, 61, 62, 110, 150, 151, 165-166, 168-169, 189, 190, 191, 197, 198, 252, 272, 274, 285-286, 288, 290, 292, 347, 349, 351, 352-353.
Unified Combatant Command (UCC): 208-209, 268, 270, 346, 385 (n.3).
Union for the Mediterranean (UfM): 41, 48, 139-147, 148, 326.
Union of Soviet Socialist Republics (USSR): 16-18, 22, 24-26, 29-30, 34-35, 41-45, 51-52, 56, 67, 68, 70, 76, 82, 84-85, 109-111, 113, 114, 118, 121, 125-126, 128-130, 151, 157-158, 165-166, 169-170, 173, 176, 192-195, 224-226, 257, 263, 266-267, 272, 276-278, 281, 287, 295, 333, 334, 336, 338, 341, 343, 347, 357.
Union Oil Company of California (UNOCAL): 118.
United Arab Emirates (UAE): 27, 153, 154, 155, 157, 159, 162, 164, 236, 241, 269, 329.
United Kingdom of Great Britain and Northern Ireland (UK): 18, 20-21, 23, 24, 30-33, 35-39, 43, 50, 55, 85, 89, 96, 112, 116-117, 118-124, 128, 130, 136, 143, 144, 154, 155, 159, 166, 171, 180, 188-189, 190, 197, 210-211, 214, 223-224, 230, 237, 239-242, 246, 247, 250, 253, 256, 257, 259-260, 269, 270, 279-280, 286-287, 288, 304-305, 315, 317, 319, 322, 323, 328-329, 331, 336, 341, 345-347, 358, 362-363.
United Nations: 20, 27, 64, 87-91, 96, 99-102, 121, 124, 145, 156, 176, 189, 212-214, 216, 222, 224, 231-235, 236, 237, 240, 242, 243, 249, 255-256, 288, 292, 295, 305, 316-319, 331, 336, 350, 353, 359.
United Nations Commission on Narcotics: 124.
United Nations Interim Force in Lebanon (UNIFIL): 316-319, 324.
United Nations-African Union Mis-

sion in Darfur (UNAMID): 214.
United Nations Interim Administration Mission in Kosovo (UNMIK): 97-98.
United Nations Protection Force (UNPROFOR): 87-89.
United Nations Security Council: 19, 21, 49, 87, 91, 117, 156, 159, 176, 180, 185, 208, 214-216, 225, 230, 239,-240, 244, 283, 344, 347.
United States Africa Command (US-AFRICOM/AFRICOM): 208, 249, 250-251, 268, 343.
US Empire (see American Empire):
United States Central Command (USCENTCOM/CENTCOM): 150, 157, 188, 228, 250, 268, 272, 306, 308, 346.
United States European Command (EUCOM): 150, 250, 268, 270, 308, 346.
United States Pacific Command (USPACOM): 250, 262, 268, 270.
United States Space Command (USSPACECOM): 200.
United States Strategic Command (USSTRATCOM/STRATCOM): 200, 385 (n.3).
Uzbekistan: 30, 58, 165-166, 172, 285-288, 290-291, 292, 294, 295, 297, 298, 303, 351.

V

van der Veer, Jeroen: 341
van den Breeman, Hendrik (Henk) Gijsbert Bernhard: 341
Vatican: 83, 329.
Vietnam War: 252-253, 260, 334.
Venezuela, Bolivarian Republic of: 55, 158, 189, 217, 223, 240, 343, 348-350, 351, 363.

W

Warsaw Pact: 16-17, 22, 25, 51-53, 60, 68, 109-111, 113, 138, 144,

195, 287-288, 291.
Washington Agreement: 87.
Washington Treaty: 20-21, 28, 30, 32, 63-65, 131, 158, 338.
Weather warfare: 206-207.
Western Bloc: 16, 29-30, 31, 35, 67-68, 72, 74, 79, 157, 166, 170, 176, 226, 276-277, 333.
Wiebes, Cees: 89.
Wieseltier, Leon: 240.
Wisner, Frank George: 336.
Wolfowitz, Paul Dundes: 130, 240.
World Bank: 43, 76, 78, 79, 217, 226-227, 232.
World War I: 75, 85, 89-90, 129, 305, 323, 366.
World War II: 16, 31, 34, 67, 68, 72, 75, 128-129, 224, 251, 255, 270, 278, 319, 331, 333, 335, 338, 365.
World War III: 127-130, 171, 198, 317-318, 345, 347, 363-366. Historiographical Definition: 128-129. Threats: 171, 198, 318, 322, 345, 347, 363-364 US Simulations of a Nuclear World War: 363.
Wörner (Woerner), Manfred Hermann: 28, 67, 195, 331.
Wurmser, David: 308.
Wurmser, Meyrav: 308, 323.

X

Xiaoping, Deng: 343.
Xinjiang Uyghur Autonomous Region: 186.

Y

Yanukovych, Viktor Fedorovych: 26, 61, 353.
Yeltsin, Boris Nikolayevich: 166, 170-171, 282.
Yemen: 130, 162, 164, 191, 225, 236, 273, 342, 363.
Yinon Plan: 309.

Yushchenko, Viktor Andriyovych:
26, 285.
Yugoslavia: 18, 24, 25, 38, 45, 53, 56,
65, 67, 75-113, 130, 170-171,
186, 194, 240, 255, 282, 285,
337, 341. Federal Republic: 24,
45, 56, 65, 80-81, 86, 87, 93-99,
104, 105, 108, 110. King-
dom: 75-76. Socialist Federal
Republic: 18, 25, 38, 45, 53, 56,
67, 76-80, 82, 83-84, 85-86, 87,
89-90, 92, 94, 99, 103, 104, 105,
108, 110, 111, 112, 113, 130,
170-171, 186, 190, 240, 250, 282,
285, 337, 341.

Z

Zapatero, José Luis Rodríguez: 142.
Zedong, Mao: 176, 343.
Zelaya Rosales, José Manuel: 348-
349.
Zemin, Jiang: 171, 282.
Zhaozhong, Zhang: 363.
Zimbabwe: 349, 351.